NATURE'S BOUNTY

NATURE'S BOUNTY

Historical and Modern Environmental Perspectives

Anthony N. Penna

M.E. Sharpe

Armonk, New York
London, England

*The background illustration on the front cover is "The Call of the Whooping Crane," by
Channing Thieme. Through its status as an endangered species earlier in this century, the
whooping crane unites the four major environmental themes in this book: woodlands,
wildlife, water, and air.*

Library of Congress Cataloging-in-Publication Data

Penna, Anthony N.
Nature's bounty: historical and modern environmental perspectives /
Anthony N. Penna
p. cm.
Includes bibliographical references and index.
ISBN 0-7656-0187-7 (alk. paper)—
ISBN 0-7656-0188-5 (pbk. : alk. paper)
1. United States—Environmental conditions—History.
2. Nature—Effect of human beings on.
3. Urban Pollution—United States.
4. Environmental quality—United States—Public Policy.
5. Ecology—Government Policy—United States.
6. Medical Policy—United States.
I. Title.
GE150.P46 1998
333.7′13′097—dc21   98-42514
CIP

Printed in the United States of America

The paper used in this publication meets the minimum requirements of
American National Standard for Information Sciences—
Permanence of Paper for Printed Library Materials,
ANSI Z 39.48-1984.

∞

BM (c)   10   9   8   7   6   5   4   3   2   1
BM (p)   10   9   8   7   6   5   4   3   2

For Channing

Contents

List of Illustrations

Foreword

Although barely twenty years old, the field of environmental history has been experiencing prodigious growth. New books and articles appear at a rapid rate, adding deeper levels to our understanding of the history of the environment. Although environmental history began essentially as a history of the West, scholars now recognize that "the environment" encompasses all of the nation's regions. Environmental history now includes examination of urban as well as wilderness and rural areas, and industrial as well as agricultural domains. It is the history of air, land, and water, of wooded and non-wooded habitats, and of animals, birds, insects, and fish. And it is the history of the men and women who shaped and altered the natural environment and who fought to restore it to its natural conditions.

Nature's Bounty by Anthony Penna presents all of the above themes within the organizing framework of forest, wildlife and habitat, water, and air quality. Beginning with the commodification, exploitation, and destruction of North America's vast forest lands, it carries the reader through the efforts of the conservation and environmental movements to protect and preserve. However, it also exposes the reader to the conflicts within those movements concerning different perspectives on the meaning of forests and the extent to which wilderness should be preserved or subject to a use ethic. The same themes surface in consideration of wildlife and wildlife habitat issues. The book investigates what value changes took place to move the society towards conservation and protection.

Penna's treatment of the issues surrounding water and air quality are illuminating because of the manner in which he clearly identifies the conflicting needs that resulted in the contamination of water and air, as well as the attempts to restore their quality. Water issues reflect different regional perspectives and disagreements over water use: upstream and downstream interests; drinking water concerns versus use of sinks for disposal of wastes, agricultural versus urban needs, preserving wild and scenic rivers versus channeling and shaping waters for commerce, trade and power production.

Air quality issues have represented some of the same user conflicts, compounded by the rise over time of the automobile as a major polluter. In both water and air regulation, local and state authority proved unable to deal with the magnitude of the problems. The result was congressional passage of a legislative agenda that created a host of laws relating to air and water quality, as well as to the land and wildlife, setting federal standards, and attempting to reshape traditional attitudes and practices in regard to common resources.

Such legislation and the approach of public policy towards environmental quality remain controversial, with various stakeholders engaged in a struggle over standards and strategies. Most Americans, however, in spite of attachment to a consumer economy, appear to be aware of the necessity of protecting the environment and hold, in various degrees of strength, a set of environmental values.

A fuller understanding and appreciation of these values can gain depth and breath through an understanding of our nation's environmental history. This book can greatly aid readers in acquiring such an understanding.

Joel A. Tarr
Richard S. Caliguiri Professor of Urban and
Environmental History and Policy
Carnegie-Mellon University

Acknowledgments

In writing this book, I have had the benefit of the scholarship of numerous historians, social scientists, and journalists of the environment. Without their writings, I would not have organized my work in this way nor been able to show the relationships among its main topics and themes. This book, an effort to synthesize the ideas, insights, and conclusions of numerous researchers and writers, relies on their work in countless ways.

Many friends and colleagues read this manuscript in various stages of development and offered moral support and criticism. Joel A. Tarr, the Richard S. Caliguiri Professor of Urban and Environmental History and Policy at Carnegie-Mellon University, a former teacher, colleague, and long-time friend, gave unselfishly of his knowledge in offering substantive and editorial advice. Irving H. Bartlett, the John F. Kennedy Professor of American Civilization at the University of Massachusetts, Boston, also a former teacher, colleague, and long-time friend, got me thinking about writing this book by sharing his environmental course syllabus with me, reading the manuscript at various stages, and offering advice over lunches and during very long bike rides through the countryside and along the seashore of southeastern Massachusetts. As the manuscript progressed, I depended on my friend and colleague at Northeastern University, Professor Clay McShane, to point out flaws and inconsistencies in my writing.

At various times, I have received invaluable assistance from graduate students in the Master's program of the history department at Northeastern University. Special thanks are due to David Brown and Antonietta Dimeo, who helped me compile the initial bibliography. Kathleen Fahey became my graduate assistant in 1995 and worked with me as a researcher, editor, and word processor until the manuscript was submitted to the publisher in the spring of 1998, long after she had received her master's degree in public history from Northeastern University. Without Kathy's attention to details, this book might not have reached the publisher in an acceptable form. Finally, Jason Eden, who entered our graduate program in the fall of 1997, did the labor-intensive work of compiling a comprehensive index and assisting me with the photographic research.

During the summer of 1997 the university provided me with an instructional development grant, which I used to prepare the manuscript for classroom trial during the fall quarter of the same year. My students in HST 1544, *Environmental History of the United States* gave me much-needed responses to the ideas contained in an earlier version of this book.

Channing, Christina, Greg, Trevor, and Brandon provided a home environment filled with activity, insightful conversation, and happiness. Without that setting, none of what follows would have been possible. My mother, Mary O. Penna, has provided guidance, support, and love throughout my life.

NATURE'S BOUNTY

Prologue

Introduction

What has been the role and place of the natural world in the lives of humans? This question is central to the work of historians who study long-term environmental trends and changes and has become increasingly important to professionals and citizens who want to understand issues of environmental change. This book attempts to address issues confronting those who want to understand the impact of long-term environmental change on their lives. It focuses exclusively on historical changes and public policy debates regarding the environment in the continental United States. Although it is not intended to encompass all environmental topics and debates, the ones selected for examination are significant because of their integral relationship to each other.

Almost fifty years ago, Aldo Leopold, a University of Wisconsin professor of game management and a wildlife biologist, whose book of essays, *A Sand County Almanac,* would become a treatise for the environmental movement in the United States, called for "an ecological interpretation of history." Such an approach, he suggested, would use the newly emerging ideas about the natural functioning of biological systems to understand our relationship to the world around us. For Leopold and those who followed him, an ecological understanding helped to explain how human activity altered the natural world in ways little understood by many who had come before. An ecological understanding of the natural history of the United States will serve as a guide for the topics and issues discussed in this book.

The four-part organization of this book, which consists of essays and primary sources, traces the complex development of the nation's ecological history. It begins with an essay on the transformation of the nation's forests by aggressive agricultural expansion and intensive commercial logging. Subsequent essays detail the environmental effects of forest depletion and

3

land development on wildlife and their habitat, water use and pollution, and air quality. Each essay, namely forests, wildlife, water, and air, deals with the complex human and environmental interactions in what is now the continental United States. Each also describes many local and national campaigns to change the environmentally destructive practices of early pioneers, settlers, colonists, and citizens. Primary sources accompany each essay in order to provide the reader with personal accounts and observations, and practices and policies that stressed environmental issues.

Forests

Extensive natural environmental changes began with the first permanent European settlements in the early seventeenth century and continue into the twentieth century. Throughout much of our colonial and national history, farmers and loggers cleared the dense forests for fuelwood, agriculture, timber, and industrial needs. These forest-clearing activities and their environmental effects, an important topic of this book, were buttressed originally by beliefs that the dense, dark forests were hostile environments, harboring dangerous animals and threatening Indians. From the early years of settlement to the coming of the Civil War in 1861, farmers cleared almost 100 million acres, while another 5 million were cleared by logging, mining, and city-building. One environmentalist has noted that "as late as 1920 logging was proceeding at nine times the rate of regrowth. It was not until 1963 that the annual regrowth exceeded the amount cut."[1] The loss of forests to agricultural cultivation, logging, and urban development is significant because of what we now know about the value of trees and the forest canopy to the natural health of soil, groundwater, and air, and their impact on weather patterns, climate stability, and change.

Wildlife and the Loss of Habitat

Retreating woodlands, the result of an expanding agricultural and industrial economy in the nineteenth century, and the suburbanization of commercial enterprise and residential development in the twentieth century, altered the country's landscape. These developments reduced the range of most wildlife and threatened their habitat. The mobility and settlement of a growing population and its passion for clearing the land also caused a shrinking wildlife habitat. Finally, the transformation of the land and the activities of market hunters who believed in the inexhaustibility of their prey accelerated species decline.

Water and Air Quality

The impact of development and habitat loss on soil erosion, groundwater depletion, and declining stream and river water quality is the third major topic in this book. Water flowing through the earth sustains plant, animal, and human life. Without water, the energy from the sun, and the chemicals of the earth and its atmosphere, the planet would become barren. Water is a matter of health or illness, life or death for each person.

Like the water we drink to nourish our bodies and enrich the planet's animal and plant life, the air we breathe is a vital life-sustaining gift of nature. When fouled by toxins and foreign particles, however, the air causes numerous respiratory ailments and life-threatening diseases. The impact on the air we breathe of increasing levels of chemical emissions into the atmosphere, coupled with a reduction in oxygen-producing forests and plants, is the fourth and final environmental issue presented in the pages that follow. Citizens, academics, and public officials have raised disturbing questions about the ways in which humankind has transformed the earth to satisfy its wants. The central question has been: "Do *Homo sapiens* have any moral obligations to the earth and its circle of life, or does that life exist merely to satisfy the infinitely expanding wants of our own species?"[2]

Early History

Although both the environmental movement and the writing of environmental history are relatively new, the topics examined in this book extend back to the arrival of European settlers in what is now the continental United States. Although some early settlements in colonial Virginia and Massachusetts Bay faced severe hardship and a few succumbed to disease, malnutrition, and an inhospitable climate, most newcomers experienced a cornucopia. In the pre-industrial world of the seventeenth century, some colonists literally believed that they had discovered the restored biblical Garden of Eden from the Judeo-Christian religious tradition. In 1954, the historian David M. Potter characterized Americans as a people of plenty.[3] This characterization aptly identified the key to understanding Americans and their relationship to their newly discovered environment. No other people in the history of humankind, according to environmental historian Donald Worster, "has ever believed, as Americans have, that they are actually living in Eden."[4]

Abundance in nature greeted most explorers and settlers. There was simply more of everything, and these newcomers wrote home to other Europeans about their newly discovered bounty. They boasted about their new

fortunes in nature and thought of themselves as "a chosen people" in the restored "garden." Their reports, diaries, letters, and travelogues spoke eloquently about the limitless abundance of the new continent. In particular, an inexhaustible land with its seemingly endless forests and its abundant wildlife were themes that would repeat themselves again and again through the centuries, as pioneers, hunters, and settlers recorded their wilderness experiences.

These observations followed an unbroken and consistent pattern from the earliest explorers almost five centuries ago to the recent past. One of the earliest descriptions of abundance in the new world was made by the Spanish explorer Don Francisco Vasquez de Coronado in the 1520s as he searched for "the lost city" of Quivira and its treasures of gold and silver. Exploring from west to east, he entered the land of the Wichita Indians and marveled at the natural bounty of the place:

> The country is the best I have seen for producing all the products of Spain, for besides the land itself being very fat and black, and being very well watered by the rivulets and springs and rivers, I found prunes like those of Spain and nuts and very good sweet grapes and mulberries.[5]

It was this bonanza from the natural world and its wealth in natural resources which captured the imagination of the earliest European explorers and was reinforced later by future pioneers in search of riches from land, forests, mining, and wildlife, as well as from rivers, streams, and coastal waters. This quest for wealth became embedded in the national character. As the environmental historian Alfred Crosby pointed out, "something as central to the American character as this ... obsession with immediate satisfaction probably has roots, deep and old, in the positive experience of common Americans, white ones, at least, in meeting life's basic demands."[6]

Centuries later, settlers in the Wabash Valley, Illinois, reiterated the Garden of Eden theme in their folklore and their songs. One particular song is worth recalling, since it repeated a message familiar to settlers, pioneers, and early nineteenth-century men and women "on the move and on the make":

> Way down upon the Wabash
> Such lands were never known.
> If Adam had passed over it,
> This soil he'd surely own.
> He'd think it was the Garden
> He played in when a boy,
> And straight he'd call it Eden
> In the State of Illinois.[7]

The Commodification of Nature

Shortages in European commodities and the transition from a mercantile–peasant to a merchant–capitalist economy turned nature's bounty into commodities in the American colonies. The mercantile–peasant economy was very much a traditional agrarian one, with forests as the main source of energy. Wood was consumed for heating and used as building material, and its charcoal was fuel for the first iron foundries. As immigrants from Europe arrived in the colonies, they witnessed the stark contrast between the resource-poor countries from which they had come and the richness of the new land. For example, a two-hundred-year shortage in fuelwood caused prices to rise and restrictions to be placed on cutting forests in England through the fourteenth and the fifteenth centuries. Thus, the dense forests of North America immediately became invested with monetary value in the eyes of the colonists, even though wood was not exported to England.

Other "merchantable commodities," such as animal furs and skins for clothing, and fish of many kinds, but especially cod for salting, quickly became major exports. With the transition to merchant–capitalism, first wood and then coal became the main combustible fuel supply. Each part of the interconnected ecosystem of trees, soils, plants, watershed, springs, ponds, streams, and rivers was exploited for its economic value. During this earlier mercantile–peasant economy, as historian William Cronon has pointed out, "explorers describing a new countryside with an eye to its mercantile possibilities all too easily fell into this way of looking at things, so that their descriptions often degenerated into little more than lists."[8] Forests became lumber and wildlife became game, with its flesh, hides, fur, pelts, meat, tallow, and bones—commodities for the emerging merchant–capitalist market economy.

The pace of the transition from an agricultural to a capitalist economy varied from region to region during the early national period from 1780 to 1830. Rochester, New York, for instance, became a merchant–capitalist boomtown between 1815 and 1825, while the economy of Concord, Massachusetts, remained agrarian and stagnant. As the economist Maurice Dobb has pointed out, however, the most significant development occurred in the system of labor. To him, the spread of capitalism was "not simply a system of production for the market . . . but a system under which labour-power had 'itself become a commodity' and was bought and sold on the market like any other object of exchange."[9] Throughout much of the nineteenth century, from about 1820 to 1900, almost all aspects of production, namely land, labor, and capital, were transformed into commodities.[10]

The commodification of nature and human labor became the bedrock of early merchant–capitalism and intensified as the nation entered its industrial–capitalist period. In the occupational structure of the changing economy, the proportion of men who listed themselves as "laborers" rose from 5.5 percent to 27.4 percent during the years from 1796 and 1855.[11] The creation of a wage-earning working class coincided with rapid population growth and urban development. Antebellum America (1830–1860) experienced a demographic explosion. While the total population of the nation was growing at about 35 percent each decade, cities with 2,500 inhabitants or more grew more than three times faster. In 1830, Boston's population of 40,000 was the result of slow growth. In the three succeeding decades, the city's population expanded to 176,000. New York City grew from a metropolis of 515,000 to 805,000 in the decade of the 1850s. Chicago grew from a muddy village in 1830 to a metropolis of 107,000 in 1860.[12] To accommodate the growth during this period, the city dredged soil from the Chicago River and elevated itself twelve feet in order to lay new water and sewer pipes across the expanding metropolis.

For hundreds of thousands of immigrants from Europe and young men and women from unproductive farms in the United States, "moving to the big city was . . . an enormously exhilarating and unsettling form of pioneering" and turned each city into "a sprawling, unmanageable metropolis."[13] With the mechanization of the workplace and the expansion of wage labor, the use of natural resources and the production of goods became central to the lives of most Americans and changed their ways of thinking and acting toward nature. As the essays and documents which follow will show, it was this new way of thinking and acting toward the land and its forests, the wildlife and their habitat, and the nation's waterways that led to the conservation movement in the late nineteenth and early twentieth centuries.

The Conservation and Environmental Movements

Forests

To conservationists, natural resources represented commodities that needed to be used wisely. As a result, they established national parks and forests and used sustained-yield forest management to attempt to protect the remaining woodlands from destruction. In fact, the current debate about preserving the forests of the Pacific Northwest represents an attempt to prevent the nation's remaining 5 percent of old-growth forests from being clear-cut, a practice that decimated the woodlands of the continental United States over a three-hundred-year period. Also, early in the nineteenth century, long before "ecology" had entered the nation's vocabulary, a few writers warned about the devastating effects of deforestation. Their early warnings showed the effects of exploiting the environment to produce wealth and suggested the relationships among three great natural systems—soil, water, and air.

Although significant differences existed among early twentieth century conservationists and post-World War II environmentalists, both groups were alarmed by the depletion of the nation's natural wealth. These early warnings point out the continuity in our thinking about ecological changes brought about by human action. More than a century ago, in 1864, a remarkable writer, diplomat, and agriculturist, George Perkins Marsh, wrote *Man and Nature: Physical Geography as Modified by Human Action.* Alarmed by the destruction of the nation's forests by farmers and loggers that he witnessed at mid-century, Marsh argued persuasively that the destruction of forests from antiquity to the modern age had disastrous effects on the countries around the world. Among the most important effects were climatic changes, including higher velocity winds whistling across a barren terrain, caused by the elimination of trees. In addition, major fluctuations in surface temperatures—freezing and thawing—caused by over-exposure to the sun's radiation, led to the inevitable erosion of topsoil, which undermined the agricultural productivity of a region. Marsh wrote about a world-wide phenomenon of overgrazing by livestock and of farming which, along with the wind and rain, eroded an already compromised surface soil. In some places, the desert encroached upon former fertile plains of the ancient eastern Mediterranean region, turning them into either a semi-arid or arid terrain. Marsh wrote about history as natural history and argued that the depletion of natural forests led to the decline of many Mediterranean civilizations including Greece, Syria, Lebanon, Palestine, Egypt, ancient Persia, and Phoenicia. Writing about the natural history of a country or a region later became known as environmental history.

While Marsh was looking back historically to find examples of the long-term negative effects of deforestation, a number of his contemporaries, both foresters and naturalists, were writing about the immediate environmental effects of forest decline. The devastation of the Great Lakes forests in the aftermath of the Civil War led to a systematic effort to document the immediate environmental effects of clear-cutting in the Wisconsin woods. A *Report on the Disastrous Effects of the Destruction of Forest Trees, Going on so Rapidly in the State of Wisconsin* (1867), a document that accompanies the essay on forests in this book, will show how prophetic the writers were in their observations. The state's changing climate, a result of intensive logging, included surface temperature changes, increased condensation and evaporation of water, and the pollution of rivers, streams, and ponds. The report's riveting conclusions confirmed the effects of deforestation on soil quality. Eliminating trees increased the dryness of the ground and led to erosion. The result was blowing sands that retarded cultivation. Finally, violent, damaging rainstorms caused the soil to run off into the rivers and streams, fouling the water and destroying aquatic life. All of these damaging effects were produced by society's voracious appetite for fuelwood and wood products.

Forest management to a later generation of conservationists meant continuous cropping of the forests and wood production for commercial and residential use. Only with the later establishment of soil conservation activities to protect land for agricultural use were efforts made to recognize the relationship of soil and forests, and the protection provided by a canopy of trees. Screening out the sun's rays, holding the soil, and preventing erosion by an extensive system of tree roots proved then to be the importance of the nation's woodlands. Forests remained commodities to conservationists, and they would not achieve the status of valued amenities until the environmental movement of the last quarter of the twentieth century.

Wildlife and Wildlife Habitat

The devastating effects of deforestation played havoc on wildlife and their habitat. The wildlife movement to protect vanishing species of birds and bison in the late nineteenth century and to end the destruction of large predators, including bears and wolves, in the late twentieth century, possessed characteristics that allowed it to serve as a bridge from the early twentieth century conservation movement to the later environmental movement. As historian Samuel P. Hays has noted:

> Interest in sustainable game populations had brought the game management movement into the orbit of "natural resources" activities in the spirit of conservation; the task of sustained-yield game management did not differ markedly from that of sustained-yield forest management. To the protectors of wildlife, however, water, land, and forests were important not in their own right but as habitat of animals.[1]

Before the first wetland habitat along the midwestern flyway of the Upper Mississippi Valley was established in the 1920s, bird and duck populations had been protected by creating "bag limits." When this age-old strategy proved to be ineffective in restoring bird populations, the focus shifted to habitat. There, birds could stop over, propagate, and feed. As the term "game" retreated from the national consciousness, an appreciative interest developed in "wildlife."

In recent years, the battle over species and habitat has been argued before the U.S. Supreme Court. Opponents of the Endangered Species Act claimed that only a direct "taking" of a species, such as hunting, constituted a threat, while disturbing habitat had no effect. Ecological scientists provided irrefutable evidence to the contrary, and the Court agreed with their conclusion. On a much broader front, the scientific knowledge of habitat has been expanded significantly in recent years as a result of radio-collar technology in tracking land animals and birds. It has been used extensively to study the range of such wide-roaming mammals as grizzly bears, elk, and the spotted owl, the most studied bird in America. Our understanding about the size of an area needed by these and other species to maintain their viability could not have developed without this research.[15]

Early in the twentieth century, some conservationists recognized the importance of a diverse habitat of forests, land, and water to sustain wildlife and insure that future generations would enjoy the commodity of the hunt. Later, protecting wildlife and their habitat became a focus of activity for the newer environmentalists, who stressed the aesthetic and regenerative qualities of the natural environment. Animal habitat served to link the interests of conservationists and environmentalists, while divisive issues about water development, harvesting trees, and soil conservation through draining wetlands and building dams pulled both groups apart. "The appreciative use of wildlife for observation came to exceed that of hunting; the majority of those who used even public game lands sought to shoot with a camera rather than a gun."[16] The goal of protecting wildlife and its habitat resulted in many new nongame preservation programs for threatened and endangered species and extended our appreciation and knowledge about biological systems.

Water and Air Quality

Engineering technology of the late nineteenth century was marshaled to conserve the nation's water and to make it available for urban and agricultural use. Earthen dams, aqueducts, and reservoirs were built in the Eastern states to provide water for a rapidly increasing urban population. Without a wholesome and plentiful supply of water, repeated outbreaks of waterborne diseases would visit urban residents, bringing industrial and business activity to a standstill. At the beginning of the twentieth century, breathtakingly large dams were built in the West under the auspices of the Bureau of Reclamation established by federal legislation in 1902. Here again, water was thought of as a commodity. Similar to earlier developments of water supply in the eastern regions of the country, building of western dams created reservoirs to provide safe drinking water for a growing urban population. Additionally, they allowed western farmers to irrigate large areas of semi-arid land for agriculture. These same dams made it possible to produce hydroelectric power, control some floods, and allow riverboats and steamships to navigate more freely. Yet, intensive land and water use degraded the quality of the soil and contaminated the water.

The effects of water and air pollution surfaced early in the nation's history, as a growing population placed enormous stress on the urban infrastructure. This book presents case studies of large American cities including New York, Philadelphia, Chicago, St. Louis, Los Angeles, and San Francisco to describe variations on a central theme: the struggles of modern cities to adjust to the tensions between urban and natural environments. As historian Joel Tarr pointed out

> . . . the spread of metropolitan populations and urban land uses has reshaped and destroyed natural landscapes and environments. The relationship . . . has actually been circular, with cities having massive effects on the natural environment, while the natural environment, in turn, has profoundly shaped urban configurations.[17]

Burgeoning city populations taxed the "carrying capacity" of natural ecosystems with mountains of human and animal waste, polluted water and air, and urban squalor. There was literally no way for the natural environment to cleanse itself of urban waste. In the early twentieth century, women's clubs took leadership positions in the efforts to eliminate the squalor. They initiated efforts to clean up local urban water supplies and rid the cities of noxious smoke. Local conservation and public health officials reduced waterborne infectious diseases by treating the water with disinfectants and imposing water purification standards, all before the middle of the twentieth century. Although national water quality standards were developed by the U.S. Public Health Service as early as 1912, enforcement remained difficult until the passage of the Clean Water Act of 1972.

Heavy pollution loads in the post–World War II decades accelerated environmental decay. Increased reliance on the automobile and suburban sprawl, along with a new generation of exotic chemical agents for pest control and agricultural production, placed additional stress on the environment. New chemical solvents and detergents for industrial and household use shifted the burden from organic pollutants to chemical toxins. Ecological diversity was reduced further by the loss of wildlife habitat to sprawling suburban residential communities. And groundwater, already compromised by pesticides and herbicides, was contaminated further by runoff from suburban shopping malls and parking lots. Sulfur emissions, produced by the smokestacks of midwestern electric power generating utilities, stunted the growth of trees in the forests of the northeastern states by leaching calcium from the soil, a necessary element in plant growth.

Reasons for Optimism: An Environmentally Friendly Future

Major environmental successes suggest that progress is being made along a number of fronts, which will continue well into the next century. The same economic growth that further polluted the environment following World War II also created unprecedented national wealth and rising incomes for a rapidly expanding middle class. The values and aspirations of this postwar middle class helped to shape the environmental movement of the last quarter century.[18] Unlike conservationists, who decades earlier espoused efficiencies in the use of resources and the end of wasteful cutting, mining, and hunting practices, environmentalists, representing a much larger share of the population than conservationists had previously, focused on the aesthetic amenities of the environment and the quality-of-life reasons for protecting nature. The concern for aesthetic quality of natural resources distinguished environmentalists from conservationists.

Rivers, for example, were seen as more than commodities for human consumption, navigation, and the production of electric power; they existed also for their scenic beauty and human enjoyment, and as habitat for aquatic life. Conservationists may have thought about sustained-yield forests as efficient sources of timber but environmentalists increasingly recognized them as locations for residences and recreation.[19] The impact of this new environmentalism can be measured in many ways, not the least of which were the federal laws passed during the 1960s and 1970s to safeguard nature and protect the growing interest of the general public in environmental matters. These laws included the Wilderness Act (1964), the National Environmental Policy Act (1969), establishing the Environmental Protection Agency, and the Clean Water and Clean Air and Endangered Species Acts of the early 1970s, and the amendments to these critical laws.

Additionally, there was increasing recognition among public officials, business executives, and industrial leaders that traditional "end-of-the-pipe" cleanup strategies, although convenient, were very costly in financial and environmental terms. Production of goods with the environment in mind can often become more effective in reducing costs and protecting the environment. For example, substituting environmentally friendly, biodegradable, or nontoxic solvents for toxic ones and using water-based solvents versus petroleum-based ones are effective ways to combat environmental degradation.

Also, recycling toxic wastes can reduce the amount of poisonous material found in the environment. Although we currently have no social or economic mechanism for collecting the nickel and cadmium in rechargeable nickel-cadmium batteries, the technology exists for recovery through a chemical engineering distillation process. By recycling cadmium, the potential health risks of human exposure to a dangerous toxic substance are reduced. Cadmium is also used as a protective coating to eliminate corrosion. Designing products with the environment in mind looks for substitutes whenever possible to replace such a hazardous material. In preventing corrosion, for example, stainless steel bolts are environmentally friendly when compared to cadmium-coated ones.[20]

Solvent substitution, recycling of toxic waste, and, finally, important technological changes such as fuel-efficient motor vehicle engines play an important role in reducing further contamination of the environment and allowing it to recover from past abuses. Also, new energy consumption standards for electronic devices including computers, printers, and recorders reduce our consumption of fossil fuel. Appliances that use less electricity and last longer protect the natural world. Products manufactured with the environment in mind require more efficient use of natural and human resources and reduce emissions and waste. They also mean lowered social costs for pollution control and environmental protection. "Social cost" means the amount that society would have to pay in cleaning up the wastes created by environmentally dangerous products, or it might mean the amount that producers would be required to pay for producing and distributing environmentally damaging products.[21]

Water consumption has been reduced. The amount used by each person in the United States quadrupled to about 450 gallons per capita by the early 1970s. Improvements in technology, the Clean Water Act of 1972, which encouraged conservation, and economic changes that raised the cost of water resulted in reductions in demand for this traditionally wasted resource. For example, the Boston area consumption of water dropped from 320 million gallons each day in 1978 to 240 million gallons in 1992.[22] Although such progress is noteworthy, water usage in the United States remains among the highest in the industrialized countries of the world. As Jesse H. Ausubel has pointed out: "In the late 1980s wastewater still made up over 90 percent of measured U.S. hazardous wastes. Importantly, as agriculture contracts spatially, its water demand will likewise tend to shrink."[23]

The Role of Local Municipalities and States in Protecting the Environment

I have attempted to point out the various ways in which efforts by the states failed to curtail the environmental excesses of the past centuries. In many instances, it took the federal government to pass and enforce laws to protect the national forests, wildlife, water, and the air. In recent years, however, pollution control, conservation of water resources, and wildlife habitat protective legislation have been enacted by the states. In fact, about 70 percent of the important environmental legislation has been written by the states and only about 20 percent of the $10 billion spent by the states on the environment currently comes from the federal government.[24]

The passage of landmark environmental legislation in the 1970s to protect wildlife, water, and air opened the way for states to pass equally strong laws. Previously, states had been under considerable pressure from business and industry either to ignore the exploitation of natural resources or to pass laws with weak enforcement provisions. The environmental movement of the 1970s and the Clean Water, Clean Air, and Endangered Species Acts changed the relationships among the different levels of government and enforcement policies. Once again, however, continued protection requires a renewed commitment to the environment.

Congressional debates about the relationship between the states and the federal government over new amendments to the Clean Water Act, new standards for protecting wetlands, and controlling pesticide runoffs from farms and pollutants from city streets point out the continuing controversies over public policy. In much the same way, discussions about the reauthorization of the Endangered Species Act by the Congress brought to the fore the issue of compensation by land developers for the losses to wildlife habitat by setting aside large tracts of land for habitat elsewhere.[25] This controversy points out that the struggle for environmental protection reflects the changing influence and power of various interest groups in conflict. In the pages that follow, you will be looking back decades and even centuries in order to understand the environment that we have changed and looking forward to the possibilities and problems facing us in the decades and centuries ahead.

1

Forests

Introduction

Virgin forests were a predominant feature in early American life. It was estimated that they covered more than 820 million acres during the early years of European settlement at the beginning of the seventeenth century. These primeval forests contained a large variety of trees and wildlife species of tremendous diversity. More than 80 percent of the land in the northeast region of the country, which presently encompasses Maine, New Hampshire, and Vermont, was dominated by hardwood, deciduous trees. Species common to the northeastern region were oak, hickory, ash, cottonwood, spruce, fir, maple, beech, and birch along with white, red, and jack pine.

More than 60 percent of the land in the southeastern region was covered with forest. Oak and hickory covered about one-third of the South. In the Atlantic and Gulf states, shortleaf and longleaf pine, oak, gum, and cypress dominated the area. Between 40 and 60 percent of the midwestern North Central states contained abundant oak and hickory forests as well as aspen, birch, maple, beech, spruce, fir, elm, ash, and cottonwood. The only remaining region of the country with more than 40 percent of the land covered with forests was in the Pacific Northwest. Then and now, redwood, Douglas fir, and hemlock–spruce dominated the region.[1]

The question, "What is a forest?" is usually answered in the following way. A forest is an area of at least one acre of land with at least 10 percent of the area covered with trees of any size. "*Forest land* is a general term that encompasses *timberland* (forest land that produces, or is capable of producing, more than twenty cubic feet per acre per year of industrial wood in natural stands)."[2] While the total area of land devoted to trees has only declined from 206 million hectares to 195.6 hectares from 1952 to 1987, the volume of hardwood growing on these reduced hectares has increased by 69 percent.[3] This is a significant growth statistic to remember as you read this essay.

The increase in hardwood volume has been accompanied by a resurgence in logging, up 27 percent from 1970 to 1986. With this increase in logging there has been a growing concern about the health of the nation's woodlands, primarily about the effects of air pollution and acid rain. Other concerns focus on cutting old-growth woodlands in the Pacific Northwest and the public policies regarding the management of our national forests, which comprise more than 25 percent of the country's forests and provide almost half of the timber available for commercial and industrial use.

The primary reason for beginning this book with changes in the forests is our knowledge that the presence or absence of trees has a direct and immediate effect on climate change and water and air quality, as well as soil composition and erosion. Many species of trees such as aspen and birch are also important as wildlife habitat. In fact, "forests provide habitats for a larger number of wildlife species than any other biome, making them the planet's major reservoir of biological diversity."[4]

Forests affect soil composition through a number of subtle processes. By growing root systems, they hold soil in place. A forested watershed (the vast area which drains into rivers, streams, lakes, and ponds) is a natural sponge, holding water which falls to earth as precipitation. Gradually, the water is released and flows into these bodies of water, replenishing them. In this natural way, water released gradually helps to control soil erosion and the flooding caused by rapid runoff. Therefore, sediment that clogs the bottoms of rivers and streams is slowed by the existence of a forested landscape.

By providing a protective canopy, forests filter light and prevent heat generated by the sun from damaging fragile groundcover. By the process of photosynthesis, trees absorb carbon dioxide and transform it into oxygen, which they release into the air that we breathe. In the global exchange of carbon into oxygen trees are critical for human existence. Massive cutting of trees releases much of the carbon stored in the soil, while burning harvested trees releases more carbon, adding to the carbon dioxide load in the earth's atmosphere. As a result, many scientists and environmentalists believe that "large scale deforestation contributes to the greenhouse warming, which will probably alter global climate, food production, and average sea levels within your lifetime."[5] We have possessed some of this knowledge for more than a century, and some have chosen to use it for the benefit of the environment, while others have ignored it to satisfy human appetites for control over the land and the material value of its natural assets.

Material value can be thought about differently, however. By one estimate, a tree with a fifty-year life span contributes $196,250 worth of economic value in reducing air and water pollution and soil erosion while aiding in climate control, protection of wildlife, and protein production. As timber, this same tree has an estimated economic value of $590.[6]

The special interests at work in logging and then raising crops on previously wooded land continued well into the twentieth century. In fact, we begin this history of the forests with some present-day examples of conflicts between logging interests intent on cutting trees and environmentalists intent on changing the historical patterns of clear-cutting and then moving on to the next old-growth stand. Despite the conflicts described in the text which follows, we should be aware of the efforts made by thousands of citizens using the best available scientific knowledge to put natural processes back in place after centuries of cutting. Efforts include restoring woodlands and planting thousands of trees.

Forests Today

Today in the United States about 650 million acres are designated as forest, and about one-fourth of that is located in forests owned and maintained by the federal government. Much of what remains is held privately and can be sold for purposes of logging or for commercial and residential development when the value of the land exceeds the price of lumber. Only claims that cutting threatens or destroys habitat under the provisions of the Endangered Species Act of 1973 can delay or prevent cutting on private lands. At present, the forests have been stabilized by replanting trees. In the last half century, the portion of timberlands cut for wood and pulp approximates the amount harvested earlier in the century. Although the amount of timberland today is comparable to that of the original old-growth forests, the quality is far inferior; the biologically rich virgin forests have been replaced by second- and third-growth forests.

Presently, only about 5 percent of the virgin forests remains from the time when Europeans appeared on these continental shores to begin three centuries of development. Ninety-five percent has been logged and harvested for purposes which will be examined in the following pages. Of the remaining old-growth forests, virtually all are located on public lands and most but not all are located in the Pacific Northwest and Alaska. The struggle in the Northwest was highlighted in April 1993 by the timber summit convened by President Bill Clinton and his Secretary of the Interior, Bruce Babbitt. The summit was held to resolve the dispute between loggers who wanted to continue cutting in the region and environmentalists determined to protect wildlife. The struggle had intensified since the spotted owl was declared endangered in 1990. The summit embraced the concept of "third-wave environmentalism," developed during the 1980s. This brand of

environmentalism endorses cooperation between warring factions and es-
chews confrontation and electoral political solutions as first and second-
wave efforts to resolve disputes.

The summit failed to end federal practices that allow timber companies
to harvest logs at below the market price on federal land. This amounts to a
federal subsidy for the loggers. Nor did the summit recommend that a
royalty fee be paid to the government for timber cut on these lands. Environmentalists regarded these proposed changes in logging policy as essential for the long-term protection of national forests and other federal lands.
Although the summit did not resolve long-standing disagreements, it did
educate most Americans about the unintended consequences of actions by
various federal agencies involved in timber policy. The summit also educated us about the uneven history of enforcing forest management and
wildlife protection policies by the federal government.

Specifically, the summit revealed that raw-log exports to foreign countries were growing, while thousands of workers who formerly worked in the
lumber mills of the Northwest were unemployed. Cutting was up, yet employment in the industry was declining. Also, cutting was accelerating in
areas where logging companies believed that federal agents were about to
enforce wildlife protection regulations. Complicating the matter were the
large number of injunctions issued by federal judges ending logging and
employment in areas where environmentalists argued that logging violated
the provisions of the Endangered Species Act of 1973. To highlight the
potential problems of cutting in the Northwest forests and encroaching on
wildlife habitat, a 1993 Forest Service report concluded that approximately
600 species lived in the Northwestern ancient forests and that many of them
were at risk. The net effect of curtailing cutting had driven lumber prices up
85 percent to $464 per 1,000 board feet by February 1993.*

Informing Americans about the activities of environmentally conscious
loggers was another way to educate the public. One such logger was Homer
T. McCrary. McCrary won the praise of The Nature Conservancy and the
Natural Resources Defense Council and was nominated by the Sierra Club
in 1990 for an award praising his forest conservation practices. Many environmentalists were elated when McCrary's Big Creek Lumber Company

---

*The Endangered Species Act of 1973 replaced the acts of 1966 and 1969 that
protected native wild species threatened with extinction. The new law contained the
concept of critical habitat. Section 7 of the law instructed the Secretary of the Interior to
prevent federal agencies from damaging threatened or endangered species and their
habitat. This section has been used by citizens in court suits to prevent encroachments
upon wildlife ecosystems.

bought 4,000 acres of redwood and fir forest above Butano Creek in the Santa Cruz Mountains of California in 1991.

The former owner had a reputation for ruthlessly clear-cutting the ancient forests. McCrary's approach avoids clear-cutting. Instead, he cuts just four old-growth trees per acre. During the timber summit in Portland, Oregon, McCrary's practices were promoted. Despite this sensitivity to ecology, McCrary's methods of conservation are not embraced by other commercial logging interests. The summit leaders tried to get a commitment from the timber industry to employ more of the low-impact techniques for which McCrary is known. The discussions stalled as federal policy makers and commercial timber interests debated how to balance wildlife protection and timber harvest rates. As the debate dragged on, lumber prices skyrocketed, largely because of logging restrictions on public land.

To government policy makers, McCrary's approach exemplified his respect for the land. Less important to him and other like-minded loggers was maximizing short-term profits. According to McCrary, "The logger has to learn that the real value out here, isn't money or fancy clothes, its the land . . . destroy the land and you've got nothing." McCrary is presented as a model woodsman, whose low-impact logging techniques work without devastating the forests and endangering its animal and human inhabitants.[7]

Although the focus of policy debates about woodlands is the Pacific Northwest and the coverage in the news media highlights events in this region, controversies regarding the use of woodlands are not limited to the Northwest. For example, one of the most important battles currently being fought is related to an effort to prevent commercial logging in about 50 percent of Allegany State Park, New York's largest state park in the Adirondack Forest Preserve. The Park contains 67,000 acres of land currently used primarily for recreation and tourism for hundreds of thousands of visitors annually. Accessible to 25 percent of the nation's population, the Adirondacks are the largest publicly owned wilderness in the Eastern United States. Efforts to harvest trees in the publicly owned areas of the 6–million-acre park system during this century have been defeated often, as New Yorkers have repeatedly opted for preservation rather than conservation.[8]

Privately owned land is actively logged in the Adirondacks but not clear-cut. General agreement exists among environmentalists and their adversaries that clear-cutting destroys wildlife habitat, and causes soil erosion and runoffs which foul lakes, rivers, and streams. The most recent chapter in the story about the Adirondack woods involved a decision to reverse this long-standing policy and to clear-cut more than 30,000 privately owned acres in areas affected by a devastating windstorm on July 15, 1995. About 95,000 publicly owned acres were also damaged in the "forever wild" region of the

Forest Preserve but were not included in this decision because of long-standing policy. In effect, the decision permits private logging companies, of which International Paper Company is the largest, owning about 300,000 acres, to harvest trees in areas damaged by the storm. The decision has broad-based support, including that of the Adirondack Park Agency and Adirondack Mountain Club, but is opposed by Citizens Campaign for the Environment.[9]

The Forests During the Period of European Exploration

Many first person and scholarly accounts discussed the composition and the vastness of the American forests prior to European exploration and settlement. When Columbus first saw the forests of Haiti, he said the land was "filled with trees of a thousand kinds."[10] Exploring the east coast of North America in 1524, Verrazano wrote of "a land full of the largest forests . . . with as much beauty and delectable appearance as would be possible to express."[11]

Some viewed the once vast and immense forests with awe and others with greed. Those who appreciated the forest for its awe-inspiring natural beauty and wildlife became part of a romantic-transcendental tradition in America. Many pioneers, probably a majority, viewed the forest as part of a public domain that provided each of them with opportunity and the possibility of free land and independence. For still others, the forests became resources and commodities, a source of riches. They were interested in profits, and that meant cutting down the forests. As settlers penetrated the forests and began to live in permanent communities, the demand for timber increased. Forests were cleared to provide land for farming or wood for home building.

Some did not perceive the forest in such a positive light and saw only its dark, mysterious, and sinister side. For them, the forest was the hinterland of the devil, since the devil was believed to lurk and live in the woods. In fact, many accounts speak of the evil proceedings late at night which took place in the forest between the devil and his worshipers. Many feared the forest's terrible wilderness. In a work entitled *New England's Prospect,* one settler stated, "some affirm that they have seen a Lyon . . . some likewise lost in the woods have heard such terrible roaring, as have made them much aghast; which must be either Devills or Lyons; there being no other creatures which use to roar saving beares, which have not such a terrible kind of roaring."[12] Governor William Bradford of the Massachusetts Bay Colony commented in 1620, the year of the landing of the Pilgrims, that there was nothing in New England "but a hideous and desolate wilderness, full of wild beasts and wild men."[13] Such fears were not unfounded, for the woods were the habitat for many wild animals and "few matters took up so much space in the records of the inland towns of New England during the early seventeenth century as the killing and maiming of livestock by wild animals."[14] These early seventeenth-century pioneers expressed their link to the wilderness with combative metaphors. The forests and the wilderness were "enemies" to be "subdued," "conquered," and "vanquished." To clear the ancient, primordial forest by cutting it down was to allow light to pour into the "clearing."

This negative view of the relationship between nature and humans did not go unchallenged as the early history of the colonies and then the nation-state unfolded. As early as the nineteenth century, James Fenimore Cooper, in both *The Pioneers* (1823) and *The Prairie* (1827), worried about the destruction of the forests. In *The Pioneers,* Judge Temple warns that trees are being cut with such reckless abandon that within twenty years fuelwood will run out. The transcendental writers of the mid-nineteenth century believed that nature was symbolic of the spiritual world and a vessel containing moral truths which transcended the known universe. The Hudson River Valley painters of the mid-nineteenth century also believed that God was present in nature. These artists revered nature and did not wish to embellish or idealize it in their paintings. Henry David Thoreau, a New England philosopher of nature, concluded that our optimum condition was a balance between wilderness, the source of our creativity, and civilization. *Read document 1.1. It contains a description of the forests and the wilderness from* New England's Prospect *by William Wood.*

The Northeast

Before you read about the history of the decline of the woodlands in the Northeast, you may wish to know that this vast region has undergone a spontaneous resurgence. After more than two centuries of cutting trees for cordwood, commercial logging, and farming, there are more wooded acres in the Northeast today than a century ago. Coal, oil, and natural gas have replaced wood as a major source of fuel. Also, as the demand for arable farmland in the Northeast diminished, the forest was renewed through its natural reproductive capacity.

For example, Maine's mature white pines have a remarkable reproductive capacity, which enables them to distribute tens of thousands of seeds as they flower each fall. This fact should not be viewed solely as a victory for nature, however. First, as a result of logging and farming over more than two centuries, the complex forest ecosystem of the region has been weakened. Second, its diverse plant system has been altered by the introduction of weedy plants and foreign species. Third, the development of large tracts of land, introduced in formerly wooded areas, has disturbed the integrity of the forest. Finally, the proliferation of the northeastern forests has not been repeated elsewhere, thereby pointing out the uniqueness of these forests.

Early History From the Colonial Period to the Civil War

In the northeast colonies, the first forests to be cut down were the great hardwood and white pine forests. Although the first lumber mills in the colonies appeared in Jamestown in 1625, the depletion of the New England forests began with the great migration of the Puritans into the interior of the Massachusetts Bay Colony. As a forewarning of the depleted forests to come, the colony passed an ordinance in 1626 to limit the cutting and sale of timber: "The statute warned of the inconvenience likely to arise from clearing too much land and exporting too many timber products."[15] This earliest of prohibitions against wanton cutting could not overcome the insatiable need for timber in an expanding Puritan community, however.

The need for timber grew with the expansion of the New England colonies. With population growth reaching 45,000 to 50,000 inhabitants, primitive shelters were replaced by the construction of 5,600 to 6,000 permanent dwellings. The survival and development of Puritan society also required timber for as many barns, outbuildings, and structures for special uses: meeting houses, mills, warehouses, and bridges. It is difficult to calculate the number of trees cut and the extent of the damage done to the forests, but wood was also used for fences, furniture, canoes, sleds, sledges, barrels, and a variety of tools and other implements.

One memoir written recalled how "the richest and straightest trees were reserved for the frames of the new houses; shingles were rived from the clearest pine; baskets, chairs bottoms, cattle bows, etc., were made from brown ash butts; . . . tables were made 2 and 1/2 feet wide from a single board without knot or blemish."[16] As early as 1691, agents of the British navy began to mark the tallest and straightest of the white pines with the symbol of a broad arrow. An early example of the "best use" theory of conservation, this mark meant to reserve these trees for their future use as masts.[17] In 1722, the White Pine Act was passed, prohibiting the cutting of white pine in the forests, regardless of size, from New England to New Jersey.

Clearing the land for farmland and townships was a multi-phased endeavor. Settlers cut away the underbrush and the smaller trees, gathered them in piles, and set fire to them. With axes, they felled larger trees in parallel lines to allow for easy plowing and so that oxen could drag the best of them out of the forest for construction material, namely for houses, barns, roads, and bridges. During dry seasons, the settler:

> learned that to pile up the trunks for burning created an overly potash-enriched patch of ground that caused the grain to grow tall with long stalks and little ear. Such piling up for burning made sense only if he wanted to collect large quantities of potash to sell to nearby urban markets. However, if the trunks were burned where they fell the potash was spread reasonably evenly over the ground and the burning trunk helped to consume the adjacent stump.[18]

Clearing the land engaged all of the human and material resources that colonial farmers could gather. As early as the 1820s, it was estimated that a 50–acre farm cost a farmer between one and six dollars per acre, depending on the quality of the land. The real cost, however, calculated in terms of the labor that a farmer would have to invest in order to turn the forested land into agricultural land was a little less than $1,000. In addition, a farmer needed a capital investment, a minimum of fifty dollars per year for about the five years that it took to turn the land into a profitable farm.[19]

Before 1850 about 114 million acres of woodland had been cleared for settlement. After that the rate of clearing land accelerated. "We know that in the ten years between 1850 and 1859 the amount cleared had risen to a colossal total of 39,705,000 acres, equivalent to roughly one-third of all clearing carried out during the preceding two centuries."[20] During the Civil War (1861–1865) and the following years of that decade, the total dropped by almost half. In the next ten years, however, clearing and settling of land by pioneers and farmers approached 50 million acres, the largest total in a single decade in the nation's history.

The large quantitative need for lumber for various purposes was small in comparison to the quantity of wood cut as firewood to protect New Englanders from the harsh and lengthy winter weather.[21] According to William Cronon in *Changes in the Land:*

> A typical New England household probably consumed as much as thirty to forty cords of firewood per year, which can be visualized as a stack of wood four feet wide, four feet high, and three hundred feet long; obtaining such a woodpile meant cutting more than an acre of forest each year. In 1800, the region burned perhaps eighteen times more wood for fuel than it cut for lumber. . . . it is probable that New England consumed more than 260 million cords of firewood between 1630 and 1800.[22]

The practice of transforming woodlands into cordwood continued through the centuries, but with each passing decade cities had to reach further into the hinterland for supplies. By the 1630s Boston had exhausted the woodlands near the city, and supplies had to be imported by boat from Cape Ann. New York experienced similar shortages by 1680 and was forced to stack wood imported from Long Island on the wharves of Manhattan. In Philadelphia, Franklin iron-plate stoves were replacing inefficient fireplaces as sources of heat.[23] As late as 1840, however, about 95 percent of the nation's energy requirements for heating, lighting, and power were supplied by wood.[24] By that time, settlers, farmers, and loggers had cut and consumed more than one billion cords of wood.[25] For the decade of the 1870s, the peak of 1.4 billion cords was reached.[26]

Although most New England forests were cut for fuel, a thriving commercial lumber industry developed in the seventeenth century in order to satisfy the construction boom. The first New England lumber mill was built in Berwick, Maine, in 1631, while a second appeared near York six years later. Within two decades, mills appeared on the sites of what are now the coastal towns and cities of Kittery, Wells, and Portland, Maine. Throughout this period, Maine became the innovator in lumbering techniques and exported experienced lumber men to other regions of the country as those regions began to harvest virgin forests.

From the 1630s onward, the largest concentration of commercial lumbering for mercantile activity and trade was in Maine and New Hampshire along the Merrimack River valley. The wide selection of trees supported the growing maritime trade with Europe. Ranging from 4 to 6 feet in diameter and 120 to 200 feet in height, the white pine trees of this region were especially suited to be used as masts. The deforested European continent no longer had trees of this height and had to splice several together to construct a mast.[27]

By 1800, Maine was the leading exporter of pine, supplying three-fourths of the United States' total export of pine.[28] As foreign shipments became important, shipbuilding as well as lumbering prospered. By the early nineteenth century, Bangor was the nation's lumber capital. As Henry David Thoreau noted in 1837, saw mills were everywhere. Bangor had more than 250 saw mills operating upstream, and the city was the principal lumber depot on this continent, with a population of 12,000. Maine's ships, stacked with lumber, sailed off to Spain, England, and the West Indies, to return overflowing with foreign goods, luxuries, and refinements.[29]

The largest forests of white pine existed in the southwest section of Maine. Its timber attracted many and produced a major incentive for permanent settlement. Also, Maine's preeminence in the forest industry was aided by forest fires in 1761 and 1762, which destroyed the fledging New Hampshire industry. New Hampshire settlers became Maine lumberjacks,

Hudson River Logging, Winslow Homer. Library of Congress
(LC-D416–29943–DLC).

according to traveler Edward Augustus Kendall, who visited Maine in 1807 and 1808.[30] Unlike Massachusetts rivers, Maine's swift-moving rivers and streams provided power for saw mills and also became arteries of inexpensive transportation, carrying logs to the mills and to the markets.

By 1840, New York exceeded Maine in the number of mills and product value. Ten years later milling logs into lumber became the number one manufacturing industry in the United States.[31] Pennsylvania and New York exceeded Maine and Massachusetts in terms of the total number of saw mills, board feet of cut timber, and total value of forest products. With the coming of the Civil War in 1861, two changes occurred in the lumber industry. First, the Lake States—Michigan, Wisconsin, and Minnesota— began to dominate the lumber industry. Second, spruce passed pine as the primary commercial timber in Maine; as a result, its timber production increased. Although the last years of the nineteenth century witnessed new levels of productivity, by then the heyday of Maine's lumber industry had passed.[32]

Early Warnings About the Effects of Deforestation

The realization that New England's forests were declining occurred in the eighteenth century, and the effort to curtail the most flagrant abuses followed almost immediately. As early as the 1780s, laws were passed to prohibit unscrupulous lumber men from cutting on public lands. The Massachusetts legislature in 1784 imposed heavy fines on those violating the ban. With timber becoming scarce, increased attention was given to building of stone fences rather than wooden ones in New England. As early as 1799, the United States Congress passed conservation legislation allowing the President to buy live oak timberland since naval officers were anxious to preserve live oak stands for the all-wooden navy. By 1827, during the administration of John Quincy Adams, a program of live oak conservation was initiated, to purchase, preserve, and increase live oak stands. In fact, the government sponsored the first forestry experimentation station on the Santa Rosa peninsula of Florida in 1828. Within a year, the forestry station had replanted 40,000 trees, constructed buildings, and built six miles of roads.[33] Nevertheless, the territorial government overseeing these lands newly acquired from Spain could not control lumber thieves from cutting on federal land, and the experiment was abandoned within a year.

Environmental concerns followed swiftly after the clear-cutting of the forests. In the early nineteenth century, public beliefs about the nation's forests began to change from the idea that forest resources were unlimited. Various experts began to express doubts that trees were capable of quick regeneration if the land was cleared for immediate agricultural use or even clear-cut and abandoned. Some prophetic observations were made by statesmen and scholars during these early years about the environmental damage done in the name of economic gain.

President James Madison, speaking to the Albemarle Agricultural Society in 1818, noted that: "none is so much to be regretted, perhaps because none is so difficult to repair, as the injurious and excessive destruction of woodlands."[34] Others raised questions about the effects on the climate of clearing the land. Two books published in the early decades of the century pointed out that clearing changed the climate. Count Volney's *View of the Climate and Soil of the United States of America* (1804) argued that the change was irrefutable:

> Longer summers, later autumns, shorter winters, lighter and less lasting snows and colds less violent were talked of by everybody; and these changes [were] not as gradual and slow, but as quick and sudden, in proportion to the extent of cultivation.[35]

The second book, more comprehensive and scientific than the first, was John Lorain's *Nature and Reason Harmonized in the Practice of Husbandry,* published after his death in 1825. Lorain believed that there was a cycle to nature. For example, the soil experienced decay, growth, rejuvenation, and change. Plowing and growing crops disrupted this natural cycle and prevented the development of decaying organic material, so necessary for the health of the soil. According to Lorain, what it took nature decades to produce, deforestation and farming destroyed in a few years. The observations by Lorain and others of the degradation of the soil caused by deforestation and farming, along with the related climatic changes, were the first signs of an environmental consciousness. "Here were the first stirrings of environmental awareness and the conservation movement, as it became known in the western world. It started in America, and it started in the forest."[36]

The publication in 1864 of a remarkable book, *Man and Nature: Physical Geography as Modified by Human Action* (1864) by George Perkins Marsh, Vermont farmer, congressman, diplomat, and scholar, signaled a change in our public attitudes about the forests. His work was the most celebrated of writings by critics of the new nation's economic practices in the woods. In this widely read and quoted text, Marsh described the decline of past civilizations caused by forest destruction. Excerpts were reprinted in magazines and read by an increasingly literate and informed public. Elected officials quoted Marsh's work when drafting legislation to protect the nation's woodlands.

Marsh pointed out that our planet was at one time covered with immense forests. The ancient landscapes of Greece, Syria, Lebanon, England, Ireland, Germany, Sweden, Haiti, and North and South America, to name a few, were covered with abundant woodlands. Ancient Phoenicians, Persians, and Macedonians used much timber for building ships and temples. Mighty civilizations were built on principles of prosperity and progress, which unfortunately were linked to the commercial value of forests. The clear-cutting of the forests in the Mediterranean region during antiquity and overgrazing by livestock contributed to a severely altered landscape and the decline of the Roman Empire and of nation–states in the region; Palestine, Syria, Egypt, Italy, France, and Spain found their most fertile land turned into arid wastelands. The forested mountains of Serbia were stripped to build the Roman fleet. They have yet to recover from this destruction. China suffered a serious woodland shortage by 1000 A.D., while India found itself in a similar condition. From the later Middle Ages to the modern period in European history, forests were ravaged, as wood was the only fuel source available for growing industries and the primary construction material used for the shelter of humans and beasts.[37]

As you read further, note that the legislation affecting the environment began to appear after the publication of Marsh's work. Nevertheless, although Lewis Mumford, a leading twentieth-century social critic, called

Logging a big load. American Forest Institute. Photographer, Jack Rottier. (LC-D4–4381 DLC)

Man and Nature the "fountainhead of the conservation movement," do not assume that we became a nation of preservationists or conservationists overnight.[38]

By the time of the Civil War, the forests of New England had largely been exhausted. The movement of the timber frontier followed a pattern that took lumber men from the Maine woods to the pineries of the Southeast and to the pine forests of the Great Lakes states beginning in the 1840s. By 1860 the Lake States had surpassed New England, New York, and Pennsylvania: "Logging . . . moved to the pineries, the cypress swamps, and the live oak stands of the Gulf South and to the pine forests of the Great Lakes region and it took only fifty years to deplete the latter."[39] After 1875 and onward, lumber men scaled the North Pacific slopes in search of new challenges. By 1900 the Pacific Northwest was replacing the Lake States in production. Many regions remained productive as sources of timber. As available timber in some older regions declined, lumber merchants moved to newer regions to cut trees. The movement west and south represented the most striking development of commercial logging in the United States in the nineteenth century. The American lumberjack epitomized the woods-man who "scattered tobacco tags and snuff boxes from Bangor, Maine, and Saginaw, Michigan to Bogalusa, Louisiana, and Portland, Oregon."[40]

Read document 1.2, a logger's recollections about working among the tall trees.

The Midwest

The lumber industry cut through the extensive Lake States timberlands with spectacular precision. The woodlands of the region were so vast that the "Big Woods" of Minnesota consisted of nearly two-thirds of the state's land area of about 51 million acres. In Michigan, 32 million acres of forest represented 96 percent of the state's total land area. The industry cut down these forests in thirty years, using a combination of seasoned lumberjacks, numbering in the thousands, and the latest tree-cutting technology and transportation. The industry's heyday was short (1860–90), but its effects on the ecology of the midwestern region of the country were long lasting.

As the northeast virgin woods disappeared, pioneer lumber men estab-lished small mills along the rivers and streams of Michigan, Wisconsin, and Minnesota, where water power could be easily utilized. These early pio-neers did not own the woodland; they logged timber on the public domain with impunity. In addition, huge blocks of land were surveyed and acquired by eastern and local lumber men, who engaged in a bitter struggle over control of the vast pine forests.[41] The military demands of the Civil War placed enormous pressures on these forests, and the struggle for control of the pine forests was intense. In Wisconsin, the exhaustion of its forests was accelerated by the growing development of the Great Plains, with their expanding population and rising standard of frontier living. Growing com-munities created an unprecedented demand for lumber of all kinds, for housing to commercial construction to railroad expansion.

After the Civil War, the cutting of the midwestern timberlands fueled the explosive growth of Chicago and its environs. The city served as the chief lumber market on Lake Michigan and thus directed the movement of white pine from forest to mill to final customer.[42] Given Chicago's favored posi-tion on Lake Michigan and its location on the edge of the western grass-lands, the city had easy access to the dense northern woods of Michigan, Wisconsin, and Minnesota. The white pines of these northern woods were among the most widely distributed in the country during the middle years of the nineteenth century.

Minnesota's first lumber mill was built in the 1820s by Fort Snelling soldiers at the Falls of St. Anthony. By 1830, and until the 1880s, lumber was a major industry. Northeastern investors, particularly from Maine, sent capital, men, and tools into the Minnesota forests as well as the Wisconsin woods to apply the techniques learned in Maine for harvesting timber. For example, John McKusick of Stillwater, Maine, founded the town of Stillwater, Minnesota, and established his lumber company of the same name in 1844. Ten years later, Samuel Hersey and Isaac Staples of Maine built Hersey–Staples Lumber. Both companies and scores of others were built in Stillwater, Minnesota, and other new lumber towns in subsequent years.

Of the 131 important lumber barons in Michigan, Wisconsin, and Minnesota, 48 came from New England, 35 from New York, and 14 from Pennsylvania.[43] As the years passed, ownership of more and more timberlands was concentrated in fewer and fewer hands. Of the estimated 2.8 billion board feet of timber left standing in the United States in 1913, 2.2 billion was held privately. In the Lake States, 215 landowners held 65 percent of all timber.[44] Much of the lumber company expansion in Minnesota was fostered by purchasing land warrants owned by Mexican War veterans. Most veterans had no intention of using their warrants and settling on the land. Ignorant of the real value of the timber in these virgin forests, they sold their warrants for the ready cash provided by these recently formed lumber enterprises.

Dominance in lumber production had shifted from the East to the Midwest during the later years of the nineteenth century. By 1870, Michigan became the nation's number one producer of timber in terms of product value. Wisconsin had leaped to number four. Ten years earlier it had not been ranked among the nation's eight largest timber states. Twenty years later, Minnesota had surpassed Pennsylvania in timber production. The mills of Minneapolis, Minnesota, sawed 500 million board feet of lumber.[45] In 1902, the mills in the state produced 2.5 billion board feet. Yet, a decade later, mills were closing permanently in Winona, Duluth, and Minneapolis.[46]

The east to west movement of the industry changed the position of timber-producing states in relationship to each other. Also, it reflected the expansion of the industry during the nineteenth century and the growing demand for forest products. The fifty years after the Civil War saw the greatest timber cutting in the country's history, concentrated in the Lake States, which were clear-cut to a degree beyond that which had been practiced in any other forest region in the United States. As one historian has noted, the demands on the forest were endless:

> Every new settler upon the fertile prairies means one more added to the vast army of lumber consumers, one more new house to be built, one more barn,

one more 40 acres of land to be fenced, one dozen corn cribs needed . . .
moreover, a vast consumption of lumber was used to build railroads, boats,
churches, new schoolhouses and stores . . . new channels of enterprise added
yearly to the increasing demand for lumber.[47]

The Use of New Technology

Response to the demand for Lake State lumber was assisted by a relatively
level topography with few natural obstacles. This allowed for the rapid
construction of logging railroads and the use of new technology in the form
of the donkey engine and the high-capacity saw mill.[48] By 1860, early
Wisconsin mills began to use circular blade saws, which were fast but made
a wasteful half-inch cut that left piles of sawdust; for example, "a circular
saw, the bite of which averaged five-sixteenths of an inch, could turn 312
feet into dust for every thousand feet of inch board sawn."[49] In 1872,
Wisconsin mills introduced band saws, which eliminated much of the
waste. These were very thin, continuous loop blades connected to pulleys
on a vertical plane.[50]

At the Philadelphia Centennial Exhibition in 1876 the Disston Saw Company exhibited its immensely large band saw, and the days of the wasteful
circular saw were numbered. Companies began to mass-produce iron
framed, adjustable cutting edge band saws. Soon thereafter, other technological innovations, ranging from various mechanical feeds which carried
logs to the saws, to mechanical carriers which transported finished lumber
from the sawmills to the storage yards, were introduced to speed up the
harvesting and processing of trees in the Lake States. The transition from
water power to steam power in the mills accelerated the movement of
lumber to consumers.

Two additional technological changes revolutionized the transportation
of logs, railroad locomotives and high-powered winches called steam donkeys.[51] By 1881, the first steam donkey was used in northwestern California by John Dolbeer, who patented his invention two years later. Within a
few years it was in general use throughout the Lake States and Gulf South
regions of the country. The design was simple: a steam-powered engine
reeled a cable onto a spool, with a log attached to the end of the line. The
engine, anchored to a sled, pulled itself along a skid road with its own
power by use of a block and tackle hung on a nearby tree or stump. The
early steam donkey engines worked side by side with animals. Gradually,
however, a more powerful version called a bull donkey replaced the animal
teams. The impact of the steam engine on the woods was profound: more
trees could be cut from more distant locations. Now, once-marginal lands

could be logged profitably. Clear-cutting became a necessity in donkey logging and in railroad building. Room was needed to maneuver without running into standing trees. Everything had to be clear-cut before moving on.[52] Depletion of the forests was swift with the development of the new technology.

The demand for wood by the prairie settlers led to the destruction of the northern Lake States forests. Ironically, without wood the prairie could not have developed. Americans who contemplated the future of the Great West at mid-century understood that settling the Western prairies meant cutting down much of the forests.[53] Yet, despite the experience in the Northeast with the destruction of the virgin forests of Maine, midwesterners regarded their forests as so extensive that their eventual destruction was inconceivable.[54]

The Costs of Clear-cutting

What were the real long-term costs of a policy of clear-cutting the Northeastern and Lakes region forests versus promoting a sustained-yield forest? The white pines and the conifers were mostly gone by the late 1920s. Despite twenty-five years of intense logging in Wisconsin's northern woods, by 1875 they still contained some 130 billion board feet of white and Norway pine and some 16 billion board feet of hardwood timber. Fifty years later, in 1925, the forest contained hardly a billion feet of white and Norway pine, and some 7 billion feet of hardwoods. Five-sixths of the 18 million acres of original northern forest were gone forever.

The selective cutting of trees rather than clear-cutting would have created a continuously productive timberland. By maintaining a sustained-yield operation, the Lake States would have avoided the need to import lumber from other regions of the country to support their industries after 1920. By 1930, Wisconsin imported 45 percent of its lumber to support its mills, box factories, furniture makers, and panel and veneer mills. The cost of the loss of its existing forest industry denied the state and the region the possibilities of growth, diversification, and flexibility.

An additional cost was the loss of land tax revenues to the region. Large-scale tax delinquency was positively correlated with the exhausted timberland. Tax delinquency occurred in 20 to 50 percent of the clear-cut land in the northern counties of the state in the 1930s as revenues from cut timber plummeted. Had the forests continued to produce through practices of sustained yield, the land would have continued to provide the state with revenue gained from taxes on timber holdings. Also, continuously productive forests sustained by prudent practices would have provided revenues from taxes on mills, equipment, inventory, and income. Clear-cutting resulted "in abandoned or under-used villages, mills, roads, and railroads."[55] Today, this capital loss to the region has not been replaced by farming on former timberland or by the tourist and resort businesses in the region. "Disappearance of the forest as a production factor also meant . . . disappearance of the wage earnings and the investment opportunities and processing and trade profits that went into an active forest-products industry."[56]

Within fifty years, the Wisconsin and Minnesota forests were depleted of their best white pines and their assortment of precious hardwoods. What had not fallen to the lumberjack's ax was destroyed by fires. The magnitude of these fires alerted citizens to the vanishing tree stands more than the methodical, consistent, day-to-day cutting. On the night of October 8, 1871, the Peshtigo fire struck the woods of northern Wisconsin. Since logging took place almost everywhere in the woods, slash on the ground had made the forest floor particularly vulnerable to fire. When the Peshtigo fire hit, it burned out of control for weeks and destroyed a million acres of woodland. In its wake fifteen hundred people lost their lives, more than in the famous Chicago fire at about the same time. The Peshtigo fire "was the worst disaster of its type in American history before, or, for that matter, since. The impact on American thought was sobering; the need for more care apparent. The nation, after all, was built with lumber."[57] When fire destroyed 2,000 square miles of forest in Michigan in 1882, an observer concluded. "The destruction of the great pine-forests . . . of Michigan and Wisconsin, rapidly as it is carried forward by the lumber man's ax, is hastened by . . . fires."[58]

The Minnesota planning board reported in 1930 that little of the virgin forest had survived the lumber man's ax. Of Minnesota's forests, which once covered two-thirds of the state, only about one-third remained, and that was a poor second growth.[59] Alarmed by the fires and the effects of clear-cutting, new conservation efforts began with the first Arbor Day on April 10, 1872, a day devoted to tree-planting.* The American Forestry

---

*Arbor Day began as a state-initiated effort to promote plantings in treeless regions caused by clear-cutting or in naturally treeless areas such as the plains. As early as 1868, Iowa, Kansas, and Wisconsin offered bounties to settlers who planted trees. Missouri, Minnesota, and Maine exempted these lands from taxation. Although the first Arbor Day in 1872 was celebrated in Nebraska, the idea spread quickly to other states. Beginning with Spain in 1896, foreign countries including Italy, England, Canada, Australia, France, Mexico, Norway, Russia, Japan, and China designated Arbor Day as a national day. For all the day became an opportunity to plant trees, orchards, flowers, and groves. Arbor Day remained a local and state affair until President Richard Nixon proclaimed it a national day in 1970. In 1972 a national Arbor Day Foundation was established with headquarters in Nebraska to promote conservation of the nation's woodlands and to continue the practice of planting. Today, Arbor Day is celebrated at different times of the year in all states.

Association was established in 1875 and began its informational campaign to alert lumbermen about the hazards of clear-cutting on private lands.* In 1881, Congress created the Division of Forestry in the Department of Agriculture for the purpose of monitoring timber supplies and demand.

By the end of the nineteenth century only 10 percent of Wisconsin's northern forest remained capable of producing salable saw logs.[60] Lumber men had cut over much of Michigan by 1892, and only Minnesota possessed timber that competed in price and quality with logs from the newly opened forests of the Pacific Northwest. In the milltown of Alpena, Michigan, the account of what remained after decades of clear-cutting could not have been more bleak:

> sawdust filled in the swamps, sawdust graded the street, sawdust extended the beach out into the lake; sawdust inclosed rows of piles or quays where the busy dockwalloper shoves the timber aboard the ship. But for the tall, fuming stack consuming the "pulverised plank" there would be a mountain like that of Cheboygan—sixty feet in height and ten acres in area. Until twelve months ago the rumble of the wheel or the beat of a hoof was never heard in Alpena. Now they have roadways on round cedar blocks.[61]

Northern Michigan, northern Wisconsin, and northeastern Minnesota had been transformed in little more than a quarter century from some of the nation's finest woods to cutover lands of indestructible pine stumps and tangled debris. Never suitable for farming, the fragile landscape was made more vulnerable by the cutting away of the protective canopy of tall pines. Soil exposed to unbroken winds, extreme temperature fluctuations, and flooding accelerated erosion. In 1897, Filibert Roth of the U.S. Division of Forestry wrote: "Logging has been carried on in almost every town of this region, and over 8 million of the 17 million acres of forest are cutover lands, largely burned over and waste brush lands, and one half of it as nearly desert as it can become in the climate of Wisconsin."[62] Lumber men left this region, crippled by the ax, in the last decades of the last century. As late as the 1930s, agriculture, which had replaced logging in the New En-

---

*Since its inception the American Forestry Association has advocated the establishment of national forests in the White Mountains of New Hampshire and in the southern Appalachians. As early as 1905, it sponsored an American Forest Congress in Washington, D.C., in which President Theodore Roosevelt gave the keynote address. In addition to supporting major federal legislation including the Weeks Act of 1911, which authorized the federal government to purchase forests, the AFA has served an important educational function through the publication of books and magazines. Its monthly journal, currently titled *American Forests,* has been published since 1898. Today, AFA has more than 80,000 members.

gland woods during the eighteenth century, had not gained a foothold in the Lake States.

The Environmental Effects on Midwest Forests

Cutover forests and repeated fires opened the midwest landscape to the natural elements of wind and sunlight. Changes in the region's microclimates followed deforestation. The temperature of the soil and ground level air rose; the climate became decidedly drier as vast woodlands were logged, exposing the surface. The temperature of the Lake States region rose several degrees Fahrenheit without the forest canopy to shade the ground. Temperatures of 100° F were not uncommon during the summer months as the heat of the sun beat upon the earth's exposed surface and ground level winds blew across the land unobstructed by trees.

Denuding the land of the Lake States affected the region's water cycle. Without the roots of trees to hold soil in place during rainy seasons or during the spring thaw, topsoil washed into the rivers and streams. Adding to the silt load in rivers was the sawdust from shoreline lumber mills. The combination of silt and sawdust clogged waterways and disrupted the natural life cycle of fish. Additionally, waterways, exposed to unbroken sunlight, became warmer, sometimes by as much as 50°F. Rainfall hitting exposed and therefore warmer soil caused it to flow uninterrupted to the rivers and streams. Since many native fish required colder water temperatures to spawn, declining fish populations were an unintended consequence of clear-cutting. *The concern about the depletion of the Wisconsin forests is described in "A Report on the Disastrous Effects of the Destruction of Forest Trees, 1867." Read document 1.3.*

As the demand for forest products began to exhaust the timber supply in the Lake States, loggers began to move to other regions of the country. Led by Frederick Weyerhaeuser, who had integrated the lumber industry in the Lake States by owning forest land, mills, transportation, and marketing establishments, they began to purchase thousands of acres of timberlands in the Gulf South as well as the Pacific Northwest. In the late 1870s, these lumber barons moved to the Gulf South—Mississippi, Louisiana, Texas, and Oklahoma.

The South

Many of the characteristics which shaped the transformation of the forests of Michigan, Minnesota, and Wisconsin into lumber commodities also shaped the development of the timber industry in the Gulf South. Northern

entrepreneurs from Illinois, Iowa, and Pennsylvania were in the vanguard of
the expansion into the South. Like the Northeast and the Lake States forests
before them, these forests were thought to be inexhaustible. At a United
States Senate investigative hearing held in 1880 to assess the future of the
nation's woodlands, it was determined that "the amount of longleaf standing timber in those states bordering the Gulf of Mexico was one hundred
and seven billion feet."[63] In the eyes of most lumber men, such a large
figure meant that the forests were limitless and therefore could be clear-cut
indiscriminately. Since farmers in the region viewed the forests as an im-
pediment to the development of farmland, it was of little wonder that woodlands virtually disappeared in a generation or two. The trees not cut for
timber or cleared for farmland were cut for fuel. In 1850, a typical 400 ton
riverboat burned 660 cords on an eleven-day round trip between Louisville
and New Orleans![64]

At the same time, settlers and travelers alike acknowledged the beauty of
the Gulf South forests. In *Harper's Monthly,* one observer described the
Texas forest as "park-like with little or no undergrowth except along the
water courses. The trees rose in stately grandeur and wildlife was abundant."[65] America's first nature essayist, William Bartram, published his
Travels in 1791. In the Carolinas, Georgia, and Florida, he described the
forests in the following way: "And now appeared in sight, a tree that
claimed my whole attention: it was the Carica papaya. . . . This admirable
tree is certainly the most beautiful of any vegetable production I know of;
the towering Laurel Magnolia, and the exalted Palm, indeed exceed it in
grandeur and magnificence, but not in elegance, delicacy, and gracefulness.
It rises erect to the height of fifteen or twenty feet. . . . Its perfectly spherical
top is formed of very large . . . leaves, supported on very long footwalks. . . . It
is always green, ornamented at the same time with flowers and fruit."[66] To
naturalist John Muir, founder in 1892 of the Sierra Club, the first organization dedicated to wilderness preservation, the forests were to be celebrated
for their impressiveness and beauty.* Their beauty was most strikingly

---

*The Sierra Club has grown during the past century from a small local club
determined to protect the Sierra Nevada Mountains in California to an organization with
more than a quarter of a million members devoted to a host of environmental issues.
Since 1892 the Club has led efforts to stop the construction of dams which flood
national lands. In some instances, they failed, as in the effort to prevent the construction
of the Hetch Hetchy Dam in Northern California in 1913. The club has also had its share
of successes, including the campaign to prevent the flooding of Dinosaur National
Monument so that a dam could be built on the Colorado–Utah border in 1952. The Club
defeated efforts to flood sections of the Grand Canyon National Park in 1968 by
building dams at Bridge and Marble Canyons in Arizona. Unfortunately, these efforts

expressed by Muir in *A Thousand Mile Walk to the Gulf* as he approached Savannah, Georgia:

> [live oaks] are the most magnificent planted trees I have ever seen, about fifty feet high and perhaps three or four feet in diameter, with broad spreading leafy heads. The main branches reach out horizontally until they come together . . . each branch is adorned like a garden with ferns, flowers, grasses, and dwarf palmettos.[67]

The Impact of Clear-cutting the Southern Forests

Fortunately, the response to clear-cutting the Gulf South forests was different from that heard earlier in the Northeast and the Midwest. The clear-cutting led experts to predict lumber shortages after the turn of the century. In 1900, the United States Bureau of Forestry estimated that the virgin yellow pine of the Gulf States might last another twenty years. More specifically, in 1908, U.S. foresters noted that "one half of the longleaf standing in Mississippi had already been converted into stumps. They forecast that in less than twenty-five years the virgin timber would be exhausted." In Georgia, where it had been estimated that a virgin forest of 36 million acres existed at the time of European colonization, almost 19 million acres had been clear-cut by 1930.[68]

By 1919 the South found itself in a position similar to that of the Lake States thirty years before. In that year the South produced 37 percent of the nation's lumber supply, as had the Lake States before them. In order to achieve this position, forests in the South had been reduced by almost 40 percent, or from 300 million acres to 178 million by 1919. Of the 178 million, only 39 million was virgin forest.[69] As R. D. Forbes noted in 1923, along the route from Virginia to Texas there existed, "Nameless Towns, their monuments huge piles of sawdust, their unwritten epitaph: 'The mill cut out!'. . . the catastrophe . . . of a vanished industry, unreplaced by any new industries remotely adequate to redeem the situation."[70] The lumber town in his account was a mere skeleton of its former exuberant self:

> the hotel was empty, the bank closed, the stores out of business: fine grain logs of Louisiana longleaf pine, the big sawmill that for twenty years had

---

cost the Sierra Club its tax-deductible, non-profit status for lobbying government officials. Its affirmation of wilderness and preservation legislation led to the establishment of the Redwood and North Cascade National Parks and the passage of the National Wild and Scenic Rivers and National Trails System Acts in the late 1960s. Today, the Sierra Club is involved in a complex set of environmental issues including public land policy, wildlife, wilderness protection, and energy conservation.

been the pulsating heart of this town, was already sagging on its foundations, its boilers dead, its decks stripped of all removable machinery. A few ragged piles of graying lumber were huddled here and there. . . . The mill had "sawed out"—had cut its last logs six months before. Within the town grass was beginning to grow in the middle of every street and broken window lights bespoke deserted houses.[71]

As a result of these predictions, the Gulf States began to monitor forest depletion by establishing departments and commissions on forestry. In Louisiana a department of forestry was established in 1904, while a state conservation commission began in 1908, and a forestry commission was created in 1918. Texas, Mississippi, Oklahoma, and Arkansas followed with similar agencies responsible for intervening to protect their forests. Policies varied from state to state. For example, the Mississippi legislature revised the tax code to encourage lumber companies to plant trees. Louisiana provided matching funds to protect against forest fires in order to take advantage of funds provided by the federal government under the terms of the Weeks Act passed by Congress in 1911.

In addition, private enterprise began a program of voluntary reforestation. In Arkansas the Crossett Lumber Company initiated the use of lightweight equipment and machinery to avoid destroying small trees and seedlings.[72] Eleven years before the state took the initiative, the company employed a trained forester. In Louisiana, the Industrial Lumber Company imposed limits on the size of trees to be cut, built fire breaks, and seeded areas with new growth. In 1922, the Great Southern Lumber Company established a seedling nursery three years before the state created its own. All of these activities demonstrated a heightened awareness of the pending crisis in the nation's forests.

Early Conservation Initiatives

Conservation initiatives by private enterprise and state policies coincided with the actions underway at the federal level. During this time public attitudes about forests were in transition. The knowledge gained by reading George Perkins Marsh's *Man and Nature* (1864) competed with traditional notions about the inexhaustibility and natural regenerative capacity of the forests. In the 1880s, Congress began to hold hearings on ways to slow forest depletion. Until then, land held by the federal government was believed to be land held as commons, meaning that everyone could use it but no person or group was responsible for its protection or upkeep. Congress believed that the way to protect land was to transfer it to private ownership. Toward this end, Congress passed the Timber and Stone Act of 1878. The revisions of the act allowed public lands in the Pacific Northwest—California, Oregon, and Washington—to be sold for no less than $2.50 an acre. The law was extended in 1892 to cover all public lands held in the states.

Federal land policy remained ambiguous throughout this early period of land policy reform. Under the provisions of the Timber and Stone Act, public lands were converted to private use for the expressed purpose of protecting the forests and making timber available to settlers. At the same time, Congress, the Interior Department, the General Land Office, and private organizations proposed that forests be appraised for their value and be managed by the government to protect against future timber shortages. This proposal represented a shift from thinking about forests as inexhaustible and began an era of management of the nation's woodlands. With the passage of the Forest Reserve Act of 1891, the president was given authority to establish forest reserves. Many states followed by creating reserves from land deeded to them from the federal government. Public ownership of woodlands gradually became the preferred way to protect the forests.[73]

The Rocky Mountain Region and the Pacific Northwest

Retaining woodlands became a new national initiative and the harbinger for the eventual national park and forest conservation policies of the government. Federal land policy remained contradictory, however, since the Timber and Stone Act was extended to all states one year after the passage of the Forest Reserve Act in 1891. The passage of the Weeks Act of 1911 established the National Forest Reservation Commission. It authorized the repurchase of private cutover and abandoned timberlands which had reverted to the states. By 1913, 4 million acres had been added to the 187 million acres of national forest land supervised by the Department of Agriculture's Forestry Division. By 1923, however, the federal government had also transferred 12 million acres of timberland from the public domain to private ownership under the provisions of the Timber and Stone Act. Even though disposal of public lands continued, the passage of the Weeks Act represented a major shift in government policy and an important milestone in an incipient conservation movement.

By the 1920s, southern forests were in decline. Forty years of aggressive clear-cutting from 1880 to 1920, using the advanced technology of power skidders to gather logs in the woods and logging railroads to transport them to massive mills for sawing and marketing, devastated the land. The technology was particularly hostile to the fragile Gulf States environment of sandy soils and bog land. The harvesting and gathering of southern pines was done by mobile Dolbeer steam donkeys outfitted with steel cables, which were described as:

> an octopus of steel with several grappling arms running out 300 or more feet. These grapple a tree of any size that has been felled, and drag it through the wood to the tram road. These become enormous battering rams and lay low everything in their way. Standing trees that are not pulled down are skinned so badly as to be worthless.[74]

Depleting the forests in New England, the Gulf South, and the Midwest had a number of negative environmental effects. Lumbering increased soil erosion. Many rivers literally became paved with the gravel and topsoil from the eroded landscape, thereby covering the natural spawning habitat for river trout and salmon. The water temperature of many streams and rivers rose because they were no longer protected by the shade of the forest. This was the world left behind by woodsmen as they turned their attention to the magnificent forests of the Pacific Northwest. By the 1880s the lumber industry from the Lake States region began to purchase thousands of acres of woodland in the Pacific Northwest.

The forests of Montana, Idaho, Northern California, Washington, and Oregon represent the largest share of the nation's remaining bounty of old-growth trees. However, that bounty, built up since the last Ice Age, is declining in the Rocky Mountain and Cascade ranges. Only 5 percent of the nearly one million acres of timberland owned by companies in the Rocky Mountain region is stocked with trees in excess of 21 inches in diameter. "A third of the volume . . . is 'pole timber.' "[75] Despite the fact that the old-growth forest is rapidly disappearing, increased cutting became the norm in the 1980s. In Montana alone, timber harvesting rose 20 percent, to nearly a quarter of a billion board feet more than it had been just ten years earlier.[76]

One explanation for the increased timber activity in the region may be the perception among lumber companies of the size of the forests and the sheer volume of available trees. The average Pacific Northwest forest is vast. Today, the region contains just under 400 tons of trees an acre, whereas some redwood forests contain 1800 tons an acre.[77] Early loggers in the region, much like their predecessors in the Northeast, Lake States, and Gulf South believed that they had finally found an inexhaustible forest. However, commercial logging and technology soon took their toll on the Pacific Northwest forest. The beginning stages of deforestation had set in. No forest is vast enough to sustain a civilization when its people are a major consumer of wood products.

Pacific Northwest trees were bigger than any that had been seen before. The majestic redwoods of California and the giant Douglas firs, cedars, spruces, and hemlocks of Oregon and Washington were incomparable. Many stretched 250 feet into the sky and measured 50 feet around the base of the trunk. The forests are the home of the massive coastal redwood. The tallest tree in the world, a coast redwood, is located in Redwood National Park in the northwest corner of California and measures 368 feet high. The tallest giant sequoias, rarely exceeding 300 feet, do not reach the heights of the coast redwoods. The sequoias, however, are known for their mass and age. For example, the General Sherman Tree in California's Giant Forest is thought to weigh 1,250 tons, and the oldest giant sequoias are about 3,200 years old, about 1,000 years older than the coast redwoods.

Weather patterns play an important role in creating and maintaining these mammoth tree stands. The climate of the area consists of wet and moderate winters followed by relatively dry and cool summers. It is a marine climate with extended frost-free seasons, with minor fluctuations between day and night temperatures. Rainfall is very heavy along the coasts, ranging from 70 to 120 inches. Further inland the precipitation falls to less than 50 inches. Most of the rain falls because of the interaction of low pressure systems from the ocean driven by the prevailing westerly winds. The Cascades, Olympic, and Klamath Mountains effectively distribute the precipitation from coastal areas to the interior valleys.

The massive size and age of the trees in western Washington and the coastal and northwestern region of Oregon are among the significant outcomes of this unique marine climate. As in other temperate forests, conifers rather than deciduous hardwoods dominate the area. "A typical Douglas fir will live 750 years or more, attain a diameter of 60 to 85 inches, and reach a height of 250 feet. The biomass accumulation per acre, meaning the total living material in an environmental space, achieved by the Douglas fir is the largest known for any plant species in the world."[78] (The botanical explorer David Douglas, for whom the fir was named, entered the Oregon woods in 1826. Sponsored by the London Horticultural Society, he traveled to the Pacific Northwest by ship for eight months and fourteen days, landing at the mouth of the Columbia River to begin his journey into the wilderness.) With such massive growths, the Pacific Northwest is crucial to the stability of the region's and the world's climate. The region's forests cause up to a third of the local precipitation, and they store more carbon than any other terrestrial ecosystem. John Muir believed that the soil of this region was the best that one could imagine for growing trees. *For a description of the forests of the state of Washington in the later years of the nineteenth century read document 1.4, an account by John Muir titled "The Forests of Washington," published in 1918.*

Early Nineteenth-Century Logging in the Northwest

The California gold rush of 1849 changed the natural ecology of the Pacific Northwest as the region's ubiquitous forests became commodities for the area's exploding population. Thousands of miners and prospectors arrived in San Francisco from late 1848 to the end of 1849. During the second half of 1849, the city's population jumped from 6,000 to 20,000 people. Construction of buildings of all kinds became the highest priority as ships laden with lumber from Santa Cruz steamed into port to meet the growing demand. Meanwhile saw mills were springing up in the Oregon Territory to satisfy San Francisco's growth. The census of 1850 noted that thirty-seven saw mills were operating there, producing nearly 21 million board feet of lumber each year.[79]

Early setters to the region were stunned by the dimensions of the virgin trees. In the 1850s, Silas Plimpton, who lived on the lower Columbia River, wrote:

> The old growth of trees are now lieing prostrate & cover a great portion of the land. I have traveled a greate distance upon ceder logs that were three & four hundred feet long & from 4 to 10 feet in diameter such trees as these would surprise you were you to see them. Most of the timber that is standing is very large & lofty. The way we clear this land is somewhat singular—we bore holes in the trees & set them on fire with a match & they will burn down few days & then after they are down they will burn the inside of the tree all out & leave nothing but the sap & bark.[80]

Although the size of these trees did not deter lumber men from cutting them down, the hazards of navigating the Columbia River forced them to look for alternative sources of supply. In the words of John Muir, the forests around Puget Sound in Washington, "as if courting their fate [came] down from the mountains far and near to offer themselves to the ax."[81] The construction of five steam powered saw mills to handle the increased volume of cut timber by the end of 1853 stimulated the population growth of Seattle.

In the northern California area that was to become Humboldt Bay, lumber was milled for the San Francisco market. In 1853, during the California gold rush, two Maine lumber men, Andrew John Pope and Frederick Talbot, opened a yard in San Francisco and sold lumber to gold diggers. Two years later they built a mill on Puget Sound in order to take advantage of its many protected harbors. They cut its shoreline timber stands and sold the lumber in the domestic and foreign marketplace. By the 1880s the Pacific lumber trade was centered on the Sound and in the Humboldt Bay area, and the Pope and Talbot Puget Mill Company became most profitable. Avoiding the boom and bust pattern of many other mill owners, they based their success on diversification. They "pursued a policy of market diversity with up to 40 percent of the cut going to overseas markets annually, and aggressively pursued new markets whether in San Diego or Hawaii."[82]

The Impact of New Technology

Throughout the remainder of the nineteenth century, many of the other lumber mills of the Pacific Northwest faced the same boom and bust pattern as those in operation earlier in the Lake States. Those that thrived did so because they possessed financial stability gained from earlier lumber-shipping ventures. In addition, they practiced industry integration by owning ships and tug boats to transport the logs and by purchasing thousands of acres of forest. Others in the lumber industry failed because of financial instability and market forces. Overproduction led to oversupply. Some producers entered the forests and made massive capital investments in logging and milling equipment, and their larger and highly trained workforces helped them replace less competitive companies. The economic effects of high capital investment in innovations such as steam power and railroad–donkey logging destroyed the small lumber operations.

This transition to more advanced forms of mechanization as logging moved from the Lake States to the Pacific Northwest led to higher productivity in harvesting trees. During the early years of the twentieth century and beyond, the internal combustion engine reduced the need for railroads. With internal combustion, harvesting of trees entered the modern age, and the railroad days in the woods came to an end. The steam donkey engine, invented in 1881, described earlier as "an octopus of steel with several grappling arms," had allowed loggers (with the aid of another invention, the steel cable), to drag logs of greater size longer distances to yards for storage before transport by railroads. Hauling logs by cable could be achieved efficiently only if the forest had been cleared of obstructions. Any new growth fell victim to the cables and the logs dragged by them. The steam donkey devastated the forest. Gasoline power replaced the steam powered donkey in the second quarter of the twentieth century, making another dramatic impact on both the woods and the men who worked there.[83]

The internal combustion engine came to logging in three distinct forms: the chain saw, the logging truck, and the caterpillar tractor. In 1927, Andreas Stihl of Germany invented the gas powered chain saw. Although these were mass-produced in the 1930s, they were not widely used in the forests until an Oregon logger named Joe Cox improved their design in 1947. They then replaced the old crosscut hand saws immediately. As a result:

> ... significant reduction of waste came through the adoption of the saw because it enabled fellers to use what became known as the Humboldt under-cut. A horizontal cut was made first, followed by an upward-sloping cut from below. In this way the wedge of the undercut was taken from the stump and not from the butt of the log, which was left with a squared end, and so between 3 and 7 percent of the best timber was saved.[84]

The general acceptance of the chain saw ended the logger's practice of cutting trees 10 to 12 feet above the ground, thereby avoiding the work of cutting through the thick bark and very large base of most trees in the Northwest forests. Both the work and the economies of the industry had encouraged wasteful cutting practices. Loggers only cut trees that yielded a minimum of three logs 24 feet long and 30 inches in diameter. With these specifications, the upper 40 to 50 feet of most trees represented debris covering the forest floor. Combined with the 10–foot stumps, the resulting sight was an ugly one. The advent of the labor-saving chain saw and the elimination of the labor-intensive whipsaw along with the disappearance of the steam donkey changed logging in accessible forests but opened more remote ones to the industry.

Caterpillar tractors replaced the old steam donkeys after World War I. They eliminated the need to construct an elaborate cable network in each section of the woods.[85] With all these inventions there was no area in the Pacific Northwest too remote for a viable logging operation. The harvesting of trees could and did occur everywhere, and more quickly. Initially, gasoline powered tractors were used to haul trailers loaded with logs out of the woods. As a result of armored tank tread design and maneuverability improvement during World War I, tractors became more adaptable to hauling in more difficult terrain. Later a number of innovations were added to make tractors even more effective logging vehicles. An A-frame hoist in the rear of tractors allowed them to lift logs and maneuver out of the forest. Larger diesel powered haulers designed after World War II were able to pick up larger redwood and Douglas fir logs.[86]

Logging trucks did not replace railroad cars until the 1930s, but then the changeover was rapid. Innovations in the design of tires and the installation of detachable trailers on trucks accelerated the decline of logging railroads, as did the soaring cost of constructing railroads. Depending on the terrain over which the railroads were built, the cost ranged from $50,000 to $1 million per mile—a cost which could be eliminated, given the availability of more cost-effective trucks. However, passable roads were needed for transporting timber in trucks:

> Between 1925 and 1940 thousands of miles of fast all-weather highway were constructed at no cost to the truck operators, with 10 different crossings of the Coast Ranges linking the interior to the Pacific Coast, 8 across the Cascades, and 10 more up into the high valleys. . . . Simply, although truck hauling was dearer than logging railroad hauling per unit mile, the public road system allowed truck operators the opportunity to disregard amortization costs on routes, which railroad operators could not ignore on their tracks. As the road system expanded, the rail system contracted. Thousands of miles of track and hundreds of locomotives were abandoned or sold, if possible, for scrap. A totally new concept of forest exploitation had evolved and now prevailed, and the western forest of the 1940s was totally different from the forest of 1900 or even that of 1920.[87]

The Conservation Movement

As one technological innovation after another entered the woods in the century after the Civil War, the conservation movement entered its modern phase. With modernization came increasing knowledge about the far-reaching implications of deforestation and awareness that the Pacific Northwest, California, and portions of the Rocky Mountain region represented "the last lumber frontier." Organizational strength came with the founding of the Sierra Club (1892), the Audubon Society (1905), and the Wilderness Society (1935), and a score of other state and national preservation and conservation associations. Governmental action entered a new phase with the creation of conservation agencies, namely the Forest and Park Services. Both became agencies for maintaining national forests and parks for public use, not private exploitation.

Inspired by George Perkins Marsh's *Man and Nature* and John Wesley Powell's *Report on the Lands of the Arid Region of the United States,* early conservationists became aware of the relationship between woodlands and water supplies, particularly in the water-starved areas of the West. Congress responded in 1872 by setting aside 2 million acres of federal land to establish Yellowstone National Park during the presidency of Ulysses S. Grant. It must be noted, however, that the Congress also passed a Mining Law (1872), which gave federal land to any person or company who claimed that minerals existed on the land. For a registration fee, the claimant took possession of the land and its minerals! To the dismay of environmentalists, this public "giveaway" of federal land exists to this very day. Federal policy in 1872 remained ambivalent when it came to protecting public land. Although a report written by President Grant's Secretary of the Interior in

1874 pointed out that illegal harvesting by individuals and companies was taking place in the nation's forests, the president did not take action against the practice.

In an attempt to halt government plans to give away public forest lands in 1877, Carl Schurz, Secretary of the Interior for President Rutherford B. Hayes, recommended that the federal government retain title to its forest lands and not "privatize" them. In effect, privatizing federal forests meant giving them away to the states, corporations, and individuals, either for nominal fees or on condition that the resources be cut, mined, or farmed. Schurz's recommendation was ignored as Congress passed the Timber and Stone Act in 1878, which legitimized the government's giveaway and its policing powers over the use of public lands. In 1889, Schurz delivered a speech to the American Forestry Association, which had become an important force in protecting our forests. In it, he observed that not only had the government given away precious forest resources but that the insatiable appetite for lumber had resulted in "enterprising timber thieves not merely stealing trees, but stealing whole forests. I observed hundreds of saw mills in full blast, devoted exclusively to the sawing up of timber from the public lands."[88]

Only with the passage of the Forest Reserve Act in 1891 was "privatization" curtailed somewhat. This act was an undebated rider to a land bill that authorized the President to create national forests where trees could be harvested under government supervision and watersheds created to provide water for municipalities and farms. "The Forest Reserve Act was a precursor to the national forest system adopted in 1905 and marked a major shift in policy away from the transferring of forested land in the public domain to private ownership and toward public ownership and management."[89] Upon its passage, President Benjamin Harrison withdrew 13 million acres and established fifteen forest reserves. Not to be outdone by his predecessor, a lame-duck president, Grover Cleveland in 1897 increased the reserve system by another 21 million acres and established another thirteen forest reserves.[90] These acts represented the most significant efforts at the national level in the nineteenth century to protect the forests within the federal domain.

After the implementation of the Forest Reserve Act to conserve woodlands, an alternative public policy, to preserve the natural landscape, was proposed. Inspired by the writings of John Muir and supported by the railroad industry, the preservationists opposed the harvesting of trees, mining, and farming. In fact, the railroad industry was one of the early supporters of the preservation of nature. Along with the growing tourist industry in the United States, preservationists viewed nature as a respite from the congestion and decay of teeming cities and their polluting factories. The Southern Pacific Railroad supported John Muir's efforts to convince Congress to pass the Yosemite Act in 1890, creating the national park, in part because it was interested in the lucrative tourist trade.

Other supporters of wildlife preserves and national parks included hunting clubs and gun manufacturers. Early preservationists were a mixture of romantics of the John Muir orientation, urban reformers who viewed nature as a release from the confinement of city life, and promoters of sport, railroad travel, and tourism.[91] The uses of the natural landscape would result in conflicts between the two government agencies responsible for the nation's forests and its parks: the U.S. Forest Service,* created in 1905, and the U.S. Park Service,** created in 1916. The Park Service would become a vehicle for promoting tourism and vacations to the national park lands where timber cutting was prohibited. The Forest Service promoted the idea

---

*Located in the Department of Agriculture, the U.S. Forest Service is the outgrowth of efforts begun as early as 1876, when the federal government began to gather statistics on forests on federal lands. In 1886, the Bureau of Forestry was established, and it became the Service on July 1, 1905. The passage of the Forest Reserve Act in 1891, giving the president authority to create forest reserves on federal lands, made forest conservation a matter of public policy and enhanced the powers of the Bureau. With the passage of the Forest Management Act in 1897, administrative guidelines were established for the management of the national reserves. The combined power of Roosevelt and Pinchot expanded the Forest Service greatly. By 1907, they expanded the federal forest system to 151 million acres. Today, the Service maintains almost 200 million acres of national forest, divided into more than 600 forest ranger districts. For a highly instructive and brief history of the Forest Service, see Harold K. Steen, "Forest Service," in *Encyclopedia of American Forest and Conservation History,* ed. Richard C. Davis (New York: Macmillan, 1983), 243–52.

**The idea of a national park is an American invention, unlike the concepts of national forests and wildlife sanctuaries, which have their origins elsewhere. The idea, first proposed by the landscape artist George Catlin in 1832, became a reality on June 30, 1864, when President Abraham Lincoln signed the Yosemite Park Act. The Yosemite Valley, California, first observed by visitors to the area in 1851, is home to giant sequoia and redwood trees. The act turned the management of Yosemite over to California. On March 1, 1872, President Ulysses S. Grant signed the act making Yellowstone the nation's first national park, supervised by the Department of Interior. By 1915, the Department held 4.75 million acres of park land in its inventory, composed of thirteen national parks and eighteen national monuments. The act creating the Service in 1915 stated its purpose as "to conserve the scenery and the natural and historic objects and the wildlife therein and to provide for the enjoyment of the same in such manner and by such means as will leave them unimpaired for the enjoyment of future generations." Today, the Park Service administers forty-two parks and ninety-six monuments as well as lake and seashores, national rivers, historic sites, national parkways, and many other places, landscapes, and objects of national importance. To read more about the history of the Service, see Alfred Runte, "National Parks and National Park Service," in *Encyclopedia of American Forest and Conservation History,* ed. Richard C. Davis (New York: Macmillan, 1983), 464–67.

of an untrammeled wilderness, where forest lands would be protected until the need for lumber exceeded the supply on private lands. The eventual clear-cutting of trees in the national forests by logging companies would become one of the many emotionally charged issues facing environmentalists, public agencies, and private enterprise in the latter years of the twentieth century.

Extensive logging in the Olympic peninsula of Washington, a forested area of 4 million acres, which today contains the Olympic National Park and National Forest, led President Grover Cleveland to place one-half of the land, or 2 million acres, in a forest reserve in 1897. On the western slopes of the Olympic Mountains, these forests are among the most productive in the country. Their high density is the result of the area's rainfall. It is the wettest region in the United States. Precipitation ranges from 90 inches on the coast to more than 220 on the upper-most parts of Mount Olympus.[92] The Forest Management Act of 1897 extended the power of the government further by granting federal officers power to monitor private lumbering, mining, and grazing activity on federal forest lands. Timber cut from dead, mature, or large-growth trees on the reserves was to be sold at or above its appraised value.

Under pressure from settlers to the Olympic peninsula and state legislators alarmed about the loss of tax revenues from the land, Cleveland's successor William McKinley removed one-third from the reserve and changed its status to "unprotected public domain." With the assassination of President McKinley in 1901, Vice President Theodore Roosevelt, a leading environmentalist, was elevated to the presidency. Gifford Pinchot, a trained forester who had been appointed by McKinley, brought the Forestry Division of the Department of Agriculture to a position of prominence in the new administration. Pinchot convinced Roosevelt to transfer the national forest reserves from the Department of the Interior to Agriculture and create the Forest Service under his leadership.

In 1905, Roosevelt transferred 159 forest reserves to the newly established Forest Service. Two years later, these reserves were renamed "national forests." These public timberlands, which had formerly been open for private use, had been removed by the president. Under Pinchot, the national forest system was enlarged to nearly its present size of 191 million acres, including 159 forests and nineteen national grasslands. However, the division of responsibility over public lands between the Interior and Agriculture departments became a source of conflict within the federal government. In addition, it caused confusion and alarm for environmentalists concerned about changing public policy. *Read document 1.5, a selection from Theodore Roosevelt's autobiography.* In his autobiography, Roosevelt justifies his case for moving the division from one federal department to another.

In 1907, Roosevelt restored 127,680 acres to the Olympic reserve and in 1909 created the Mount Olympus National Monument, with 615,000 acres in the central part of the national forest. Roosevelt's actions were prompted not only by pressure from local citizens regarding poaching of Olympic elk but also by a recommendation from the U.S. Biological Survey. Yet Roosevelt's Director of Forest Services, Gifford Pinchot, wrote the proclamation in such a way that it not only established the national monument* but also permitted logging. The struggle to decide the extent of the logging began immediately. To curtail it, preservationists advocated turning the monument into a national park. On the other hand, administrators from the National Forest Service supported legislation which would eliminate the largest woodlands from the monument, thereby making it available for logging. With the support of President Woodrow Wilson's Chief Forester Henry S. Graves, they achieved their goal in 1915. The monument was reduced in size by one-half, thereby removing the best woodlands from the monument and changing their status to "unprotected public domain," in much the same way that President McKinley had reduced the size of public lands held in reserve. The final disposition of the woodlands, mountains, and herds of elk that would eventually become the Olympic National Park would have to await the presidency of Theodore Roosevelt's second cousin, Franklin Delano Roosevelt, in 1938.

In the interim, a major conflict surfaced when preservationists remained firm in their opposition to the flooding of the Hetch Hetchy Valley in Yosemite National Park, California. The flooding of Hetch Hetchy was proposed in order to provide a water reservoir for the city of San Francisco. The conflict pitted John Muir, the preservationist who advocated the idea of unspoiled wilderness, against Gifford Pinchot, the conservationist who supported "wise use" of the nation's woodlands. The majority of newspapers and leading magazines, including *Outlook, Nation,* and *Collier's,* opposed

---

*On June 8, 1906, the American Antiquities Act became law. With it, authority was granted to presidents to establish national monuments. National monuments can include historic landmarks, structures, and other objects of historic significance. Spearheaded by Representative John F. Lacey of Iowa, the act placed the federal government at the center of efforts to eliminate the plunder and destruction of national places by thieves and vandals. A large number of national monuments have been established since the passage of the act, and presidents from Theodore Roosevelt to William Clinton have used the act to protect special lands and places, ranging from cliff dwellings to fur-trading posts and geological formations. National monuments, parks, and forests share similar goals. Congress creates parks and forests and may recommend the establishment of national monuments; however, it is by presidential proclamation that monuments are created.

the flooding of the Valley. The Museum of Natural History in New York hosted a conference opposing the project. Letters opposing it poured into the offices of Congressmen and the president. Despite the overwhelming public opposition to the project, President Wilson and Congress deleted the valley from the park's lands in December 1913. An embittered John Muir concluded: "Nothing dollarable is safe, however guarded."[93] Although public opinion remained divided about the proper use of the country's natural treasures, on the fate of the Hetch Hetchy Valley public opinion had been galvanized on the side of the preservationists. The consciousness of a segment of the society had been awakened.

Despite losing the Hetch Hetchy battle, the preservationists won their fight to establish the National Park Service over the opposition of the National Forest Service. On August 25, 1916, Congress established the agency. Initially created to protect wilderness areas from development, the Park Service shifted its mandate to promoting tourism after the automobile made the parks more accessible to visitors. More tourist-related facilities with support from Congress and industry shaped the future activities of the Service.[94] Making the parks more accessible to tourists also meant making them safer. Park rangers stalked, trapped, and shot all predators believed to threaten travelers in the parks, and "Throughout the 1920s . . . the Park Service eliminated wolves, cougars, coyotes, and other predators from the major parks of the West."[95]

After the Hetch Hetchy controversy, efforts to expand the Mount Olympus National Monument and establish a national park were opposed by the U.S. Forest Service, the logging industry, and the National Park Service. The Forest Service argued that the economic stability of the region depended on an active lumber industry, which the Service maintained provided income to 19,400 people in the area. Preserving woodlands for future logging was vital to the lumber industry. In addition, the U.S. Park Service opposed preservationist arguments on the grounds that the monument was not park quality. Leadership for creating a park came from the Emergency Conservation Committee, established in 1930 by Willard Van Name, a zoologist from the American Museum of Natural History. Along with philanthropist Rosalie Edge and newspaperman Irving Brant, they campaigned against both the U.S. Forest Service and the Park Service for their failure to protect the forests.

Conservation and the New Deal

President Franklin Roosevelt tried to break the impasse by transferring the monument from the Forest Service to the Park Service without the advice or consent of either. Pressure from Roosevelt's Secretary of the Interior, Harold Ickes, resulted in the passage of a 1938 law creating the Olympic National Park, with 648,000 acres. Executive orders by Roosevelt and his successor Harry Truman expanded the park to 898,000 acres by 1952. Under Ickes and his successors, the Department of Interior purchased hundreds of thousands of acres of private land in the Northeast and merged them with existing national forests or established new ones. In the West and Northwest, they claimed ownership over millions of acres. By 1950, some of this land would be incorporated into the Grand Teton National Park.[96]

The establishment of Olympic National Park in 1938 was important for a number of reasons. First, the park area contained a substantial number of valuable old-growth trees, which if allowed to be cut would have generated a high price on the open timber market. Since it lost its forest holdings in Olympic National Park to the National Park Service, the plans of the Forest Service to work with the pulp and lumber industry to harvest the hemlocks on the western slopes of the Olympic peninsula were thwarted. The Forest Service had wanted the park area restricted to the peninsula's interior, leaving them in control of the western region. By controlling the valuable tree stands of the western slopes and monitoring cutting, they could maintain price stability for lumber. Lastly, preventing timber harvesting and future exploitation of the Olympic National Park would cause an eventual confrontation between the Forest Service and preservationists. With declining stands of old-growth trees on privately held lands, increased harvesting in national forests would become the new arena for controversy and conflict between preservationists and the Forest Service along with its ally, the lumber industry. Efforts by the paper and pulp industry to acquire valuable timberlands in the 1940s and again in the 1950s failed to reduce the size of the park. This failure permanently hampered industry expansion in the region.

A major theme of conservation during Franklin Roosevelt's presidency was "scientific forestry." This was practiced most effectively in two regions of the country, the states located in the Tennessee Valley and those Dust Bowl states on the Plains ravaged by drought, high winds, and soil erosion during the 1930s. The Tennessee Valley region had been cutover by settlers and farmers, who cleared the land of much of its ancient oak and hickory stands during the early nineteenth-century trek through the Cumberland Mountains to the Valley. By the 1890s commercial loggers had cut vast tracts of its ancient cedar and cypress woods. While about one-half of the region remained wooded with second- and third-generation trees, their quality was inferior, and much of the land was reduced to wasteland. As a result, much of rural America during the Great Depression from 1929 to 1938 looked like an underdeveloped country, with a growing number of landless people struggling to survive and feed their families.

To salvage the land, Roosevelt instituted a long-term conservation policy of scientific forestry, which combined programs of tree and pasture planting carried out by the Civilian Conservation Corps. Soil regeneration, scientific farming, land reclamation, and bringing electricity to the rural sections of this seven-state region became the goals of federal agencies working with each other. The Tennessee Valley experiment demonstrated that although once destroyed natural forests can never be completely restored, much can be accomplished.

Nothing symbolized the impact of scientific forestry more than the Shelter Belt Program, designed to prevent the Great American Desert from encroaching on the Great Plains states, many of which had been devastated by the dust storms of the 1930s. With the enthusiastic support of Franklin Roosevelt, an avid tree planter on his New York estate, the Forest Service planted 220 million trees and saplings on 30,000 farms. The trees were planted along a 100–mile strip of land that separates the tallgrass prairie from the shortgrass plains, extending from Childress, Texas, to the Canadian border.[97]

Major conservation initiatives ended in 1941 with the American entrance into World War II. *Read document 1.6. This is a speech by President Franklin Roosevelt, who proposed sweeping improvements in the nation's forest policy.* The wartime objective of defeating our enemies placed extraordinary demands on all human and natural resources. To meet the military demands for lumber, increased cutting of trees commenced in the national forests. Until the beginning of the war, clear-cut logging competed with sustained-yield management. However, the war brought many logging companies to the point of acknowledging that cutting in the far western pine country represented the closing of the lumbering frontier. The recognition that a frontier had been reached signified to some that "cut and run" timber practices would not go unchallenged.[98] The war years disrupted the debate between conservationists and members of the timber industry about the percentage of clear-cutting and sustained-yield cutting which should occur in the national forests, however. In the fifteen years after the war, clear-cutting and sustained-yield harvesting of trees had begun to exhaust the woodlands on private lands. By 1960, the timber industry, with the support of the U.S. Forest Service, looked to the national forests as the source of the nation's lumber needs. In that year, cutting in the national forests represented only 22 percent of the nation's timber harvest.

The Environmental Movement and Its Aftermath

During this entire period the preservationists, including the Sierra Club and the Wilderness Society, became more vocal in their efforts to establish national wilderness areas.* Recalling the controversy over the creation of the Olympic National Park, they defeated efforts to flood the Dinosaur National Monument and create the Echo Park Dam along the Utah border in northwestern Colorado. This represented a great victory for the preservationists in the earliest post–World War II years. This victory "set the stage for the proposing and eventual passage of the Wilderness Act in 1964."[99]

The passage of the Wilderness Act of 1964 provided the vehicle for preserving additional woodlands. Soon thereafter, the creation of the North Cascades National Park and Alpines Lakes Wilderness in western Washington in 1968 and 1976, respectively, added forests to the wilderness category. The creation of the Endangered Wilderness Act for western Oregon in 1978 further extended the scope of the 1964 Wilderness Act.

The movement to preserve the nation's woodlands came from several distinct sectors. Preservationists wanted to protect the remaining old-growth forests in their pristine state. However, the lumber industry, aided by the Forest Service, sought to maintain lumber price supports by curbing the supply of lumber in a declining market for wood products. "Part of the explanation for slower growth can be found in the secular drop in the per capita consumption of wood products that began in 1906."[100] Curtailing cutting on public lands represented the industry's way of preserving America's forests.

An active national wilderness movement in the Pacific Northwest became one of the positive outgrowths of the last decades of the century. The wilderness movement's philosophy was embodied in the words of David Brower, executive director of the Sierra Club in the 1960s:

> Wilderness is no longer extensive enough to protect itself. Man must now protect it from himself. He must supply the sense, the hearing, the taste, the smell, the touch, the seeing, making sure that he does not blindly oppose

---

*"Wilderness," as defined by the act of Congress which bears its name, is "an area of undeveloped Federal land retaining its primeval character and influence, without permanent improvements or human habitation, which is protected and managed so as to preserve its natural conditions and which (1) generally appears to have been affected primarily by the forces of nature . . . (2) has outstanding opportunities for solitude or a primitive and unconfined type of recreation; (3) has at least five thousand acres of land or is of sufficient size as to make practicable its preservation and use in an unimpaired condition; and (4) may also contain ecological, geological, or other features of scientific, educational, scenic, or historical value." (William O. Douglas, *A Wilderness Bill of Rights,* Boston: Little, Brown, 1965, 28–29).

progress but that he never lets blind progress go unopposed. What progress seems to have achieved is so spectacular that it preempts our attention; it lets us forget the most important element of all—the life force, the unbroken link to the beginning of life on earth, that from the long-ago beginning on down to each of us has never failed to reproduce itself well and move on. That force, in two billion years, has also produced a miraculous complexity of living things each more dependent upon the others than we know. It has produced organic wholeness, and Robinson Jeffers would have us "love that, not man apart from that."[101]

It was during the 1960s that public interest in the environment, as we know it today, began to take shape. The "environmental movement" of the sixties differed from the earlier "conservation movement." The conservation movement stressed efficiency and sound management in the exploitation of our natural resources, including national forests. The "new environmentalists" shared the ideals of the early preservationists, which advocated the removal of public lands from future use by establishing permanent wilderness areas and national monuments and parks. Both stressed environmental quality and ecology. As for the nation's woodlands, new environmentalists also advocated policies long espoused by preservationists, namely using them for outdoor recreation and for living space and not for lumber production.

What caused the new environmentalism, with its concern for the ecological quality of American life? First, Americans experienced an unprecedented post-war economic boom, which affected all aspects of social and personal life. A rising standard of living for most Americans meant higher salaries and wages, improved housing, a more diversified and more nutritional diet, and more leisure time. For the first time in the nation's history, more Americans were able to meet their basic consumer needs and could place a higher value on amenities, especially nonwork activities. The quality of the surrounding natural environment became a highly valued aspect of an enriched life.

Second, focus on the quality of the environment occurred at a time when the amenities that many Americans enjoyed had come about through technological advances. Electrical power created by burning fossil fuels and by nuclear fission, transmission lines built to service new industrial plants, and new housing developments in a sprawling suburban nation became the symbols of post-war America. The newly constructed roads and highway systems not only connected the country together but also cut deeply into the natural landscape. Many Americans remained ambivalent about these changes while others, the new environmentalists, saw these developments as threats to their enjoyment of leisure and recreation.

Last, the use of chemicals experienced a marked increase, particularly in the growing petroleum and plastics industries and in the availability of chemical agents for household use. The wastes from these products as well as other industrial wastes contaminated the land, air, and water and threatened the health and well-being of insect, mammal, aquatic, and human life. The ranks of the environmental movement swelled, as the knowledge about the potential and real harm to the environment caused by chemical waste became available to an increasing number of Americans.

The passage of the National Environmental Policy Act in 1969 was a victory for the new environmentalists. The new law required each federal agency to assess the environmental impact of a proposed action and offer alternatives if such proposed action was deemed to have a negative impact on the environment. The environmental impact statement would become a powerful tool, used by environmentalists in court to press their cases for protection of nature.

Major environmental legislation protecting the nation's forests emerged from the U.S. Congress during the early years of the new environmental movement. In addition to the National Environmental Policy Act of 1969, the National Forest Management Act of 1976 was passed in response to the federal court decision to prohibit clear-cut logging in the Monongahela National Forest. The Izaak Walton League of America* had sued the U.S. Forest Service and private logging companies on the grounds that clear-cutting violated the Forest Management Act of 1897. The court ruled that in order to allow clear-cutting, new legislation would be required. The 1976 legislation endorsed the concept of multiple use of the forests and included protection of the diversity of plant and animal life in the forests. In addition, the law redefined "sustained yield" to include the notion of nondeclining yield for each of the national forests. Clear-cutting was also redefined as an acceptable silvicultural (meaning care and cultivation of trees) practice. Each of these provisions was steeped in controversy because their net effect was to slow the cutting of trees on public lands.

The environmental movement of the 1970s was slowed considerably during the presidency of Ronald Reagan (1981–1988). Although Congress thwarted many of the administration's efforts to weaken federal environ-

---

*Named for the author of *The Compleat Angler* (1653), the League was founded in Chicago in 1922 to protect fishing waters from water pollution and wetland drainage. Recognizing early the effects of cut-and-run logging on rivers and streams, the League has supported multiple use and sustained-yield forestry. With a membership of more than 50,000, it remains a forceful advocate of clean water, wild and scenic rivers, and a national wilderness system.

mental legislation, millions of acres of national forest were clear-cut by companies who were subsidized by the government. The Department of Agriculture departed from the policy of sustained-yield forestry, which had remained in effect since the days of Gifford Pinchot, in favor of clear-cutting. This aggressive reversal in policy was slowed only by the sluggish demand for lumber during much of the decade of the 1980s. Despite this sluggishness, the department accelerated its program of road building in the national forest system and sold logs to companies at below-cost prices, including the cost of road construction and cutting. Throughout the decade, similar policies were carried out in the Tongass National Forest of Alaska, and in the ancient forests of Washington, Oregon, and California. Although the president and members of his cabinet remained hostile to expanding environmental regulations and tried to roll back initiatives taken by their predecessors by proposing new legislation and budget cuts, a bi-partisan Congress prevented a debacle.

Although President Reagan's successor, George Bush (1989–1992), promoted himself as "the environmental president," his zeal for environmental tasks waned soon after taking office. During his presidency, the Forest Service continued the policy initiatives begun by President Reagan, namely increased road building in the national forests and increased cutting of trees. The size of the public domain increased by 100 million acres when President Carter (1977–1981) signed the Alaska National Interests Lands Act (1980) but stagnated under President Bush. The legacy of the Reagan years, at least in terms of the forests and parks, lived on for an additional four years.

Today, the Forest Service estimates that twelve old-growth national forests in Washington, Oregon, and northern California have 4 million acres of old growth left. Adding in national parks, the total of old-growth forest is 5.4 million acres, of which one million acres are under permanent protection. According to the Wilderness Society, however, the Forest Service has greatly exaggerated the amount of remaining old-growth forest.

One of the first acts of the presidency of William Clinton (1993–) was to address the dispute in the Northwest between loggers and environmentalists. The Northwest Forest Plan was a President Clinton sponsored compromise, which resulted from the 1993 timber summit. The summit was attended by the president, Vice President Gore, nearly a third of the president's cabinet, including Secretary of the Interior Bruce Babbitt, a leading environmentalist, lumber company executives, and Forest Service rangers. The intent was to reduce logging by 80 percent on the last 6 million acres of ancient forests on federal lands in the Northwest. The plan also pledged to spend $1.2 billion to retrain loggers displaced by the plan and restore cutover forests. In addition, the president proclaimed the plan would protect wildlife, while limiting the enforcement of wildlife protection regulations on private lands. In effect, the plan proposed a relaxation of the restrictions on cutting of private timberlands imposed by the Endangered Species Act. This provision of the plan threatened woodland species such as the spotted owl.

The plan opened up other areas, previously closed, for harvesting, and prohibited protesters from seeking court injunctions against contracted tree cutting, a tactic which had either slowed or stopped the sale of woodlands to timber companies. As a result of the agreement, the U.S. Forest Service, along with private loggers, planned to clear-cut woodlands in at least sixty different parts of several national forests. Less timber harvesting would occur in Oregon and more in Washington. The plan had the support of preservationists, loggers, and the government. In the summer of 1995, however, the 104th Congress, the first Congress controlled in both houses by the Republican Party in forty-two years, passed a budget appropriations bill which contained a rider exempting much of the logging in the Pacific Northwest from environmental laws, thereby overturning the provisions of the Clinton Plan reached by the participants at the 1993 summit. After initially opposing the bill, President Clinton signed the bill into law, assuming that administrative regulations would be sufficient to curtail the spirit of the rider. The test of this assumption was made in the federal courts.

A federal court interpreted the new law broadly, giving logging interests a license to begin logging again in areas that the president had vowed to protect. Vice President Al Gore noted:

> That was, indeed, our biggest mistake and it never would have happened except for the miscalculation on our part about the magnitude of what was wrong with the provision. We were genuinely surprised, indeed shocked by the court decision which vastly expanded the scope of something we thought could be muted by administrative action. We knew it was not a good policy. But it was one of those examples of one thing imbedded in a huge, overall measure that had to pass.[102]

This law and the court's interpretation had no effect on the U.S. Forest Service's long-standing practice of auctioning federal woodlands to logging companies. These auctions represent subsidies to logging companies, who purchase timber at below-market prices and also get to use logging roads built by the Forest Service at public expense to enable companies to harvest trees. According to the Wilderness Society, the Forest Service lost $195 million in 1995 by selling under-market-priced trees to loggers. To date, environmental groups who want to purchase woodlands at auction prices and preserve them rather than cut them have been denied access by the Service.

In a separate but related case on January 8, 1995, the United States Supreme Court intervened to protect the forests in the Northwest region. It supported an earlier ruling by the Ninth Circuit Court that Bruce Babbitt, the Secretary of Interior had acted according to the National Environmental Policy Act (NEPA) of 1976. Secretary Babbitt had designated 6.8 million acres of federal land and old-growth forest in 1992 in the states of Oregon, Washington, and California as protected "critical habitat" for the Northern spotted owl. Lawyers for the opposition in Douglas County, Oregon, had argued that Secretary Babbitt had failed to file an environmental impact statement as required by the 1976 Act before making his decision.

The Supreme Court rejected the appeal by Douglas County, a heavily forested region in southwestern Oregon, on grounds that the Endangered Species Act implicitly exempts the secretary from the NEPA in designating a habitat as threatened or endangered. Since Douglas County receives about two-thirds of its annual budget from the receipts of federal timber sales and its property tax base is dependent on a thriving lumber industry, the decision undoubtedly created economic hardship for the county's citizens. The decision by the Supreme Court to let stand the ruling of the Ninth Circuit Court reaffirmed the policy of the federal government to view the land as an integrated entity, an entity which it believes is made up of plant life and wildlife, and upholds a conviction that disruptions in either or both threaten or endanger other parts of the life-sustaining mosaic called the natural world.

During much of the twentieth century, forest management involved curtailing the most flagrant abuses of past centuries. The wholesale clear-cutting of primal woodlands destroyed the canopy which protected vulnerable plant species from the harmful effects of the sun's rays. Root systems which held the earth's protective topsoil in place rotted away after tree stands were felled by the ax and saw. Unshaded and unsecured soils hardened in the sweltering sunlight and were washed away in torrential rain storms. As the hardened ground surface became less able to absorb rain water, the runoff carried topsoil to the nearest streams and rivers, which in turn became clogged with silt.

The destruction of the forests and their conversion to agriculture and later to commercial and residential development has been highly destructive to wildlife and wildlife habitat. The modern conception of the forest as a complex ecosystem of plants, animals, insects, and soil systems, and not as a simple system for the production of wood and the management of the tree stands, will require changes in the ways we define and value the nation's forests.

Document 1.1

New England's Prospect (1634)

William Wood

The next commoditie the land affords, is good store of Woods, & that not onely such as may be needfull for fewell, but likewise for the building of Ships, and houses, & Mils, and all manner of water-worke about which Wood is needefull. The Timber of the Countrey growes straight, and tall, some trees being twenty, some thirty foot high, before they spread forth their branches; generally the Trees be not very thicke, though there be many that will serve for Mill posts, some beeing three foote and a halfe o're. And whereas it is generally conceived, that the woods grow so thicke, that there is no more cleare ground than is hewed out by labour of man; it is nothing so; in many places, divers Acres being cleare, so that one may ride a hunting in most places of the land, if he will venture himself for being lost: there is no underwood saving in swamps, and low grounds that are wet, in which the *English* get Osiers, and Hasles, and such small wood as is for their use. . . .

Though many of these trees may seeme to have epithites contrary to the nature of them as they grow in *England,* yet are they agreeable with the Trees of that Countrie. The chiefe and common Timber for ordinary use is Oake, and Walnut: Of Oakes there be three kindes, the red Oake, white, and blacke; as these are different in kinde, so are they chosen for such uses as they are most fit for, one kind being more fit for clappboard, others for fawne board, some fitter for shipping, others for houses. These Trees affoard much Mast for Hogges, especially every third yeare, bearing a bigger Acorne than our *English* Oake. The Wallnut tree is something different from the *English* Wallnut, being a great deal more tough, and more servicable, and altogether as heavie: and whereas our Gunnes that are stocked with *English* Wallnut, are soone broaken and cracked in frost, being a brittle Wood; we are driven to stock them new with the Country Wallnut, which will endure all blowes, and weather; lasting time out of minde. These trees bear a very good Nut, something smaller, but nothing inferiour in sweetnesse and goodnesse to the *English* Nut, having no bitter pill. There is likewise a tree in some part of the Countrey, that beares a Nut as bigge as a small peare. The Cedar tree is a tree of no great growth, not bearing above a foot and a half square at the most, neither is it very high. I suppose they be much inferiour to the Cedars of *Lebanon* so much commended in holy writ. This wood is more desired for ornament than substance, being of colour red and white like Eugh, smelling as sweete as Iuniper; it is commonly used for seeling of houses, and making of Chests, boxes, and staves. The Firre and Pine bee trees that grow in many places, shooting up exceeding high, especially the Pine: they doe afford good masts, good board, Rozin and Turpentine. Out of these Pines is gotten the candlewood that is so much spoken of, which may serve for a shift amongst poore folkes; but I cannot commend it for singular good, because it is

---

From William Wood, *New England's Prospect,* 1865 edition (New York: Burt Franklin, 1967), 16–20.

something sluttish, dropping a pitchie kinde of substance where it stands. Here no doubt might be good done with saw mils; for I have seene of these stately high-growne trees, ten miles together close by the River side, from whence by shipping they might be conveyed to any desired Port. Likewise it is not improbable that Pitch and Tarre may be forced from these trees, which bear no other kind of fruite. For that countrey Ash, it is much different from the Ash of *England,* being brittle and good for little, so that Wallnut is used for it. The Horne-bound tree is a tough kind of Wood, that requires so much paines in riving as is almost incredible, being the best for making bolles and dishes, not being subject to cracke or leake.

❧

Document 1.2

Cutting Down the Big Woods—
for Twenty Dollars a Month

Louis Blanchard

The old-time logging camps in the early 1880's when I first went into the pineries weren't very big, maybe a dozen men or something like that. I've knowed a crew to go into the woods in the fall, cut the logs for a cabin the first day, put it up the next day, and start cutting timber the day after that. But before I quit logging to settle down on a farm, I worked in camps that had a hundred men—Swedes, Germans, Norwegians, Bohemians, Frenchies, and a lot of others, including some half-breeds and one Negro. The camps got big. We had cook shacks, bunkhouses, blacksmith shops, carpenter shops, barns, hay sheds, and a slew of other log buildings. In them days we even had an outhouse that made life better in the camps over what it was in the early days.

Crosscut and Ax

The first lumberjacks chopped down every tree with a double-bitted ax, but by the time I went into the woods we had crosscut saws and a man who didn't do anything but sharpen saws and repair tools. The sawyer was the king of the camp. He could size up the lay of the land, spit a few times to see where the wind was blowing from, and drop a tree that would drive a stake into the ground when it fell. Sawing was dangerous in some ways. Limbs would fall down sometimes or a tree might kick back when it fell. It might hit another tree on the way down and the butt would jump back awful fast. If the sawyer didn't get out of the way pretty quick, he'd be

Reprinted with permission from Walker D. Wyman, *The Lumberjack Frontier: The Life of a Logger in the Early Days on the Chippeway, Told from the Recollections of Louis Blanchard* (River Falls, Wisconsin: University of Wisconsin–River Falls Press, 1994), 36–47. (Originally published in 1969.)

killed dead as a doornail. That's why the sawyer always broke a trail in the snow around the tree and back away from it so he could get away if he had to.

One season I sawed straight through the winter. That was in 1897 when I worked for Dick Falin on the Couderay River. He paid sawmen twenty to twenty-two dollars a month, and every man had to file his own saw, too. We used a seven-foot saw, and one with that many teeth took a lot of filing every night when we got back to camp. I worked with a feller named Pete King, or that was what we called him since he was French and his name meant "king." Frenchmen were mostly axmen, and the Germans and Norwegians were mostly sawyers. Pete had grown up in Canady and had worked in the logging camps in Massachusetts before drifting out to Wisconsin. He had dropped a lot of fir trees in his day when they did everything with an ax, and so was an awful good man to work with in the woods. He was better with the ax than I was when it come to trimming off branches, and could chop like the devil. He weighed around 175 pounds and I weighed only 150, but we hit it off pretty well and I don't believe I ever rode on the saw much or he would have let me know about it. Maybe we got along because we both had French blood in our veins, and that kind of blood running a crosscut saw on the Chippeway was about as good as there was in any of the camps. . . .

One time I heard about a feller who worked in a camp up on the north shore of Lake Superior. They had just finished cutting every tree up to the line where the next logging rights started. The logger who had the contract always cut up to the line where a tree is blazed. That tree is right on the line, so the one who gets there first cuts the tree. So this feller come to the blazed tree on the line and got ready to saw it down. There was a big limb hanging up there in the tree that had broke off of another tree when it fell against it, and it looked like it might fall anytime. This sawyer's partner said, "Let's leave that tree. It looks like a widow-maker to me. I don't like the looks of it with that big limb hanging up there. It's liable to come down at any time and hit us fellers on the head. Let's leave it and let the fellers on the other side have the darn thing. Its time to quit anyway. This job is done." The little German said it was all right with him, so they went back to camp, and the next morning they were paid off and started down the road home.

The next year the little German feller worked for the same logger, and he started cutting where they left off the year before. Well, they come to that same tree with the same big limb hanging up there. The head sawyer said to them, "Remember when you left that tree last spring?"

"Yes," said the German, "but we was afraid to cut it because of that big limb hanging up there. But if the limb has hung there all year, I guess it's safe to saw the tree down."

There was no wind a blowing when they stepped up to the tree and started sawing it down with their crosscut. All at once that big limb fell straight down and killed one of the men deader than a doornail. He was the man who had said to leave it the year before. That's the way things happen sometimes. I never had any close calls that way, but when the snow is deep and the trees thick, you sure have to watch yourself when a tree falls.

Swampers and Skidders

All the work in the woods was done along the tote road or the branches leading off from it. A pair of sawyers worked out a branch of the tote road for a quarter of a mile, then started out another branch. It was hard to skid logs much farther than that.

The swamper was the man who brushed out the roads so the sawmen could get to their trees, and he made a trail for every tree that had to be skidded to the tote road. Then there was the chain tender, who barked off the tree and put the chain on the log and helped get it on the go-devil. The round-nosed go-devil was a sledlike thing made out of the crotch of a hardwood tree. It looked like the wishbone of a chicken, with a crossbar bolted on. The butts of two or three logs would be loaded on the crossbar and the other end dragged on the snow. A team was hitched to the top of the wishbone, and they could pull two or three big logs at the same time to the skidway.

At the logging road the big trees was piled up so they could be loaded on the sleighs without too much trouble. The skids at the side of the road was made of two tall tamarack trees, maybe seventy or eighty feet long. The butt end was farthest from the road, so the skidder drove up on the road with his go-devil, and then with the help of the swamper rolled the logs onto the skids. The sleighs loaded from there. It kept one skidder busy following two sawyers, and he might skid seventy-five logs a day. . . .

Sleighs on the Tote Roads

The skidway might be four or five miles, maybe more, from the lake or crick that flowed into the old Chippeway River. The crew that come up early in the fall laid out the road and tried to make one that didn't have much of a hill to go up and down with the loads of logs. In the winter water tanks pulled by four horses sprinkled the roads about every night and made them as slick as a piece of greased lightning. We had a piece of iron to put on the runners of the sleighs that we used to cut deep ruts in the ice. This made a good track for the sleighs when they had a load of logs, maybe twenty thousand to thirty thousand board feet.

One of the first jobs I ever had in a logging camp was a flunky for the water tank teamster. We'd have to cut a big hole in the ice, fill our barrels with ice-cold water, and heist them up to the tank on the sleigh runners. It was sixteen feet wide and thirty feet long and maybe held one hundred barrels of water. When the tank was full, the driver started the four-horse team up the road. Two of us flunkies sat on top and pulled the plugs and let the water run into the ruts. Most of the time the water froze right away. This kept a good glare of ice for another day or two, all depending on the weather and how much hauling we did on the road. In the little camps the logs was hauled over snow-packed roads, and contractors like my father never could have bought contraptions like water tanks and horses to pull them.

The job I liked best in the woods was driving the teams hauling the logs from the skidway to the river. It was a cold job, riding on the sleighs most of the time and not exercising the way the men on the end of an ax did from daylight to dark. Teamsters had to get up early to feed and harness their horses and they had to look after them when they come in at night. When I started, I "geehawed" a yoke of oxens a few years, but I always like to work with horses more than oxens. . . .

We had one old teamster that was different. He would go out in the morning barefooted to harness and feed his horses, then come in, shake the snow off his feet, and put on his socks and shoes. He believed that this kept his feet warm all day even if it was forty below.

A good teamster in the woods is a man who can get a good pull out of a horse and not abuse him. He has to know how to handle lines good and drive four horses down a crooked tote road covered with ice so the sleigh will slide along easy even when loaded with half the logs of the Chippeway Valley. I call a good pull when the four horses get right down with their bellies on the ground and get the load moving again, and do it with only the driver talking to them and not beating them in any way. I seen horses pull so hard that they pull themselves right out from under their shoes, breaking the nails that hold their shoes on and leaving the shoes right there on the ice. I seen this several times when a horse would kind of twist his foot and every nail in the hoof would break off right there and he'd leave his shoe on the icy road. If horses are broke right and not overloaded in the beginning, they will gradually pull bigger and bigger loads. You just keep putting on a few more logs, and talk to them and tell them, "Come on there, boy, you've got a good pull. . . ." They get to know every word you say and will work hard to do what you want them to do. . . .

The sleighs used in hauling logs down to the river over the tote roads got bigger as the camps got bigger. Some of the sleighs was awful big. They had sixteen-foot bunks that the logs went on and was sixteen feet wide. Then there was corner bind chains to hold the logs on tight, and you could put on as much as five or six or seven thousand feet on a load. Horses, maybe two teams of big ones, took the place of oxens. Somebody in Eau Claire or Chippeway Falls would go down to Illinois or Ioway and buy up a bunch of horses and ship them up by train. The loggers would buy them all the way from three hundred to seven hundred dollars a team. They was mainly Percherons and Belgians, big, heavy horses that could pull big loads, and it took a good teamster to handle horses like these.

A loading crew was made up of three men. One man was put on top of the load, one man rolled the logs down the skidway to the sled, and the other man kept the log even as the team pulled the log up on top. The teamster told the men when he had enough and moved down the icy road with his load. When he pulled out, another sled moved in. Sometimes you might have a little time between the loads, but mostly it was pretty steady. If you got cold, you'd make a little fire. You knowed that the quicker you got the load on, the quicker you were done, so you'd hurry to get the logs on the sleigh.

When I worked in the woods we loaded with a single line, a loading line we called it. It was a small chain that run over the load and was anchored on one side to a tree. We'd skid the logs on the tamarack skids to the edge of the sleigh and hitch a chain to it, and the horses would pull it up on the load. One man would stand at each end with a cant hook and keep it straight as it went up. Suppose you had a sixteen-foot log and your load was four tiers of logs high. This meant the sleigh would be about three and a half feet above the ground. The team would pull the log up and the men didn't have much trouble keeping it straight. But when the sleigh was loaded up seven or eight tiers and the top was twice as far from the ground, it took a man who knowed his business with a cant hook to keep the log straight as it was pulled up. The man who made the load on top had to be pretty good, too. He had to build up a square load so he could get on a lot of logs. If he brought it up to a peak, he soon run out of room for more logs. Maybe the teamster wanted to put on a load bigger than the other man hauling to the river, and he'd say, "Put on some more." The man on top would have to say that he was out of room unless he had built a good square load as wide on the bottom as it was on top. Keep it straight, build it straight, and you can get on a big load. That's the way it was in the logging business in the old days.

We didn't ride on top of the load, but on the crosspiece connecting the runners where the tongue hooked on. There was a chain there that held up the tongue and another that went to the neck yoke on the horses. We made a little box there and put a gunny sack filled with marsh hay in it to stand on. it helped keep the feet warm, you see, in the long hauls of several miles. There was a camp halfway to the landing. If there was two of you hauling, you would haul your load from the woods to the halfway camp, and the other driver would take over there. Maybe you'd get there at eight in the morning, unhook the team from the big load, and hitch onto the empty sled and head back to the woods while the other man would hitch onto the full load and take it to the river.

It was pretty near impossible to make a road that didn't have a little hill some-where so you had to hitch on another team to get to the top, and then you had the problem of the sleigh load moving too fast going down the other side. Hay was scattered in the tracks on the downhill side to slow up the sled. The teamster could take some of it off if the sled was slowed down too much. I've seen horses hurt bad when the load moved downhill too fast. Sometimes a horse fell down and the sled rolled over his back legs and he had to be killed. That happened every now and then, and to lose a horse in the woods was a real loss. Loads never tipped over because the sleigh runners was so wide and couldn't get out of the ruts. . . .

Over in the St. Croix River camps, they used to haul loads of eight or ten thousand feet. The men didn't ride on the load but walked on a trail along the side of the tote road. The main reason was because of the danger. It was dangerous to ride on a big load, since you could get squashed to death if a chain broke. I seen them break, too. One broke over on Mud Brook and a hell of a good man was on top of a big load when it broke. He was coming down a grade pretty fast and the logs went off in all directions. He was crushed to death and the team went on down to the landing all alone with what was left of the sleigh. The landing man knowed something was wrong and went back up to look, and there he was, deader than a mackerel.

Some of the loggers drowned when the ice broke under their loads. They would drive right out on the ice to unload if they could, and sometimes the ice give way and down they went. If the banks was too high, they put their loads in the rollways. Suppose your logging road come on top of a hill where you could see the river. Well, they'd roll the logs right down the hill until there was a big pile of logs standing there like a keg of nails. In the spring when the drive started, you had to break the rollways by getting down in front of them and work on them with cant hooks or peaveys and get out of the way when they started rolling toward the river. Many a lumberjack got caught and was crushed to death by a hundred logs rolling down the hill hell-bent for election.

In the old days, getting logs out of the woods to the river bank was hard and cold work. It got better when the camps got bigger. Then we had a blacksmith shop to keep our things in good shape. The woodbutcher was handy with a saw and a plane, and could make most anything out of wood. He made cant hook handles, singletrees and eveners for the sleighs, and maybe even a go-devil or a new runner for the sleighs. Something was always getting busted in the woods, but the blacksmith or the woodbutcher could fix it or make a new one. They worked together, and the crew kept them busy every night repairing the things that got broke that day in the woods. By morning you always knowed that they'd have things ready to go, and so you never had any excuse for not getting up when the cook hollered, "Come and get it."

When the Loggers Moved Out

When the spring come and the ice went out of the lakes and rivers, the logging camp crew scattered. Some of the men went down with the drive. Others went home to families and started clearing land and planting and making 160 acres of stumps into a farm. A little crew closed up the camp and brought the pots and pans and the horses down to Chippeway Falls. They left behind a sorry-looking land: miles of stumps and brush, piles of branches where the swampers and skidders trimmed the trees, roads that never growed up again. I suppose we should have burned our brush as we cut off the trees, so forest fires couldn't get going so easy. But we never knowed much about such things in them days. Most of us lumberjacks just worked in the winter for the big contractors so we could feed the family and get ourselves a little farm or a house somewhere. It seemed good business to cut down the pine. It give us jobs, and the lumber went down river to the sawmills and was used to build homes and cities. The government shouldn't have let them companies take off the little trees that wouldn't make anything bigger than a two by four. Us loggers thought the big woods would last forever. I guess we can't expect the government to be much smarter than us.

Document 1.3

Report on the Disastrous Effects of the Destruction of Forest Trees, Now Going on so Rapidly in the State of Wisconsin (1867)

I.A. Lapham, J.G. Knapp, and H. Crocker

The Effect of Clearing the Land of Forest Trees Upon the Climate of the State

Temperature.—To become convinced that the destruction of the forests would increase the temperature of the ground in summer one has only to ride in an open conveyance, on a hot day, across a prairie or cleared country, and then enter the depths of a dense forest. The change is at once apparent from the burning heat of the sun we pass to the cool shade of the trees, and find a contrast so great that it must have been observed by every one; it is the difference between sunshine and shade; and is so obvious that . . . *clearing the land of trees increases the temperature of the ground in the summer.*

It is not to be supposed that the sun supplies a less amount of heat upon a given surface of forest than upon the same area of cleared ground; but in the former case the heat is intercepted by the leaves of the trees, and therefore does not reach the ground. Hence, although the mean temperature of the summer as measured by the thermometer in the shade in the usual way, may not be affected by the clearing away of forests, yet the quantity of heat that actually reaches the ground is vastly increased; and it is this temperature of the ground, perhaps as much as that of the air above it, that affects the growth of farm crops.

Again, if one should pass in an open conveyance from an exposed or prairie country into one covered with trees, at a time when the winter cold is the most severe, he would immediately find a degree of comfort and relief, that renders all arguments needless, to show that *clearing away the trees from the land diminishes the temperature of the gronnd [sic] in winter.* It is familiarly known that frost does not penetrate the ground to the same depth in the woods as in the fields. . . .

In the state of Michigan it has been found that the winters have greatly increased in severity within the last forty years, and that this increased severity seems to move along even-paced with the destruction of the forests. Thirty years ago the peach was one of the most abundant fruits of that state; at that time frost, injurious to corn at any time from May to October, was a thing unknown. Now the peach is an uncertain crop, and frost often injures the corn. . . .

It is quite evident, therefore, that a forest is a great equalizer of temperature,

Reprinted from I.A. Lapham, J.G. Knapp, and H. Crocker, *Report on the Disastrous Effects of the Destruction of Forest Trees, Now Going on so Rapidly in the State of Wisconsin* (Madison, Wisconsin: The State Historical Society of Wisconsin, 1967), 9–12, 14–18, 23–24. Reprint of the 1867 edition. Author's footnotes have been omitted.

modifying both the extreme heat of summer and the extreme cold in the winter; its removal makes the climate more *excessive;* the range of the thermometer being increased; and many crops, fruits, &c., that could be raised under the protection of the forests, are killed, either by this excessive heat or extreme cold.

Humidity.—No constituent of the atmospheric air is more important, or less understood, than aqueous vapor, the greater or less amount of which regulates not only the growth of plants, but also to a considerable degree the health and comfort of the inhabitants. It prevents the undue radiation of heat from the ground, and thus aids materially in maintaining that equitable degree of temperature so essential to many of the processes of nature. Here again, it will be found upon passing, on a very dry day, from an open to a well-wooded country, that a very marked change occurs; in the woods the air is more nearly saturated with vapor, the ground is moist, and not hardened by the loss of water, and hence no further arguments need be adduced to show that *clearing away the forests from a country will increase the dryness of the ground. . . .*

Trees have a very decided effect upon the temperature and humidity of the air by the evaporation constantly going on from the surface of the leaves. It is a principle in chemical science, that evaporation produces cold . . . To absorb heat from any medium is to make it cold; and the amount of heat absorbed from the atmosphere by the evaporation of water from leaves of trees must therefore be very considerable. . . .

The process of evaporation of water is very much accelerated by wind; for when the air is still it soon becomes so nearly saturated with moisture that no more can be absorbed from the soil, or from leaves: but when this moist air is removed by the wind the absorption of moisture continues.

The ground under the forests being shaded and kept cool, the evaporation from the surface is very much diminished, and the water of rains remains longer in the ground to supply the absorption of roots, within the forests, than upon open fields.

Another source of increased moisture under trees is the coolness of the leaves at night causing a deposition of dew, sometimes in such quantities as to cause drops of water to fall to the ground like rain.

How Trees Affect the Springs, Streams and Rain of a Country

From what has already been said it is evident that clearing away the forests diminishes the flow of water from springs. In the woods the water is retained in the soil, evaporation being prevented by the shade, while in the fields the water is rapidly evaporated, or, not being impeded by vegetation, runs off to the river and watercourses more rapidly, thus giving less time to penetrate the soil and supply subterranean passages to springs. There are well attested instances where springs have been dried up in consequence of the clearing of adjacent forests. . . .

It follows also, from the facts above recited, that clearing a country of trees increases the suddenness and magnitude of floods and torrents; trees causing the surplus water to pass off through the rivers more uniformly throughout the season. As the trees are removed, the waters of heavy rains rush unimpeded directly to the valleys and are carried off within a short time, leaving the bed almost or quite destitute of water during the dry season. About one fourth of the water falling in the form of rain, snow and hail in this state is carried off by rivers.

We need not have gone beyond our own state, nor referred to times longer than our own limited experience to find examples of the evils resulting from this change in the flow of rivers from one of regularity and uniformity to one of periodic floods and dry or nearly dry beds. Such has been the change in the flow of the Milwaukee river, even while the area from which it receives its supply is but partially cleared, that the proprietors of most of the mills and factories have found it necessary to resort to the use of steam, at a largely increased yearly cost, to supply the deficiency of waterpower in dry seasons of the Year. Until this was done many large mills were closed for want of water in the latter part of summer and early autumn; while the floods of spring are increased until they are sufficient to carry away bridges and dams before deemed secure against their ravages. The Menomonee river, a small tributary of the Milwaukee, has been effected in the same way and to a still greater degree, because a larger proportion of the water supplying area has been stripped of its forest trees. Several of the mills that formerly found sufficient power on this stream, have been entirely abandoned; others are propelled a large share of the time by steam. Down its channel during and immediately following heavy rains, great floods sweep along, doing more or less damage; followed in a very few days by dry pebbly, or muddy banks, and bed, in which only an occasional pool of water can be found. . . .

What has happened to the Milwaukee river and to these smaller streams, has happened to all the other water courses in the state from whose banks the forests have been removed; and many farmers who selected land upon which there was a living brook of clear, pure water, now find these brooks dried up during a considerable portion of each year.

How Trees Protect the Soil

Another serious evil resulting from clearing away the forests *is the washing away of the soil* by the rains. The degradation of the soil by rains, especially on side hills, commences when the trees are removed. At first a slight break is made, along which the descending currents flow, carrying with them the softened earth, to be deposited upon the plains below, or carried off by rivers. The removal of the natural turf or sod of the prairies has the same effect upon the soil, especially in those districts where the particles are fine, and therefore more easily suspended in water and washed away by the rain. Even the slight interruption of the protecting vegetable carpet, caused from an Indian trail, is often sufficient to cause frightful gullies in a very few years. All steep hill-sides are liable to this evil when the trees or the sod are removed. On the margin of the steep banks of lake Michigan these deep gullies are formed, making it necessary to remove the "lake shore road" from time to time farther from the water. . . .

To realize the importance of this constant absorption of the soil, we have only to refer to the deep and broad valleys every where excavated, and to the deltas of large rivers, where whole states owe their very existence to the accumulations of earthy matter brought down from their channels above, including among its particles the richest soil of the uplands. The quantity of sand and mud carried into the Mississippi river by the principal tributaries from this state, especially the Wisconsin and Chippewa, is such that the current of this great river is checked in its onward flow, and formed into lakes. . . . Already has the amount of earthy matter, brought into the Mississippi river from the surface of our state, been so much increased, by the destruction of the forests, and the breaking of the sod, that it begins to disturb the former condition of things; the water is no longer clear and dark, from decomposed vegetable matter, as it used to be, more sand accumulates in the stream, and a noticable [sic] quantity of saw-dust and chips from the lumber regions of the St. Croix, Chippewa and Wisconsin is also deposited along the banks. . . .

How Trees Affect the Winds

Besides the very important influence forests exert upon the temperature and humidity of the air, they afford protection from the bad effects of high winds; both from the cold north-west winds of winter, and the hot, dry, south-west winds of summer. Any one exposed to the full blasts of either of these winds upon a high prairie, would very gladly welcome the friendly protection of forest-trees, among which he could pursue his avocation with comparative ease and comfort, listening to the whistling of the fierce winds above the tree-tops, but free from their evil consequences. To clear away the forests from the state is *therefore to expose it and all its inhabitants to the biting and blighting effects of these winds which will sweep over the surface with unabated violence.*

   If the trees would not stop entirely the strong currents of the wind to which the state of Wisconsin is subjected from its vicinity to the great lakes on the one hand, and the greater plains and prairies on the other, being itself in part a prairie; and that which was not prairie at the first settlement fast becoming so, they would certainly have great influence in modifying those currents. Whether we adopt the theory that the motion of the wind be that of a soft body rolling over the surface of the earth, or of a body sweeping along like the current of a river, slightly retarded by contact with the upholding surface, need not be discussed or decided. In either case the moving current must rise above the tree tops, and leave the surface almost undisturbed. Very much of this effect will be produced by belts of trees, especially if they be closely planted. . . .

   The effect of a very slight obstruction to the operation of the wind, will have been noticed by every observing man who has planted his winter wheat with a drill. Mr. Lyon, the secretary of the state board of Agriculture of Michigan, in 1865, says: "It is presumed that during the seasons from 1861 to 1865, few of us failed to observe that even the protection of a ridge or dead-furrow, running north and south through a field of wheat, was sufficient to preserve a streak of green where all else was brown and bare; and that the shelter of a fence was the means of preserving a still greater breadth while the interposition of a hedge of oak grubs, or a body of timber invariably secured the preservation of a fair crop over a still greater breadth of ground, often amounting to an entire field. . . ."

Summary View of Facts and Consequences

. . . From the facts already given above it must be quite evident that clearing away the forests of Wisconsin will have a very decided effect upon the climate and productions, and therefore upon the inhabitants themselves. The summers will become hotter and more oppressive; the winters colder; both the cold blasts of winter and the hot winds of summer will have full unobstructed sweep over the land; the dryness of the ground will be increased; springs dried up; rivers cease to flow at some seasons of the year, and become great floods at others; the soil on sloping hills washed away; loose sands blown over the country preventing cultivation; snow will accumulate in great drifts in some places, while other places are left bare and unprotected; the ground becomes frozen to great depth; vegetation retarded in the spring; the productiveness of the soil diminished; thunder-storms will be increased in number and violence; and there will be more hail and more heavy, damaging rains.

☙

Document 1.4

The Forests of Washington (1918)

John Muir

When we force our way into the depths of the forests, following any of the rivers back to their fountains, we find that the bulk of the woods is made up of the Douglas spruce . . . , named in honor of David Douglas, an enthusiastic botanical explorer of early Hudson's Bay times. It is not only a very large tree but a very beautiful one, with lively bright-green drooping foliage, handsome pendent cones, and a shaft exquisitely straight and regular. For so large a tree it is astonishing how many find nourishment and space to grow on any given area. The magnificent shafts push their spires into the sky close together with as regular a growth as that of a well-tilled field of grain. And no ground has been better tilled for the growth of trees than that on which these forests are growing. For it has been thoroughly ploughed and rolled by the mighty glaciers from the mountains, and sifted and mellowed and outspread in beds hundreds of feet in depth by the broad streams that issued from their fronts at the time of their recession, after they had long covered all the land.

The largest tree of this species that I have myself measured was nearly twelve feet in diameter at a height of five feet from the ground, and, as near as I could make out under the circumstances, about three hundred feet in length. It stood near

Reprinted from John Muir, *Steep Trails*, William Frederic Báde, ed. (Boston: Houghton Mifflin, 1918), 227–31, 235–39, 242–45. Editor's footnotes have been omitted.

the head of the Sound not far from Olympia. . . . I have heard of some that were said to be three hundred and twenty-five feet in height and fifteen feet in diameter, but none that I measured were so large, though it is not at all unlikely that such colossal giants do exist where conditions of soil and exposure are surpassingly favorable. The average size of all the trees of this species found up to an elevation on the mountain-slopes of, say, two thousand feet above sea-level, taking into account only what may be called mature trees two hundred and fifty to five hundred years of age, is perhaps, at a vague guess, not more than a height of one hundred and seventy-five or two hundred feet and a diameter of three feet; though, of course, throughout the richest sections the size is much greater.

In proportion to its weight when dry, the timber from this tree is perhaps stronger than that of any other conifer in the country. It is tough and durable and admirably adapted in every way for shipbuilding, piles, and heavy timbers in general. But its hardness and liability to warp render it much inferior to white or sugar pine for fine work. In the lumber markets of California it is known as "Oregon pine" and is used almost exclusively for spars, bridge-timbers, heavy planking, and the frame-work of houses.

The same species extends northward in abundance through British Columbia and southward through the coast and middle regions of Oregon and California. It is also a common tree in the canons and hollows of the Wahsatch Mountains in Utah, where it is called "red pine" and on portions of the Rocky Mountains and some of the short ranges of the Great Basin. Along the coast of California it keeps company with the redwood wherever it can find a favorable opening. On the western slope of the Sierra, with the yellow pine and incense cedar, it forms a pretty well-defined belt at a height of from three thousand to six thousand feet above the sea, and extends into the San Gabriel and San Bernardino Mountains in southern California. But, though widely distributed, it is only in these cool, moist northlands that it reaches its finest development, tall, straight, elastic, and free from limbs to an immense height, growing down to tide-water, where ships of the largest size may lie close alongside and load at the least possible cost.

Growing with the Douglas we find the white spruce, or "Sitka pine," as it is sometimes called. This also is a very beautiful and majestic tree, frequently attaining a height of two hundred feet or more and a diameter of five or six feet. It is very abundant in southeastern Alaska, forming the greater part of the best forests there. Here it is found mostly around the sides of beaver-dam and other meadows and on the borders of the streams, especially where the ground is low. One tree that I saw felled at the head of the Hop-Ranch meadows on the upper Snoqualmie River, though far from being the largest I have seen, measured a hundred and eighty feet in length and four and a half in diameter, and was two hundred and fifty-seven years of age.

In habit and general appearance it resembles the Douglas spruce, but it is somewhat less slender and the needles grow close together all around the branchlets and are so stiff and sharp-pointed on the younger branches that they cannot well be handled without gloves. The timber is tough, close-grained, white, and looks more like pine than any other of the spruces. It splits freely, makes excellent shingles and in general use in house-building takes the place of pine. I have seen logs of this species a hundred feet long and two feet in diameter at the upper end. . . .

The oaks, so far as my observation has reached, seem to be most abundant and to grow largest on the islands of the San Juan and Whidbey Archipelago. One of the three species of maples that I have seen is only a bush that makes tangles on the banks of the rivers. Of the other two one is a small tree, crooked and moss-grown, holding out its leaves to catch the light that filters down through the close-set spires of the great spruces. It grows almost everywhere throughout the entire extent of the forest until the higher slopes of the mountains are reached, and produces a very picturesque and delightful effect; relieving the bareness of the great shafts of the evergreens, without being close enough in its growth to hide them wholly, or to cover the bright mossy carpet that is spread beneath all the dense parts of the woods.

The other species is also very picturesque and at the same time very large, the largest tree of its kind that I have ever seen anywhere. Not even in the great maple woods of Canada have I seen trees either as large or with so much striking, pictur-esque character. It is widely distributed throughout western Washington, but is never found scattered among the conifers in the dense woods. It keeps together mostly in magnificent groves by itself on the damp levels along the banks of streams or lakes where the ground is subject to overflow. In such situations it attains a height of seventy-five to a hundred feet and a diameter of four to eight feet. The trunk sends out large limbs toward its neighbors, laden with long drooping mosses beneath and rows of ferns on their upper surfaces, thus making a grand series of richly ornamented interlacing arches, with the leaves laid thick overhead, rendering the underwood spaces delightfully cool and open. Never have I seen a finer forest ceiling or a more picturesque one, while the floor, covered with tall ferns and rubus and thrown into hillocks by the bulging roots, matches it well. The largest of these maple groves that I have yet found is on the right bank of the Snoqualmie River, about a mile above the falls. The whole country hereabouts is picturesque, and interesting in many ways, and well worthy a visit by tourists passing through the Sound region, since it is now accessible by rail from Seattle.

Looking now at the forests in a comprehensive way, we find in passing through them again and again from the shores of the Sound to their upper limits, that some portions are much older than others, the trees much larger, and the ground beneath them strewn with immense trunks in every stage of decay, representing several generations of growth, everything about them giving the impression that these are indeed the "forests primeval," while in the younger portions, where the elevation of the ground is the same as to the sea-level and the species of trees are the same as well as the quality of the soil, apart from the moisture which it holds, the trees seem to be and are mostly of the same age, perhaps from one hundred to two or three hundred years, with no gray-bearded, venerable patriarchs forming tall, majestic woods without any grandfathers.

When we examine the ground we find that it is as free from those mounds of brown crumbling wood and mossy ancient fragments as are the growing trees from very old ones. Then, perchance, we come upon a section farther up the slopes towards the mountains that has no trees more than fifty years old, or even fifteen or twenty years old. These last show plainly enough that they have been devastated by fire, as the black, melancholy monuments rising here and there above the young growth bear witness. Then, with this fiery, suggestive testimony, on examining those sections whose trees are a hundred years old or two hundred, we find the same fire-records, though heavily veiled with mosses and lichens, showing that a century or two ago the forests that stood there had been swept away in some tremendous fire at a time when rare conditions of drouth made their burning possible. Then, the bare ground sprinkled with the winged seeds from the edges of the burned district, a new forest sprang up, nearly every tree starting at the same time or within a few years, thus producing the uniformity of size we find in such places; while, on the other hand, in those sections of ancient aspect containing very old trees both standing and fallen, we find no traces of fire, nor from the extreme dampness of the ground can we see any possibility of fire ever running there.

Fire, then, is the great governing agent in forest-distribution and to a great extent also in the conditions of forest-growth. Where fertile lands are very wet one half the year and very dry the other, there can be no forests at all. Where the ground is damp, with drouth occurring only at intervals of centuries, fine forests may be found, other conditions being favorable. But it is only where fires never run that truly ancient forests of pitchy coniferous trees may exist. When the Washington forests are seen from the deck of a ship out in the middle of the Sound, or even from the top of some high, commanding mountain, the woods seem everywhere perfectly solid. And so in fact they are in general found to be. The largest openings are those of the lakes and prairies, the smaller of beaver-meadows, bogs, and the rivers; none of them large enough to make a distinct mark in comprehensive views. . . .

Notwithstanding the tremendous energy displayed in lumbering and the grand scale on which it is being carried on, and the number of settlers pushing into every opening in search of farmlands, the woods of Washington are still almost entirely virgin and wild, without trace of human touch, savage or civilized. Indians, no doubt, have ascended most of the rivers on their way to the mountains to hunt the wild sheep and goat to obtain wool for their clothing, but with food in abundance on the coast they had little to tempt them into the wilderness, and the monuments they have left in it are scarcely more conspicuous than those of squirrels and bears; far less so than those of the beavers, which in damming the streams have made clearings and meadows which will continue to mark the landscape for centuries. Nor is there much in these woods to tempt the farmer or cattle-raiser. . . .

For many years the axe has been busy around the shores of the Sound and chips have been falling in perpetual storm like flakes of snow. The best of the timber has been cut for a distance of eight or ten miles from the water and to a much greater distance along the streams deep enough to float the logs. Railroads, too, have been built to fetch in the logs from the best bodies of timber otherwise inaccessible except at great cost. None of the ground, however, has been completely denuded. Most of the young trees have been left, together with the hemlocks and other trees undesirable in kind or in some way defective, so that the neighboring trees appear to have closed over the gaps made by the removal of the larger and better ones, maintaining the general continuity of the forest and leaving no sign on the sylvan sea, at least as seen from a distance.

In felling the trees they cut them off usually at a height of six to twelve feet above the ground, so as to avoid cutting through the swollen base, where the diameter is so much greater. In order to reach this height the chopper cuts a notch about two inches wide and three or four deep and drives a board into it, on which he stands while at work. In case the first notch, cut as high as he can reach, is not high enough, he stands on the board that has been driven into the first notch and cuts another. Thus the axeman may often be seen at work standing eight or ten feet above the ground. If the tree is so large that with his long-handled axe the chopper is unable to reach to the farther side of it, then a second chopper is set to work, each cutting halfway across. And when the tree is about to fall, warned by the faint crackling of the strained fibers, they jump to the ground, and stand back out of danger from flying limbs, while the noble giant that had stood erect in glorious strength and beauty century after century, bows low at last and with gasp and groan and booming throb falls to earth.

Then with long saws the trees are cut into logs of the required length, peeled, loaded upon wagons capable of carrying a weight of eight or ten tons, hauled by a long string of oxen to the nearest available stream or railroad, and floated or carried to the Sound. There the logs are gathered into booms and towed by steamers to the mills, where workmen with steel spikes in their boots leap lightly with easy poise from one to another and by means of long pike-poles push them apart and, selecting such as are at the time required, push them to the foot of a chute and drive dogs into the ends, when they are speedily hauled in by the mill machinery alongside the saw-carriage and placed and fixed in position. Then with sounds of greedy hissing and growling they are rushed back and forth like enormous shuttles, and in an incredibly short time they are lumber and are aboard the ships lying at the mill wharves.

ॐ

Document 1.5

The Natural Resources of the Nation (1913)

Theodore Roosevelt

All the forest which belonged to the United States were held and administered in one Department, and all the foresters in Government employ were in another Department. Forests and foresters had nothing whatever to do with each other. The National Forests in the West (then called forest reserves) were wholly inadequate in area to meet the purposes for which they were created, while the need for forest protection in the East had not yet begun to enter the public mind.

Such was the condition of things when Newell and Pinchot called on me. I was a warm believer in reclamation and in forestry, and, after listening to my two guests, I asked them to prepare material on the subject for me to use in my first message to

Reprinted from Theodore Roosevelt, *An Autobiography* (New York: Macmillan, 1913), 430–31, 435–44.

Congress, of December 3, 1901. This message laid the foundation for the development of irrigation and forestry during the next seven and one-half years. It set forth the new attitude toward the natural resources in the words: "The Forest and water problems are perhaps the most vital internal problems of the United States. . . ."

In my first message to Congress I strongly recommended the consolidation of the forest work in the hands of the trained men of the Bureau of Forestry. This recommendation was repeated in other messages, but Congress did not give effect to it until three years later. In the meantime, by thorough study of the Western public timberlands, the groundwork was laid for the responsibilities which were to fall upon the Bureau of Forestry when the care of the National Forests came to be transferred to it. . . .

In 1903, so rapidly did the public work of the Bureau of Forestry increase, that the examination of land for new forest reserves was added to the study of those already created, the forest lands of the various States were studied, and cooperation with several of them in the examination and handling of their forest lands was undertaken. While these practical tasks were pushed forward, a technical knowledge of American Forests was rapidly accumulated. The special knowledge gained was made public in printed bulletins; and at the same time the Bureau undertook, through the newspaper and periodical press, to make all the people of the United States acquainted with the needs and the purposes of practical forestry. . . .

The men upon whom the responsibility of handling some sixty million acres of National Forest lands was thus thrown were ready for the work, both in the office and in the field, because they had been preparing for it for more than five years. Without delay they proceeded, under the leadership of Pinchot, to apply to the new work the principles they had already formulated. One of these was to open all the resources of the National Forests to regulated use. Another was that of putting every part of the land to that use in which it would best serve the public. Following this principle, the Act of June 11, 1906, was drawn, and its passage was secured from Congress. This law throws open to settlement all land in the National Forests that is found, on examination, to be chiefly valuable for agriculture. Hitherto all such land had been closed to the settler.

The principles thus formulated and applied may be summed up in the statement that the rights of the public to the natural resources outweigh private rights, and must be given its first consideration. Until that time, in dealing with the National Forests, and the public lands generally, private rights had almost uniformly been allowed to overbalance public rights. The change we made was right, and was vitally necessary; but, of course, it created bitter opposition from private interests.

One of the principles whose application was the source of much hostility was this: It is better for the Government to help a poor man to make a living for his family than to help a rich man make more profit for his company. This principle was too sound to be fought openly. It is the kind of principle to which politicians delight to pay unctuous homage in words. But we translated the words into deeds; and when they found that this was the case, many rich men, especially sheep owners, were stirred to hostility, and they used the Congressmen they controlled to assault us—getting most aid from certain demagogues, who were equally glad improperly to denounce rich men in public and improperly to serve them in private.

The Forest Service established and enforced regulations which favored the settler as against the large stock owner; required that necessary reductions in the stock grazed on any National Forest should bear first on the big man, before the few head of the small man, upon which the living of his family depended, were reduced; and made grazing in the National Forests a help, instead of a hindrance, to permanent settlement. . . .

Up to the time the National Forests were put under the charge of the Forest Service, the Interior Department had made no effort to establish public regulation and control of water powers. Upon the transfer, the Service immediately began its fight to handle the power resources of the National Forests so as to prevent speculation and monopoly and to yield a fair return to the Government. On May 1, 1906, an Act was passed granting the use of certain power sites in Southern California to the Edison Electric Power Company, which Act, at the suggestion of the Service, limited the period of the permit to forty years, and required the payment of an annual rental by the company, the same conditions which were thereafter adopted by the Service as the basis for all permits for power development. Then began a vigorous fight against the position of the Service by the water-power interests. The right to charge for water-power development was, however, sustained by the Attorney-General. . . .

One incident in these attacks is worth recording. While the Agricultural Appropriation Bill was passing through the Senate, in 1907, Senator Fulton, of Oregon, secured an amendment providing that the President could not set aside any additional National Forests in the six Northwestern States. This meant retaining some sixteen million of acres to be exploited by land grabbers and by the representatives of the great special interests, at the expense of the public interest. But for four years the Forest Service had been gathering field notes as to what forests ought to be set aside in these States, and so was prepared to act. It was equally undesirable to veto the whole agricultural bill, and to sign it with this amendment effective. Accordingly, a plan to create the necessary National Forest in these States before the Agricultural Bill could be passed and signed was laid before me by Mr. Pinchot. I approved it. The necessary papers were immediately prepared. I signed the last proclamation a couple of days before, by my signature, the bill became law; and, when the friends of the special interests in the Senate got their amendment through and woke up, they discovered that sixteen million acres of timberland had been saved for the people by putting them in the National Forests before the land grabbers could get at them. The opponents of the Forest Service turned handsprings in their wrath; and dire were their threats against the Executive; but the threats could not be carried out, and were really only a tribute to the efficiency of our action. . . .

The idea that the Executive is the steward of the public welfare was first formulated and given practical effect in the Forest Service by its law officer, George Woodruff. The laws were often insufficient, and it became well nigh impossible to get them amended in the public interest when once the representatives of privilege in Congress grasped the fact that I would sign no amendment that contained anything not in the public interest. It was necessary to use what law was already in existence, and then further to supplement it by Executive action. The practice of examining every claim to public land before passing it into private ownership offers a good example of the policy in question. This practice which has since become general, was first applied in the National Forests. Enormous areas of valuable public timberland were thereby saved from fraudulent acquisition; more than 250,000 acres were thus saved in a single case.

This theory of stewardship in the interest of the public was well illustrated by the establishment of a water-power policy. Until the Forest Service changed the plan, water-powers on the navigable streams, on the public domain, and in the National Forests were given away for nothing, and substantially without question, to whoever asked for them. At last, under the principle that public property should be paid for and should not be permanently granted away when such permanent grant is avoidable, the Forest Service established the policy of regulating the use of power in the National Forests in the public interest and making a charge for value received. This was the beginning of the water-power policy now substantially accepted by the public, and doubtless soon to be enacted into law. . . .

The natural result of this new attitude was the assertion in every form by the representatives of special interests that the Forest Service was exceeding its legal powers and thwarting the intention of Congress. Suits were begun wherever the chance arose. It is worth recording that, in spite of the novelty and complexity of the legal questions it had to face, no court of last resort has ever decided against the Forest Service. This statement includes two unanimous decisions by the Supreme Court of the United States (U.S. vs. Grimaud, 220 U.S., 506, and Light vs. U.S., 220 U.S., 523).

In its administration of the National Forests, the Forest Service found that valuable coal lands were in danger of passing into private ownership without adequate money return to the Government and without safeguard against monopoly; and that existing legislation was insufficient to prevent this. When this condition was brought to my attention I withdrew from all forms of entry about sixty-eight million acres of coal land in the United States, including Alaska. The refusal of Congress to act in the public interest was solely responsible for keeping these lands from entry.

❧

Document 1.6

Call for a Joint Congressional Committee on the Forest–Land Problem (1938)

Franklin D. Roosevelt

To the Congress of the United States:

I feel impelled at this time to call to the attention of the Congress some aspects of our forest problem, and the need for a policy and plan of action with respect to it.

Forests are intimately tied into our whole social and economic life. They grow on more than one-third the land area of the continental United States. Wages from

Reprinted from *Forest Lands of the United States,* Senate Doc. 32, 77th Congress, 1st session, 1941.

forest industries support five to six million people each year. Forests give us building materials and thousands of other things in everyday use. Forest lands furnish food and shelter for much of our remaining game, and healthful recreation for millions of our people. Forests help prevent erosion and floods. They conserve water and regulate its use for navigation, for power, for domestic use, and for irrigation. Woodlands occupy more acreage than any other crop on American farms, and help support 2 1/2 million farm families.

Our forest problem is essentially one of land use. It is a part of the broad problem of modern agriculture that is common to every part of the country. Forest lands total some 615,000,000 acres.

One-hundred-and-twenty-odd million acres of these forest lands are rough and inaccessible, but they are valuable for the protection of our great watersheds. The greater proportion of these protection forests is in public ownership. Four hundred and ninety-five million acres of our forest lands can be classed as commercial. Both as to accessibility and quality the best four-fifths, or some 396,000,000 acres of these commercial forests, is in private ownership.

This privately owned forest land at present furnishes 96 percent of all our forest products. It represents 90 percent of the productive capacity of our forest soils. There is a continuing drain upon commercial forests in saw timber sizes far beyond the annual growth. Forest operations in them have not been and are not now conducive to maximum regrowth. An alarming proportion of our cut-over forest lands is tax delinquent. Through neglect much of it is rapidly forming a new but almost worthless no man's land. . . .

I have thus presented to you the facts. They are simple facts; but they are of a character to cause alarm to the people of the United States and to you, their chosen representatives. . . .

Creation of the national-forest system, which now extends to 38 States, has been a definite step toward constructive solution of our forest problem. From national-forest lands come domestic water for more than 6,000,000 people. Forage, occurring largely in combination with timber, contributes stability to one-fourth of the western range livestock industry. Through correlated and co-ordinated public management of timber and all other resources these public properties already help support almost a million people and furnish healthful recreation to more than 30,000,000 each year. By means of exchanges and purchases the Congress has for many years encouraged additions to this system. These measures should very definitely be continued as funds and facilities are available.

The Congress has also provided that the National Government shall cooperate with the various States in matters of fire protection on privately owned forest lands and farm woodlands. The States are in turn cooperating with private owners. Among other measures the Congress has also authorized an extensive program of forest research, which has been initiated and projected; Federal cooperation in building up a system of State forests; cooperative activities with farmers to integrate forest management with the general farm economy; the planting of trees in the Prairie-Plains States—an activity which has heretofore been carried on as an emergency unemployment relief measure with outstanding success and material benefit;

and, under the omnibus flood-control bill, measures to retard run-off and erosion on forested and other watersheds.

Progress has been made; and such measures as these should be continued. They are not adequate, however, to meet the present situation. We are still exploiting our forest lands. Forest communities are still being crippled; still being left desolate and forlorn. Watersheds are still being denuded. Fertile valleys and industrial cities below such watersheds still suffer from erosion and floods. We are still liquidating our forest capital; still cutting our accessible forests faster than they are being replaced. . . .

I recommend, therefore, study by a joint committee of the Congress of the forest-land problem of the United States. . . .

First. The adequacy and effectiveness of present activities in protecting public and private forest lands from fire, insects, and diseases, and of cooperative efforts between the Federal Government and the States.

Second. Other measures, Federal and State, which may be necessary and advisable to insure that timber cropping on privately owned forest lands may be conducted as continuous operations, with the productivity of the lands built up against future requirements.

Third. The need for extension of Federal, State, and community ownership of forest lands and of planned public management of them.

Fourth. The need for such public regulatory controls as will adequately protect private as well as the broad public interests in all forest lands.

Fifth. Methods and possibilities of employment in forestry work on private and public forest lands and possibilities of liquidating such public expenditures as are or may be involved.

Facilities of those technical agencies that, in the executive branches of the Government, deal with the many phases of our forest problem will of course be available to such committee as the Congress may appoint. These technical agencies will be glad to assist the committee in assembling and interpreting facts, indicating what has been done, what still needs to be done, and in such other ways as the committee may desire.

I make this suggestion for immediate study of our forest problem by the Congress in the belief that definite action should be taken by the Congress in 1939. States, communities, and private capital can do much to help—but the fact remains that, with some outstanding exceptions, most of the States, communities, and private companies have, on the whole, accomplished little to retard or check the continuing process of using up our forest resources without replacement. This being so, it seems obviously necessary to fall back on the last defensive line—Federal leadership and Federal action. Millions of Americans are today conscious of the threat. Public opinion asks that steps be taken to remove it.

If the preliminary action is taken at this session of Congress, I propose to address letters to the Governors of those States in which the amount of State and privately owned forest land is substantial, enclosing to them a copy of this message to the Congress and asking their full cooperation with the Congress and with the executive branch of the National Government.

2

Wildlife and Wildlife Habitat

Introduction

Before European exploration and colonization in America almost four hundred years ago, a tremendously diverse wildlife lived on a correspondingly diverse land and in its forests. According to one scholar, since colonization, "At least 500 species have become extinct: an average of one or two per year. During the Pleistocene period (a period of glaciation, more than 10,000 years ago, when many natural extinctions occurred), fewer than 100 species were known to have been destroyed in North America."[1] Although nearly one-third of the United States is forest land today, much of the wooded landscape is a homogeneous second and third growth. The old-growth forest, commonplace before the opening of the frontier in the seventeenth century, is largely gone, and with it the habitat for much wildlife.

The fragile and important connection between mature forests and wildlife habitat disappeared as large virgin woodlands fell to the logger's ax and saw and became agricultural land. As the living space for animal life shrank and became fragmented, many species of wildlife became endangered, even as the amount of land devoted to agriculture declined in the twentieth century. As agricultural land decreased, residential and commercial development of the land accelerated at a breathtaking rate, further depleting wildlife habitat.

The remaining fragmented forest consisted of small patches of woodland unable to support its original biotic communities. Patches create forest edges, homes for predators who thrive on animals who live in the densely wooded areas. Altered microclimates caused by the loss of forest canopies occurred, with higher and lower seasonal ground temperatures and higher wind velocities.[2] Additionally, many of the virgin hardwood forests have been replaced by conifers planted for harvesting, which is detrimental to wildlife. In this new woodland environment, "snags," or standing dead or dying trees and downed deadwood, have no lumber value and are therefore removed. Snags are important for maintaining an ecological balance in the forest because they are habitat for some wildlife. As a result:

> Wildlife species that depend upon mature forests are vulnerable to the policies of production forestry that view climax forests as decadent. The passenger pigeon's extinction in the early 1900s, though due largely to commercial exploitation, was hastened by the elimination of the large virgin stands of mast-bearing beech and oak trees in the Midwest. More recently, the demise of the ivory-billed woodpecker was linked to widespread reduction of mature southern hardwood forest.[3]

The spotted owl controversy of the 1980s and 1990s in the Pacific Northwest pitted protectors of this endangered species and the logging industry against one another. Since spotted owls use for nests the natural cavities found in old-growth hardwoods, in snags, or in the roosts of other nesting wildlife, continuous cutting of old growth destroys some of the spotted owl's natural habitat.

Although it is not confined to old growth for nests, a number of additional explanations have been offered to explain why this sub-species of owls favors old-growth tree stands. Old growth provides better protection from extreme weather fluctuations—harsh winters and hot summers. Although the plumage of the owls provides protection in the winter, old-growth canopies may provide summer protection from the heat. Also, the spotted owl preys on the flying squirrel and other animals abundant in the old growth. It may require a large forest range in which to search for its needed supply of food. Finally, old-growth canopies may provide the protection that this sub-species needs from its larger aggressive predator, the great horned owl.[4]

The Loss of Habitat

There are obvious connections to help us to explain the losses in forest lands and the subsequent losses of wildlife and wildlife habitat. After all, "forests and wildlife were among the most useful components of the New World environment."[5] However, deforestation and changes in the composition of existing forests provide only a partial explanation for wildlife destruction. Multiple causes are necessary to explain this loss over the last four hundred years. There were countless commercial and sporting excesses, much of them originating in ideas about limitless bounty and the inexhaustibility of various wildlife species. Both nonenforcement of existing game laws and wanton violations contributed to the losses, as well as human ignorance about the complexities of the natural world. Most importantly, however, wildlife populations declined as habitats and the home range of game birds and mammals were eliminated, not only by logging but also by agriculture, mining, and commercial and residential construction. Government policy at all levels also played a role.[6]

The concept of a wildlife home range is a topic of much current discussion and controversy, as we extend the range of our living space and narrow the home range of wildlife species. In the past, we tried to protect wildlife by creating sanctuaries, national parks, and designated wilderness. We now know that many species need large unrestricted areas for their general well-being. We are beginning to understand the impact of restricting wildlife living space.

Of the 171 species of birds who have become extinct in the last four hundred years, 155 extinctions occurred in island communities. As David Quammen has pointed out: "That's 90 percent—despite the fact that only about 20 percent of the planet's bird species are island dwellers. Clearly, island birds face a much higher probability of extinction than mainland birds do. It's true also among animals and plants overall: Island species are more readily extinguished than mainland species."[7] The reasons for the vulnerability of island species are as complex as the reasons that spotted owls need an extensive home range in order to thrive. The populations of island communities are small, and their size makes them more vulnerable to changing environmental conditions. Severe weather in the form of drought, famine, heat, and cold can cause small populations to disappear. On nature's islands, birds, plants, and other species are more vulnerable to change.

The impact on wildlife of humankind's artificial islands such as designated wilderness, refuges, and national parks is more severe. Small designated areas cannot sustain the larger populations of many species that were once protected by living on larger islands and on the vast mainland. Research by William Newmark, published in *Conservation Biology,* cites the impact of these protected areas on endangered species by reporting that:

> 29 mammal populations have disappeared from national parks in western North America due to no other factor than the island syndrome. The red fox is missing from Bryce Canyon National Park in southern Utah. The mink is gone from Yosemite. The river otter, the spotted skunk and the ermine are absent from Crater Lake National Park in Oregon—not hunted out, not poisoned out, but apparently squeezed out by the sheer insularity of their situation.[8]

These findings reinforce those of earlier wildlife researchers. In 1947, the federal government established the Everglades National Park in Florida "to protect the finest assemblage of large wading birds on the continent."[9]

By 1989 these bird populations had declined by 90 percent. Investigations of the causes for these catastrophic losses demonstrated that the ecosystems for these birds were either too small or had been changed by land development outside their borders. These changes altered adjacent biotic communities and microclimates. In addition, these alterations over time brought about subtle changes in the nature reserves and made them less suitable for many original species. Efforts to segment, fragment, and compartmentalize nature and its species haven't worked. Isolation is fatal to diverse nature and wildlife.

Early History

Our discussion of human–wildlife relationships in North America in prehistory begins long before the age of European exploration. With the retreat of the mile-thick glaciers of the last Ice Age about 12,000 years ago, the North American continent became nature's paradise. As Hal Glen Borland describes it:

> Normal melt from the Big Ice filled every brook and river, created new lakes, perpetuated old marshlands. Grass grew everywhere, more grass than the new arrivals and the native herds of horses, camels, and pronghorn antelope together could eat. Trees were beyond counting—pines and cedars and hemlocks and cypress along the waterways. Farther still from the ice were maples, elms, chestnuts, sycamores, beeches, birches, and cottonwoods, with leakage, nuts, seeds, and fruits for the squirrels, mice, and rats that were native here. And for such migrants from South America as the porcupine and the armadillo. Bison began to swarm over the vast grasslands and into the woodlands to the east. Deer were in every thicket. Moose and elk were on the flatlands and in the thin woodlands. Beaver, some as big as black bears, swarmed in the streams. And the birds, the fish, the insects filled the land's niches. Wild geese crowded the lakes, the ponds were filled with ducks, the rivers teemed with huge trout and sturgeon, the bordering oceans with cod and salmon and all the lesser fish. Whales and seals and walruses fed and migrated in the offshore waters. Whales even ran up the big rivers, up the Hudson a hundred miles. The skies were beginning to darken with passenger pigeons.[10]

It is customary to think about prehistoric humans and the aboriginal peoples who followed them as living under subsistence conditions, taking from the land and from the flocks and herds only the necessities to sustain life. They killed wildlife for food, for their skins, furs, and bones, for rituals and ceremonies, but not for sport. They took less, not more, for "To kill more was simply to create excess baggage."[11] However, one hypothesis about the decline of prehistoric wildlife suggests that the hunting practices of early prehistoric humans led to the extinction of many species. For example:

> Pleistocene overkill by Paleo-Indians* is one explanation proposed to account for the mass extinction of large mammals in North America 10,000 to 11,000 years ago. According to this hypothesis, a small band of humans arrived in southern Canada about 11,500 years ago. From there, these big game hunters and their descendants spread throughout the ice-free portion of the continent along an arc-shaped "front" of human occupation. They killed off much of the megafauna as they advanced, moving relentlessly as the big-game animals were depleted. People remaining in the less densely populated region behind this advancing front lived on smaller game and those large plant-eating mammals that remained. Carnivores that had been the herbivores' natural predators were probably driven by hunger to seek out the last remaining prey.[12]

More than a century ago, the zoologist Alfred Russel Wallace wrote about overhunting by prehistoric humans as an important factor in the extinction of a number of species at the end of the Ice Age. Fossil remains suggested that the relentless human hunting of large mammals by driving them over cliffs and into canyons caused many of them to be crushed or trampled to death. In his analysis of these remains, Wallace pointed out that "the uppermost animals were butchered, the remainder were left untouched. If so, this is an early example of the extreme waste of wildlife."[13]

A second hypothesis suggests that extreme fluctuations in temperature throughout the Pleistocene era shrank the size of the range land and reduced the amount of food available for big mammals. Simply put, the habitat for mammals was destroyed by climate change. A third and more recent hypothesis links the decline in prehistoric mammals to diseases carried by rats, birds, parasites, and domesticated dogs traveling with the new migrating humans. All three hypotheses may contribute to our understanding of the reasons for the decline: overhunting, dramatic climate changes, and pestilence.

------

*Paleo-Indians or prehistoric Indians who migrated across the Bering land bridge from Asia to the North American continent beginning about 11,200 years ago are known as the Clovis people. Clovis is a town in New Mexico where stone arrowheads attributed to Paleo-Indians were found early in the twentieth century. Since a similar arrowhead was found in the last decade at a Siberian site approximately 1,200 miles from the Bering Strait, it is now a subject of debate whether such willow-shaped arrowheads were the product of Asian or North American technology. ("American Arrowhead Found in Siberia," *The New York Times,* August 2, 1996, A6.)

The overhunting hypothesis suggests that prehistoric hunting societies and the premodern generations who followed them were not frugal in their hunting patterns. To distinguish them from modern humans, who we characterize as profligate and wasteful, may not be an appropriate way of distinguishing one group from another. The overhunting of large game animals by humans went on during the thousands of years of prehistory. The extinction of various species such as camels and horses in North America, the depletion of the long-horned bison and musk oxen, and the declining numbers of big cats, dire wolves, and cave bears are testimony to that fact.

Europeans who explored and settled North America many thousands of years later during the sixteenth and seventeenth centuries still encountered a bountiful and tremendously diverse continent, although one of mostly small land mammals. The passage of thousands of years and the relatively sparse settlements of Native Americans on this vast continent contributed to the existence of this bounty, newly discovered by European settlers.

Early American Hunting and Trapping

As the forests had been viewed as inexhaustible by early settlers in America, the woodlands rich in mammals, rodents, and roosts for birds were seen in much the same way. Wildlife became a subject that early explorers and settlers accustomed to the scarcity of European life described in detail. Virginia's early Jamestown settlers in 1607 described 6–foot sturgeon in the James River. Captain John Smith stated, "We had more Sturgeon than could be devoured by Dog and Man."[14] Bountiful ducks, geese, wild turkey, and grouse inhabited the marshes and woods. Off the coast of Cape Cod, early settlers in Massachusetts Bay described a "great store of cod fyshes the bigeste & largest I ever Saw or any man in our Ship." Equally abundant were "scallops, muscles, cockles, lobsters, crabs, oysters, and welks, exceeding good and very great."[15] The waters surrounding Manhattan Island were noteworthy for their abundance of fish, including salmon, sturgeon, shad, and mullet, as well as 10–inch by 3–inch oysters.

In what would become the future American West, the early French explorers and trappers described Mississippi River catfish so large that when one struck a boat, it was thought to be a large tree about to smash the hull to bits and pieces. Early trappers already knew the value of many shoreline animals, as they shipped skins and pelts to Europe as early as 1626. In that year, one Dutch West India Company vessel shipped 7,246 beaver and 675 otter skins.[16]

The plight of the North American beaver provides a riveting example of the carnage animals experienced at the hands of early fur trappers. Before

European exploration, it was estimated that approximately 60 million beavers* lived on the continent. However, more than two centuries of trapping brought beavers to the brink of extinction. For example, a Virginia price list in 1621 showed that an extensive fur trade in beaver, mink, marten, otter, and wildcat brought between seven and ten shillings apiece for prime fur and pelts.[17] The beaver's fate was sealed by England's Charles II in 1638, when he decreed that its dense fur be used in the manufacture of hats. Trapping by French fur traders was also relentless. In 1743 the pelts and furs of 127,080 beaver, 30,325 martens, 1,267 wolves, 110,000 raccoons, 16,512 bears and many other animals were shipped to the French port of Rochelle.[18] The effects of excessive hunting were felt into the next century. The naturalist John Godman, writing in 1831, lamented the passing of beavers:

> It is a subject of regret that an animal so valuable and prolific should be hunted in a manner tending so evidently to the extermination of the species, when a little care and management on the part of those interested might prevent unnecessary destruction, and increase the sources of their revenue. . . . In a few years, comparatively speaking, the beaver has been exterminated in all the Atlantic and in the western states . . . and the race will eventually be extinguished throughout the whole continent. A few individuals may, for a time, elude the immediate violence of persecution, and like the degraded descendants of the aboriginal of our soil, be occasionally exhibited as melancholy mementos of tribes long previously whelmed in the fathomless gulf of avarice.[19]

Godman was responding to hunting beyond the Mississippi River as far as the Pacific Northwest, especially by the German immigrant John Jacob Astor. In the first decade of the nineteenth century, Astor convinced the state legislature of New York that trapping in the newly acquired lands of the Louisiana Purchase should become a monopoly for American interests. Through the support of his powerful benefactor, DeWitt Clinton, the legislature granted him charter rights to establish the American Fur Company in 1808. For the much of the nineteenth century, American fur trap-

---

*Beavers are the largest North American rodents. They are recognizable by their size of about 3 1/2 feet and weight of between 35 and 40 pounds, and the reddish-brown color of their hair. Their habitats consist of dams, lodges, burrows, artificial canals, and tree cuttings. Their most distinctive characteristic, however, is the two large, constantly growing incisors in the jaw, used to gnaw wood into small particles. Socially, beavers live in pairs, raising their young until they reach maturity at age two or three. Each family possesses its own lodge and burrows. Prior to European colonization, beavers were found throughout the wet and wooded regions of the continent. By the middle of the nineteenth century, they had virtually disappeared from the United States east of the Rocky Mountains. With the decline in beaver hunting during the last century, they have returned to the eastern regions of the country.

A Beaver Dam in South Dakota. American Forest Institute. Photographer: Jack Rottier.

pers, including those in Astor's employ, mountain men and Native Americans, extended their reach to the Pacific Northwest and the Oregon Territory. Once there, they competed with each other and the British fur-trading interests for supremacy in the Oregon country. *The practice of trapping beavers was described by the naturalist Lewis Morgan in 1868. That description appears as document 2.1.*

With the development of a market economy, trappers "found it advantageous to kill as many beavers as possible. The pelts made their way back to St. Louis and ultimately to the heads of fashionable gentlemen in Philadelphia and London. In return, supplies flowed west to sustain the trappers. No wonder the beaver virtually disappeared from western streams in only twenty years of intensive trapping."[20] The popularity of beaver hats ended in the late 1830s, as fashions in hats changed from fur to silk. By the 1840s, the buffalo had replaced the beaver as the nation's most hunted species. The popularity of beaver coats sustained the trappers and traders, however, and beavers continued to be hunted for their fur and pelts. The North American beaver population, estimated at 60 million at the time of European colonization, had been reduced to only about 100,000 by the nineteenth century's end.[21] Although beaver coats became the rage again during the Great Depression of the 1930s, anti-trapping sentiments in the country made renewed trapping a short-lived and illegal, clandestine activity.

Early Wildlife Laws

The efficiency and determination with which early settlers hunted, trapped, and fished their new-found bounty did not go unnoticed. Alarmed by the slaughter of deer, some early settlers tried to restrain the avarice of others. As the felting fur of beavers was made into hats, so deerskin breeches became fashionable at home and abroad. Once again, trapping and hunting followed fashion. "A first-quality buckskin was worth a dollar, and this probably was the source of the ... slang expression—calling a dollar a buck."[22] As a commodity, deer meat as well as skins became a source of hard currency in a newly developing country, where cash was scarce but the goods needed to acquire it were plentiful. To acquire the much valued hard currency, early settlers engaged in what proved to be a lucrative transatlantic trade. "From 1699 to 1715, South Carolina traders alone shipped an average of 54,000 buckskins to England each year. In the peak year of 1748 they shipped 160,000 skins. Small wonder that a closed season had been established by law in all states except Georgia by 1776."[23] Earlier, in 1694, Massachusetts had led the way, by establishing the first closed season on the hunting of deer. Farmers in the colony remained ambivalent about deer. They regarded them both as pests who ate corn from their fields and also as a tasty dinner of venison for their hungry and growing families. In 1717, Massachusetts banned deer hunting for a five-year period in an effort to protect the colony's severely depleted herds.

Estimates of the number of deer across the continent during the age of exploration and colonization range between 24 and 34 million. By 1900, only 1 to 2 percent of that original total remained. During the last century, however, deer herds have grown to about 14 million as the result of conservation measures, including enforcement of laws similar to the ones attempted during the colonial period. Abundance, decline, and now a resurgence have characterized the history of deer in North America.[24]

Early game laws that attempted to restrict hunting to specific times of the year or for many years proved to be unenforceable. In colonies where population densities measured in the tens and twenties per square mile, enforcement of restrictive game laws was impeded by the absence of witnesses. The colonies became a poacher's paradise, since violations of the local and state laws went unpunished. As the Commissioner of Fisheries in Massachusetts reported in 1868: "People complain, and the legislature passes game laws, and nobody pays any attention to them after they are passed. Why? Because we insist on considering wild animals as our remote forefathers considered them, when men were scarce and wild animals were plenty."[25]

The colonies experienced the same outcome when they tried to impose restrictions on hunters' enthusiasm for killing game by limiting the number of game animals the hunters were allowed to kill during a hunting season. The bag limit, as it was called later, became a modern method of game management. (Initially, seasonal hunting limitations were as unenforceable in the early years of the twentieth century as they had been in colonial times.) By the 1730s game wardens were employed for the purpose of enforcing the game laws. However, most of the early game wardens were part-time employees of the state, who were charged with the responsibility of enforcing poorly written laws and who faced constituencies who believed in the principle of free taking. "Free taking" meant that animals located on public land were free and fair game and could be hunted without bag limits. As an alternative to the game laws, local laws were enacted, which limited hunting of specific species only to townspeople. In this way: "Colonies often prohibited the export of favorite species, allowing residents to monopolize a limited resource, such as raccoons prized for making a good sort of hats."[26] In the end, however, the marketplace became the final arbiter of wildlife protection. As eating habits and fashions changed, the taking of certain species of wildlife changed. The marketplace provided the only restriction on the taking of wildlife that was obeyed until the early years of the twentieth century.

For popular species little could be done to curb hunting. John Josselyn observed in 1672 that as a result of decades of overhunting wild turkeys, hunters had "now destroyed the breed so that 'tis very rare to meet with a wild turkie in the woods." This was the fate of the bird that William Wood a few years earlier in *New England's Prospect* (1643) counted in flocks of one hundred or more in the local woods.[27] Deer, bear, elk, and lynx virtually disappeared from all but the northern reaches of New England.

The plight of predators, especially the gray wolf,* was even more dra-

---

*The natural habitat of wolves and efforts to exterminate them will be discussed in detail in this essay. Today our knowledge of wolves has been increased immensely as a result of scientific research. For the last few years, the reintroduction of wolves into the national park system has been underway. The return of a large predator into a large ecosystem like Yellowstone National Park, Wyoming, has resulted in some dramatic ecological changes. In the two years since their reappearance, gray wolves have killed

matic in colonial America. Since it competed with settlers for the commodities of the hunt such as deer, elk, raccoon, and other species, the wolf was singled out by the colonists for elimination. Again, the chronicler William Wood noted in his *New England Prospect* that:

> there is little hope of their utter destruction, the country being so spacious, and they so numerous, traveling in the Swamps by Kennels: sometimes ten to twelve are of a company. Late at night, and early in the morning, they set up their howlings and call their companies together, at night to hunt, at morning to sleepe; in a word, they may be the greatest inconvenience the Countrey hath, both for the matter of damage to private men in particular, and the whole Countrey in generall.[28]

In order to provide incentives to eliminate gray wolves, Massachusetts Bay Company established in 1630 the first bounty system in the colonies, offering one penny for each slain wolf. A half century later, in 1697, New Jersey offered bounties of twenty shillings for each slain wolf to white hunters and ten to African and Native American hunters. By 1717, gray wolves remained so much in the consciousness of Massachusetts residents that some proposed making the Cape Cod peninsula a sanctuary for livestock, by building a fence from Sandwich to Wareham to prevent wolves from destroying domestic animals. The plan failed to gain the support of residents living on the "wrong" side of the proposed fence.[29] Ultimately, bounty hunting removed wolves from the entire Northeast and Southeast. Hunters killed the last wolf in Maine in 1860, and by the turn of the century wolves were gone from New York, Pennsylvania, and North Carolina. Cougars were gone in various areas by the beginning of the nineteenth century or had disappeared by mid-century.[30]

---

half of the Park's coyote population. Also, a wolf pack kills an elk every few days, leaving most of its 900–pound carcass for other predators. For every one hundred elk chased by wolves in the park about two or three are caught and killed. For example, it is not uncommon to see grizzly bears feeding simultaneously with ravens, coyotes, fox, and bald and golden eagles on wolf-killed elk. The significant decline in the coyote population has caused the rodent population to increase, creating a boon for other predators, including hawks and bald eagles. As a result, overall biodiversity in Yellowstone has increased so dramatically in so short a time as to surprise even Park scientists and rangers. In addition, we know that an average-sized 150–pound wolf needs about 5 pounds of meat per day to survive in the wild. They are intelligent creatures, able to focus on prey miles away and keep a protective eye on their young simultaneously. The social lives of wolves fascinate researchers. They tend to be monogamous, mating for life with a single partner. They live in packs and care for each other by feeding the young and weak and attending to their dead.

Hunting and Conservation

Game Birds

Hunting was not limited to predators or to game mammals. Initially, some hunting was carried out for the purpose of removing flocks of birds that colonial farmers believed destroyed their crops and fields. As the nation grew westward, the abundance and eventual destruction of these birds became symbolic of the nineteenth century carnage of wildlife and helped to energize the early beginnings of a late nineteenth- and early twentieth-century conservation movement.

In the 1880s, the New York City Zoological Society estimated that the nation's bird populations had dropped by 46 percent during the last one hundred years. Included in these estimates were the nation's twenty-eight states and its territories. The diet of Americans and related overhunting help to explain this precipitous decline.

The Saturday night before Thanksgiving, a game dinner was served by a fashionable Chicago restaurant in the Grand Pacific Hotel. It provides one example of the eating habits of America's genteel class. The first such dinner was in 1885, and thereafter it became an annual event. The custom lasted for thirty years and was emulated by hotels across the country. The prominence of game birds on the menu was striking. The menu below was printed in the Chicago Tribune, November 22, 1886. In addition to game birds the meal included main courses of bear, buffalo, deer, sheep, elk, and rabbit.

Procession of Game[31]

Roast
    Wild Goose, Quail, Redhead Duck, Canvasback Duck, Bluewing Teal, Partridge, Widgeon, Brant, Pheasants, Mallard Duck, Prairie Chicken, Wild Turkey, Spotted Grouse, Wood Duck, Sandhill Turkey, Ruffled Grouse

Broiled
    Bluewing Teal, Jacksnipe, Blackbirds, Reed Birds, Partridges, Pheasants, Quails, Butterballs, Ducks, English Snipe, Rice Birds, Red Wing Starling, Marsh Birds

Entrees
    Fillet of Grouse

Salads
    Prairie Chicken

Ornamental Dishes
    Boned Duck au Naturel, Pyramid of Wild Goose Liver in Jelly, Boned
    Quail in Plumage, Red Wing Starling on Tree, Partridge in Nest,
    Prairie Chicken en Socle

Birds were plentiful and they were cheap. For pennies per pound, Americans could satisfy their appetites with a succulent and varied diet of wild game birds.*

The Extinction of Passenger Pigeons

The symbol of these abundant flocks was the passenger pigeon,** which an astonished John Josselyn in 1631 described during one of the semiannual flights as "millions of millions . . . that to my thinking had neither beginning nor ending, length nor breath, and so thick that I could see no Sun."[32] In 1643, the pigeons destroyed the crops of Plymouth Plantation and nearly caused a famine. Yet, five years later, they provided residents with an ample food supply during a poor harvest. Then they became the prey of market hunters and would remain so until their near extinction at the end of the nineteenth century. As early as 1672 Josselyn noted: "of late they are

---

*The game supper was a popular culinary event in many American homes of the nineteenth century. In 1873, Chicago grocers and retailers received 50,000 dozen prairie chickens at $3.25 per dozen, 25,000 dozen quail at $1.25 per dozen, 5,000 dozen pigeons at $1.00 per dozen, 30,000 pounds of elk, 400,000 pounds of buffalo, 450,000 pounds of venison, 10,000 pounds of bear, 225,000 pounds of antelope, at five, seven, eight, and ten cents per pound respectively. The total estimated value was $500,000. (James Tober, *Who Owns the Wildlife*, Westport, CT: Greenwood Press, 1981, 77.)

**Passenger pigeons, also called migratory pigeons because they traveled such long distances in search of food, possessed a colorful plumage, with a gray-blue head and back and a distinctive pink neck and throat. Their undercarriage was mostly reddish brown at the top, with a white down lower in the body. The tails were long, the same gray-blue color as the heads, and the pigeons' eyes were ringed with red. With a wing spread of about 2 feet, the pigeons were strong flyers. They lived in enormous flocks and were accustomed to traveling great distances in search of food. Although they nested in the great oak and beech forests of eastern and central North America, they ate mostly nuts, fruits, grains, seeds, and earthworms from the ground. Like all pigeons, they mated for life with a single partner and shared the task of incubating a single, glossy white egg for two weeks. Once numbering in the "millions of millions," the passenger pigeon has been extinct for most of this century. The smaller mourning dove is its closest living relative.

much diminished, the English taking them with Nets."[33] Although they may have been disappearing in New England, hunters continued to sell them at six for a penny in the markets of Boston in 1736; and as settlers moved across the Appalachians they were astonished by their encounters with the great flocks of migrating passenger pigeons along the midwestern flyways.

The ornithologist Alexander Wilson witnessed a flight in 1806 that he believed was 40 miles wide and contained two billion birds. His classic description remains to this day a marvel for wildlife conservationists, ornithologists, and amateur bird watchers:

> The most remarkable characteristic of these birds is their associating together, both in their migrations and also during the period of incubation, in such prodigious numbers as almost to surpass belief . . . These migrations appear to be undertaken rather in quest of food, than merely to avoid the cold of the climate, since we find them lingering in the northern regions around Hudson's Bay so late in December . . . I have witnessed these migrations in the Genessee country—often in Pennsylvania, and also in various parts of Virginia, with amazement; . . . when compared with the congregated millions which I have since beheld in our western forests, in the states of Ohio, Kentucky, and the Indiana territory. These fertile and extensive regions abound with the nutritious beech nut, which constitute the chief food of the Wild Pigeon. . . . It sometimes happens that having consumed the whole produce of the beech trees in an extensive district, they discover another at the distance perhaps of sixty or eighty miles, to which they regularly repair every morning and return as regularly . . . in the evening, to their . . . roosting place. . . . The ground is covered to the depth of several inches with their dung; all the tender grass and underwood destroyed; the surface strewed with large limbs of trees broken down by the weight of the birds . . . and the trees themselves, for thousands of acres, killed as completely as if girdled with an axe.[34]

John James Audubon* also witnessed migrations as he traveled through the Midwest selecting birds to paint for his *Birds in America* collection. In the autumn of 1813, he described the flight of passenger pigeons on the

---

*John James Audubon's (1785–1851) legacy to wildlife was primarily his richly colored album, *Birds of America.* For this alone, he is regarded as the nation's greatest bird painter. Along with his five-volume *Ornithological Biography,* he left a magnificent record of anecdotes, vivid descriptions of birds and their habitats, and an enthusiasm for birds unknown during his time. Those who followed him established their reputations as champions of preservation by creating the various state Audubon Societies. Although he condemned the massive killing of birds, he shot birds in large numbers and in the case of the starling, he shot hundreds of them. The birds of his magnificent paintings were found, observed, and then shot by Audubon in order to paint them.

Ohio River as he traveled 55 miles from Hardensburgh and Louisville, Kentucky. The flight was so dense that "the light of the noonday sun was obscured as by an eclipse."[35] On this trip, Audubon crossed back and forth to determine the width of the flight and estimated that it was about three miles. He described trees so crowded with birds that those two feet in diameter were splintered at the trunk and their limbs came crashing to the ground under the weight of the pigeons. He wrote, "with a noise that sounded like a gale passing through the rigging of a close-reefed vessel, thousands alighted everywhere, one above another, until solid masses as large as hogsheads were formed on the branches all around. . . . It was a scene of uproar and confusion."[36] He believed that he had witnessed the migration of about one billion birds.

Hunting of passenger pigeons was marked by excess. During a two year span from 1867 to 1869, one town in Michigan sold 15,840,000 birds. Hartford, Michigan, sent three railroad car loads of pigeons per day during one forty-day period, for a grand total of 11,880,000 birds.[37] In 1869, Michigan passed the first law protecting passenger pigeons but to no avail. In 1878, hunters discovered the last major colony of passenger pigeons near Petoskey, Michigan. Within two weeks, using nets, they captured 1,107,800,066 pigeons. This episode marked the end of the passenger pigeon as a viable species.[38] To satisfy the demands of the market for bird meat, hunters used nets to capture and clubs to destroy tens of thousands during a single catch. When hunters fired into migrating flocks, thousands more were slaughtered. In addition to the aggressive practices of market hunters, the commercial logging of beech and oak trees in the midwestern forests of Michigan, Wisconsin, and Minnesota destroyed the pigeons' natural roosts along the midwestern flyways.

Earlier, in 1846, Rhode Island had passed game laws designed to stop spring shooting of wood and black ducks. Still earlier, New York had banned the use of multiple gun emplacements, called "batteries," to hunt waterfowl. The passage and eventual repeal of these early game protection laws indicated that hunters and consumers of game would be slow in accepting changes that limited their freedom. The final fate of passenger pigeons, whose estimates were placed at about 6 billion at the time of European settlement, came when the last one died in the Cincinnati Zoo in 1914.

Market hunting of the passenger pigeon, once so plentiful that it was thought to represent about one-fourth of all native American land birds, to the point of extinction in the nineteenth century played a major role in the creation of efforts to conserve native birds. The pigeon was not the only bird either forced into extinction or endangered by voracious hunters, how-

Market and Pot Hunting. Library of Congress, William T. Hornaday Collection (LC-USZ62–94584).

ever. Millions of Carolina parakeets,* the only member of the parrot species native to the United States, were wiped out because the bird was regarded by farmers and hunters alike as an agricultural pest. The last pair also died in the Cincinnati Zoo, in 1917, after a twenty-year effort to breed them in captivity. The country's last heath hen** died on Martha's Vineyard in the 1930s.

---

*Carolina parakeets formerly lived along the eastern coastal region of the United States from southern Virginia through Florida and west to the forests of east Texas, Oklahoma, Kansas, and Nebraska. It was the only parrot native to North America and possessed the following markings: a large pale yellow bill and yellow head with rich orange cheeks; green throughout, with a long pointed green tail; some yellow and dark blue on the wings. They were hunted as cage birds, captured for their colorful plumage, but were mostly shot by farmers because they descended in flocks on apple orchards, destroying the fruit to get at the seeds, and ate corn and grain from the fields. Audubon observed that they were "always an unwelcome visitor to the planter, the farmer, or the gardener. . . . I have seen several hundreds destroyed . . . in the course of a few hours, and have procured a basketful of these birds at a few shots." (John James Audubon, *Ornithological Biography,* vol. I, Philadelphia: J. Dobson, 1831, 136.)

**Heath hens lived in the salt marshes and open heathland of the eastern coast from New England to the Carolinas. They were hunted by early colonists for food and became a rarity by the end of the eighteenth century. The heaths had become farmland, and the

Early Conservation Movement to Save the Birds

The destruction of birds of all shapes and sizes was so extensive that it caused Theodore Roosevelt to write to his friend, the distinguished naturalist Frank Chapman, owner and editor of *Bird Lore* from 1899 to 1935, about the loss: "When I hear of the destruction of a species I feel just as if the works of some great writer had perished."[39] The losses in the last quarter of the nineteenth century cannot be explained solely in terms of game birds killed for food or sport, or the waste associated with the use of rapid-fire rifles by a growing population of Americans who turned bird hunting into a national pastime. The carnage also received a boost from the millinery trade and fashion industry.

As beaver and deer were hunted to satisfy changes in clothing fashions, the plumage of wild birds as well as whole stuffed birds was valued for the decorative quality it added to women's hats. Five million birds were killed each year in the last forty years of the nineteenth century to satisfy changing fashions promoted by the millinery industry. In 1866, Frank Chapman walked the streets of New York City, taking an inventory of the birds used to enhance a woman's head gear. By his count, "Five hundred and forty-two out of seven hundred hats brandished mounted birds. There were twenty-odd recognizable species, including owls, grackles, grouse, and a green heron."[40] The many ways women's hats displayed birds and their feathers in the last quarter of the nineteenth century was described by the fashion magazine *Harper's Bazaar*. For the fall 1881 fashions, the magazine described hats with "A profusion of feathers, especially breasts, wings, and parts on turbans, large round hats and upon the sides of bonnets."[41] The plumage of fourteen different birds, including scarlet ibis, kingfishers, parroquets, and hummingbirds, were used to create this effect of "profusion." For the spring 1893 fashions, *Harper's Bazaar* described dinner evening wear of black duchesse "bordered with tiny swallows with outspread wings."[42] As late as summer 1899, long after the campaign to curtail the use of plumage in hats was underway, the magazine described the "Fad for whole birds on walking hats; wings, feathers on golf hats and horse-show costumes."[43]

Since plumage of many song and wading birds matures during breeding season, feather hunters attacked the nests of breeding birds and killed them,

---

hen's survival was threatened by cats and rats. By 1830, it was extinct on the mainland. It survived on Martha's Vineyard island, Massachusetts, until March 11, 1932. Exposure to disease and fire on the island revealed the vulnerability of heath hens or any species, for that matter, when they are restricted to a single location.

leaving their young to starve or fry in the summer heat or to be eaten by predators. With the price of some plumes higher than that of an equal weight in gold, the slaughter continued unabated. When it was coupled with the carnage of game bird populations, the loss of wildlife was staggering.[44]

The movement to ban the killing of birds for nongame purposes began with the protest against the plume trade. The combat that ensued marked the addition of aesthetic reasons promoting conservation, along with the existing economic and utilitarian reasons. Alarmed by the devastation to wildlife caused by sophisticated firearms and the avarice of hunters, a number of new organizations dedicated to conservation came into existence. In 1866 the American Society for the Prevention of Cruelty to Animals and the American Ornithologists' Union (AOU) were established. These organizations were intended to alert the public about the destruction of wildlife. The AOU entered the fray against the millinery trade with lectures, publications, and lobbying for legislation to promote public awareness and changed behavior.

At the same time, the state Audubon Societies were increasing their membership. By the beginning of the twentieth century, these separate societies had become incorporated into the National Association of Audubon Societies for the Protection of Wild Birds and Animals.* By 1888, its membership swelled to more than 38,000. Beginning in 1889 its official magazine, titled *Bird Lore,* became a clearinghouse for news about state efforts to protect and preserve birds and their habitats. In 1941, the magazine changed its name to *Audubon Magazine* and then to simply *Audubon* in 1961.

Women activists became central figures in the crusade to save the birds. Those who wrote for *Bird Lore* were popular authors. One contributor, Mabel Osgood Wright, president of the Connecticut Audubon Society, was the author of *The Friendship of Nature* (1894), *Birdcraft* (1895), *Birds of Village and Field* (1898), and articles on preservation for the *New York Times* and the *Evening Post.* By 1905, women had become active in all twenty-eight states, many of them where Audubon Societies were prominent. Many of these states passed the National Audubon Society's Model Predatory Bird Protection Law. The "model law," as it became known,

---

*The Audubon Society was named for the naturalist John James Audubon. Today, the Society numbers over 500,000 members in more than 500 local chapters across the country. In addition to its advocacy of legislation to protect wildlife and its habitat, it began in the 1920s to establish a system of privately held wildlife preserves, which is the largest in the world. Throughout its history the Society has been an innovator in research on endangered species, in creating summer nature camps and centers, and in producing wildlife films. The scope of its present activities extends far beyond its original mandate to protect birds and wildlife and encompasses such environmental matters as land, water, and air quality as well as energy policy and population.

protected birds, hawks and owls from hunters. In addition, the activists waged war on the transatlantic plume trade, centered in Britain. They tried to ban the importation of birds and feathers into the United States, and by October 1913 succeeded, with the passage of a new tariff act banning the import of wild bird feathers.

In addition, the Plumage League was created by women intent on destroying the millinery practice of using plumage for ornament. Thousands of women signed pledges not to purchase or wear these "fashionable" hats. "Two days after the new law went into effect, Audubon Save the Birds Hats were being advertised in New York for $5 to $15 apiece. Congratulations poured in from all over the world for the Audubon Society's great victory."[45] Bird protection became highly publicized. At the International Animal Protection Congress held in Geneva, Switzerland, in 1913, bird protection and the campaign against vivisection dominated the agenda.

Bird books captured the attention of many Americans in the late nineteenth and early twentieth centuries. John Burroughs,* the naturalist and writer, was affectionately called "John o'Birds" as John Muir** had become known as "John o'Mountains." Burroughs' books, including *Birds and Bees, Sharp Eyes,* and *A Bunch of Herbs,* became staples in the education of American school children. More than three hundred thousand copies were purchased for classroom use between 1889 and 1906. Within a few years, John Burroughs' societies sprang up in classrooms across the country. The combined effect of Burroughs' writings and the societies prompted students to study nature and support efforts to protect birds and their habitat. By the turn of the century, many Americans had become infatuated with nature, and nature essays became important reading material during the

---

*John Burroughs (1837–1921), naturalist, poet, and preservationist, wrote extensively about birds and their habitat. His early works, *Wake Robin* (1871) and *Birds and Poets* (1877), were romantic books about the sights and sounds of birds and his own emotions and memories. Later, his observations and the details of his written descriptions became scientific. To acknowledge his lifetime contributions to wildlife, the Museum of Natural History in New York City awards the Burroughs Medal periodically to individuals who make outstanding contributions to conservation and natural history. One of his biographers wrote that "his nature-books express the joie de vivre of the intelligent, healthy outdoor man walking over his acres in the sunlight and the breeze." (William S. Kennedy, *The Real John Burroughs: Personal Recollections and Friendly Estimate,* New York: Funk and Wagnalls, 1924, 5.)

**John Muir (1838–1914), successful farmer, naturalist, traveler, and preservationist, was instrumental in the creation of Yosemite National Park in 1890. As the first president of the Sierra Club, he publicized his ideas about the detrimental effects of deforestation and overgrazing. Forest and park land preservation became important dimensions of his life's work.

Market Hunting or Legitimate Recreation—Which? Courtesy The Bancroft Library, The University of California: Berkelely.

MARKET HUNTING OR LEGITIMATE RECREATION—WHICH?
The first spells extinction for the game birds.   The second means a benefit conferred on every citizen.

early conservation movement. Much younger than Muir or Burroughs, a Boston professor, Dallas Lore Sharp, became one of the most popular and prolific nature writers of the early twentieth century. *Read document 2.2, a sample of Sharp's work, titled* The Nature Movement.

In 1873 the scientist Louis Agassiz* initiated nature study on Penikese, one of the Elizabeth Islands off Massachusetts's southern coast. The

---

*Louis Agassiz (1807–1873), called the star of nineteenth-century American science, immigrated to the United States from Switzerland in 1846. As a zoology professor in Switzerland and then at Harvard University, he pioneered the classification of fossil fish in glacial deposits. At Harvard, he established the Museum of Comparative Zoology and became an innovator in the teaching of zoology, ecology, and natural history. Agassiz and his students were instrumental in establishing the nation's first research stations. The Florida Keys station was established only decades after the nation acquired the peninsula from Spain in 1821. Soon thereafter, Florida's biota were found in the museums and laboratories of American universities.

Agassiz Association, established in 1875, became an early promoter of science education in the nation. The group flourished, and "By 1887 the association was composed of 986 local societies with a total membership of more than ten thousand."[46] The study of nature became a favorite topic in progressive elementary and secondary schools until the 1920s. The negative reaction to progressive educational ideas, which its critics viewed as permissive, ended nature study in the schools during that decade.

Faced with the decimation of some wild birds and the extinction of others in the latter years of the nineteenth century, state governments restricted the activities of market hunters who killed for food, pelts, fur, and feathers. At the same time, they passed laws to protect the rights of sportsmen who hunted for trophies and amusement. Sportsmen and naturalists alike viewed market hunters and those who hunted for their dinner or, as they were called, "men who shot for the pot" with equal disdain. To gentlemen hunters, the others were "selfish, heartless, disgusting and disreputable." "By the twentieth century, in fact, 'pot shot' had entered American slang as an act of cowardice and ill-breeding."[47] This dual policy of restricting market hunters and protecting sportsmen remained in effect through much of the twentieth century. State and federal wildlife legislation reinforced each other. By establishing the world's first national park at Yellowstone in 1872, the government created the "first federal preserve and as such benefited wildlife by eliminating local hunting and preserving natural habitat."[48]

Ideas about preserving some portion of the nation's land in the vast federal territories for public use rather than permitting private development for either farming, mining, or logging were first put forth by the artist and naturalist George Catlin as early as 1833. After Meriwether Lewis and George Clark explored and surveyed the vast acquisition known as the Louisiana Purchase, Catlin traveled west, sketching and painting landscapes, wildlife, and Native Americans. He and others promoted their ideas about the use of public lands until the national park idea began to receive wider support. In 1894, the Park Protection Act was passed to secure the natural resources of the parks, including wildlife, from the avaricious market hunters.

State and federal legislators found ready allies among the growing number of sport hunters, who were repelled by the slaughter now being publicized by their four national periodicals: *American Sportsmen* (1871), *Forest and Stream* (1873), *Field and Stream* (1874), and *American Angler* (1881). The popularity and rapid increase of sport hunting during the period after the Civil War came about for exactly the same reasons that had made market hunting so efficient. The population of sport hunters rose as the middle class expanded during the nation's late nineteenth-century industrial and urban boom. With rising incomes, middle-class sport hunters purchased many of the products of this boom, including technologically improved, afford-able, mass-produced guns, ammunition, and fishing gear. In addition, the new railroad system brought the hunters to the hunt faster than ever before.

What they encountered when they arrived at the site of the hunt con-vinced them that the "golden age" of market hunting had to end. Market hunters had "killed big game for hides, waterfowl for flesh, wading birds for plumage, and ocean fish for oil and fertilizer. Quick money, sometimes large amounts, could be made by men like the plume hunters who shot the snowy egret into extinction."[49] When sport hunters arrived in the comfort of vehicles and trains with their newly improved hunting gear and equipment, they discovered that market hunters had laid waste to the area's wildlife. *Read document 2.3, a description of the market hunting of prairie chickens in Kansas in 1876.*

In response to this realization, editors of sport hunting magazines began a massive campaign to educate sportsmen and citizens alike about the car-nage to wildlife and the impending dangers if policies were not changed and current practices curtailed. Their publications preached to a growing mem-bership the need for uniform game laws and the importance of observing habitat and migration patterns; of forest conservation and watershed protec-tion; of maintaining game fish reserves and restocking depleted waterways; and of saving and increasing the nation's fur-bearing animals. Sport hunters and magazine publishers were important advocates of the newly emerging conservation movement.

The conservation movement grew incredibly during the last decades of the nineteenth century; there were thirty-four organizations in 1878 and as many as 308 within a decade. All were devoted to the preservation of wildlife and their habitats. In addition, hundreds of clubs were interested in both hunting and conservation. If one were to include these, the number of clubs devoted to conservation would have approached 1,000 in total.[50] When the Audubon Society was founded in 1886 by George Bird Grinnell, he made a passionate appeal to club members, naturalists, and sportsmen on the editorial pages of *Forest and Stream.*

Although all of these clubs did not rise up in unison and establish a national conservation movement, the editor of the *American Sportsman,* Wilbur F. Parker, could proudly state: "the sportsmen of America are . . . roused to the importance of banding themselves together for the purpose of checking and controlling the wanton and wasteful destruction of nature's best gifts intended for the heritage of universal man, and not for the benefit of the reckless and the greedy few."[51]

The impact of the efforts to save game birds was far-reaching. Sportsmen published magazines, journals, and bulletins devoted to wildlife conservation. Their clubs created esprit among members and the desire to combat the market hunters and poachers and to promote the establishment of private and public space earmarked for game preservation. The creation of New York's Adirondack Preserve of 715,000 acres in 1885 for the conservation of forest and wildlife habitat represented an important victory for sportsmen and advocates for the wilderness alike. Getting rid of the "game hogs," as market hunters and poachers were called, as well as establishing preserves where wildlife could flourish, were two prescriptions used by nineteenth-century conservationists to save game birds.

The loss of birds became a mark of environmental degradation. It would become a theme echoed by protectors of wildlife through the nineteenth and early twentieth centuries. This theme would be repeated most eloquently to a future generation in 1962 by Rachel Carson.* In the introduction of *Silent Spring,* one of the nation's most influential books of the twentieth century, she muses: "It was a spring without voices. On the mornings that had once throbbed with the dawn chorus of robins, catbirds, doves, jays, wrens, and scores of other bird voices there was now no sound; only silence lay over the fields and woods and marsh."[52]

National fervor over protecting birds was increased by the efforts of the American Society for the Prevention of Cruelty to Animals (ASPCA) and its state affiliates such as the Massachusetts SPCA. Much of the earlier work of the SPCAs had focused on protecting beasts of burden—urban horses and dogs who pulled wagons, trams, and carts—from being abused by owners and workmen. By 1884, numerous SPCA magazines, including its famous *Animal World,* warned that destroying birds would have dire effects on humans: "Decimate the feathered population . . . and a plague of grubs and weevils will consume our sustenance. Only the ravenous appetite of millions of small birds maintained the balance of nature and kept starvation from the door."[53]

William T. Hornaday was one of the first among the early conservation-

---

*Rachel Carson (1907–1964), educated as an aquatic biologist, wrote *Under the Sea Wind* (1941), *The Sea Around Us* (1951), and *The Edge of the Sea* (1956) before *Silent Spring* (1962). Before devoting her life to writing full time, she was a biologist for the nation's Bureau of Fisheries in the 1930s and editor-in-chief of the Fish and Wildlife Service from 1949 to 1953. *Silent Spring* was a vigorous indictment of the chemical pesticide industry and the government agencies who defended the use of pesticides to control insects. Only the support of President John F. Kennedy and his Secretary of the Interior, Stewart Udall, however, resulted in curtailing pesticide use and the banning of DDT after 1970 by the Environmental Protection Agency.

ists to see the "web of life" concept in the activities of settled and migratory birds. In *Our Vanishing Wild Life,* he summarized the research on the number of weed seeds and destructive insects eaten in a day by various birds. For example, "bob-white" quail consumed 115,000 weed seeds of different varieties and more than 3,000 insects each day.[54] The next generation of wildlife advocates would invest heavily in establishing organizations dedicated to wildlife research.

The views expressed in *Animal World* and in *Our Vanishing Wild Life* gained acceptance slowly by conservationists. The traditional concept of a great "chain of being," which linked humans to other forms of life in a rigid hierarchy with humans at the top, had been accepted for centuries. Although the views expressed by SPCAs about human linkages to other species were imperfectly understood, a new ethic, about humanity's interconnected relationship to other life forms rather than its dominance over other species, was beginning to take hold among a small group of educated Americans. As the quote above points out, this newer ethic was articulated initially in terms of the devastation of bird populations and its potential disastrous consequences for humans. The American Ornithologists' Union, the national and local Audubon societies, the American Society for the Prevention of Cruelty to Animals, and many small local clubs had been established by avid bird watchers and sports hunters to save the birds from extinction. Their members were among the early advocates of the new ethic regarding the interdependence of animal and human life.

Beginning in 1912, Hornaday became one of the many vigorous supporters of protection for wild birds, fighting for laws to protect migratory birds and the ending of trade in game birds and their plumage. The Weeks–McLean Migratory Bird Act of 1913 and the international migratory bird law protecting 1,022 species of continental birds from the North Pole to Mexico, signed by Canada, England, and Mexico in 1918, were written to end such practices. In 1919, the U.S. Migratory Bird Conservation Act created fourteen migratory bird sanctuaries from California to New York. Hornaday's *Our Vanishing Wild Life,* published in 1913 by the N.Y. Zoological Society and sent to every congressman and to influential state legislators across the country, gave a poignant, assertive, and uncompromising voice to the growing national conservation movement.

As societies and clubs advocated the protection of birds, the conservation of large game animals was promoted by the Boone and Crockett Club, founded in 1887 by sportsmen and led by Theodore Roosevelt. It had responded to the slaughter of the Great Plains bison herds, estimated to range in total size from 6 to well over 30 million in 1870. Thirteen years later, in 1883, the herds hovered on the brink of extinction. Along with the passenger pigeon, the bison became the most visible example of the devastation of wildlife in the last quarter of the nineteenth century.

Hunting Bison

The destruction of the Great Plains bison* was the second major episode which set in motion the late nineteenth-century conservation effort on behalf of wildlife. As late as the 1700s, the range of these one-ton grazers, who could run thirty-five miles per hour, extended from the South to the Rocky Mountains. During European exploration and colonization, it was believed that 30 million roamed across the national landscape. With the westward movement in the 1800s, "Pioneers reported herds five miles wide galloping past a given point for half a day."[55]

As early as 1832 George Catlin, the artist and naturalist, described the sight of herds of bison on the western prairie. His descriptions are worth remembering:

> the congregations of bison . . . [crowded] into such masses in some places, as literally to blacken the prairies for miles together. . . several thousands in a mass, eddying and wheeling about under a cloud of dust . . . the whole mass . . . in constant motion; and all bellowing (or roaring) in deep and hollow sounds; which, mingled together, appear, at the distance of a mile or two, like the sound of distant thunder.[56]

Catlin witnessed also the plundering of the herds by Native Americans, pioneer hunters, and the slow steady stream of market hunters whose infiltration into the Great Plains accelerated quickly with the coming of the continental railroads. He predicted the demise of the bison unless the government intervened to protect them, even before the railroads made it easier to traverse the continent. St. Louis merchants were paying three dollars for a 150–pound bison hide in 1849. As the Union Pacific railroad extended its routes into Nebraska and Wyoming in the 1860s, the retail market for robes made of bison hides expanded greatly.

In the next twenty years, the transcontinental railroad system was completed. During its construction, bison were hunted to feed the railroad workers.

------

*The bison is North America's native bovine, which adapted over the millennium to the harsh, arid climate of the Great Plains. Bison live by eating grass of various quality, drink water only once every three days, and avoid shelter during the harsh winters of the open plains. In winter, their metabolism slows, and they require less food to survive. They possess 2–inch-thick skin and 4–inch-deep fur. They refuse to be herded like cattle and sheep on the range, and have been known to gore horses and dogs. If agitated, they are capable of jumping a 6–foot fence and running for half an hour at a speed of thirty-five miles per hour.

Charles Rath's Buffalo Hide Yard in Dodge City, Mid 1870s. Courtesy Kansas State Historical Society, Topeka, Kansas.

Once the railroad was in operation, bison were killed by passengers from passing trains, who left their dying and dead carcasses to rot in the summer sun. One meat hunter employed by the railroads was William F. Cody, who during his rodeo career became known as "Buffalo Bill." He offered the following description of his work as a hunter:

> I started in killing buffalo for the Union Pacific Railroad. I had a wagon with four mules, one driver and two butchers, all brave, well armed men, myself riding my horse "Brigham."
>
> I had to keep a close and careful lookout for Indians before making my run into a herd of buffalo. It was my custom in those days to pick out a herd that seemed to have the fattest cows and young heifers. I would then rush my horse into them, . . . shooting them down, while my horse would be running alongside of them. . . . I have killed from twenty-five to forty buffalo while the herd was circling, and they would all be dropped very close together; . . . in a space covering about five acres.
>
> I killed buffalo for the railroad company for twelve months, . . . the number I brought into camp was kept account of . . . that period I had killed 4,280 buffalo.[57]

Not long after Bill Cody wrote this account, in 1870 Philadelphia tanners learned how to turn bison hides into fashionable leather for the growing retail market in leather boots, clothing, and accessories. To supply the growing demand, professional hunting parties, made up of a shooter, two skinners, and a cook, descended on the herds with ferocity. They were linked to a support system of collection points and smokehouses in western towns established to dry and cure the hides before shipping them east to the tanneries. The market system had made the killing, curing, distribution, and tanning of hides efficient and highly profitable.

Richard Dodge, a member of the U.S. military assigned to the western territories, described the carnage. "Where there were myriads of buffalo the year before, there were now myriads of carcasses. The air was foul with sickening stench, and the vast plain, which only a short twelvemonth before teemed with animal life, was a dead, solitary, putrid desert . . . The buffalo melted away like snow before a summer's sun."[58]

In less than six years after the coming of the railroad, more than 4 million bison were killed on the southern plains. Dodge City, Kansas, became a major depot for hides. They sold for $1.25 each; tongues for 25 cents apiece; and hindquarters for one cent a pound. Professional hunters killed hundreds of bison each day. One named Brick Bond killed 250 in a day and 5,855 in one three-month period. In 1872 and 1873 alone more than 1,250,000 hides were shipped from Kansas to the tanneries in Philadelphia and New York State.[59]

The remnants of the southern bison herd were located in Texas from 1874 to 1878, and by the end of this four-year period nothing was left of them. The remnants of the northern herd were located on the Dakota, Montana, and Canadian prairies. By 1883, nothing but stragglers remained, and the great herds were gone from the plains. By this time herds of longhorn cattle driven up the Chisholm Trail from Texas had replaced the bison on the western plains. Ranch land was beginning to replace open prairie.

Early Conservation: The Bison

In 1897, taxidermists destroyed one of the last small bands of bison, in Lost Park, Colorado. The federal government, however, saved a small band of about twenty bison when their grazing land was included in the nation's first national park at Yellowstone. Two years later, the pioneer zoologist William Hornaday estimated that only eighty-five wild buffalo survived on the western plains.[60] By 1905 he had interested President Theodore Roosevelt in helping him to form the American Bison Society to protect and propagate bison in the national preserves.

Before the establishment of this society, however, Roosevelt was invited by George Bird Grinnell to assist him in creating the Boone and Crockett

Club, dedicated to protecting large mammals including bears, elk, mountain sheep, and bison from further devastation. Grinnell was the founder of the influential wildlife magazine *Forest and Stream* and the National Audubon Society, and was a leader in the fight to save game birds from market hunters. Grinnell had also written a widely read article titled "The Last of the Buffalo," which appeared in *Scribner's Magazine*. It became a focal point in discussions about the buffalo. *Read document 2.4, "The Last of the Buffalo."*

In December 1887 the Boone and Crockett Club was founded at a dinner meeting in Manhattan attended by Roosevelt, Grinnell, and a number of active sportsmen from elite New York families. The goals of the club, named for two of the nation's more celebrated pioneer hunters, included the following: "To promote manly sport with the rifle . . . To work for the preservation of the large game of this country, . . . to further legislation for that purpose, and to assist in enforcing the existing game laws."[61]

During the early years of its existence, the club became embroiled in a controversy over a Congressional initiative to permit a private company, Montana Mineral, to build a railroad line through Yellowstone National Park. For club members Yellowstone symbolized the first step in an effort to set aside public land for recreation and as a preserve for threatened wildlife species. The idea of the intrusion of a private railroad crossing land set aside for conservation and wildlife preservation angered members of the Boone and Crockett Club. In an effort to pass the bill quickly, the railroad lobby pressured the Speaker of the House to bring it to a vote, but it was defeated ultimately because Grinnell exposed this tactic in a *Forest and Stream* editorial, which brought to Congress an avalanche of mail opposing the bill to Congress.

Public support of club goals, however, can be attributed to an earlier incident involving poaching at Yellowstone and the recognition that enforcement of wild game laws was either lax or nonexistent. In March 1894, a poacher named Edgar Howell was captured by federal agent Felix Burgess and an associate but only after he had beheaded six bison and begun to skin another five or so. The entire incident was reported by Emerson Hough, a novelist and reporter for *Forest and Stream*. In its editorial about the capture titled "Save the Park Buffalo," the magazine appealed to every sportsman in the following way:

> It is but a short time since we announced the capture of the poacher in the National Park, and the fact that he had killed eleven buffalo, and this announcement greatly surprised and alarmed all who are interested in the National Park and all public-spirited citizens as well.

In another column we quote statements contained in a private letter received from our staff correspondent in the National Park, and these statements show that the condition of things there, so far as the buffalo are concerned, is infinitely worse than any one had supposed. Besides the buffalo known to have been killed by Howell, Messrs. Hough and Hofer, of the *Forest and Stream* Yellowstone Park Game Exploration, discovered in another place eight buffalo carcasses scattered over the hillside and buried under 4 ft. of snow. The date at which these were killed has not yet been determined, as it was impossible with the means at hand for the travelers to get to the carcasses.

There seems now to be little doubt that within the last year or two a wholesale slaughter has been taking place among our buffalo preserved in the Yellowstone Park. It was believed that these, if they had been protected, would by natural increase have reached four or five hundred by this time, but if the herd has been preyed on by poachers in other years as it has in the winter of 1893–4, we can well imagine that two hundred or two hundred and fifty is the outside limit for the buffalo in the Park.

As we stated a few days ago, Congress has put a premium on the head of every one of these great beasts. Any man is free to enter the National Park and kill them, and knows that—even if taken in the act—no punishment can be inflicted on him. The chances against his capture are considerable, and even if taken, the only inconvenience that he suffers is a confiscation of his outfit, amounting to but a few dollars in value, and a few weeks discomfort in the guard house. Against this there is the prospect of selling for $200 or $300 the head of every buffalo which he has killed, and in the deep snows of winter there would be no difficulty in killing in the course of three or four days, all the buffalo in the Hayden Valley, which, as our correspondent reports, are now not more than from seventy-five to one hundred head.

It is not surprising that sportsmen and many of the newspapers of the country are stirred up about this matter, nor that the number of police bills have been introduced in Congress to remedy the existing state of things. Most of the bills introduced thus far are entirely inadequate, partly because they have been drawn by persons who are not familiar with the condition of things in the Park, and so are ignorant of what is required in such a bill. It is somewhat absurd to provide the penalty of a fine of $100 for killing a buffalo, when it is perfectly well known that if a man kills one and succeeds in getting its head out of the Park, he can obtain for it three times the amount of the possible fine. On the other hand the penalties should not be so severe as to excite sympathy for the law breaker, and so to render the law inoperative.

We have already said that these animals are Government property, and that injury to them should be punished in the same way as injury to any other Government property. The Yellowstone Park has by law been distinctly set aside as a public Park or pleasuring ground for the people, and the natural objects in it, whether animate or inanimate, belong to the public. It is the business of the Government, which acts for the people, to protect this property which belongs to those whom it represents. The executive branch of the Government has done and is doing all in its power to furnish this protection, but the legislative branch has failed and continues to fail to do its duty, for it refuses to provide methods and means for enforcing the protection which it has authorized in the organic act in establishing the Park.

We suggest that every reader of *Forest and Stream* who is interested in the Park or in natural history, or in things pertaining to America, should write to his Senator and Representative in Congress, asking them to take an active interest in the protection of the Park. In no other way can Congress be made to feel the force of public opinion, and be induced to enact the necessary laws for the protection of the National Park.[62]

To dramatize the matter, the magazine's next issue included photographs of the captured poacher and his victims, with a comment that the herd would have been wiped out if the culprit had not been apprehended.

Almost immediately after the reporting of the Howell incident John Lacey,* congressman from Iowa and a member of the Boone and Crockett Club, submitted a bill to protect the birds and animals in Yellowstone National Park. Passed quickly by Congress, the law prohibited the killing of animals except to protect human life. It also banned all trafficking in wildlife. Enforcement was emphasized by establishing a system of federal marshals, with powers to arrest anyone possessing dead wildlife. A federal park commissioner for Yellowstone was appointed by the U.S. Circuit Court and served as judge. Convictions for violations included fines of $1,000 and prison terms of up to two years. The law was signed by President Grover Cleveland on May 7, 1894, only a few short months after the poaching episode in Yellowstone. The passage of this first Lacey law preceded the establishment of the National Park Service by one year. Once the service was established, this precedent-setting law provided the National Park Service with a ready-made mechanism for the future protection of wildlife in the park system. As a legal precedent, the first Lacey law served as a forerunner to all subsequent legislation written to protect threatened and endangered species.

The passage of this first law was followed by the Lacey Act in May of 1900, which ended market hunting for the interstate shipment of wildlife or

---

*John F. Lacey (1841–1913), a Civil War veteran, was a lawyer and expert on railroad law. As a congressman for sixteen years, 1889–1891 and 1893–1902, he served as a member and then as chairman of the House Committee on Public Lands. In this capacity, he became involved in significant conservation issues, including the establishment of forest and wildlife refuges as well as national parks and monuments. Under his legislative leadership, market hunting for hides, horns, food, and feathers ended officially. Thereafter, he was referred to as the "father of federal game legislation." As a founding member of the Boone and Crocket Club, he joined Theodore Roosevelt, George Grinnell, William Hornaday, and others in advocating increased federal involvement in wildlife administration and law enforcement.

wildlife products. The law included the plumage, eggs, and flesh of birds as well as the meat, pelts, and antlers of mammals taken in violation of state game laws. The Lacey Act of 1900 authorized the Department of Agriculture to stop interstate traffic of illegally killed wildlife. The administration of the law was placed with the U.S. Biological Survey, forerunner to the present Fish and Wildlife Service. Enforcing the law was difficult. An illegal market grew and the killing continued, until the murder of a Florida game warden, Guy Bradley, by a plume hunter. The hunter's eventual acquittal caused a national outrage and helped to turn the tide against market hunters and hatters.

The Lacey Act of 1900 represented the culmination of a generation's attempts to control commercial hunting and poaching. Getting rid of "game hogs" as market hunters were called, was one prescription for saving wildlife. The second, which will be examined now, was to establish a system of game refuges where game could reproduce unimpeded. Once their numbers reached acceptable levels, they would naturally extend their range to adjacent areas. These areas would then become hunting grounds or zones for sportsmen.

The Nation's First Refuges for Wildlife

As a former big-game hunter and first director of the New York Zoological Park, William T. Hornaday became one of the most vocal spokesman of big-game preservation. He advocated a permanent moratorium on hunting in order to avoid another disaster like the extinction of the passenger pigeon and the near extinction of the bison. During his presidency, Theodore Roosevelt, influenced by Hornaday and others, created over fifty wildlife refuges in order to translate this prescription into a reality. A public policy of establishing refuges stimulated private philanthropy. Initiated by John D. Rockefeller, Jr., land philanthropy became an important early twentieth-century activity among the nation's elite men and women. Their wealth purchased mountain tops, woodlands, highlands and lowlands, wetlands, palisade overlooks, islands, and open space, and they donated private estates for park and wildlife preservation.

The impact of private individual philanthropy and private group activity was striking. The matter of wetlands and their relationship to wildlife is a case in point. Many of the marshes and lands owned by private duck clubs were purchased by a conservancy or organization dedicated to conservation. Then the group donated the property to the national wildlife refuge system, for it to be managed either by the U.S. Fish and Wildlife Service or by a state wildlife agency. Today, such public holdings represent more than half of the nation's remaining wetlands. On the other hand, "Most private marshes . . . that were not acquired by a conservation agency . . . have long since been drained and desiccated."[63]

Preservation of space led naturally to land and wildlife management in the early decades of the twentieth century. Order, stability, and efficiency were important early concepts in the Progressive ideology of Theodore Roosevelt and his contemporaries. Their ideas included the management of industrial time, production, and people along with performance measures to quantify achievements on the job and in school. Alongside municipal research conducted for the evaluation of local government, these innovations would became important legacies of the Progressive era of the early twentieth century. Organizations dedicated to the protection of wildlife, the conservation of federal land, and the management of both were established during these early years.

In 1911, the American Game Protective Association (AGPA), forerunner to the American Wildlife Institute, was founded in New York by sportsmen. Of its sponsors, the Sporting Arms and Ammunitions Manufacturers' Institute (SAAMI) was the most visible. The association correctly saw the devastation of game as detrimental to business, and the pages of its quarterly newsletter, the *Bulletin*, were devoted to issues of game conservation. AGPA was a federation of local and state affiliates established to increase membership, get members appointed as local and state game wardens, and serve as "watchdogs" to enforce local and state laws protecting wildlife and their habitat. In 1915, AGPA began sponsoring an annual American Game Conference on preservation and restoration. It was responsible for getting tough new state game laws passed and many new small state game refuges established.

At the same time that members of Roosevelt's Progressive coalition were at work establishing refuges for wildlife in nature, Roosevelt, as president of the Boone and Crockett Club of New York, initiated discussions about creating a zoological park in New York City. As conceived, the park would become a large wildlife preserve in an urban setting. The New York state legislature chartered the New York Zoological Society with authorization to operate a zoo in 1895. This inspired a movement to create zoological parks in many urban areas that were far removed from the natural habitats of the protected species.

Believing that natural habitat loss could be partly compensated by establishing "artificial" habitats for threatened species, the New York Zoological Society's first statement of purpose read: "no civilized nation should allow its wild animals to be exterminated without at least making an attempt to preserve living representatives of all species that can be kept alive in confinement."[64] Its conservation goals were apparent in its early annual reports: "living creatures can be kept under conditions most closely approximating those with which nature usually surrounds them ... [and could] serve a good purpose in this community by extending and cultivating in every possible manner the knowledge and love of nature."[65]

The "Bronx Zoo," as the New York Zoological Park was called because of its location in the Bronx borough of New York City, was directed for thirty years, from 1896 to 1926, by William T. Hornaday. As also founding director of the National Zoological Park in Washington, D.C., Hornaday became an active and outspoken advocate for wildlife preservation. Along with Roosevelt, he established the American Bison Society. He initiated a plan to use bison stock from the Bronx Zoo and place bison on several government-owned western lands. As a result, "Bronx bison" were placed on the Wichita Mountain Preserve in Oklahoma (1907), the Montana National Bison Range (1908), and the Wind Cave Bison Range in Dakota and the Fort Niobarra Bison Range in Nebraska (1913).

Efforts to preserve wildlife and restore depleted herds were fostered by a number of new permanent organizations. For example, the American Wildlife Institute, founded in 1935, had its origins in 1911 as the American Game Protection Association. When it became the Wildlife Management Institute in 1946, it had already trained a generation of modern biologists and managers of wildlife. The Nature Conservancy, a national organization of conservation-minded businessmen, purchased "small, quiet, nooks typical of wild America" and turned them over to government agencies or local groups for management and supervision.[66] The Izaak Walton League of America, founded in 1922, was dedicated to the preservation of waterways and fish life. In the 1930s, a new host of organizations dedicated to wildlife preservation and restoration were created. The Federation of Western Outdoor Clubs was founded in 1932, followed by the North American Wildlife Foundation in 1935, and the Wildlife Society and Ducks Unlimited in 1937. In 1934, the Wilderness Society was created to protect primitive areas from the government-financed skyline drives into park and forest reserves. And, in 1935, the National Wildlife Federation "came into being to correlate the activities of thousands of local sportsmen's clubs which were the Boone and Crockett Clubs of grassroots America. The federation has helped to educate a whole generation in the use of firearms and the tenets of conservation."[67]

Hunting Predators

Hornaday was also an outspoken advocate of the third prescription, namely predator control, along with establishing refuges for wildlife in nature and by building man-made habitats such as zoos, for enhancing the stock of wildlife. In Hornaday's extensive lexicon of wildlife preservation was the categories of "good" wildlife and "bad" wildlife. There were good game birds and bad game birds: the prey and the predators. The prey were to be protected and the predators eradicated. In referring to hawks that should be "shot on sight," Hornaday stated: "There are two small, fierce, daring, swift-winged hawks both of which are so destructive that they deserve to be shot whenever possible. They are Cooper's Hawk . . . and the Sharp-shinned Hawk . . . The Goshawk is a bad one, and so is the Peregrine Falcon, or Duck Hawk. Both deserve death . . . . The Great Horned Owl was an aerial robber and murderer."[68]

Hornaday's views about some hawks, falcons, and owls were those expressed generally by a generation of conservationists who were committed to saving wildlife from extinction. As a group, with few exceptions such as John Muir and Joseph Grinnell, their view of the natural world excluded predatory animals, who might prevent the restoration of game animals to their former robust numbers. John Muir in 1910 pointed out the absurdity of coyote hunts in California's San Joaquin Valley. To Muir, "The loss of a few chickens from hawks and a few calves and sheep from coyotes amounted to nothing" when compared to the crops destroyed by rabbits, a staple in the coyotes' diet.[69]

War on predators was nothing new in the nation's history. After all, the colonies had "declared war" on wolves in the seventeenth century. Recall that as early as 1630, Massachusetts Bay and Virginia offered a penny bounty for the killing of each grey wolf. By the beginning of the nineteenth century wolves had all but disappeared from New England; the last New England wolf was killed in Maine in 1860. The method used to help eradicate the wolf was the bounty: "The bounty system spread with settlement, remaining an almost ubiquitous feature in state statutes into the twentieth century."[70]

However, predators continued to thrive on the western plains. During the era of the buffalo hunters, carcasses left by hunters provided carnivore mammals, including wolves, cougars, coyotes, and mountain lions, with an ample supply of fresh meat. Once grazing herds of livestock replaced bison on the western plains during the last quarter of the nineteenth century, cattlemen and sheep herders hired professional "wolfers," who made extensive use of newly invented steel traps and strychnine poison to "wage war on wolves." To Hornaday, the wolf was a "master of cunning and the acme of cruelty."[71] In some western states, officials gave strychnine away freely, and in others the sale of poisons in drugstores was unregulated.[72]

Cowmen and sheep ranchers began their assault on wolves, coyotes, and mountain lions with guns, traps, and arsenic in the late nineteenth century as their herds and flocks replaced the vanishing herds of bison on federal lands in the western plains. At the same time, they complained to government land officials about the killing of their grazing animals by predators. In 1896, the manager of the Standard Cattle Company complained that:

> the number of wolves has become so considerable that all means of extermination used for the last five years have only succeeded in keeping them at a standstill ... I consider that the extent of the loss to the community is much greater than is commonly supposed, and that it is much greater than that from cattle thieves ... to a state like Wyoming, ... I should judge it to be not far from a million dollars a year, four times the entire revenue needed to run the state government.[73]

A year earlier, the Department of Agriculture's Office of Economic Ornithology and Mammalogy began to study efficient ways to poison rodents, predatory birds, and mammals. During the early twentieth century, the federal government sponsored several predator control programs. As a result, the population of carnivores and their habitats declined significantly.

In the early years of the twentieth century, the strategies used by practitioners of game management included controlling predators as well as protecting, restoring, and even restocking forests, parks, and refuges with animals from elsewhere. Also, they licensed hunters, imposed "bag" limits on them, and limited the seasons for hunting to months, weeks, and even days. In a political world dominated by Progressive ideas, controlling nature became a priority for conservationists.

Dedicated to providing protective natural environments in the form of refuges and artificial environments in the form of zoological parks, conservationists also supported predator control programs as part of the restoration process. To them, predators were a major cause for the decline in the numbers of wildlife. Understanding the hatred directed against predators is important to understanding the aggressiveness of government policies against them during the first three decades of this century. In addition, the active role of sheep and cattle ranchers in lobbying the government helps us to understand the public policy of eliminating predators, despite information about its contrary environmental effects.

Conservationists were convinced that predator control and wildlife restoration were equal parts of a coherent program. Combined with powerful farming, ranching, and sheep-herding interests, they sealed the fate of predators. The Bureau of the Biological Survey (BBS), in the Department of Agriculture, became the federal agency chosen to carry out the control program. Established in 1905 as a successor to the Division of Economic Ornithology and Mammalogy, BBS focused on the economic impact of damage to crops done by insects and of loss of livestock due to predatory carnivores. One year after its founding, BBS became a clearinghouse for information about the effectiveness of state bounty systems. Also, it began to issue pamphlets about predators, "suggesting the best kinds of scents and poisons to use against each species. Just two years after its founding in 1907, the Bureau supervised the killing of 1,800 wolves and 23,000 coyotes in the National Forests, a policy that was soon extended to the National Parks as well."[74]

At approximately the same time, government policy had resulted in a new program to save deer on the Kaibab Plateau* in northern Arizona's national forest. The Grand Canyon National Game Preserve, established to restore and protect the Kaibab deer, represented the implementation of the national conservation wildlife policy. By 1906, in response to a national campaign by sportsmen and wildlife conservationists to protect the shrinking herd of mule deer, President Roosevelt designated the Kaibab area as the Grand Canyon National Game Preserve. In addition to establishing the preserve, one of the many wildlife refuges established during his administration, Roosevelt ordered a predator control program to protect the vulnerable deer. Two years earlier, the Forest Service had employed trappers to kill wolves on its grazing land. The effectiveness of these trappers in killing wolves and cats was devastating to the predator population.

After the last twenty-five years of the nineteenth century, the habitat for wolves had shrunken to the northern woods of Michigan, Wisconsin, and Minnesota. As one report noted: "Between 1906 and 1923 it was estimated that Forest Service employees killed 674 cougars, 11 wolves, 3,000 coyotes, and 120 bobcats on the Kaibab. Roosevelt himself came in 1913 with his sons Archie and Quentin and his nephew Nicholas, and led them on predator hunts."[75] In 1915, Congress provided funds to the Bureau of Biological Survey to help ranchers eliminate wolves from their range. By the mid-1920s, the last breeding wolves in the western United States had been killed. In recent years they have been reintroduced into Glacier and Yellowstone National Parks.

At the time of European colonization, the range of the North American

---

*The Kaibab Plateau is about 8,000 feet above sea level in the Arizona National Forest. It is surrounded on three sides by mile-deep canyons, Grand and Marble Canyons to the south and east respectively and the Kanab Creek to the west. Its name, "Kaibab," is taken from the Indian word meaning "mountain lying down." Originally the home for about 3,000 deer, the area, about 1 million acres of open woodland and meadows, became a favorite place for hunters. The intrusion of about 9,000 head of cattle and about 20,000 sheep in the later part of the nineteenth century caused a dramatic decline in the population of deer.

wolf was approximately 7 million miles. Human population growth, deforestation, agricultural production, and hunting altered the habitat, range, and
numbers of wolves directly. "By 1908 the wolf population had shrunk to
200,000, and only 2,000 of these were living in the Transmississippi West,
once its stronghold. . . . [In 1928] out of tens of thousands of carnivores
killed in western states, only eleven were listed as gray wolves."[76] Government policy was so effective in eliminating wolves that it took only fifteen
years before wolves all but disappeared from the West. For much of the
twentieth century, the poisoning of predators was the most common and
controversial control technique. A revision in public policy took place,
however, once it became clear that a lack of food and shelter was the
primary cause for the decline in wild game and livestock, not predation.

The first signals that predators were not the primary problem for wild
game occurred on the Kaibab Plateau. Eighteen years after the government
had established the preserve and instituted its predator control program in
1906, the depleted deer herd of 4,000 approached nearly 100,000. It appeared that Progressive conservation policy had been a major success.
However, during the winters of 1924–1925 and 1925–1926, thousands of
deer died of starvation. Within a decade, the remaining herd numbered only
10,000. What had happened to this seemingly stunning success in wildlife
restoration and management? Simply put, the plateau had a maximum "carrying capacity" of only about 20,000 deer; 100,000 deer had overgrazed,
overbrowsed, and highlined all the trees (meaning that they ate the twigs on
the branches they could reach). The result was malnutrition and eventual
starvation. Predators played no roll in this catastrophe. Although it was not
known at the time, predators, if there had been any on the plateau, would
have eliminated the old, ill, and young deer, reducing the magnitude of the
eventual disaster.*

The disaster did not bring about an immediate change in the public
policy regarding predators. The eradication program on the Kaibab Plateau,
begun in 1906, continued unabated as late as 1939. For example, "During
the period from 1916 to 1931, [government hunters] trapped or shot 781
mountain lions, 30 wolves, 4,889 coyotes, and 554 bobcats."[77] Additional

---

*Today, about 27 million deer live in the forests and in rural and suburban areas of
the United States, many more than were alive when the Pilgrims arrived in 1620. When
Walt Disney's *Bambi* appeared on the movie screen in 1942, only about 500,000 deer
existed in the United States. With no natural predators and restricted hunting seasons,
and with numerous new habitats on the edges of suburban and commercial
developments, the population of deer has exploded. In 1996, nearly 500,000 automobile
collisions involved deer, resulting in more than 100 human fatalities. ("Bambi the Pest,"
New York Times, July 26, 1997, 22.)

evidence about the impact of eradication programs on the "balance of nature" went largely unheeded by the Bureau of Biological Survey and the hunters in its employ.

In 1924–1925 and again in January 1927, the BBS, at the request of farmers in Kern County, California, began a program of poisoning coyotes on the grounds that coyotes were killing large numbers of chickens and other barnyard animals. This program of killing caused a major outbreak of mice in the county. Hordes of mice "overran stores and homes; a slick coating of crushed rodents made roads impassable. Traps and poison yielded incredible numbers—two tons at one warehouse. Stories circulated about housewives who had spent a week on the furniture, never touching the floor."[78]

Investigators from BBS and university mammalogists disputed the causes of the outbreak. E. Raymond Hall, a mammalogist and student of Joseph Grinnell, argued that plentiful food and shelter were important factors in creating the hordes of mice but the absence of their natural enemies was the most important ingredient in their increase. Since BBS predator control efforts were running in high gear in the 1920s, with government appropriations to fuel the programs, BBS officials vehemently disputed the mammalogists' claims. With the growing support of the National Wool Growers Association, coupled with that of western representatives and senators, appropriations for programs to eliminate "useless" animals continued. With the passage of the Animal Damage Control Act in 1931, initially planned as a ten-year program to control predators and rodents, Congress provided the legal basis for a program that would remain in effect until the 1970s.[79] Since most wolves, mountain lions, and grizzly bears had been eliminated from the western states by the time of the law's passage, coyotes became the major object of BBS control programs. From 1915 to 1947, almost 2 million were killed, and in recent years about 90,000 have died from poisoning each year.[80]

Such government programs did not continue without conflict and controversy. With the expansion of BBS programs in the 1920s, the organization continued to defend its practices despite opposition. However, other government agencies curtailed their programs, either because of opposition or because they began to doubt their programs' effectiveness. From 1924 to 1931, members of the American Society of Mammalogists criticized the BBS for its reckless use of poisons, which indiscriminately killed nontarget animals while threatening entire target species. The National Park Service, many of whose rangers viewed the national parks as sanctuaries for all species of wildlife, responded to the criticism directed at the BBS by curtailing its predator control program.

At the Park Service annual conference in 1925, "park superintendents reduced the money that rangers received from the sale of pelts and cut the list of predators to three species: wolves, coyotes, and cougars. Three years later—following a speech by Joseph Grinnell—they passed a resolution opposing trapping in the parks."[81] The work of the small, well-organized, and aggressive Anti-Steel Trap League,* forerunner of the present Defend-ers of Wildlife organization, helped to mobilize opposition to this inhumane method of killing carnivores in the 1920s. By 1931 the Director of the Park Service, Horace Albright, declared that "all animal life should be kept inviolate ... examples of the various interesting North American mammals under natural conditions for the pleasure and education of the visitors and for the purpose of scientific study."[82]

By 1936, the National Park Service banned the killing of predators on the lands under its jurisdiction. Many of its rangers endorsed the principle of limited sanctuaries rather than total extermination. However, enforcing this policy remained a problem; illegal hunting and poaching threatened predators, while BBS field agents made "secret raids into park lands to get their varmints anyway. And it was not uncommon thereafter to find the borders of the park bristling with cyanide-loaded coyote getters."[83] The "coyote getter" was a mechanical device that fired sodium cyanide into the mouth of an animal once it bit into loaded meat.

Finally, with most other predators eliminated, the Bureau of Biological Survey and its branch, the Office of Predator and Rodent Control (PARC), focused on the coyote. The coyote was the only predator that existed in large enough numbers for it to be identified as a menace to sheep by the Bureau and the wool growers. Until World War II, PARC had used poisoned fat and horse meat injected with strychnine to kill coyotes. In addition, the Biological Survey then began using thallium sulfate, a most effective poison but one which caused a slow agonizing death. The evi-

---

*The Anti-Steel Trap League (1925–1942) was an important part of the humane movement in the United States. Along with the Society for the Prevention of Cruelty to Animals and the American Humane Society, the League sought to educate the public about the violence committed against animals in the United States. In addition to education, the League was responsible for the introduction of ninety-nine anti-trapping codes in eighteen states. Five of these states eliminated either all trapping or the leg-hold trap. Led by upper- and middle-class women, the League formed associations with other organizations, including the Massachusetts Rod and Gun Club, to try to bring trapping under control. The League disappeared during the early years of World War II. The conflict between the "environmental–ecological idea and the anti-killing idea," as exemplified by the League, however, did not end. One group accepted hunting as a way to promote environmental stability, while the latter opposed all killing. (Thomas R. Dunlap, *Saving America's Wildlife,* Princeton: Princeton University Press, 1988, 92–97).

dence of such inhumane death created much controversy among the agencies and wildlife conservationists and much bad publicity for PARC.

During World War II, Monsanto Chemical Company developed the poisonous compound sodium fluoroacetate, referred to by its laboratory number, 1,080, to kill rodents. In 1945 the Fish and Wildlife Service,* created by the Congress in 1940, began using 1,080 on coyotes and found it to be highly effective as a killer. For example, "A lethal dose for coyotes was a few mouthfuls of a bait treated at the rate of 1.6 *grams* of 1,080 per hundred *pounds* of meat."[84] It was "one of the most lethal poisons ever devised, a single pound of it sufficient to kill a million pounds of animal life. In recent times at least 90,000 coyotes have been killed each year in the United States by such means."[85] The powerful chemical, with no known antidote, was also deadly to humans. Its opponents believed that, because it was water-soluble, it would contaminate waterways: rivers, streams, ponds, and lakes.

To limit the environmental impact of 1,080, Monsanto agreed to sell the compound to the Fish and Wildlife Service only. The Service agreed to limit use of 1,080 for coyote extermination to west of the 100th meridian. This area represented the sparsely settled section of the country where other methods of control were failing. In addition, the poison was to be used only when poisoned winter bait was placed away from roads, communities, and waterways. Since much of the federal program for coyote control was funded privately by the wool growers, however, the use of 1,080 proved to be more extensive than originally intended.

By 1949, E.R. Kalmbach, employed by the Denver office of the Fish and Wildlife Service, argued that the use of the poison was widespread. He pointed out that "The 15,289 [locations] in 1949 and 16,668 in 1950 'covered' about half of the West," and that the increased use of 1,080 "had

---

*The Fish and Wildlife Service was established as the independent Bureau of Fisheries in 1871. Later it was placed in the Department of Commerce, with the mandate to promote commercial fishing. In 1939, it was transferred to the Department of Interior and a year later merged with the Bureau of Biological Survey. It finally became the Fish and Wildlife Service. In 1956 the Service was divided into the agencies of Commercial Fisheries and Sport Fisheries and Wildlife; these agencies reported respectively to the Department of Commerce and the Department of Interior. The latter was renamed the U.S. Fish and Wildlife Service in 1974 and remained in the Department of Interior. Its mandate was to assure the maximum opportunity for the American people to benefit from fish and wildlife resources as part of the natural environment. Waterways and wetlands make up the largest number of the nation's 390 wildlife refuges and fall under the jurisdiction of the Service. Also, such reserves as the Kenai National Moose Range in Alaska, the Wichita Mountain Reserve in Oklahoma, and many wildlife sanctuaries in the Pacific Northwest contain forests, so as a result the U.S. Fish and Wildlife Service is involved in forest management as well.

taken place without reducing the use of traps, guns, and strychnine."[86] By the early 1950s, use of the poison was growing. By the end of the decade, reports of declining coyote attacks on sheep on the open range, grazing without herders or dogs for supervision and protection, convinced PARC staffers and ranchers that their joint program of eradication was working. Even though opposition to poisoning was building slowly and the numbers of coyotes in the West were shrinking, poisoning continued unabated.

Efforts to Protect Wildlife and Waterfowl Habitat

A product of Progressive zeal to reshape the natural environment and make the world safe for "good" species by eliminating "bad" ones, the extermination of predators was identified by some wildlife researchers as a dubious practice during the 1930s. First, the failure of the government's effort to protect mule deer on the Kaibab Plateau undermined common assumptions about predation. Second, it was found that eliminating predators did not increase the numbers of game animals. Third, the creation of predator-free refuges closed to all hunting, for which Hornaday had argued so forcefully as a way to preserve wildlife, did not prevent some species from continuing to decline. Nor did shorter or closed hunting seasons have much effect. Equally ineffective or impractical for improving wildlife populations were winter feeding lots, cover plantings to protect ground animals and fowl from extreme temperatures, and water catchments to provide mammals and fowl with an adequate supply of water.

Most clearly, predator programs were failures, regardless of the support by their advocates. On an economic basis alone, the programs could not be sustained: "in 1962, for instance, the value of sheep lost on the National Forest land in California was $3,500 while the control program there cost over $90,000."[87] At the state and federal levels spending to eradicate coyotes reached $8 million in 1971, one year before President Richard Nixon announced a ban on federal use of poisons to kill predators as part of his environmental state of the union address in February 1972.

Additional evidence had presented itself during the 1920s and 1930s to demonstrate that predator control was not protecting and perpetuating wildlife. The Kaibab Plateau experience was played out again and again. This led Aldo Leopold, noted conservationist who will be discussed later in this essay, to reflect that: "It is amazing how little is known about the life histories of game. About the role of wild life in the ecology of the forest, we know even less. Yet we cannot manage either game, forest, or forage without such knowledge . . . it is important to avoid the extermination of predators."[88] If eradicating predators did not protect mammals on the range, then what did? In addition, evidence that the nation's waterfowl population was declining, despite efforts to control hunting, confused conservationists.

Proposed policies to eliminate hunting versus those preserving and protecting waterfowl habitat competed with each other. In 1913, the Weeks–McLean Act regulated hunting seasons and vested regulatory authority in the BBS. In 1918, the Migratory Bird Act was signed by the United States, Canada, and Great Britain. After its passage, waterfowl populations experienced sudden but brief changes. Even though waterfowl were protected by new federal legislation and international agreements, their populations along the midwestern flyways fluctuated in the 1920s and 1930s. Many states passed laws during the Progressive era protecting wildlife and waterfowl within their boundaries. Some of these state laws served as prototypes for future federal regulations; others were passed in anticipation of federal laws that would have required state compliance. Although Progressive era laws spurred brief recoveries of some species, bird populations still fell in the 1920s. The economic boom of that decade aggravated the ongoing loss of waterfowl habitat:

> Prosperity brought good roads, automobiles, improved firearms, more leisure time, and millions of new sport hunters. Simultaneously, agricultural expansion expropriated breeding, feeding, and resting grounds across the continent. The shrinkage of habitat was especially acute in the northern wet prairies, where vital marshes, potholes, river bottoms, and peatlands were being drained off the map. . . . To make matters worse, drought was beginning to dry up the northern breeding grounds.[89]

With the onset of the Great Depression in 1929, neither the states nor the federal government were able to provide the funding needed to protect various species. Bird populations, for example, "reached their nadirs between 1929 and 1934, only to rebound again in the late 1930s."[90] These situations led to two major changes in thinking about wildlife management in the 1920s and 1930s. Protecting waterfowl from hunters was one change; the other, protecting waterfowl habitat, required a quite different approach. "Gradually, conservationists made the same connection between wildlife and habitat that foresters had seen between trees and land two decades before."[91]

Aid to promoting habitat preservation and restoration came from the Sporting Arms and Ammunitions Manufacturers' Institute (SAAMI), which had recently withdrawn its financial support from the American Game Protection Association (AGPA). The leaders of SAAMI believed that fifteen years of backing AGPA had resulted in few tangible gains for either sport hunters or for the duck population. Through its Committee on Game Restoration, SAAMI used money formerly given to AGPA to finance programs to propagate waterfowl, small game, and upland birds. In addition, it funded a game survey and convinced Aldo Leopold to design and conduct it. What he discovered during the early months of the survey changed the approach to restoration and protection programs forever and added depth, breadth, and substance to what he had begun to suspect about the importance of habitat and its place in a comprehensive conservation program. He found that:

> the intensification of agriculture was eliminating food and cover plants required by upland game species. Fence rows, borders, woodlots, and wetlands were disappearing from the midwestern landscape, and the quail, prairie chicken, grouse, snipe, woodcock, and in some localities even rabbits and squirrels, were disappearing with them.[92]

In addition, the Congress passed the Duck Stamp Act in 1934, which required all waterfowl hunters to purchase a special stamp for one dollar. The proceeds were used to restore waterfowl breeding grounds and refuges. Eventually, the stamps cost five dollars. Over the next forty years, the U.S. Fish and Wildlife Service collected $150,000,000 for these purposes. In 1935, President Franklin Roosevelt appointed Jay Norwood "Ding" Darling as his new environmental chief of the Bureau of Biological Survey. (In addition to his national stature as a conservationist, Darling was a Pulitzer Prize-winning cartoonist.)

In his home state of Iowa, Darling had established his reputation as a conservationist by developing a system of fish and wildlife education. This became the prototype for the new federal program, the Cooperative Wildlife Research Unit, which Darling would use to revolutionize wildlife conservation at the national level. First, Darling had to convince industrialist–philanthropists of the value of the proposed new directions and seek their financial support. Upon meeting a group at New York City's fashionable Waldorf-Astoria Hotel on April 3–5, 1935, he was able to convince them to participate in a number of new initiatives, including support for the new American Wildlife Institute, which would replace the American Game Protection Association. In addition, they agreed to support the Cooperative Wildlife Research Unit Program, created to conduct studies of the interrelationship of wildlife and habitat and to train professional biologists for careers in wildlife work. Federal funds to ten land grant colleges, state funds to conservation departments, and private philanthropic funds to the nonprofit American Wildlife Institute were used to begin the cooperative program.

Darling encouraged President Franklin Roosevelt to call conservationists, biologists, agency administrators, and sportsmen to the First North

American Wildlife Conference, February 3–7, 1936, for the purpose of discussing the condition of wildlife in the nation. Twelve hundred attendees debated about wildlife across a range of issues, including management, farmer–sportsman impacts on wildlife populations and habitats, and ways to remain informed about recent research developments. One initiative which has had long-standing effects was the creation a year later of the Wildlife Society* and its *Journal of Wildlife Management.* In subsequent years, the North American Wildlife Conference continued to meet.

In 1937, Congress passed the Federal Aid in Wildlife Restoration Act, an act known by the name of its congressional sponsors, Pittman and Robertson ("P–R"), whose purpose was to conduct game surveys and wildlife research and to acquire habitat for wild game. To fund the program, a federal excise tax of 5 percent (by 1993 the tax was set at 11 percent) was placed on firearms and ammunition sales. These revenues were apportioned to states based on their land area and the number of hunting licenses issued by them. States are required to spend one dollar for every three dollars that they receive from the federal excise tax. In addition:

> any state that diverts revenues derived from hunting license sales to activities unrelated to wildlife is not eligible for P–R funds. This provision was instrumental in ensuring that wildlife funding is actually used for wildlife projects. State legislatures can no longer tamper with state wildlife funding, or hold wildlife budgets hostage, so wildlife management at the state level is assured of financial stability.[93]

These new federal initiatives reflected the evolution of environmental thinking from "conservation" in 1900 to "ecology" in the 1930s. Ecologists began to recognize the complex interactions of soil, water, plants, animals, and humans. To many conservationists, the land existed isolated from its environment. It was soil in one context such as farming or grazing; it was habitat when referring to refuges or sanctuaries. To ecologists, the land and all of its species was a complicated web of being. By 1950, the principles of Pittman–Robertson were extended to fish with the passage of the Federal Aid in Fish Restoration Act, with sponsorship by Representative John

---

*The Wildlife Society began with a solid base of five hundred members in 1937, which expanded to more than ten thousand in the 1990s. From its inception, it has served as a clearinghouse for technical, scientific, and statistical information on wildlife-related matters. Its mission, to promote the wise use and conservation of wildlife worldwide, is pursued by publishing papers, giving testimony, writing curricula, upholding standards, and certifying the qualifications of biologists who specialize in wildlife management and resources. In addition to its journal, the society publishes *Wildlife Society Bulletin* and *Wildlife Monographs.*

Dingell from Michigan and Senator Lyndon Johnson from Texas. Dingell–Johnson applied the same 3:1 federal-to-state dollar ratio and placed an excise tax of 10 percent on selected fishing tackle.

One important outcome of the new federally funded research on wildlife was an end to refuges as conservationists had originally conceived of them. Refuges had been thought of as a means to protecting and managing resident game animals. The practice was abandoned after World War II, when researchers discovered that big game on refuges did not overflow into surrounding areas in sufficient numbers so that they could be hunted by sportsmen. Also, it was learned that wildlife in refuges was protected only to the extent that their habitat was protected and managed specifically for their benefit. If their habitat was damaged, then wildlife was threatened. The person identified more closely than any others with these ideas, who developed and implemented them into a land, human, and animal ethic, was Aldo Leopold, who played an important early role in the development of scientific ecology.

Aldo Leopold and the Advent of an Environmental Consciousness

Aldo Leopold (1887–1948) was instrumental in introducing scientific ecology into the university curriculum and into the popular consciousness. He symbolized the transition from Progressive era conservation to New Deal ecology. Educated as a conservationist, he studied forestry at Yale University in a program established by funds donated by Gifford Pinchot's family in 1900. Pinchot dominated the field of forestry in the early years of the twentieth century as Theodore Roosevelt's Director of the Division of Forestry in the Department of Agriculture. He became an articulate spokesperson for the utilitarian approach to conservation, which meant that humans had the right to use natural resources and also the obligation to use them wisely.

When Leopold entered Yale's School of Forestry in 1906, forestry was a new profession. It was destined to confront the lumberjack's legacy of cutover forests from Massachusetts to Minnesota. Leopold spent his early career in the southwestern region of the country employed by the National Forest Service created by Roosevelt in 1905 and headed by Pinchot. As a twenty-five-year-old, he was managing a million acres of forestland in Colorado. In 1933 he became the first professor of game management at the University of Wisconsin and began a career of writing about the delicate balance of animals and plants in their environments. As the man who turned "game" into "wildlife" in America, he became as influential as Grinnell, Pinchot, Muir, Burroughs, and others.

Leopold, educated in the latest ideas about sustained yields* as they applied to the management of the national forests, began to apply these ideas to the management of wildlife. As a conservationist with Progressive ideas about a controlled environment, he was a vocal proponent of predator control. At the American Game Conference in New York in 1925, he made a strong argument for a controlled wildlife environment through the extermination of wolves and mountain lions throughout the West. Within a few short years, however, Leopold had changed his thinking about predator control. In 1930 he again spoke at the American Game Conference and this time supported the adoption of the first comprehensive American wildlife policy. The policy stated that:

> The public, not the sportsman, owns the game.
>   The public is (and the sportsman ought to be) just as much interested in conserving non-game species, forests, fish, and other wild life as in conserving game. . . .
>   To this end sportsmen must recognize conservation as one integral whole, of which game restoration is only a part. In predator control and other activities where game management conflicts in part with other wild life, sportsmen must join with nature-lovers in seeking and accepting the findings of impartial research.[94]

In addition, the policy statement argued for the establishment of a wilderness system.** It distinguished itself in this way from earlier conservationist policy statements about refuges that would provide cover, food, and protection for wildlife. Five years later, in 1935, Leopold aided Robert Marshall in founding the Wilderness Society. Through its publication, *The Living Wilderness,* later simply titled *Wilderness,* it lobbied at the state, regional, and federal levels for the preservation and expansion of the nation's wilderness system.

---

*The concept of sustained yield remains a principle idea in the professions of forestry and wildlife management. It means that you should not harvest more trees than the number reaching maturity, either by natural growth or by planting, each year, nor hunt more game in a season than the number coming into the population each season. Such factors as diseases that limit timber yields and death to game caused by predation need to be observed, controlled and prevented where possible. An important corollary to the idea of sustained yield as applied to game is that a surplus may be produced each year, exceeding the carrying capacity of the natural habitat. Sport hunting can therefore harvest the surplus.

**Leopold defined wilderness as "a continuous stretch of country preserved in its natural state, open to lawful hunting and fishing, big enough to absorb a two weeks' pack trip, and kept devoid of roads, artificial trails, cottages, or other works of man." (Curt Meine, *Aldo Leopold: His Life and Work* (Madison: University of Wisconsin Press, 1988), 196.)

The policy statement also called for the training of professional wildlife managers, to be distinguished from gamekeepers, a term borrowed from Great Britain. It advocated an expansion of the national wildlife refuge system and further cooperation with Canada in protecting migratory birds. And, most important, "it called for emphasis on the natural production of wildlife through habitat development and for a more understanding and sympathetic attitude toward predators, in an age when game farms and predator controls were common practice."[95] Three years after Leopold's plea to the American Game Conference that "The only really new thing which this game policy suggests is that we quit arguing over abstract ideas, and instead go out and try them," he published *Game Management*.[96]

This was a major text for the education of new managers and the professional development of those already in the field. With its publication, Leopold established himself as the leading proponent of Progressive wildlife principles, some of which were already dated, however, given his presentation at the 1930 Game Conference. Leopold articulated his views about ways to manipulate nature for economic goals. Game was similar to a crop in that it could be cultivated, improved, and even harvested. Using agricultural metaphors, he stated "game management produces a crop by controlling the environmental factors which hold down the natural increase or productivity of the seed stock.[97] This influential volume was intended to teach its readers about the ways to manage game for productive human use and to satisfy our needs for food, sport, and amusement.

Somewhat ironically, the publication of *Game Management* reflected Leopold's past thinking. At the time of its publication in 1933, he was questioning prior assumptions and developing his ideas about a conservation and land ethic. He criticized earlier conservation theory as "based solely on economic self-interest [and] hopelessly lopsided. It tends to ignore, and thus eventually to eliminate, many elements in the land community that lack commercial value, but that are ... essential to its healthy functioning."[98]

Leopold changed his view of predators when he and his companions attacked an old female wolf and her pack of young. As Leopold approached the dying female, she grasped the butt of his rifle in her teeth and he witnessed "a fierce green fire" in her eyes. That sight changed Leopold. The change in his attitude toward wolves was poignantly described in his short essay titled "Thinking Like a Mountain":

> A deep chesty bawl echoes from rimrock to rimrock, rolls down the mountain, and fades into the far blackness of the night. It is an outburst of wild defiant sorrow, and of contempt for all the adversities of the world.

Every living thing . . . pays heed to that call. To the deer it is a reminder of the way of all flesh, . . . to the cowman a threat of the red ink at the bank, to the hunter a challenge of fang against bullet. Yet behind these obvious and immediate hopes and fears there lies a deeper meaning, known only to the mountain itself. Only the mountain has lived long enough to listen objectively to the howl of a wolf.

Those unable to decipher the hidden meaning know nevertheless that it is there, for it is felt in all wolf country, and distinguishes that country from all other land. . . . Only the ineducable tyro can fail to sense the presence or absence of wolves, or the fact that mountains have a secret opinion about them.

My own conviction on this score dates from the day I saw a wolf die. . . . When she [a wolf] climbed the bank toward us and shook out her tail, we realized our error: [Leopold and members of his party had thought initially that the wolf was a buck] it was a wolf. A half-dozen others, evidently grown pups, sprang from the willows and all joined in a welcoming mélée of wagging tails and playful maulings. What was literally a pile of wolves writhed and tumbled in the center of an open flat at the foot of our rimrock.

In those days we had never heard of passing up a chance to kill a wolf. . . . [He goes on to describe shooting into the pack.]

We reached the old wolf in time to watch a fierce green fire dying in her eyes. I realized then, and have known ever since, that there was something new to me in those eyes—something known only to her and to the mountain. I was young then, and full of trigger-itch; I thought that because fewer wolves meant more deer, that no wolves would mean hunters' paradise. But after seeing the green fire die, I sensed that neither the wolf nor the mountain agreed with such a view. . . .

I now suspect that just as the deer herd lives in mortal fear of its wolves, so does a mountain live in mortal fear of its deer. And perhaps with better cause, for while a buck pulled down by wolves can be replaced in two or three years, a range pulled down by too many deer may fail of replacement in as many decades.

So also with cows. The cowman who cleans his range of wolves does not realize that he is taking over the wolf's job of trimming the herd to fit the range. He has not learned to think like a mountain. Hence we have dust bowls, and the rivers washing away the future into the sea.[99]

Leopold's transformation coincided with the debate between proponents of sustained-yield conservation policies and their more ecologically minded critics. This latter group's defense of the predator is fundamental to understanding modern environmental thought:

This new defense of the varmint . . . has been put on an ecological footing. It is at the very center of the shift that has occurred in twentieth-century environmental thought toward a broader, popular ecological consciousness. . . . The story of the varmint's changing reputation is thus the story of the movement in American conservation toward an ecological point of view: an attitude grounded not only in science but in a moral philosophy of interdependence and tolerance.[100]

Although many of the early twentieth-century Progressive era conservation ideals remained in practice throughout the first half of the century, Leopold's transformation marked the end of one era and the beginning of another. "He was perhaps the first person to articulate the need to conserve biological diversity in its entirety."[101] Not only did this transformation help to bring about the federal wildlife and wildlife habitat legislation of the 1930s, it also prepared the ground for the receptivity of the ecological ideas in Rachel Carson's *Silent Spring* and Barry Commoner's *The Closing Circle: Nature, Man and Technology,* which appeared during the revival of environmentalism in the 1960s and 1970s. *Document 2.5 presents Aldo Leopold's ideas about the conservation of wildlife.*

The Environmental Movement and the Protection of Wildlife

World War II and the period extending through the 1950s were particularly difficult times for wildlife and habitat preservation. The war taxed the nation's human capacity and its natural resources. In the decades that followed, the nation focused on its Cold War struggles with the now defunct Soviet Union and the disappointments of a failed post-war peace strategy. By the end of World War II, however, 34 percent of the nation's larger mammals, bison, bears, panthers, elk, antelope, and others, were protected in the country's national parks, forests, and refuges, encompassing more than 184 million acres. Efforts by Secretary of the Interior Douglas McKay and his replacement Frederick A. Seaton during the 1950s to open up federal refuge and park lands to mineral exploration and military use were curtailed by Congress during the presidential administration of Dwight D. Eisenhower (1953–1960). In addition, industrial wartime creativity and inventions were translated into post-war domestic applications. One of these applications, however, had deleterious effects on the nation's wildlife.

Endangered Species

Dichlorodiphenyl-trichloroethane or DDT, discovered in the 1930s, had a number of wartime applications, including the killing of fleas, lice, and the mosquitoes that spread malaria and typhus. After the war, DDT and a number of other chlorinated hydrocarbons were used to control outbreaks of farm pests which destroyed crops. The use of DDT spread rapidly, until Rachel Carson published *Silent Spring* in 1962 and demonstrated that these chemical agents damaged wildlife and possibly compromised human health.

Not until 1972, however, did the newly created Environmental Protection Agency finally ban the use of DDT in the United States. By that time millions of tons of the chemical compound had entered the environment and become embedded in the land and water as well as in the tissues of water-fowl, fish, and mammals.

Rachel Carson's *Silent Spring,* the National Environmental Policy Act of 1970, and the passage of federal Endangered Species Preservation Acts (ESA) first in 1966 and again in 1973 brought the nation to focus once again on the ecological effects of human efforts to change the environment. The ESA required the approval of environmental impact statements before changes proposed to the existing natural world could be made. Thought of as one of the world's most important pieces of environmental legislation, the Endangered Species Act has been reauthorized five times by Congress since its passage in 1973.

ESA is considered by many environmentalists as a bill of rights for animals and plants. In 1973, the list of endangered and threatened wildlife contained 103 species. Since then, the list has grown to more than 600 species in the United States and more than 1,400 worldwide. In addition, there are 3,700 species waiting for a full review by two agencies, the Fish and Wildlife Service and the National Marine Fisheries. These agencies decide whether a species is placed on the threatened or the endangered list or not listed at all.

Originally, the lists consisted mostly of mammals and birds, but presently the lists contain many plants and invertebrates. "For example, the U.S. has 297 different kinds of freshwater mussels, the greatest variety in the world, concentrated mainly in the Southeast. Of these, 56 are listed as threatened or endangered, 74 more are seriously declining, and 21 may already be extinct."[102] More aquatic life has been placed on the endangered list because of the realization that pollutants ultimately affect the water as well as the land. For example, southeastern mussel filter feeders help to keep the water clean and store important water nutrients. Unfortunately, they also absorb the toxins from pesticide run-off, industrial spills, waste treatment, and other contaminants that pollute fresh water. In this regard, the status of mussels is an effective indicator of water quality.

Congress appropriates about $50 million each year to fund ESA. An equivalent amount is spent by twelve other federal agencies and individual states to protect the 648 species on the threatened and endangered species lists. Expenditures, however, are weighted toward a very few of the species on the list. For example, heading the list are the following species, given with the annual expenditures on their behalf:[103]

1. Northern Spotted Owl	$9,687,160
2. Bell's Vireo	9,168,800
3. Grizzly Bear	5,882,540
4. Redcockaded Woodpecker	5,195,030
5. Florida Panther	4,113,580
6. Mojave Desert Tortoise	4,091,400
7. Bald Eagle	3,150,740
8. Ocelot	2,980,200
9. Jaguarundi	2,893,100
10. Peregrine Falcon	2,873,320

More than $45 million, or almost half of the total expended, is designated for these ten species, and the remaining half is spent on the rest in decreasing sums. The first fish on the endangered list, the Chinook or king salmon, receives $2,306,470 to help it spawn in western rivers. The Columbia and the Snake rivers once raced to the Pacific but were long ago stilled by the construction of massive hydroelectric dams and artificial lakes to provide electricity to western cities and towns. These changes to the natural flow of many western rivers jeopardizes the reproductive capabilities of many sub-species of salmon. In the early years of the twentieth century, Chinook salmon, the largest of the salmon species, weighed from 50 to 60 pounds each. Local citizens called them "hogs." Salmon of this size are gone proba-bly forever. In 1991 the Chinook in the Snake River were declared an endan-gered species and placed under the protection of the 1973 act.

The Endangered Species Act owes its existence to a generation of ecolo-gists who believed that an ecosystem is a complex puzzle in which every living thing has the potential of affecting every other living thing. This very important belief fuels Congressional disputes over the intent of ESA and threatens the act each time it is up for reauthorization. The act is also overshadowed by litigation over single species such as the Northern spotted owl. However, the controversy raises issues that transcend the spotted owl. It encourages us to shift our thinking from a local species perspective to larger environmental questions about our nation's biodiversity policies and the protection of its larger landscapes. Saving the last old-growth trees in the Pacific Northwest's temperate rain forest ensures the viability of spotted owls. Cutting the old growth down places an entire ecosystem at risk. Seen in this larger context:

> The case [of the spotted owl] personifies the end of forest management based on exploiting presettlement forests, and the need to shift to a set of policies grounded in concepts of long-term environmental and economic sustainabil-

ity. It bears witness to the need to change organizations and decision-making processes, and indicates the problems and opportunities attending a change in national politics and a changing world economy. How we manage these transitions has considerable meaning for the quality of human and nonhuman life in the next century.[104]

Section 7 of the ESA is the most important and controversial provision in the act. It requires the Secretary of the Interior to guarantee that federal land policies of any kind do not threaten to disrupt the habitat of wild and plant life. Specifically, the section acknowledges the critical importance of habitat and the ecological impact of proposed changes in the land on the lives of creatures and plants. Supporting these ecological ideas are the broad mandates and policies of the National Environmental Policy Act of 1969. The language of NEPA acknowledges basic ecological thinking and recognizes the "responsibilities of each generation as trustee of the environment for succeeding generations," and "the profound impact of man's activity on the interrelations of all components of the national environment."[105] The language of both laws has resulted in numerous challenges in the federal courts, the most famous of which has been Hill *v.* TVA (1976). In this case the Tennessee Valley Authority was prohibited from building the Tellico Dam because this would threaten an endangered fish, the snail darter.

Challenges to the Endangered Species Act are neither aberrations nor are they simply forecasts of a gloomy future for wildlife. The obstacles to protection and restoration are real, and vigilance is required, of the kind that prevented market hunters in the late nineteenth century from shooting more species of waterfowl and game birds into extinction. Today, ranchers oppose the practice of reintroducing wolves into national parklands in the West. Powerful special interest groups, such as the Endangered Species Roundtable, representing mining, timber, petroleum, and large farm interests, want to narrow the scope of the present ESA legislation by eliminating sub-species from protection. In effect, this would eliminate the Northern Spotted Owl from the list of endangered species because other subspecies of the spotted owl thrive in California and Mexico. A group of hikers calling themselves Residents Against Grizzlies in our Environment (RAGE) believe that the bears should be eliminated from the North Cascade Mountains. A loosely knit movement called Wise Use advocates eliminating restrictions on wetlands development and rewriting ESA guidelines to eliminate from protection species like the California condor, a "nonadaptive" species that cannot survive in an unfamiliar environment.

Understanding the role of the nation's court system in interpreting the provisions of the Endangered Species Act demonstrates the changing and sometimes unpredictable nature of environmental law. In a 1997 Supreme

Court decision, the nation's highest court ruled that citizens can sue the federal government for doing too much to protect endangered species. This decision reversed a previous trend in which the court system had encouraged the executive branches of government to comply fully in protecting endangered species. The reversal originated in a suit brought by a group of Oregon ranchers against the federal Fish and Wildlife Service. The Service had decided to maintain higher water levels in two of the reservoirs in the Klamath Irrigation Project near the Oregon and California borders in order to protect two endangered species of fish, the Lost River sucker and the shortnose sucker. The ranchers, who wanted more water released for their herds, argued that the evidence used by the Fish and Wildlife Service did not support the contention that the fish were endangered or that higher water levels were needed to support them. Having lost their case in the lower federal courts, including the United States Court of Appeals for the Ninth Circuit, the ranchers appealed to the Supreme Court of the United States.

The Supreme Court ruled unanimously that there is no limitation in the Endangered Species Act that prevents citizens from challenging the way in which the Secretary of the Interior or the secretary's agents execute the law. The ruling does not apply only to cases of "underenforcement." It can also be applied to cases like the one under consideration, which is one of "overenforcement." Environmental groups did not oppose the ruling because they have argued for a long time that the Court should interpret the ESA broadly. In this case, Bennett v. Spear, the Court for the first time broadened the interpretation of environmental law.[106]

Continuing debates about the future status of endangered and threatened wildlife and the role of government in protecting them will continue into the next century. The reintroduction of wolves into the nation's park system and its wilderness areas has stimulated the debate, since so much of this land had been touted as safe for tourists by the Park Service and other government agencies. Although high-profile policies of government for reclaiming park land and wilderness areas for wildlife activate public debates about the relationships of wild and human species, a more significant threat to wildlife is urban geographic expansion, which occurs as much as 50 percent more rapidly than the growth in the size of urban populations. As the density of urban populations decreases, the total amount of living space consumed by urban residents expands. Highway systems, including beltways and freeways, and the paved land used up to rent, lease, sell, and park millions of automobiles make expansion feasible; the shopping malls and the many related services associated with urban sprawl take millions of acres of grasslands and woodlands. In addition, new housing developments are cut out of former meadows, pastures, and farmland. When adjourning land is intensively cultivated for agricultural production, the living space for birds, mammals, fish, and plants is placed under severe restrictions.

Research into the geographic distribution of endangered species in the United States points out that areas similar in characteristics to those described above are "hot spots" of the four groups of endangered species, plants, birds, fish, and mollusks. The areas identified represent a relatively small amount of the total land mass of the country, but the size of the area should not be interpreted to mean that the problems are minimal. "The greatest numbers of endangered species occur in Hawaii, southern California, the southeastern coastal states, and southern Appalachia."[107] Although areas containing different groups of endangered species seldom overlap, research has pointed out that two counties, San Diego (fish, mammals, and plants) and Santa Cruz (arthropods, reptiles, and plants) in California are hot spots for three groups. Nine counties* are hot spots for two groups.

The research also points out that (with the exception of these counties) the existence of an endangered species in one group does not mean that other species are also endangered, with one exception. Endangered birds serve as an indicator of the presence of other endangered species. Studies of the kind described here increase our understanding of the relationships that exist between our penchant for "developing" the land and its consequences for the natural world. With this knowledge, our ability to plan for harmony with the natural world is enhanced.

---

*The nine counties are Hawaii, Honolulu, Kauai, and Maui, (plants and birds); Los Angeles, California (arthropods and birds); San Francisco, California (arthropods and plants); Highlands, Florida (reptiles and plants); Monroe, Florida (birds and mammals); and Whitfield, Georgia (fish and mollusks).

Document 2.1

The American Beaver and His Works (1868)

Lewis H. Morgan

A knowledge of the habits of beavers is necessary to the trapper to enable him successfully to pursue his vocation. . . . After the colonization of North America commenced, a new value was given to the beaver for his fur, which was chiefly used, as is well known, for making hats. From their excessive numbers and wide distribution, their pelts were among the first, and for a number of years the largest, exportations of the colonists. The settlers as well as the Indians united in the business of trapping, which they pursued with such diligence that, about the year 1700, beaver pelts ceased to be exported, to any considerable extent, from the New England and Middle States. At this early period, their numbers had become so greatly reduced by capture and dispersion that the business of the trapper, within these areas, ceased to be remunerative. In the regions around Hudson's Bay and Lake Superior; upon the head waters of the Missouri and Siskatchewun [sic], and upon the Columbia and its tributaries, it has continued through all the intermediate period to be, and still is, a profitable vocation. After the substitution of silk for fur in the manufacture of hats, the value of beaver peltry greatly declined; thus affording a respite to this persecuted animal, under the effects of which he is now increasing in numbers in certain localities. This is particularly the case on the Upper Missouri and in the great forests around Lake Superior: but it is not at all probable that they will ever recover, in any locality, their former numbers. In 1802, beaver pelts were worth, at Fort Benton, on the Upper Missouri, one dollar and a quarter per pound against seven and eight dollars per pound fifty years ago. They are now worth two dollars per pound on the south shore of Lake Superior. An ordinary pelt weighs from 1 1/2 to 1 3/4 pounds.

The Hudson's Bay Company, chartered May 2d, 1682, and the American Fur Company, organized in the early part of the present century, have been the principal organizations engaged in the fur trade in North America. Instead of ravaging their districts, as the colonists did, they early adopted a protective system, not only with reference to the beavers, but also to other fur-bearing animals, that their numbers might not become exhausted. Among other regulations of the Hudson's Bay Company, an interval of five years is allowed to elapse, after a season's hunt in a particular beaver district, before it is again resumed. While these companies have prosecuted their operations upon a vast scale, they have by no means enjoyed a monopoly of the business. Private adventurers in large numbers have engaged in trapping, and followed it year after year as a regular pursuit. Our Indian nations, also, whose territories produce furbearing animals, trap more or less for the means

Reprinted from Lewis H. Morgan, *The American Beaver: A Classic of Natural History and Ecology* (New York: Dover Publications, 1986), 227–31, 235–38, 243–46. (Reprint of the 1868 edition. Author's footnotes have been omitted.)

of subsistence. Within our national limits there are hundreds, and even thousands of men, who now make trapping their exclusive business.

As success in trapping depends very much upon the knowledge the trapper has of the habits and mode of life of the several animals he seeks to capture, an examination of the methods resorted to in trapping beavers will develop some of the habits of this animal not before introduced. It is for this reason exclusively that the subject will be considered.

The steel trap came into use when the systematic pursuit of the fur-bearing animals commenced. Its form is well known. The most perfect instrument, however, is of recent introduction, and is known as the "Newhouse Trap," . . .

The jaws are smooth, and spread six inches and a half, of the size best adapted for taking beavers. Its chief merits, as an improvement upon the old form, are said to consist in such an adjustment of the form of the jaws, and of the bow of the spring to each other, and the further adaptation of the power of the spring to both, as to secure in the highest degree the two qualities of a good catcher and a sure holder. These traps are used without bait, and operate on the principle of an inadvertent tread upon the pan.

The trapping season commences about the first of November and ends about the first of April, during which period the different fur-bearing animals are in the best condition with respect to their fur. But it is pursued more or less at all seasons of the year, by persons who are more reckless of the waste of animal life than the regular trappers. In the spring, summer, and fall, the usual place of setting traps for beavers is upon the dam. The trapper avails himself of the well-known habit of this dam builder to repair at once any breach made in the structure, over which his supervision is constant. He therefore makes one or more openings in the crest of the dam, four or five inches deep, and sets a trap in the pond at each one, about a foot back of the breach and a few inches below the surface of the water. By means of a chain the trap is then secured to a stake driven into the bed of the pond, about four feet back of the trap and out in the pond, where the water is of some depth. When a beaver ascertains that the level of his pond is subsiding, which is shown by the fall of the water in the lodge entrances, he goes to the dam, after night has set in, and commences its repair. While thus engaged, he is in constant danger of springing the trap by stepping on its pan inadvertently. If taken by either of the fore feet, he is very apt to break the bones in turning around the trap, thus freeing himself; but if caught by either hind leg, his case is hopeless. He immediately plunges into the deep water of the pond, where his course is soon arrested by the stake and chain. It is a part of the trapper's merciless plan to drown the animal, for the double purpose of preventing him from breaking away and of saving his body under water, where it will be inaccessible to beasts of prey. To accomplish this end, two contrivances are resorted to, of which the most simple is an extra stake set a short distance beyond the first, around which the beaver is quite certain to coil the chain, and thus drown himself, in his attempts to escape; and the other is the pole-slide. A dry pole, ten or twelve feet long, with a prong at one end to prevent the ring of the chain from slipping off, is secured to the bank or dam by a hook driven down into the ground near the trap. The small end of the pole—the ring being run up to the large end near the hook—is then immersed in the pond as far out as it will reach. When a beaver is caught, he dives and swims in the direction to which the pole leads, the ring sliding down to the end. In the deep water thus reached, the weight of the chain and trap, by which his motions are embarrassed, prevents his rising to the surface, and he is soon an unresisting victim of the trapper's art. . . .

In the winter, which is the season for trapping, after the ponds are frozen over and the beavers are housed for the winter, other methods are resorted to, among which is the following: the trapper selects a place in the vicinity of a lodge, cuts a hole through the ice, and puts down into the pond a fresh-cut pole of birch or poplar about ten feet long. While the small end is pushed out into the water, the large end is securely fastened in the edge of the bank, and a trap is set immediately under the place where it is secured. This fresh cutting the trapper knows will soon be discovered, and seized with avidity for transportation to the lodge. When a beaver has thus found it, and ascertained that it is fast at one end, he follows it up for the purpose of cutting it off—very naturally desiring to secure the whole of the stick. This brings him immediately over the trap; and if the trap is judiciously placed, it will be next to a miracle if the unsuspecting victim does not step upon its pan before the stick is severed. This has always been found one of the most successful methods of trapping. After a trap has been set in this way, the trapper throws snow into the hole cut through the ice, to hasten the freezing over of the opening, and leaves the place to quiet until his next round among his traps brings him again to the spot. . . .

In trapping bank beaver, they use various kinds of scents to attract them to the place where the trap is set, which is usually near the bank, and a few inches below the surface of the water. Gum camphor is one, a piece of which is inserted in the split fork of a stick, and the latter is then set in the bank so as to bring the camphor immediately over the trap, but above the water. A beaver, when he scents the pungent odor of the camphor, follows it up until he discovers the substance; whereupon he rises up to reach it, in doing which he is liable to step on the pan of the trap with his hind foot, and thus pay for his curiosity with his life. Trappers also use castoreum, cinnamon, cloves, and oil of juniper for the same purpose. Cloves and cinnamon are dissolved in alcohol and made into a kind of paste, which, when smeared over a stick adjusted in the same manner, is found to answer equally well as a bait. Traps are also set, at a venture, upon their run-ways, particularly on their solid-bank dams, which always, by some depression, show where they pass in going up and down stream. When set in such places, it is necessary to make a slight excavation for the reception of the trap, and to cover it with leaves. They are also set in the water at points where the land juts out into the pond, along which beavers are apt to pass in going up or down the pond. Whenever the trapper discovers a trail, or well-marked line on which beavers travel, either on land or in the water, he avails himself of the knowledge to conceal a trap under their footsteps. . . .

The number of beavers taken during a season's hunt varies, of course, with the skill of the trapper and the supply within his district. On the south shore of Lake Superior, an Indian family of four effective persons will capture from seventy-five to one hundred and fifty, if their hunting grounds are well stocked. Fifty and a hundred are not an uncommon number. But the business must be assiduously followed to secure any degree of success.

The statistics of the fur trade sufficiently prove that beavers existed in immense numbers in different parts of North America at the several epochs of their settlement. A brief reference to some of the figures will make this apparent ... in January and August, 1854, 509,240 beaver skins; in January and August, 1855, 62,352; and in January, 1856, 56,033; making in the aggregate the enormous number of 627,625 beaver skins in the course of two and a half years. It is to be inferred that the large number sold in 1854 was the accumulation of a few previous years, and that the numbers sold in 1855 and in the first half of 1856 show the average annual production at this late period.

The foregoing statistics are sufficient to indicate the numerical extent to which the species had become developed and increased in North America, as well as to mark the areas in which they were the most abundant. A statement before made may be here repeated, that the beaver, with his life, has contributed in no small degree to the colonization and settlement of the British Provinces and the United States.

∾

Document 2.2

The Nature Movement (1908)

Dallas Lore Sharp

I was hurrying across Boston Common. Two or three hundred others were hurrying with me. But ahead, at the union of several paths, was a crowd, standing still. I kept hurrying on, not to join the crowd, but simply to keep up the hurry. The crowd was not standing still, it was a-hurrying, too, scattering as fast as it gathered, and as it scattered I noticed that it wore a smile. I hastened up, pushed in, as I had done a score of times on the Common, and got my glimpse of the show. . . . It was Billy, a gray squirrel, taking peanuts out of a bootblack's pocket. And every age, sex, sort, and condition of Bostonian came around to watch the little beast shuck the nuts and bury them singly in the grass of the Common.

"Ain't he a cute little cuss, mister?" said the boy of the brush, feeling the bottom of his empty pocket, and looking up into the prosperous face of Calumet and Hecla at his side. C. and H. smiled, slipped something into the boy's hand with which to buy another pocketful of peanuts for Billy, and hurried down to State Street.

This crowd on the Common is nothing exceptional. It happens every day, and everywhere, the wide country over. We are all stopping to watch, to feed, and—to smile. The longest, most far-reaching pause in our hurrying American life to-day is this halt to look at the out-of-doors, this attempt to share its life; and nothing more significant is being added to our American character than the resulting thoughtful-

---

Reprinted from Dallas Lore Sharp, *The Lay of the Land* (Boston: Houghton Mifflin, 1908), 114–22, 124–26.

ness, sympathy, and simplicity—the smile on the faces of the crowd hurrying over the Common.

Whether one will or not, he is caught up by this nature movement and set adrift in the fields. It may, indeed, be "adrift" for him until he gets thankfully back to the city. "It was a raw November day," wrote one of these new nature students, who happened also to be a college student, "and we went for our usual Saturday's birding into the woods. The chestnuts were ripe, and we gathered a peck between us. On our way home, we discovered a small bird perched upon a cedar tree with a worm in its beak. It was a hummingbird, and after a little searching we found its tiny nest close up against the trunk of the cedar, full of tiny nestlings just ready to fly."

This is what they find, many of these who are caught up by the movement toward the fields; but not all of them. A little five-year-old from the village came out to see me recently, and while playing in the orchard she brought me five flowers, called them by their right names, and told me how they grew. Down in the loneliest marshes of Delaware Bay I know a lighthouse keeper and his solitary neighbor, a farmer: both have been touched by this nature spirit; both are interested, informed, and observant. The farmer there, on the old Zane's Place, is no man of books, like the rector of Selborne, but he is a man of birds and beasts, of limitless marsh and bay and sky, of everlasting silence and wideness and largeness and eternal solitude. He could write a Natural History of the Maurice River Marshes.

These are not rare cases. The nature books, the nature magazines, the nature teachers, are directing us all to the out-of-doors. I subscribe to a farm journal (club rates, twenty-five cents a year!) in which an entire page is devoted to "nature studies," while the whole paper is remarkably fresh and odorous of the real fields. In the city, on my way to and from the station, I pass three large bookstores, and from March until July each of these shops has a big window given over almost continuously to "nature books." I have before me from one of these shops a little catalogue of nature books—"a select list"—for 1907, containing 233 titles, varying in kind all the way from "The Tramp's Handbook" to one (to a dozen) on the very stable subject of "The Farmstead." These are all distinctively "nature books," books with an appeal to sentiment as well as to sense, and very unlike the earlier desiccated, unimaginative treatises.

There are a multitude of other signs that show as clearly as the nature books how full and strong is this tide that sets toward the open fields and woods. There are as many and as good evidences, too, of the genuineness of this interest in the out-of-doors. . . .

There is no way of accounting for the movement that reflects in the least upon its reality and genuineness. It may be only the appropriation by the common people of the world that the scientists have discovered to us; it may be a popular reaction against the conventionality of the nineteenth century; or the result of our growing wealth and leisure; or a fashion set by Thoreau and Burroughs—one or all of these may account for its origin; but nothing can explain the movement away, or hinder us from being borne by it out, at least a little way, under the open of heaven, to the great good of body and soul.

Among the cultural influences of our times that have developed the proportions of a movement, this so-called nature movement is peculiarly American. No such general, widespread turning to the out-of-doors is seen anywhere else; no other such body of nature literature as ours; no other people so close to nature in sympathy and understanding, because there is no other people of the same degree of culture living so close to the real, wild out-of-doors.

The extraordinary interest in the out-of-doors is not altogether a recent acquirement. We inherited it. Nature study is an American habit. What else had the pioneers and colonists to study but the out-of-doors? and what else was half as wonderful? They came from an old urban world into this new country world, where all was strange, unnamed, and unexplored. Their chief business was observing nature, not as dull savages, nor as children born to a dead familiarity with their surroundings, but as interested men and women, with a need and a desire to know. Their coming was the real beginning of our nature movement; their observing has developed into our nature study habit.

Our nature literature also began with them. There is scarcely a journal, a diary, or a set of letters of this early time in which we do not find that careful seeing, and often that imaginative interpretation, so characteristic of the present day. Even the modern animal romancer is represented among these early writers in John Josselyn and his delicious book, "New England's Rarities Discovered."

It was not until the time of Emerson and Bryant and Thoreau, however, that our interest in nature became general and grew into something deeper than mere curiosity. There had been naturalists such as Audubon (he was a poet, also), but they went off into the deep woods alone. They were after new facts, new species. Emerson and Bryant and Thoreau went into the woods, too, but not for facts, nor did they go far, and they invited us to go along. We went, because they got no farther than the back-pasture fence. It was not to the woods they took us, but to nature; not a-hunting after new species in the name of science, but for new inspirations, new estimates of life, new health for mind and spirit.

But we were slow to get as far even as their back-pasture fence, slow to find nature in the fields and woods. It was fifty years ago that Emerson tried to take us to nature; but fifty years ago, how few there were who could make sense out of his invitation, to say nothing of accepting it! And of Thoreau's first nature book, "A Week on the Concord and Merrimack Rivers," there were sold, in four years after publication, two hundred and twenty copies. But two hundred and twenty of such books at work in the mind of the country could leaven, in time, a big lump of it. And they did. The out-of-doors, our attitude toward it, and our literature about it have never been the same since.

Even yet, however, it is the few only who respond to Thoreau, Emerson, and Burroughs, who can find nature, as well as birds and trees, who can think and feel as well as wonder and look. Before we can think and feel we must get over our wondering, and we must get entirely used to looking. This we are slowly doing,—slowly, I say, for it is the monstrous, the marvelous, the unreal that most of us still go out into the wilderness for to see—bears and wolves, foxes, eagles, orioles, salmon, mustangs, porcupines of extraordinary parts and powers. . . .

The present great nature movement is an outgoing to discover . . . its trees, birds, flowers, its myriad forms. This is the meaning of the countless manuals, the "how-to-know" books, and the nature study of the public schools. And this desire to know Nature is the reasonable, natural preparation for the deeper insight that leads to communion with her,—a desire to be traced more directly to Agassiz, and the hosts of teachers he inspired, perhaps, than to the poet-essayists like Emerson and Thoreau and Burroughs.

Let us learn to see and name first. The inexperienced, the unknowing, the unthinking, cannot love. One must live until tired, and think until baffled, before he can know his need of Nature; and then he will not know how to approach her unless already acquainted. To expect anything more than curiosity and animal delight in a child is foolish, and the attempt to teach him anything more at first than to know the out-of-doors is equally foolish. Poets are born, but not until they are old.

But if one got no farther than his how-to-know book would lead him, he still would get into the fields—the best place for him this side of heaven—he would get ozone for his lungs, red blood, sound sleep, and health. As a nation, we had just begun to get away from the farm and out of touch with the soil. The nature movement is sending us back in time. A new wave of physical soundness is to roll in upon us as the result, accompanied with a newness of mind and of morals.

For, next to bodily health, the influence of the fields makes for the health of the spirit. It is easier to be good in a good body and an environment of largeness, beauty, and peace—easier here than anywhere else to be sane, sincere, and "in little thyng have suffisaunce." If it means anything to think upon whatsoever things are good and lovely, then it means much to own a how-to-know book and to make use of it.

This is hardly more than a beginning, however, merely satisfying an instinct of the mind. It is good if done afield, even though such classifying of the out-of-doors is only scraping an acquaintance with nature. The best good, the deep healing, come when one, no longer a stranger, breaks away from his getting and spending, from his thinking with men, and camps under the open sky, where he knows without thinking, and worships without priest or chant or prayer.

The world's work must be done, and only a small part of it can be done in the woods and fields. The merchants may not all turn ploughmen and wood-choppers. Nor is it necessary. What we need to do, and are learning to do, is to go to nature for our rest and health and recreation.

❧

Document 2.3

An Amusing Story of a Prairie Chicken Hunt (1878)

The prairie chicken, as all Kansans term it, is . . . the same bird familiar to ornithologists as the pinnated grouse, the most conspicuous of all the American grouse family. Though hardly a handsome bird from its rather dusky feathering, . . . the delicate pencilings of its feathers, and its bars of different shades of yellow and

---

Reprinted from *Osborne County Farmer* (August 9, 1878): 3.

brown across the breast. It is a larger bird than the ruffed grouse, its flesh quite dark, and as many an epicure knows of exquisite flavor when "cooked to a turn." The pinnated grouse or prairie chicken has the power of inflating the two yellow sacks which he carries on the side of his neck, and during the mating season the cocks are often seen, . . . "strutting and swelling in mimic grandeur, with expanded wings and tail and making a trumming noise with their wings, striving to please by their pompous ways." At these times they court conflict, and two cock birds never meet without having it out. They spring into the air, striking at each other with feet and wings and continue the animated condition of things generally until the one proves his claim to first choice, and the other sadly concludes to put up with what may be left. . . .

No sooner were we robed and ready for the fray than Rick . . . had his team at the door, and hardly were the suburbs of Sterling reached before we had a taste of something in the way of the wagon locomotion, Rick letting his ponies out until they plunged forward on a dead run. . . . It could not have been possible to make a finer hunting ground than the grand expanse of swelling prairie, the thickly matted buffalo grass, just high enough to afford excellent cover for the chickens and not too high for the dogs to work in, to the utmost satisfaction both as to themselves and the men folk behind them. Morton had his favorite pointer Bang, and Burlingame his crack setter, Ranger, and the constant bantering between the two as to the respective merits of setters and pointers bid fair to receive new impetus from the day's doings. While never agreeing on the dog question, there was no disputing judgment as to character of ammunition used by these old hands at chicken shooting. . . .

Hardly had the dogs been commanded to "hie on" before Bang struck the faint scent where a covey of the birds had recently been hiding, and, in an instant reached them with every vein in his sleek brown body standing out like whipcords. The birds were running in the grass, and hardly had Bang come to a full point, before Ranger, some fifteen yards distant crouched in the tangled growth carpeting the prairie until his long, fleecy and brilliant coat, looked like some bunch of autumn verdure. The weather was warm and clear, and, with a grandly proportioned cornfield near at hand, the fowl were loth to exert themselves. They laid close, and so many steps did we advance ahead of the dogs, that to one not conversant with the cunning of the prairie chicken, the conviction would almost, if not quite, force itself upon the mind that both pointer and setter had played us false. Just as something of this kind was creeping over your most obedient, swish! flashed an old cock bird so close to my nose that I involuntarily made a lunge at him with my gun, so bewildered that I never dreamed of shooting. The Judge, not daring to shoot owing to my being in range, held up until the bird flew beyond his reach, but Burlingame let fly, shot clean over, and thus the laugh was on all three of us. Auter, in the meantime, bagging a young 'un with that cool and satisfied bearing so dreadfully provoking to those whose powder but scented the open air. . . . Sure enough, up popped a youngster not twenty feet distant, and he was my meat. It had not touched the grass before the Judge flushed a pair and nipped them both in exceedingly pretty style. Another chick up only to go back to mother earth again, when the parent bird broke cover, and, making a sudden dart almost in Burlingame's face, gave that gentleman a chance for a difficult shot which he accomplished with a grunt of satisfaction that demonstrated his keen desire to get even with the Judge. Only the first bird breaking cover escaped in the entire covey of thirteen, and then onward we moved for new fields to conquer. In the meantime Rick had marked down a large flock flying from the feeding ground to the open prairie, and, speeding his ponies to us, made the new field for sport in a jiffy. Out on the long sweeping prairies of Kansas, one drives at will, there being no fences but such as are easily circumvented, and streams so readily forded as to offer no obstacle to the driver's desire to go anywhere and everywhere. As my companions were starting off behind the dogs, Rick, who remained in the wagon, called me and suggested that I try him and the team as pointers, and promising me three or four fine opportunities for "single" birds rising one at a time. Nothing loth, I assented, and walking at the horse's heads, soon had the satisfaction of seeing a cock bird break cover with a rush, and, taking my time, brought him to the grass at fifty yards. Following on a few steps another took wing and, flying directly in the line with the team, I had another chance for distinguishing myself. Of the seven birds Rick had marked down I bagged six and knocked feathers out of the seventh. In the meantime the rivalry between Burlingame and the Judge waxed exceedingly warm, and upon picking them up for the return to town for dinner, we found Morton had twenty-six, Burlingame twenty-six, and Auter, who had talked least of all, thirty-one; the sum total of the morning's sport reaching ninety-seven.

Somewhere about three o'clock in the afternoon we went south of the river for a change, and had the best of luck, especially as night approached, the birds becoming almost as tame as domestic fowl as the twilight fell over the beautiful valley. . . .

The chicken season, the present year, is of such glorious promise as to fairly make the boys ache over the enforced delay until Aug. 1. The season throughout southwest Kansas is fully a month in advance of previous years, and the young birds are growing so rapidly and are in such remarkably large numbers that it does appear hard that we should have to wait so many weeks yet before taking the field. But it is this very adherence to the letter, as well as the spirit of the game laws, that has led to the amazing increase of both quail and chickens, old settlers declaring they never before saw anything like it. . . . The young birds are plumper and heavier than ever before known at this stage of their growth, and the opening day of the shooting season—Aug. 1—will, unquestionably be one long to be remembered in the game annals of Kansas.

Document 2.4

The Last of the Buffalo (1892)

George Bird Grinnell

On the floor, on either side of my fireplace, lie two buffalo skulls. They are white and weathered, the horns cracked and bleached by the snows and frosts, and the rains and heats of many winters and summers. Often, late at night, when the house is quiet, I sit before the fire, and muse and dream of the old days; and as I gaze at these relics of the past, they take life before my eyes. The matted brown hair again clothes the dry bone, and in the empty orbits the wild eyes gleam. Above me curves the blue arch; away on every hand stretches the yellow prairie, and scattered near and far are the dark forms of buffalo. They dot the rolling hills, quietly feeding like tame cattle, or lie at ease on the slopes, chewing the cud and half asleep. The yellow calves are close by their mothers; on little eminences the great bulls paw the dust, and mutter and moan, while those whose horns have grown one, two, and three winters are mingled with their elders.

Not less peaceful is the scene near some river-bank, when the herds come down to water. From the high prairie on every side they stream into the valleys, stringing along in single file, each band following the deep trail worn in the parched soil by the tireless feet of generations of their kind. At a quick walk they swing along, their heads held low. The long beards of the bulls sweep the ground; the shuffling tread of many hoofs marks their passing, and above each long line rises a cloud of dust that sometimes obscures the westering sun. . . .

The early explorers were constantly astonished by the multitudinous herds which they met with, the regularity of their movements, and the deep roads which they made in travelling from place to place. Many of the earlier references are to territory east of the Mississippi, but even within the last fifteen years buffalo were to be seen on the Western plains in numbers so great that an entirely sober and truthful account seems like fable. Describing the abundance of buffalo in a certain region, an Indian once said to me, in the expressive sign language of which all old frontiersmen have some knowledge, "The country was one robe."

Much has been written about their enormous abundance in the old days, but I have never read anything that I thought an exaggeration of their numbers as I have seen them. Only one who has actually spent months in travelling among them in those old days can credit the stories told about them. The trains of the Kansas Pacific Railroad used frequently to be detained by herds which were crossing the tracks in front of the engines, and in 1870, trains on which I was travelling were twice so held, in one case for three hours. When railroad travel first began on this road, the engineers tried the experiment of running through these passing herds, but after their engines had been thrown from the tracks they learned wisdom, and gave the buffalo the right of way. Two or three years later, in the country between the Platte and Republican Rivers, I saw a closely massed herd of buffalo so vast that I

Reprinted from George Bird Grinnell, "The Last of the Buffalo," *Scribner's Magazine* 12 (September 1892): 267–70, 281–82, 284–86.

dare not hazard a guess as to its numbers; and in later years I have travelled for weeks at a time, in northern Montana, without ever being out of sight of buffalo. . . .

To the white travellers on the plains in early days the buffalo furnished support and sustenance. Their abundance made fresh meat usually obtainable, and the early travellers usually carried with them bundles of dried meat, or sacks of pemmican, food made from the flesh of the buffalo, that contained a great deal of nutriment in very small bulk. Robes were used for bedding, and in winter buffalo moccasins were worn for warmth, the hair side within. Coats of buffalo skin are the warmest covering known, the only garment which will present an effective barrier to the bitter blasts that sweep over the plains of the Northwest. . . .

The dismal story of the extermination of the buffalo for its hides has been so often told, that I may be spared the sickening details of the butchery which was carried on from the Mexican to the British boundary line in the struggle to obtain a few dollars by a most ignoble means. As soon as railroads penetrated the buffalo country, a market was opened for their hides. Men too lazy to work were not too lazy to hunt, and a good hunter could kill in the early days from thirty to seventy-five buffalo a day, the hides of which were worth from $1.50 to $4 each. This seemed an easy way to make money, and the market for hides was unlimited. Up to this time the trade in robes had been mainly confined to those dressed by the Indians, and these were for the most part taken from cows. The coming of the railroad made hides of all sorts marketable, and even those from naked old bulls found a sale at some price. The butchery of buffalo was now something stupendous. Thousands of hunters followed millions of buffalo and destroyed them wherever found and at all seasons of the year. They pursued them during the day, and at night camped at the watering places, and built lines of fires along the streams, to drive the buffalo back so that they could not drink. It took less than six years to destroy all the buffalo in Kansas, Nebraska, Indian Territory, and northern Texas. The few that were left of the southern herd retreated to the waterless plains of Texas, and there for a while had a brief respite. Even here the hunters followed them, but as the animals were few and the territory in which they ranged vast, they held out here for some years. It was in this country, and against the very last survivors of this southern herd, that "Buffalo Jones" made his very successful trips to capture calves.

The extirpation of the northern herd was longer delayed. No very terrible slaughter occurred until the completion of the Northern Pacific Railroad; then, however, the same scenes of butchery were enacted. Buffalo were shot down by tens of thousands, their hides stripped off, and the meat left to the wolves. The result of the crusade was soon seen, the last buffalo were killed in the Northwest near the boundary line in 1883, and that year may be said to have finished up the species, though some few were killed in 1884 to 1885.

After the slaughter had been begun, but years before it had been accomplished, the subject was brought to the attention of Congress, and legislation looking to the preservation of the species was urged upon that body. Little general interest was taken in the subject, but in 1874, after much discussion, Congress did pass an act providing for the protection of the buffalo. The bill, however, was never signed by the President.

During the last days of the buffalo, a remarkable change took place in its form, and this change is worthy of consideration by naturalists, for it is an example of specialization—of development in one particular direction—which was due to a change in the environment of the species, and is interesting because it was brought about in a very few years, and indicates how rapidly, under favoring conditions, such specialization may take place.

This change was noticed and commented on by hunters who followed the northern buffalo, as well as by those who assisted in the extermination of the southern herd. The southern hunters, however, averred that the "regular" buffalo had disappeared—gone off somewhere—and that their place had been taken by what they called the southern buffalo, a race said to have come up from Mexico, and characterized by longer legs and a longer, lighter body than the buffalo of earlier years, and which was also peculiar in that the animals never became fat. Intelligent hunters of the northern herd, however, recognized the true state of the case, which was that the buffalo, during the last years of their existence, were so constantly pursued and driven from place to place that they never had time to lay on fat as in earlier years, and that, as a consequence of this continual running, the animal's form changed, and instead of a fat, short-backed, short-legged animal, it became a long-legged, lightbodied beast, formed for running.

This specialization in the direction of speed at first proceeded very slowly, but at last, as the dangers to which the animals were subjected became more and more pressing, it took place rapidly, and as a consequence the last buffalo killed on the plains were extremely long-legged and rangy, and were very different in appearance—as they were in their habits—from the animals of twenty years ago.

Buffalo running was not a sport that required much skill, yet it was not without its dangers. Occasionally a man was killed by the buffalo, but deaths from falls and from bursting guns were more common. Many curious stories of such accidents are told by the few real old-timers whose memory goes back fifty years, to the time when flintlock guns were in use. A mere fall from a horse is lightly regarded by the practised rider; the danger to be feared is that in such a fall the horse may roll on the man and crush him. Even more serious accidents occurred when a man fell upon some part of his equipment, which was driven through his body. Hunters have fallen in such a way that their whip-stocks, arrows, bows, and even guns, have been driven through their bodies. The old flintlock guns, or "fukes," which were loaded on the run, with powder poured in from the horn by guess, and a ball from the mouth, used frequently to burst, causing the loss of hands, arms, and even lives. . . .

It was on the plains of Montana, in the days when buffalo were still abundant, that I had one of my last buffalo hunts—a hunt with a serious purpose. A company of fifty or more men, who for weeks had been living on bacon and beans longed for the "boss ribs" of fat cow, and when we struck the buffalo range two of us were deputed to kill some meat. . . .

At length I saw my companion slowly bend forward over his horse's neck, turn, and ride back to me. He had seen the backs of two buffalo lying on the edge of a little flat hardly a quarter of a mile from where we stood. The others of the band must be still nearer to us. By riding along the lowest part of the sag which separated the two buttes, and then down a little ravine, it seemed probable that we could come within a few yards of the buffalo unobserved. Our preparations did not take long. . . . We skirted the butte, rode through the low sag and down into the little ravine, which soon grew deeper, so that our heads were below the range of vision of almost anything on the butte. Passing the mouth of the little side ravine, however, there came into full view a huge bull lying well up on the hillside. Luckily his back was toward us, and, each bending low over his horse's neck, we rode on, and in a moment were hidden by the side of the ravine. Two or three minutes more, and we came to another side ravine which was wide and commanded a view of the flat. We stopped before reaching this, and a peep showed that we were within a few yards of two old cows, a young heifer, and a yearling, all of them to the north of us. Beyond, we could see the backs of others all lying down. . . .

Of the millions of buffalo which even in our own time ranged the plains in freedom, none now remain. From the prairies which they used to darken, the wild herds, down to the last straggling bull, have disappeared. In the Yellowstone National Park, protected from destruction by United States troops, are the only wild buffalo which exist within the borders of the United States. These are mountain buffalo, and, from their habit of living in the thick timber and on the rough mountain sides, they are only now and then seen by visitors to the Park. It is impossible to say just how many there are, but from the best information that I can get, based on the estimates of reliable and conservative men, I conclude that the number was not less than four hundred in the winter of 1891–92. Each winter or spring the Government scout employed in the Park sees one or more herds of these buffalo, and as such herds are usually made up in part of young animals and have calves with them, it is fair to assume that they are steadily if slowly increasing. The report of a trip made last January speaks of four herds seen in the Hayden Valley, which numbered respectively 78, 50, 110, and 15. Besides these, a number of single animals and of scattering groups were seen at a distance, which would perhaps bring the total number up to three hundred. Of course, it is not to be supposed that all the buffalo in the Park were at that time collected in this one valley.

In the far Northwest, in the Peace River district, there may still be found a few wood buffalo. Judging from reports of them which occasionally reach us from Indians and Hudson's Bay men, their habits resemble those of the European bison. They are seldom killed, and the estimate of their numbers varies from five hundred to fifteen hundred. This cannot be other than the merest guess, since they are scattered over many thousand square miles of territory which is without inhabitants, and for the most part unexplored.

On the great plains is still found the buffalo skull half buried in the soil and crumbling to decay. The deep trails once trodden by the marching hosts are grass-grown now, and fast filling up. When these most enduring relics of a vanished race shall have passed away, there will be found, in all the limitless domain once darkened by their feeding herds, not one trace of the American buffalo.

Document 2.5

Conservation (1953)

Aldo Leopold

Conservation is a bird that flies faster than the shot we aim at it. . . .Conservation is a state of harmony between men and land. By land is meant all of the things on, over, or in the earth. Harmony with land is like harmony with a friend; you cannot cherish his right hand and chop off his left. That is to say, you cannot love game and hate predators; you cannot conserve the waters and waste the ranges; you cannot build the forest and mine the farm. The land is one organism. Its parts, like our own parts, compete with each other and co-operate with each other. The competitions are as much a part of the inner workings as the co-operations. You can regulate them—cautiously—but not abolish them.

The outstanding scientific discovery of the twentieth century is not television, or radio, but rather the complexity of the land organism. Only those who know the most about it can appreciate how little we know about it. The last word in ignorance is the man who says of an animal or plant: "What good is it?" If the land mechanism as a whole is good, then every part is good, whether we understand it or not. If the biota, in the course of aeons, has built something we like but do not understand, then who but a fool would discard seemingly useless parts? To keep every cog and wheel is the first precaution of intelligent tinkering.

Have we learned this first principle of conservation: to preserve all the parts of the land mechanism? No, because even the scientist does not yet recognize all of them.

In Germany there is a mountain called the Spessart. Its south slope bears the most magnificent oaks in the world. American cabinetmakers, when they want the last word in quality, use Spessart oak. The north slope, which should be the better, bears an indifferent stand of Scotch pine. Why? Both slopes are part of the same state forest; both have been managed with equally scrupulous care for two centuries. Why the difference?

Kick up the litter under the oaks and you will see that the leaves rot almost as fast as they fall. Under the pines, though, the needles pile up as a thick duff; decay is much slower. Why? Because in the Middle Ages the south slope was preserved as a deer forest by a hunting bishop; the north slope was pastured, plowed, and cut by settlers, just as we do with our woodlots in Wisconsin and Iowa today. Only after this period of abuse was the north slope replanted to pines. During this period of abuse something happened to the microscopic flora and fauna of the soil. The number of species was greatly reduced, i.e. the digestive apparatus of the soil lost some of its parts. Two centuries of conservation have not sufficed to restore these losses. It required the modern microscope, and a century of research in soil science,

Reprinted with permission from Aldo Leopold, *Round River: From the Journals of Aldo Leopold,* ed. Luna B. Leopold. (New York: Oxford University Press, 1953, 145–52, 155–57.)

to discover the existence of these "small cogs and wheels" which determine harmony or disharmony between men and land in the Spessart.

American conservation is, I fear, still concerned for the most part with show pieces. We have not yet learned to think in terms of small cogs and wheels. Look at our own back yard: at the prairies of Iowa and southern Wisconsin. What is the most valuable part of the prairie? The fat black soil, the chernozem. Who built the chernozem? The black prairie was built by the prairie plants, a hundred distinctive species of grasses, herbs, and shrubs; by the prairie fungi, insects, and bacteria; by the prairie mammals and birds, all interlocked in one humming community of co-operations and competitions, one biota. This biota, through ten thousand years of living and dying, burning and growing, preying and fleeing, freezing and thawing, built that dark and bloody ground we call prairie.

Our grandfathers did not, could not, know the origin of their prairie empire. They killed off the prairie fauna and they drove the flora to a last refuge on railroad embankments and roadsides. To our engineers this flora is merely weeds and brush; they ply it with grader and mower. Through processes of plant succession predictable by any botanist, the prairie garden becomes a refuge for quack grass. After the garden is gone, the highway department employs landscapers to dot the quack with elms, and with artistic clumps of Scotch pine, Japanese barberry, and Spiraea. Conservation Committees, en route to some important convention, whiz by and applaud this zeal for roadside beauty.

Some day we may need this prairie flora not only to look at but to rebuild the wasting soil of prairie farms. Many species may then be missing. We have our hearts in the right place, but we do not yet recognize the small cogs and wheels.

In our attempts to save the bigger cogs and wheels, we are still pretty naive. A little repentance just before a species goes over the brink is enough to make us feel virtuous. When the species is gone we have a good cry and repeat the performance.

The recent extermination of the grizzly from most of the western stock-raising states is a case in point. Yes, we still have grizzlies in the Yellowstone. But the species is ridden by imported parasites; the rifles wait on every refuge boundary; new dude ranches and new roads constantly shrink the remaining range; every year sees fewer grizzlies on fewer ranges in fewer states. We console ourselves with the comfortable fallacy that a single museum-piece will do, ignoring the clear dictum of history that a species must be saved *in many places* if it is to be saved at all.

The ivory-billed woodpecker, the California condor, and the desert sheep are the next candidates for rescue. The rescues will not be effective until we discard the idea that one sample will do; until we insist on living with our flora and fauna in as many places as possible.

We need knowledge—public awareness—of the small cogs and wheels, but sometimes I think there is something we need even more. It is the thing that *Forest and Stream,* on its editorial masthead, once called "a refined taste in natural objects." Have we made any headway in developing "a refined taste in natural objects"?

In the northern parts of the lake states we have a few wolves left. Each state offers a bounty on wolves. In addition, it may invoke the expert services of the U.S. Fish and Wildlife Service in wolf-control. Yet both this agency and the several conservation commissions complain of an increasing number of localities where there are too many deer for the available feed. Foresters complain of periodic damage from too many rabbits. Why, then, continue the public policy of wolf-ex- termination? We debate such questions in terms of economics and biology. The mammalogists assert the wolf is the natural check on too many deer. The sportsmen reply they will take care of excess deer. Another decade of argument and there will be no wolves to argue about. One conservation inkpot cancels another until the resource is gone. Why? Because the basic question has not been debated at all. The basic question hinges on "a refined taste in natural objects." Is a wolfless north woods any north woods at all?

The hawk and owl question seems to me a parallel one. When you band a hundred hawks in fall, twenty are shot and the bands returned during the subsequent year. No four-egged bird on earth can withstand such a kill. Our raptors are on the toboggan.

Science has been trying for a generation to classify hawks and owls into "good" and "bad" species, the "good" being those that do more economic good than harm. It seems to me a mistake to call the issue on economic grounds, even sound ones. The basic issue transcends economics. The basic question is whether a hawkless, owlless countryside is a livable countryside for Americans with eyes to see and ears to hear. Hawks and owls are a part of the land mechanism. Shall we discard them because they compete with game and poultry? Can we assume that these competi- tions which we perceive are more important than the co-operations which we do not perceive?

The fish-predator question is likewise parallel. I worked one summer for a club that owns (and cherishes) a delectable trout stream, set in a matrix of virgin forest. There are 30,000 acres of the stuff that dreams are made on. But look more closely and you fail to see what "a refined taste in natural objects" demands of such a setting. Only once in a great while does a kingfisher rattle his praise of rushing water. Only here and there does an otter-slide on the bank tell the story of pups rollicking in the night. At sunset you may or may not see a heron; the rookery has been shot out. This club is in the throes of a genuine educational process. One faction wants simply more trout; another wants trout plus all the trimmings, and has employed a fish ecologist to find ways and means. Superficially the issue again is "good" and "bad" predators, but basically the issue is deeper. Any club privileged to own such a piece of land is morally obligated to keep all its parts, even though it means a few less trout in the creel.

In the lake states we are proud of our forest nurseries, and of the progress we are making in replanting what was once the north woods. But look in these nurseries and you will find no white cedar, no tamarack. Why no cedar? It grows too slowly, the deer eat it, the alders choke it. The prospect of a cedarless north woods does not depress our foresters; cedar has, in effect, been purged on grounds of economic inefficiency. For the same reason beech has been purged from the future forests of the Southeast. To these voluntary expungements of species from our future flora, we must add the involuntary ones arising from the importation of diseases: chestnut, persimmon, white pine. Is it sound economics to regard any plant as a separate entity, to proscribe or encourage it on the grounds of its individual performance? What will be the effect on animal life, on the soil, and on the health of the forest as an organism? Is there not an aesthetic as well as an economic issue? Is there, at bottom, any real distinction between aesthetics and economics? I do not know the answers, but I can see in each of these questions another receding target for conservation. . . .

❧

We shall never achieve harmony with land, any more than we shall achieve justice or liberty for people. In these higher aspirations the important thing is not to achieve, but to strive. It is only in mechanical enterprises that we can expect that early or complete fruition of effort which we call "success."

The problem, then, is how to bring about a striving for harmony with land among a people many of whom have forgotten there is any such thing as land, among whom education and culture have become almost synonymous with landlessness. This is the problem of "conservation education."

When we say "striving," we admit at the outset that the thing we need must grow from within. No striving for an idea was ever injected wholly from without.

When we say "striving," I think we imply an effort of the mind as well as a disturbance of the emotions. It is inconceivable to me that we can adjust ourselves to the complexities of the land mechanism without an intense curiosity to understand its workings and an habitual personal study of those workings. The urge to comprehend must precede the urge to reform.

When we say "striving," we likewise disqualify at least in part the two vehicles which conservation propagandists have most often used: fear and indignation. He who by a lifetime of observation and reflection has learned much about our maladjustments with land is entitled to fear, and would be something less than honest if he were not indignant. But for teaching the fresh mind, these are outmoded tools. They belong to history.

My own gropings come to a dead end when I try to appraise the profit motive. For a full generation the American conservation movement has been substituting the profit motive for the fear motive, yet it has failed to motivate. We can all see profit in conservation practice, but the profit accrues to society rather than to the individual. This, of course, explains the trend, at this moment, to wish the whole job on the government.

When one considers the prodigious achievements of the profit motive in wrecking land, one hesitates to reject it as a vehicle for restoring land. I incline to believe we have overestimated the scope of the profit motive. Is it profitable for the individual to build a beautiful home? To give his children a higher education? No, it is seldom profitable, yet we do both. These are, in fact, ethical and aesthetic premises which underlie the economic system. Once accepted, economic forces tend to align the smaller details of social organization into harmony with them.

No such ethical and aesthetic premise yet exists for the condition of the land these children must live in. Our children are our signature to the roster of history;

our land is merely the place our money was made. There is as yet no social stigma in the possession of a gullied farm, a wrecked forest, or a polluted stream, provided the dividends suffice to send the youngsters to college. Whatever ails the land, the government will fix it.

I think we have here the root of the problem. What conservation education must build is an ethical underpinning for land economics and a universal curiosity to understand the land mechanism. Conservation may then follow.

3

Water and Drinking Water Quality

Introduction

The significance of water to the health of the environment is acknowledged by almost everyone; for the water flowing through the earth is equivalent to the flow of blood in the human body. For each person, water is a matter of health or illness, life or death. Seventy percent of each human's body is water. To sustain a healthy body, we must constantly consume liquids with a high water content to replenish ourselves during a normal day of walking, talking, thinking, and all other daily activities.

Each person needs about two quarts of drinking water every day to prevent dehydration, physical fatigue, and illness. Healthy humans can survive for nearly a month without food but they will die of thirst in less than a week without water. Until recently, Americans have thought little about the sources of their drinking water. How does it flow on and beneath the earth's surface? How does it reach the earth? Where is it collected, and how does it get from there to our homes? For all too many of us, water "arrives" when we turn on the faucet and it "disappears" when we pull the plug. According to Benjamin Franklin, "we know the worth of water only when the well runs dry."[1]

Human Consumption

Each day residents of the United States use about three times more water than Europeans, despite the fact that both are members of the urban, industrial, developed world. Each person in the United States uses about 1,400 gallons each day for all uses. Ten percent is used for tap water supplies. Eleven percent is used for industry, 38 percent for cooling electric generating plants, and 41 percent for irrigated agriculture.[2] For people living in the undeveloped parts of the world, the difference in water usage is even more pronounced. In underdeveloped countries, grains and legumes rather than animal products make up a higher percentage of each person's diet. Both use less water during the growing season than cattle and sheep raising. Industrial usage is an important part of the total quantity of water consumed in the United States, since many goods that we purchase require the use of water in the manufacturing process. The industrial use of water has been declining since the passage of the Clean Water Act in 1972, but unfortunately, residential usage has not seen a similar drop since the 1970s.

One might argue that our nation uses excessive water for personal functions.* This pattern began as residential water systems were designed, constructed, and put into use in many eastern cities during the early nineteenth century. Water, like so many other resources, including trees and wildlife, was thought to be plentiful to the point of inexhaustibility. Once it became available, water was used with abandon; water use was not monitored nor was it measured by mechanical meters. To prevent pipes from freezing in winter, water spigots were often left open to allow a constant flow. As a result of such practices, inefficiency and waste were commonplace in operating early modern waterworks.

Today, an average American family of four uses about 233 gallons of water each day. Seventy-four percent of that total is used in the bathroom. Toilets consume about 40 percent of the total, with original equipment toilets using from 5 to 7 gallons of water with each flush. More modern appliances use from 1 1/2 to 3 gallons per flush. Bathing uses another 34 percent, with showering taking up about 60 percent of that 34 percent.[3] Now, however, we possess the technological know-how to reduce water consumed in showers by up to 70 percent by replacing older fixtures with water-reducing shower nozzles. Technological innovations have the capacity for changing traditionally inefficient water delivery systems into more effective ones without requiring drastic lifestyle changes.

To date, however, we have been slow to replace older water-consuming fixtures with new water-efficient systems. New building and household renovation codes do require the installation of bathroom water fixtures that consume less water. Despite water reduction technology, however, consumption of water by Americans has been increasing for decades. At the

---

*The average American takes seven showers in ten days. The average number of showers per household is 2.4 per day. Showering accounts for 19.4 percent of indoor residential water use, or an average of 11,000 gallons of water annually per household. Doing your laundry consumes between 35 and 50 gallons of water. Shaving adds 5 to 10 gallons, if you leave the water running; only one gallon is used if you fill the basin. (Thomas Vinciguerra, "Forget the Game: Here Are the Shower Statistics," *New York Times,* May 29, 1997, C6, and Allen Hammond, ed., *The 1993 Environmental Almanac,* Boston: Houghton Mifflin, 1993, 6.)

turn of the century, Americans consumed water at the rate of about 95 gallons per person per day. Fifty years later, the rate of consumption had increased by almost 50 percent. In the largest American cities, namely New York, Philadelphia, Chicago, Baltimore, and Detroit that average had been exceeded before the outbreak of World War II in 1941. Water usage had jumped to about 155 gallons each day. In calculating this total amount, water used for drinking, cooking, laundry, personal cleanliness, and toilet flushes was included, as well as the approximately 25 gallons used for a bath daily in a tub.[4]

The Natural Water Cycle

What does all of the water usage on the planet add up to each day? Approximately 339 billion gallons of water is withdrawn from the ground and from the surface of the earth each day by humans for agricultural, industrial, and personal use. To accommodate this heavy demand, about 4 trillion gallons falls on us each day in the form of precipitation as rain or snow. Much of this precipitation evaporates and therefore does not replenish the groundwater supply, and much is runoff into canals, rivers, and streams.[5]

The earth's atmosphere holds about a ten-day supply of fresh water, which amounts to about one inch of rain spread around the planet's surface. "Each day on earth almost 250 cubic miles of water evaporates from the sea and the land. Its stay in the air is short; it is always seeking particles to stick to and fall with as rain or snow."[6] This natural cycle of evaporation and precipitation represents the earth's endless interaction with the sun's energy. In thinking about the earth as a natural and dynamic entity:

> All is movement, from the endless flex of freeze and thaw that breaks mountains down to sand, to the enormous aquifers in which water oozes slowly but inexorably through the ground, to the great heave of fresh into salt at the river's mouth. Every day the Yukon River [in northwestern Canada] dumps an average of 145 billion gallons into the Bering Sea [in the northern Pacific Ocean] and the sun pumps vapor right back into the sky, and the [water] cycle roars on.[7]

The daily flow of the Columbia River, for example, will provide an additional perspective on the magnitude of the flow of fresh water to the ocean, where water is captured by the energy of the sun and transformed into vapor to again become rainfall on the land. Its water is collected from a 258,200 square mile area and moves along a 1,214-mile route, pushing its 100 millions of gallons of fresh water many miles out into the Pacific Ocean each day from its mouth in western Oregon.

Major Pathways of the Runoff of the Hydrological Cycle. Adapted from Figure 4.1 in *Handbook on the Principles of Hydrology,* **ed. D.M. Grey, 1970. Courtesy National Research Council, Ottawa, Canada.**

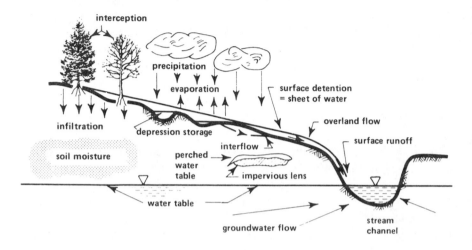

There is a physics to the drama . . . at the river's mouth, and it leads outward beyond the earth to the sun and the moon. Lunar gravitation causes the tides, but virtually all the rest of the energy manifest at the Columbia's mouth originates in the sun. The sun in effect, provides fuel for a great atmospheric heat engine which evaporates water from the oceans and produces winds that move the moisture over the land. As the clouds cool, the moisture falls as rain. Without solar energy to move the water inland and uphill, rivers would never begin; without gravity to propel the water downhill back toward the ocean, rivers would never flow.[8]

There are many mighty rivers on earth that dump hundreds of millions of gallons of fresh water into the oceans each day, with much of it to be recycled back onto the land. Water is constantly moving and being replaced by this natural process of atmospheric change.

It is this process that replenishes the earth with fresh water. Most of that which is not vaporized by the energy of the sun becomes groundwater. It percolates into the earth's surface, filling the spaces between geological rock and sub-strata soil. There, it remains stored in subterranean groundwater aquifers, constantly moving, filling new voids, and recharging areas depleted by pumping. Eighty-five percent of all fresh water stored on the earth is found in these groundwater aquifers. The remaining 15 percent is located on the earth's surface in rivers, streams, ponds, and lakes. Of the water we remove from aquifers annually for agriculture and personal use, it is estimated that only about 3 percent is replenished annually by the natural processes described above. The recharge rate, as it is called, is very slow, and it takes hundreds of years to replace the total volume contained in an aquifer.[9]

Most of our country's surface water network is composed of rivers, streams, lakes, and ponds, thousands of which were created by the expansion and retreat of the last North American glaciers more than ten thousand years ago. "The greatest legacy of this glacial activity is the Great Lakes, five major lakes that collectively contain about twenty percent of the fresh water on the surface of the world."[10] These natural surface water networks, to which we now add man-made reservoirs, are recharged by the same cycle of evaporation and atmospheric precipitation as the groundwater aquifers. Although both surface and groundwater are replenished by rainfall and snow, surface water is particularly susceptible to changes in the land. When the land contains a diverse vegetation of trees, plants, and litter left from the accumulation of years of growth and decay, it intercepts and absorbs precipitation. For example:

> Plant material reduces the kinetic energy of falling rainwater and water flowing downhill and alters the chemical composition of the incoming water. Thus vegetation both minimizes soil erosion and regulates nutrient flow to water. . . . [If the land mass surrounding the surface water, called the watershed] is stressed by pollution [and] deforestation, not only is the water flow altered but these conditions change the nutrient flow and cycling with the terrestrial part of the ecosystem.[11]

Unfortunately, the natural replacement rate of groundwater and the quality of that water is compromised by excessive demands. Ecological changes in the land cause deteriorating water quality. This knowledge helps to put into perspective the enormous consumption by Americans of 25 billion gallons of fresh water each day.[12] We are entering an era in which the supply of plentiful and affordable water may be coming to an end. Clearly, we are withdrawing water from the earth at an alarming rate, a rate in which the supply is diminishing faster than its replacement by natural processes. The water problem can be defined in terms of supply and demand. It is made all the more extreme by the uneven distribution of water; some regions of the country, not necessarily those with the highest demand, possess more than others. To renew the balance, we need to conserve more and use less, a policy at odds with much of our history.

The Contribution of Beavers

During the colonial period of our country's history, water policy was decidedly local. Concerns focused mostly on the availability of water for residents in the various neighborhoods for domestic use and for fighting fires. As colonial towns and cities grew, deciding how to transport supplies of water for household and commercial use became a matter of concern for public agencies and private enterprise. As potable water became more available to urban areas, populations grew and usage skyrocketed. The demand for water coincided roughly with ecological changes caused by the systematic hunting and trapping of beavers by Native Americans, French trappers, and English pioneers. As was described in the essay on wildlife and the loss of wildlife habitat, beavers were hunted for their pelts, which were used for the manufacture of felt hats, the fashion for both Americans and Europeans during the eighteenth century. Millions of beavers were killed until silk hats replaced felt ones as the new fashion statement.

Although the ecological effects of this massive slaughter were seldom acknowledged, a few naturalists, most notably John Godman, writing in 1831, lamented the near extermination of beavers. Yet, even he was unaware of the environmental impact of the carnage, particularly in the loss of a species whose natural dam-building instincts elevated water tables and created ponds, which served the important ecological purpose of catching melted snow and preventing widespread soil erosion. In order to engage in these activities, however, beavers inadvertently created forest clearings, which enabled hunters and trappers to penetrate the dense forests, as well as pioneers and settlers who logged the extensive timberlands.

The ecological effects of simultaneous trapping and logging were witnessed as early as the middle of the eighteen century. The lower water tables, the destruction of ponds, and the drying of the land were just some of the effects of slaughtering beavers. The French expatriate J. Hector St. John de Crevecoeur, a New York farmer from 1769 to 1778, observed the effects without knowing the cause. He wrote in his "Thoughts of an American Farmer on Various Rural Subjects" (1782) that:

> I could show you in this country the ruins of eleven grist-mills which twenty years ago had plenty of water, but now stand on the dry ground, with no other marks of running water about them than the ancient bed of the creek, on the shores of which they had been erected. This effect does not surprise me. Our ancient woods kept the earth moist and damp, and the sun could evaporate none of the water contained within their shades. Who knows how far these effects may extend.[13]

Crevecoeur was explaining one of the natural pathways that rainfall takes once it falls to earth. If it comes in contact with direct sunlight, water evaporates back into the atmosphere. If water is shaded by tall trees, its cycling back into the air is impeded and slowed. What Crevecoeur did not know was that accelerating much of the water loss was destruction by farmers, who were clearing the land of its trees and draining the marshes and upland watersheds. These watersheds had been created by the more than 200 million beavers living in the rivers and streams of the continental United States during the era of European exploration and settlement. Once they had been hunted nearly to the point of extinction, their dams, which flooded meadows and flatlands, turning them into swamps and marshes, began to disintegrate. The process was accelerated by farmers intent on turning the land to crops and pasture.

The destruction of ninth-tenths of the beavers beginning in the early eighteenth century placed increasing stress on the ability of the water to clean itself. Over the previous millennium, the compulsive dam-building behavior of beavers had resulted in the development of rich new ecosystems sustained by rainwater. Beaver dams transformed forests into meadows and these same meadows into wetlands, collecting silt from upland stream runoffs.

Water contained in this way percolates into the ground, where it is either absorbed by plants and trees or where it recharges the underground aquifers. In either instance, wetlands soak up water during rainy seasons and release it during dry spells. All of these important ecological developments were destroyed by hunting and trapping beavers. Beaver dams, built, maintained, reinforced, and rebuilt by "eager beavers," collapsed, releasing snowmelt into the rivers and streams much too quickly. Rich nutrients formed mainly from decaying plants in wetlands, which eventually would have become rich topsoil, were carried along with the rushing water, adding unnecessary silt to the river bottoms, clogging channels and shallow streams. The continuous decline in the nation's wetlands over the last centuries can be traced to the early destruction of beaver habitat. With the decline came an alteration in the natural water cycle and its capacity to filter water naturally.

History of Urban Water Use

A minimal number of water supply systems existed in the United States in 1800. Philadelphia built the first waterworks in 1802, followed by New York, Boston, Detroit, and Cincinnati. Construction of water systems was slow through most of the nineteenth century until the 1870s and early 1880s, when municipalities began to invest heavily in public waterworks. Before the 1870s, only cities with larger populations, facing major problems such as the outbreak of infectious disease and large urban fires, invested in water supply systems. Later, smaller municipalities, influenced by the public health movement in America which promoted the germ theory for the spread of disease, also invested in these water supply systems. And the municipalities that built waterworks experienced a reduction in their fire insurance rates.[14]

Artificial filtering of water began in the early nineteenth century. The first slow sand filter was used in London, England, by the Chelsea Water Works in 1827. A few short years later, in 1832, Richmond, Virginia, applied the same process to its drinking water. Early industrial applications occurred in textile mills, where plentiful clear and potable water was needed in generating power for mechanical looms.

Boston

Early seventeenth-century American cities gathered water from local wells, springs, ponds, and cisterns. Cisterns were located in carefully chosen places to collect rainwater before it hit the ground. As the cities grew in size and population, these local sources became inadequate, both in terms of availability and quality. The first two hundred homes in Boston, for example, drew their water from a spring located near the Common. By 1652, not much more than twenty years after its founding, this water supply could not meet Boston's growing demand. In response to the increasing demand, the General Court of the Massachusetts Bay Colony established a public works water supply system, one of the oldest in the nation, by granting a charter to a "Water Works Company."

Once incorporated to supply the city with water, the company built a large cistern, twelve feet square (by today's standards a very small reservoir), to hold water carried by way of a conveyer named the Conduit. Made of bored logs, the Conduit carried water from the wells and springs near today's Haymarket Square section of the city to Beacon Hill and the area around the Boston Common. As the city's population grew to about 7,000 in 1690, additional cisterns or small reservoirs were built to hold supplies of water for household and commercial use. Over approximately the hundred years that followed, in addition to using the downtown cisterns and the Conduit, Boston's citizens dug more than 2,000 wells to satisfy their water demands. One of the city's more popular public wells in 1774 was located in Dock Square.

Unfortunately, many of these wells became contaminated not long after they were put to use. City dwellers dug cesspools and privies (outhouses) to hold human waste near water supplies. As a result, the waste seeped into the groundwater and drinking water became putrid. By 1835 Boston's City Council selected the engineer Loammi Baldwin to survey the quality of the city's water. His survey concluded that of the 2,767 wells inspected, "only seven supplied water that was soft enough to be used in washing clothes. In 682 wells the water was too polluted to drink. The smell in many cases is extremely offensive and I should think it probable that they have an injurious effect on the water of wells contiguous."[15]

While well water had been contaminated by human waste, cistern water was darkened by airborne particles. In 1833, the city's mayor noted that "not only a greater accumulation of soot ... takes place on the roofs of houses, but dust and other foul matters blow up from the streets and lodge or collect in the gutters and stain and contaminate the water."[16] To escape from malodorous local wells and contaminated cisterns, citizens of Boston reached further away from the city for their water supply, beginning a quest for plentiful, clean, and cheap water from sources other than underground wells and rainwater collected in cisterns.

This quest, with intermediate solutions, would continue in stages well into the twentieth century. In 1795, the Jamaica Plain Aqueduct Company was incorporated to bring water from Jamaica Pond to Boston. By this time, the city's population had reached 19,000. The company agreed to lay 4-inch log pipes, buried below the surface, a distance of five miles to deliver water to part of the city by gravity. By 1846, the water from city wells and Jamaica Pond failed to meet the demands of Boston, now with a population of 180,000 residents.

The demand for more water was accentuated by the rash of devastating fires which roared through Boston and other densely populated cities in the eighteenth century. Major fires swept through the city in 1711, 1760, 1794, and 1825. Lack of water for fire fighting led to such drastic procedures as using dynamite to combat the spreading flames. The Massachusetts legislature, called the General Court, described the "Great Fire of 1760" in the following way:

> On the best information that could be obtained in so short a time there were consumed one hundred seventy-four dwellings and tenements, one hundred and seventy-five warehouses, shops and other buildings, with so great part of the furniture, besides quantities of merchandise and the stock and tools of many tradesmen. That the loss upon a moderate computation cannot be less than 100,000 pounds sterling, and the number of families inhabiting the aforementioned houses was at least two hundred and twenty.[17]

If uncontrollable fires were not a sufficient reminder of the need for more available water, outbreaks of disease among the residents of the tightly arranged tenements revealed that the available water was polluted. The sanitary habits and personal hygiene of most residents met the standards of

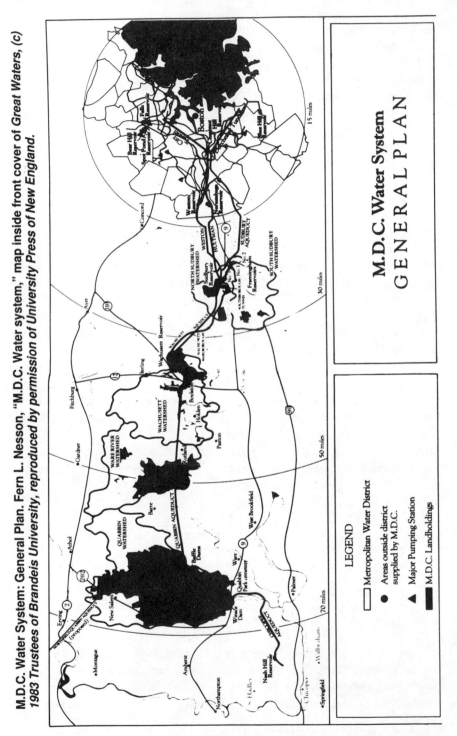

M.D.C. Water System: General Plan. Fern L. Nesson, "M.D.C. Water system," map inside front cover of *Great Waters*, (c) 1983 Trustees of Brandeis University, reproduced by permission of University Press of New England.

LEGEND

☐ Metropolitan Water District

● Areas outside district supplied by M.D.C.

▲ Major Pumping Station

■ M.D.C. Landholdings

M.D.C. Water System

G E N E R A L   P L A N

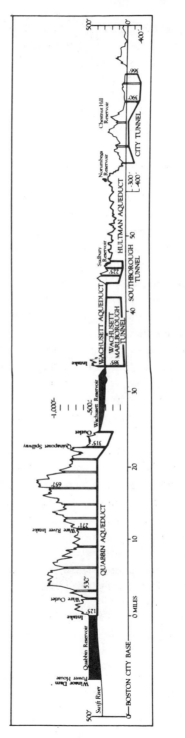

A ground-level side view of the M.D.C. Water System, showing the distance from the Quabbin to Boston, noting the elevation of important aqueducts, reservoirs, and tunnels.

the day, which were hardly comparable with present-day knowledge about public sanitation. Although Boston escaped the worst of the epidemics, namely outbreaks of yellow fever, cholera, and smallpox, the association of disease with filthy living conditions soon led to a number of practices to combat the personal habits of city dwellers. The most prominent of these practices was the cleansing of the city's streets, gutters, alleys, and the like with water. Regularly, residents disposed of garbage, human waste, and horse manure into the streets and alleys. Washing away the accumulated fifth was considered the most effective way to combat the spread of disease.[18] In turn, this created an increased need for water.

In 1854 in London, England, it was discovered that water from a certain public pump, the Broad Street Pump, was responsible for the cholera epidemic ravaging the people of that city. The next year London authorities required that all water be filtered before distribution. Although the germ theory of disease had to await the pioneering discovery of Louis Pasteur in 1857, the transition from believing that "filth" was the source of infectious disease to a germ theory had been made in Europe and in North America by the 1870s. In many ways, however, this transition was very slow, and the complete acceptance of the germ theory did not occur until the twentieth century.

While quality was an important issue in Boston, as in many other cities, the primary concern of engineers was the quantity of water they had to deliver. This was a problem of hydraulics, or how to move millions of gallons of water by the pull of gravity or under pressure to its users. The matter of the quality of this water became a major concern only after the Broad Street episode and Pasteur's discovery. In the meantime, Bostonians, running out of water, looked westward to satisfy their unquenched thirst.

In response to the growing demand for water, the city, with the support of the Commonwealth, tapped the water located in Long Pond, later renamed Lake Cochituate, in Wayland, a western suburb of the city. Construction of an aqueduct to convey the water to the Brookline reservoir bordering Boston began in 1846 and was completed two years later. In the city lead and cast-iron pipes were installed along with "a network of smaller distributing reservoirs"[19] to deliver water to many sections of Boston. The official arrival of Cochituate water was marked by a day of celebration, including:

> the simultaneous roar of 100 cannons and the ringing of every church bell in the town and beyond. There would be no commerce that day, nor work, nor learning. . . . The parade terminated at the Common where a crowd estimated at between 50,000 and 100,000 were gathered around a fountain in the center of the famous Frog Pond. . . .

"Do you want water?" Mayor Quincy shouted to the ... people as ... dusk fell.

"Yes!" they roared back and with a mighty pull on the lanyard, a sluice shot open and a geyser leaped 70 feet into the air. Beyond the Common on the crest of Beacon Hill rockets burst into the air, setting off a display of multicolored fireworks of intricate design. It was, all in all ... a wonderful party in the end.[20]

For Bostonians, tapping the Cochituate and leaving its polluted former sources of water behind established a pattern of consumption which would carry the city into the late twentieth century and beyond. Like other major cities looking for space for residential expansion, Boston annexed a number of neighboring towns, beginning with Roxbury in 1868. Roslindale was annexed in 1873, and in 1874, Charlestown, Dorchester, Brighton, and West Roxbury. By annexing Charlestown, Boston captured the town's much-needed water supply from the Mystic Lakes.

In Boston, a city whose services were growing much slower than its population, appeals from its fire chief, John Stanhope Damrell, "to install new hydrants with multiple outlets and for larger pipes to relieve a drastic water shortage"[21] were rejected by the City Council. This was the era when gaslights were installed to illuminate cities after dark. Gaslights were, however, also a fire hazard. When the great fire of November 12, 1872, a roaring conflagration, enveloped 65 acres of the city's financial district, Boston was as unprepared as Chicago had been a year earlier, when it was consumed by its memorable "Great Fire."

Despite the annexation of Charlestown, with its proximity to the Mystic Lakes, Boston's expansion stretched the limits of the city's water resources. To alleviate the shortages, the Sudbury Aqueduct, a 17–mile conveyance that stretched from a reservoir on the Sudbury River to Boston, was completed in 1880. It added to the city's sources of pure and wholesome water. Further west in Massachusetts, expansion of the city's water system was achieved by building a dam across the south branch of the Nashua River, creating the Wachusett Reservoir in 1906.* With the construction of the

---

*The Wachusett Reservoir, located in central Worcester County, currently provides drinking water to about half of Massachusetts's population. Water travels by aqueduct from the larger Quabbin Reservoir in the western part of the state to the Wachusett Reservoir, is disinfected and then sent on to the 2.5 million metropolitan Boston residents. Suburban sprawl and increasing population around the Wachusett Reservoir have placed the water supply at risk. Storm water runoff into the Wachusett Reservoir degrades the water supply. Scientists have shown that increasing storm water runoff flowing into surface water decreases water quality and causes about 3 million cases of

Wachusett aqueduct in 1925, the system became fully operational. By then Bostonians believed that water was plentiful, pure, and very cheap. In 1931, however, the Cochituate Reservoir was eliminated as a functional source of pure water. The metropolitan area had grown significantly during the past decades, and the waters of the Cochituate had become polluted.

Each move westward to tap a new supply took Bostonians to more elevated terrain, from which it was easier to operate a gravity water system. Throughout the nineteenth and for most of the twentieth century, the cost of water for the consumer was exceedingly cheap. Availability and low cost encouraged waste. In 1860, as the city's population approached 200,000, it used about 17 million gallons each day or about 100 gallons for each person. Since indoor plumbing had been introduced during this period, increased consumption was inevitable.

The cost of water remained so low throughout the nineteenth century that Bostonians paid only twelve cents for 1,000 gallons of water. The cost remained low for most of the twentieth century. As immigration nearly doubled the population of Boston and its surrounding suburbs, the Commonwealth established the multi-municipality Metropolitan Water District to manage water resources in 1895. This new agency, with powers to make water policy and establish water rates as well as enforce its decisions, represented an innovation in governmental organization. To curtail waste in Boston, all water was metered after 1907. *A description of the advantages of water meter use is provided in document 3.1.*

After nearly a half-century of continuous growth spanning the last decades of the nineteenth and the first decades of the twentieth century, the Quabbin Reservoir, located in the far western region of the state, was completed in 1939, to provide water for the twenty cities and towns in the Metropolitan District. Quabbin became operational seven years later, in 1946, because it took that long to fill the reservoir to its water capacity of 490 billion gallons. As one of the largest reservoirs in the world, its area covers 39 square miles, with 118 miles of shore and a watershed of 186 miles.[22] Currently, the Massachusetts Water Resources Authority (MWRA), the Commonwealth's agency responsible for delivering approximately 168

intestinal disease every year in the United States. The Wachusett water's best protection is the 75,000–acre watershed drainage basin around the Reservoir, made up of a forest which serves as a natural water filter. By continued building on the lands of the watershed, the natural filter is altered and water quality deteriorates. The solution is either to protect the watershed by acquiring land valued at about $22 million around the reservoir or to construct a $500 million filtration plant. (Jack Clarke and Deborah Cary, "State Must Move Fast To Protect Our Water Supply," *The Boston Globe,* April 23, 1997, A19.

gallons of water every day to each of its 2.5 million customers, plans to
build a new water tunnel between the Massachusetts towns of Framing-
ham and Weston to relieve the Hultman Aqueduct. The Hultman carries
about 85 percent of the water into the greater Boston area. It currently
leaks in 27 places, with the largest leak spilling about 90,000 gallons of
water each day. When completed, the MetroWest Water Supply Tunnel,
as it is called, will be 14 feet in diameter and 17 miles in length, boring
through solid rock at depths ranging from 200 to 500 feet below the
surface. It will have the capacity to deliver as much as 300 million
gallons of water each day.[23]

New York

Before the arrival of the British, Manhattan Island was controlled by Dutch
settlers. Called New Amsterdam by the Dutch, the city's water came from a
public well dug in front of a fort in 1658, located south of the present-day
Bowling Green section of the city. When the British replaced the Dutch,
they dug six additional wells. As the city's population grew, more wells
were dug to accommodate its inhabitants. Because of an abundance of fresh
groundwater in Manhattan Island's porous sub-strata, created by the last
glacier more than twelve thousand years ago, New Yorkers were able to dig
many private wells to satisfy their daily needs. Not counting the wells
owned by residents and businesses, the city had 249 public wells in 1809,
and there were numerous private cisterns constructed to catch rain water
from the roofs of buildings.

As population density increased, the city's residents became victims of a
common early modern urban experience. Many private and public wells
became contaminated by seepage from privies and cesspools. Much of the
contamination began as earlier as 1750. In 1748, Peter Kalm, a visitor to
the city, recorded in his diary: "There is no good water in the town itself,
but at a little distance there is a large spring of good water, which the
inhabitants take for their tea, and for uses of the kitchen. Those, however,
who are less delicate on this point make use of the water from the wells in
town, though it be very bad."[24]

The first attempt, in 1774, at supplying water from a public waterworks
failed for various reasons. First, contaminated well water was pumped into
the reservoir, some 40 feet in diameter and 50 feet deep. Also, the bored-log
water mains laid below the surface of the city's streets were inadequate for
the demands by residents. In addition, the American Revolution interrupted
the progress of the project. After the revolution New York City's population
tripled, in thirty years reaching 96,373 persons living on Manhattan Island.

Most were concentrated below Canal Street. Above the present 14th Street, one found woodland with hills and valleys, a few roads, and a clearing here and there for small farms.[25]

Fires and epidemics served as a catalyst for municipal action on the city's unwholesome and inadequate water system. Water for fires was sometimes directed at the blaze by drilling directly into the bored-log pipes, releasing water in great quantities. This proved to be a wasteful technique, since there was no way to control the flow once the fire was either extinguished or had leaped across the drilled logs, forcing the firefighters to abandon their positions. To close the holes, wooden plugs, later to be known as "fireplugs," were driven into the logs. Yet, the amount of available water did not save the city from devastating fires. Cities needed more water, and they needed to be able to deliver it under pressure to a blaze. Fire fighting was stymied by being limited to feeble streams of water pumped by hand from the earliest fire engines. The New York fire of 1776 destroyed almost one-quarter of the city. The fire of 1835:

> leveled twenty blocks and was stopped by blowing up buildings in its path. Before it was extinguished it had destroyed 674 buildings, 530 of which were stores or commercial establishments. Estimates of property loss were as high as $40,000,000. More than fifteen hundred merchants were ruined; several thousand clerks and laborers were thrown out of work. Nearly all the fire insurance companies in the city went bankrupt.[26]

Fouled water and deplorable sanitation exacerbated the filthy conditions that residents encountered each day. The outbreak of infectious disease threatened the city's residents repeatedly. Two thousand died of yellow fever in 1790. Annually, New Yorkers died from cholera and typhoid fever, the worst years being 1798 and 1799. Dr. Joseph Browne, a physician who admonished the Common Council about its failure to provide better sanitation, stated: "it may be laid down as a general rule that the health of a city depends more on its water than all the rest of the eatables and drinkables put together."[27]

New York passed Philadelphia as the nation's largest city in 1810, and it was growing at such an alarming rate that it was feared that all of the well water on Manhattan Island would become polluted. With the New York state legislature giving authority to the city to establish a waterworks, a plan was developed to convey water from the Bronx River across the Harlem River to Manhattan. The city, still without a public waterworks, executed this plan by contracting with the newly formed Manhattan Company to deliver water to the island's residents. Privatized water as opposed to municipal water was the idea of Assemblyman Aaron Burr, who wanted the newly constituted Manhattan Company to function as a financial institution as well as a waterworks. As a bank, the company would be able to use any "surplus capital" in "moneyed transactions."[28]

The impact of joining these dual functions, a water company and a bank, was to deprive New Yorkers of a modern waterworks for the first forty years of the nineteenth century. The Manhattan Company invested in no capital improvements; it took its surplus capital held in the bank that would grow to become Chase Manhattan Bank, and loaned it with interest to private investors. Aside from laying about 40 miles of bored-wood water mains through city streets, which it was required to do in order to fulfill the requirements of its charter with the city, the company did little to bring clean water to Manhattan. In fact, residents complained that the company extended service to residents very slowly while it left city streets torn up for months. Instead of constructing conduits to bring clean Bronx River water to residents, the company, using a steam engine, pumped water from an existing well.

Manhattan Company water smelled bad and tasted even worse. Many residents would drink it only with whiskey, perhaps an excuse for drinking by some, but an indication of the water's foul taste. Vendors regularly sold spring water door to door to householders in need of clean water, at an average cost of $273.75 per year. Smell and taste were one thing; disease was another. In 1835, a cholera epidemic struck New York. It killed 3,500 residents and caused almost half of the city's 202,589 residents to flee the city. Although the "germ theory of disease" was decades away in terms of professional and public acceptance, human and animal refuse were thought to be the source of organisms carrying diseases. With as many as 150,000 residents dependent on well water, it is clear why disease spread through the city's population so rapidly. Sanitary conditions in Manhattan offer a ready explanation:

> ... scientists in 1830 estimated one hundred tons of human excrement were being put into the porous soil of lower Manhattan Island daily. New York City then had a population of 202,589. There was no citywide sewer system. Privies, cesspools, and open pits were the only provisions for disposal. In addition to this seepage of human excrement contaminating the wells, there was the seepage from graveyards and the drainage from stables and the filthy streets. Dead animals and offal were carelessly disposed of with no notion that such refuse might become the host of disease-breeding organisms. The stench arising from the streets was appalling. Travelers frequently declared they could smell the city two or three miles away.[29]

The opposition of the Manhattan Company to any waterworks improvements was overcome by the devastating effects of the cholera epidemic during the summer months of 1832 and by the report commissioned by the city's Common Council in the same year in regard to new sources of fresh water for the city, written by Colonel DeWitt Clinton, Jr., a civil engineer. The Croton River, almost 40 miles away, was recommended as a source of continuous fresh water for the city. In Clinton's words: "This supply may . . . be considered as inexhaustible, as it is not all probable that the city will ever require more than it can provide."[30] The Council's acceptance of Clinton's recommendations placed New York City on the road to a plentiful, pure, wholesome, and cheap source of water into the early years of the twentieth century. Later, the city would reach further away, to the Catskill Mountains, for its water.

The proposal to send Croton River water to New York City required the construction of a masonry and earth dam about 270 feet long and about 50 feet high. Croton Lake, about 400 acres in total area, was created by the dam. The lake had a holding capacity of 600 million gallons and provided 36 million gallons to New York City's 300,000 residents each day. The Croton Aqueduct, a closed stone conduit, built to carry water to the city, was thought to be one of the engineering marvels of the nineteenth century. Extending from the dam at the mouth of the Croton River to the north side of the Harlem River, the water was carried across the river at High Bridge, built specifically for the aqueduct, in 8–foot diameter wrought-iron pipes. The Aqueduct then continued from the south side of the Harlem River into Manhattan to a reservoir at Murray Hill, the present location of the New York Public Library. At a total cost of almost $5.5 million the Croton System provided the city with most of its water from 1842 to 1890.

Before New York could reap the benefits of a plentiful water supply, which not only provided residents with wholesome drinking water but also with the volume sufficient to fight fires, in 1835 the city was ravaged by its worst fire. On December 17, the merchant Philip Hone, a former city mayor, wrote in his diary:

> How shall I record the events of last night, or how attempt to describe the most awful calamity which has ever visited these United States? The greatest loss by fire that has ever been known. . . . I am fatigued in body, disturbed in mind, and my fancy filled with images of horror which my pen is inadequate to describe. Nearly one-half of the first ward is in ashes, five hundred to seven hundred stores, which with their contents are valued at $20,000,000 to $40,000,000 are now lying in an indistinguishable mass of ruins. There is not, perhaps in the world the same space of ground covered by so great an amount of real and personal property as the scene of this dreadful conflagration.[31]

In addition, the public response to the new supply of pure and plentiful water was to consume more and more. Per capita daily consumption jumped from 30 to 78 gallons. Excessive use placed extraordinary demands on the city's reservoirs and the Croton delivery system. Water shortages became a common experience for New Yorkers. The city's Department of Public Works, which had replaced the private Manhattan Company, and the Croton Aqueduct Department responded in two ways. The former initiated a policy of placing water meters in stores, factories, hotels, other business establishments, and public buildings to curtail water usage. The latter built more dams, tapped the Bronx River and streams further north, and began construction of an aqueduct three times the size of Old Croton.

Metering water was initiated in buildings that served the public. As the city's public works commissioner pointed out in his 1880 report, "One large hotel which on the first application of a meter was found to be consuming, or rather wasting, 115,000 gallons of water daily was reduced to 45,000 gallons."[32] The failure to meter water consumption in private households, however, caused repeated shortages. Instead of being based on use, the water rates for private dwellings were based on the measured frontage of one's property. Since property, not consumption, was the basis for water rates, consumers still left taps running, especially in winter to prevent frozen pipes, and failed to repair leaking pipes and dripping faucets.

The city also added about 50,000 people through immigration and annexation of land and property each year. In response, the city constructed approximately 30,000 buildings yearly in the last two decades of the nineteenth century. This population and building boom placed an enormous burden on the city's public works. The city simply couldn't keep up with the rapid increase, despite efforts to curtail water consumption. The annexation of Brooklyn in 1898, at the time the seventh largest city in the nation, placed additional burdens on services, despite the added property tax revenues collected by New York City. By 1898, the city's boundaries expanded to include much of the Bronx, and all of Brooklyn, Queens, and Richmond boroughs. The population had swelled to 3.5 million people, consuming 372 million gallons of water each day. Increased immigration along with annexations increased New York City's population by another 1.25 million between 1900 and 1910.[33] In 1873, the Croton Aqueduct Department, with authority from the state, constructed dams at Boyd's Corner, along the West Branch of the Croton, creating a reservoir of more than 2.75 million gallons of water. In subsequent years, the department placed additional dams across Rye Pond and the Bronx, Byram, and Wampus rivers making one billion gallons of pure water available to the residents of New York City by the turn of the century.

The city's advantageous location, just south of and just lower than the water resources of Westchester and Putnam counties to the north, proved essential to New York City's growth. In both northern counties there were once "thirty-one lakes and ponds fed by springs and rivers at an elevation sufficient to provide a gravity flow to the heart of the city. The water from this enormous watershed was pure and immediately usable without filtration. The supply was ample for years to come—if it was not allowed to escape."[34] The major objective of the Croton Aqueduct Department with the assistance of the State of New York was to manage this watershed, contain its runoff, dam its rivers, divert its flow into reservoirs, and deliver its bounty to the growing metropolis. All of the dams, flooded areas, and conduits, in the form of aqueducts, pipes, and siphons, worked because of advances in construction technology and the use of new fast-drying, durable cement. In the process of such building, the ecology of the region, the composition of its soil, its forests and wildlife, and its aquatic life were changed forever. Damming prevented free-flowing rivers from carrying soil downstream. As a result, the bottom of the dams became laden with silt, salt, and other minerals. The natural habitat for waterfowl along the river and stream banks and for fish in the rivers and streams was damaged or destroyed.

The search for more water continued, however. With each passing year in the last decade of the nineteenth century, a new dam, more modern in its technological and structural engineering, was brought into service. As one writer noted: "It is not unreasonable to assert that the construction of the Croton system of dams sparked the widespread system of dams that began in the United States at this time. At any rate, New York City was the outstanding pioneer in this country in this field of engineering."[35] In 1906, the new Croton dam and aqueduct began delivering water to the city. The reservoir created by the dam was 19 miles long with a storage capacity of almost 34 million gallons. The new system completely overshadowed the Old Croton aqueduct; in fact, the old dam was completely submerged beneath the new reservoir.

As the city entered the new century, however, conservation of existing water supplies was never considered by most New Yorkers as an alternative to finding new sources. The earlier century's "habit of wasteful water use," a phrase used by the Croton Aqueduct Commission's chief engineer, Alphonse Fteley, was as applicable as ever. Per capita use in New York exceeded 100 gallons daily, and the antiquated system of exempting private dwellings from metering remained in effect. In such an environment, the only solution was to develop new distant sources of supply beyond the Croton watershed. The Catskill Mountains, a retreat for many New Yorkers, became the ultimate source of supply. Some of the Catskill's summer residents were so impressed by the quality of the water from Catskill springs and ponds that they had it bottled and delivered to them in the city.

Built between 1907 and 1917 and fully operational in 1928, the Catskill water system consisted of four large reservoirs and 126 miles of aqueduct counting the 18 miles of City Tunnel No. 1, completed in 1917, much of which was bored through solid rock below the Harlem and East Rivers and some of Manhattan Island. To hold the water once it arrived in the vicinity of the city, a 36–inch pipeline was placed under the Narrows, leading to Silver Lake Reservoir on Staten Island.[37] Combined, the Croton and Catskill systems provided the city with 870 million gallons of water daily, with the new Catskill operation providing 614 million gallons of the total. City Tunnel No. 2 was completed in 1937. Despite conflicts with Pennsylvania over the diversion of Delaware River water, the inclusion of this river system increased the daily amount available to city residents to over one billion gallons, which turned out to be the amount used in 1949. The supply and demand curves for water always intersected. Fears about probable water shortages resulted again in searches for new supplies, not water conservation.

In 1997, the city opened Tunnel No. 3, connecting the Brooklyn and Queens boroughs. The new tunnel allowed the city to inspect Tunnels Nos. 1 and 2 for the first time since they had gone into service in 1917 and 1937 respectively. Because of the demands placed on them for water, neither had ever been shut down for inspection. Shutting them down for inspection would have required engineers to close the huge valves leading to the tunnels. Since the population of the city had soared since the completion of these original tunnels, both now carried more than 60 percent more water than they had been designed to transport. During days with the greatest demand, as much as 1.5 billion gallons of water flowed from the system's reservoirs to the city. Once Tunnel No. 3 becomes fully operational, Nos. 1 and 2 will be closed, inspected, and repaired where necessary. Then they will be put back into service, and construction of three additional tunnels will commence, with completion dates for all three set for the year 2020.

Throughout the nineteenth century, New Yorkers increased their daily consumption of water. Indoor plumbing, particularly the introduction of the flush toilet in the 1860s, followed by the bathtub and shower, promoted personal hygiene. Beginning in the later nineteenth century and extending well into the twentieth century, the "germ theory of disease" became the impetus for personal hygiene such as washing hands and food, and boiling bottles and milk. These activities required the use of water. At the same time, sewer systems, which used ample amounts of water, were built to dispose of the waste. Also, with the knowledge that objectionable microorganisms were

The Progress of Water Tunnel No. 3, *New York Times Graphics,* **The New York Times Company, 229 West 43rd Street, 9th Fl, New York City 10036.**

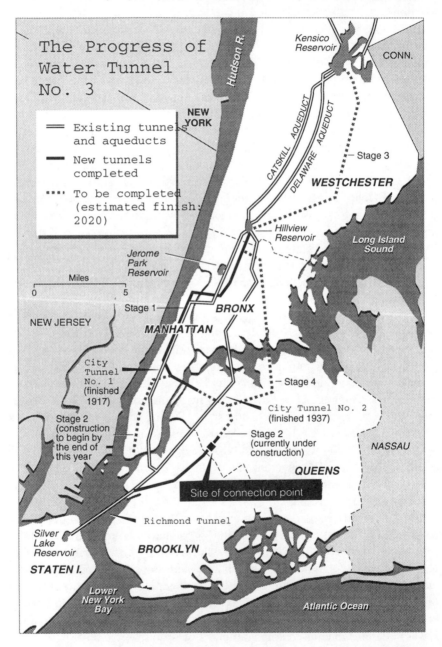

the causes of typhoid fever and cholera in the last decades of the nineteenth century, water treatment became customary. First, municipalities used slow and then fast sand filtration. In 1912, chlorine and copper sulfate were used for the first time. As a result, life expectancy began its dramatic rise. In 1900, U.S. life expectancy was 49 years of age; today it is 76. The existence of safe or pure water encouraged the use of tap water for cooking and bathing. It was also cheap and plentiful for most consumers. As a result, waste was encouraged in New York and in other large and small communities.

Philadelphia

Philadelphia experienced similar needs for ample cheap water for drinking, cooking, disease prevention, and fire protection as other growing cities in the early years of the country's history. As other cities did, Philadelphia faced conflicts over private versus public control of its waterworks. The outcome of this controversy in Philadelphia was settled through public referendums and the weight of public opinion, through which the citizenry expressed its willingness to support the construction and maintenance of public waterworks with taxes. The experience of Philadelphians was similar to that of New Yorkers and Bostonians in the manner in which they faced their respective water crises. The crises bore similar characteristics. None of these early cities possessed a central water supply; residents either drilled wells on their property or collected water from the wells located in the public squares. Volunteer fire brigades, hampered by the inefficiencies of fighting fires with buckets and low-pressure hand pumps, sprang into action whenever a fire broke out. Great epidemics threatened the vitality of each city. In their wake, the epidemics left a population of survivors weakened, frightened, and demoralized by the death toll and the fear of the next unexpected outbreak. A growing population in each city turned refreshing well water into a foul-tasting and -smelling liquid, contaminated by unsealed privies and piles of manure and excrement that were allowed to seep into the groundwater.

In 1790, Philadelphia was the new nation's largest city, with about three hundred public pumps and wells and many more private ones for a population of 43,000; New York City had 10,000 fewer residents. Philadelphia thus faced all the urban environmental ravages associated with massive human concentrations and a natural carrying capacity problem, along with bottomless demands for water and the disposal of wastes. Fortunately, Philadelphia lay between the Delaware River on the east and the Schuylkill River to the west. Of the two, only the tidal Delaware was contaminated with sea water. The western Schuylkill was far enough away and elevated enough for it to be protected from the sea. However, early nineteenth-century proposals to build a canal connecting both rivers for the purpose of delivering water to the city failed. Private investors and elected officials who could provide public finance could not reach agreement on the capital investment required for such an ambitious undertaking or the eventual monetary gains, if the canal were to become operational.

The proposed quasi-public canal project to be funded with both private and pubic money was abandoned for a publicly financed plan to pump water, using a steam engine, from the Schuylkill River. The Philadelphia waterworks:

> had its source in a marble-paved basin, eighty-four feet wide and two hundred feet long, extending eastward from the Schuylkill River at the foot of Chestnut Street. . . . From its primary basin the water passed . . . into a second and somewhat smaller basin and then into an oval-shaped tunnel, three hundred feet long, cut through solid rock nearly the whole distance. From this, the water emptied into a well ten feet in diameter and thirty-nine feet deep.
>
> Above this well stood the so-called Lower Engine House, which raised the water into a brick tunnel six feet in diameter and 3,144 feet in length, extending . . . to the Centre Square, or Upper, Engine House. Here the water was pumped fifty feet from the bed of the tunnel, into two wooden tanks with a total capacity of over twenty thousand gallons.[37]

From this point in Centre Square, where City Hall is located now, connected 4–inch wooden water mains began carrying water through the city's central streets in January 1801. Problems with the new waterworks surfaced almost immediately. The pumping engines could not keep up with the demands of a growing city, and when they malfunctioned, the city was left without water from a central source.

The original waterworks lasted less than twenty years. By 1822, a new waterworks became operational, with a dam of about 900 feet in width, built of logs, earth, and stone diagonally across the Schuylkill. The river's reputation for floods required engineers to construct a barrier to control such unpredictable events. A diagonal dam across the river created an overfall of 1,200 feet as a precaution against the dam being broken through by a flood. The effect of this dam was to back the river upstream for six miles.[38] Six water wheels lifted water up into the city's four reservoirs, which held upwards of 22 million gallons of water. Within eight years, ten thousand Philadelphians were receiving water from the new works, paying a flat rate of between five and ten dollars a year. Average daily use passed 2 million gallons in 1830. By 1837, "98 3/4 miles of iron pipes had been laid, 19,678 tenants were supplied with 3,122,164 gallons of water daily. . . . 1,492 Philadelphians enjoyed the luxury of bathrooms with running water; three thousand citizens, on the other hand, still patronized the free pumps in the streets."[39]

The delivery of pure and plentiful water represented a level of success achieved by Philadelphia early in the nineteenth century and nowhere else. Boston had ignored the upstream waters of the Charles as a source of supply, and New York had done the same with the Bronx and Harlem rivers. Both looked further away for a supply in order to guarantee its purity. New Yorkers at this time were also struggling with public versus private control of the waterworks. By 1850, however, Philadelphians used about 5 million gallons of water per day, while its reservoirs contained a supply for only three days. The continuing population growth of the city, and the potential for floods and droughts which could cripple water wheels and pumps, left the city and its residents at risk. As in Boston, New York, and other cities, improvements in the waterworks were necessary to prevent a breakdown in municipal services.

To alleviate the growing demand on the main sources of water supply, the Schuylkill and Delaware rivers, Philadelphians built additional reservoirs and more powerful pumping stations, and proposed impounding water as far as twenty-five miles upstream. All but the last solution were implemented in the last quarter of the nineteenth century. As the city's population continued to grow and outlying areas became populated, Philadelphia faced the startling reality that its drinking water was becoming contaminated with sewage. Each year the "destroying angel," typhoid fever, visited the city and "annual epidemics . . . gave grim warning to the citizens that to continue to drink their untreated water was to invite death."[40]

In the following years, Philadelphians and residents of others cities who drew their water from rivers and nearby lakes and streams changed their view that nature would continue to supply a unlimited amount of wholesome water. Between 1881 and 1900, Philadelphia's annual typhoid fever death rate never dropped below 35 per 100,000 and was often above 70. In 1906, at a time when the city had begun to construct filtration plants, 1,063 persons died of the fever in Philadelphia, representing a high death rate of 80 persons for every 100,000 residents.

Women's clubs across the country were among the most ardent groups initiating urban water reform policies at the turn of the century. In Philadelphia, the Women's Health Protective Association became important in getting the city to clean up its polluted water supply. One of thousands of local women's clubs across the country, the Philadelphia Association, founded in 1893 with more than 100,000 members in the 1890s, was active in efforts to build drinking water filtration plants and centralized sewer systems.[41] In the words of one historian, late nineteenth century Philadelphia had become:

one great cesspool. . . . The filth of the city littered the streets and the banks of the creeks, which eventually found its way into the drinking water of the city. . . . The garbage, the refuse and the sewage that overflowed the streets, the manure of the thousands of horses left behind by the street cleaners on poorly paved streets, washed into the open creeks and culverts which by-passed the intercepting sewers that were designed to carry sewage below the Fairmont Pool, the site of the city's water source.[42]

The Philadelphia Association hired Allen Hazen, an expert on water filtration from Boston, to study the Philadelphia situation and make recommendations for improvement of the city's drinking water problem. Hazen recommended sand filtration as the answer to the city's contaminated water. Although the association urged the city in 1897 to adopt Hazen's plan, not until 1911 was filtered water supplied to residents throughout the city.[43]

About the same time, Philadelphia, following the lead of Jersey City, New Jersey, began to use liquid chlorine as a method for purifying drinking water drawn from its two major rivers. Throughout the early decades of the twentieth century, Philadelphia continued to filter and chlorinate its drinking water. Although safe, its water became notorious for its smell and poor taste. Not until after 1945 did the city begin to increase its water supply, taking more water from the upper Delaware River, thus further removing the supply from potential sources of contamination nearer to the city. As a result, the Schuylkill River, badly compromised by city sewage, became a secondary source of supply.

Chicago

Midwestern cities, particularly those in the Great Lakes region, and including Chicago, possessed a readily available supply of drinking water. Unlike many cities in the East, which had to transport their water great distances by aqueduct and tunnel, many midwestern cities drew their water from one of the Great Lakes. However, since the lakes also received sewage from these and neighboring cities, outbreaks of disease became commonplace. Cholera and typhoid epidemics, in particular, became more severe and long lasting as sewage carrying pathogenic microbes continued to pour into the lakes from which drinking water was drawn.

Most Chicagoans during the city's early history depended on residential wells, cisterns, and public pumps located in the city's growing neighborhoods. The Chicago Hydraulic Company, a small, privately owned waterworks serving a limited clientele, began operations in 1842. Using an antiquated system of pumps and pipes, it drew water from the contaminated Chicago River. After the cholera epidemic of 1852, the Chicago Hydraulic

Company stopped operations, and the city assumed control of its water supply by drawing water from Lake Michigan. The city tried to avoid the "domestic sewage, fat and animal carcasses, steel and coke-making wastes such as quenching liquors, acids, phenols, benzene, tars, oils and iron fines" that were dumped into the Chicago River, which in turn flowed into the lake, by locating its intake pipe some 600 feet from the shoreline.[44]

Chicago functioned for decades without filtration plants to purify Lake Michigan water and without sewage treatment facilities to keep dangerous bacteria out of the lake. The lake had become the city's "ultimate sink" along with the Chicago River, used by industries along its course to dump untreated wastes. The environmental damage done to the river by the slaughterhouses, tanneries, breweries, and gasworks who dumped their solid and liquid wastes into the river was noted by a citizen during an epidemic in 1864. "That a city of nearly two hundred thousand inhabitants ... should quietly permit a river running through its entire limits to be converted into a gigantic sewer ... here red with blood, there slimy with grease, and black with filth and putrid matter, turning what is itself a noble and beautiful object into a sight so foul and loathsome as to excite only thoughts of a 'River of Death' is a matter of profound astonishment."[45] To eliminate the contamination of the lake caused by the flow of sewage in the river, city officials contemplated a plan to reverse the flow of the Chicago River from Lake Michigan to the Mississippi River.

First, Chicago needed to build a new sewer system. Beginning in the 1850s and finishing within a decade, Chicago had constructed the first comprehensive sewer system in the United States. The new system, drained by gravity, required elevating the city. Engineers laid sewer pipes at a high enough level to achieve gravitational flow, packed them with fill dredged from the Chicago River, and constructed new streets above them. Once it was completed, the new combined sewer system carried storm water and sewage into the Chicago River. As the river's pollution became a threat to the city's water supply, the need to reverse the flow became crucial. Before undertaking the digging of the world's largest canal for sewage and shipping, Chicagoans were encouraged by the thought of the potential benefits from such a project, the most important of which was the protection of its Lake Michigan water supply.

It is important to note that the Chicago River was connected to the Des Plaines River in the west by a small lake filled to capacity during the rainy season. In addition, a canal, built to divert sewage from the Chicago River to the Illinois River, was completed in 1848. The canal was fed by the Des Plaines River and also connected Lake Michigan to the Illinois River. As a result, the canal allowed traffic between the lake and the Chicago River. It did not take much for the engineers to consider the possibility of enlarging and deepening the Lake Michigan–Illinois River Canal and by a series of pumping stations reversing the flow of the Chicago River. By 1871, the pumping stations became operational and the reverse flow of the river became continuous regardless of the amount of rainfall.

By 1880 the diversion canal became overwhelmed by domestic and industrial waste. For decades, Chicago's political leaders and business elite had refused to assume the costs of water filtration and sewage treatment, appealing to the public to boil its water during epidemics. In 1889, the Metropolitan Sanitary District (MSD) was created to address the pollution problem. Initially, the MSD chose to enlarge the size of the sewage diversion canal to carry waste to the Illinois River, far enough away from Chicago to protect the city's inhabitants. In the two-year period from 1890 to 1892, however, typhoid fever took 4,494 lives, and the city's death rate from infectious disease climbed to 159 persons for every 100,000 residents.[46] In 1900 the Sanitary and Ship Canal was opened; and after hearing evidence about the harmful health effects of dangerous microbes, the city's aldermen approved the use of hypochlorite (bleaching powder) in two of the pipes taking drinking water from Lake Michigan. Substantial declines in the number of typhoid cases proved without a doubt the remarkable success of this form of treatment. In 1908 Chicago became the first city to chlorinate sewage, and by 1918 the city's water was treated with the chemical, reducing deaths caused by typhoid to a total of 38 for the year.[47]

Atlanta

In the American South recovering from the ravages of the Civil War, the experience of Atlanta, Georgia, followed a pattern similar to that of other American cities drawing their water from inland rivers. In 1870, with a population of about 20,000, the city built its own waterworks, after two commercial companies failed to meet the city's growing fire-fighting and industrial needs. The waterworks drew water from Atlanta's South River, which flowed below the city's downtown district. When completed in 1876, the waterworks distributed water over an 8–mile area by way of a single 16–inch pipe from one pumping station. However, the waterworks was constructed only for the city's safety and commercial needs, and never provided residents with an adequate supply of water. Its more affluent citizens purchased water from upland springs, while the city's less fortunate, living in the lowland sections of Atlanta, used water from local wells. As in other cities, these wells were fouled by the drainage flowing from the upland districts of the city.

By the last decade of the nineteenth century, water shortages and contamination had reached critical levels in the city. Atlanta abandoned the
South River for the safe mountain water of the Chattahoochee River. With a
pumping station and a 176–million-gallon reservoir, 3 1/2 miles from the
city, the new system began operating in September 1893. The river water
was safe but filled with red clay and sand particles. As a result, it had to be
treated and filtered before it could be consumed by Atlantans. As in many
other American cities, demand for cheap water far outran the supply. In
1908, 40 percent of the population survived without modern sanitation facilities—no water mains and no sewers. The city also lacked a sewage
treatment facility. For a city without a modern sanitation infrastructure, the
effects were predictable. In 1910, Atlanta had the second highest death rate
from typhoid fever in the country, 62 persons for every 100,000 people.
With the construction of sewage treatment plants, water purification facilities, sewer pipes and water lines, the fortune of Atlanta's citizens changed
significantly in the second decade of the century. Typhoid rates dropped as
low as 17 per 100,000 residents.[48]

Water Works, Sewage Treatment, and Public Health

Increased water availability led to a rapid growth in consumption. Many
cities saw their water usage expand three or four times in a period of twenty
to thirty years. From a very few waterworks located in Philadelphia, New
York, Boston, Detroit, and Cincinnati, the number of waterworks in the
United States continued to increase unabated through the first eighty years
of the nineteenth century. By 1860, the nation's sixteen largest cities had
waterworks, and twenty years later the number of municipalities with waterworks had increased to 598.[49] While there were as many as 600 waterworks by the 1880s, there was no simultaneous development of sewer
systems to carry away the waste-bearing water. Sewer systems that did exist
were designed primarily to carry away storm water, not household effluent.
Cities that built combined sewer systems for storm water and household
wastes learned that the high volume of wastewater, especially after the
public's enthusiastic acceptance of the flush toilet, made treatment and
recovery expensive. (Previously, these toilets had flooded the outdoor privies and cesspools to which they were connected, adding to the municipal
health risks.) By 1880 about one-quarter of urban households possessed
flush toilets.[50]

Brooklyn, Chicago, and Jersey City built the first municipal sewer systems in the 1850s. By 1910, the nation's municipalities had constructed
18,361 miles of combined sewers, 5,258 miles of sewers for the disposal of

human waste, and 1,352 miles of storm water sewers. Smaller cities built separate sanitary sewers and allowed the storm water to run over the land to be absorbed by the ground. Since storm water needed to be diverted away from the heavy traffic of city streets and human waste needed to be kept away from the drinking water supply, larger cities generally built combined sewers for storm water and human waste.[51]

Where did the waste carried away from these cities by the new sewer systems go? By 1910, 88 percent was disposed of in waterways—the rivers, streams, and lakes—without treatment. The effect of this dumping was to contaminate the supply of downstream drinking water; this was the way that downstream Philadelphians suffered from those who contaminated the upstream Schuylkill. In this instance it was argued that the self-purifying nature of running water had not been allowed to have its effect, since "upstream" Philadelphians lived too close to the "downstream" Philadelphians.

The "purifying nature" argument remained the principal justification for dumping sewage into the waterways well past the time when microbiologists had discovered a new and powerful scientific explanation for the outbreaks of cholera and typhoid in downstream communities. In the 1880s, the German scientist Dr. Robert Koch isolated the bacteria that caused tuberculosis. The isolation of other bacteria followed, including those carried in contaminated water such as the cholera, typhoid, and diphtheria bacteria. For a while, the germ theory of disease coexisted with the theory that disease was spread by miasmas or putrid air emanating from decaying organic material and inhaled by humans. If one cleaned up the surrounding environment of this filth, then the spreading of disease would be curtailed. Identifying specific microbes as the cause of contagious disease did not seem to nullify efforts to clean up the environment because the piles of decaying matter that caused miasma were breeding areas for microbes in many instances. Ultimately, however, the germ theory proved to be so powerful as an explanation for the spread of disease that it required significant changes in disease prevention and treatment.[52]

Some cities, including Boston, New York, Newark, and Jersey City, reached far beyond their familiar boundaries to a distant and protected watershed for pure and wholesome water. In other cities, particularly those that drew their water downstream from other cities, filtration was required to eliminate deadly bacteria. Once the germ theory of disease was accepted and water was tested for purity before use, those American cities that either filtered their water, chlorinated it, or went to a protected watershed experienced a dramatic decline in deaths due to drinking water contaminated with sewage. Death from typhoid fever declined from an average of 58 per 100,000 in 1889 to less than one death per 100,000 in 1938.[53] *For a de-*

scription about the need for clean water, read the excerpt from a speech given by George C. Whipple in 1911, the year he was appointed by Harvard University as its first professor of sanitary engineering. This appears as document 3.2.

A revolution had occurred. Pure drinking water and pasteurized milk contributed greatly to improved health. Eliminating the breeding places of disease-carrying flies by moving piles of manure away from households, and by installing window and door screens, provided added protection.* Advances in water filtration and sewage treatment restored public confidence in local water supplies. Cities began the continuous chlorination of their urban water supplies to disinfect suspicious water. Renewed confidence in the water supply led to increased bathing, flushing, and general household use. As a result, however, eastern, midwestern, and southern cities faced the seemingly insurmountable task of locating new sources of water and purifying existing supplies throughout the decades of the twentieth century. With population growth and increased household water use on a per capita basis, a lengthy list of discarded domestic and industrial wastes entered the nation's streams and rivers on a scale previously unknown. Water quality deteriorated and aquatic life suffered, as the pressure continued to build more dams and aqueducts, divert more rivers, and alter the ecological balance of the environment in search of new sources of fresh water.

By the beginning of the twentieth century, forty-four states and territories had passed laws to limit water pollution. Yet few of them empowered state agencies with regulations to penalize polluters. Legislators in Connecticut, Massachusetts, Minnesota, New Hampshire, New Jersey, New York, and Vermont had enacted restrictive laws. For decades New England textile and paper mills had been accustomed to flushing sewage, dyes, and acids into the region's water system. The rivers of Massachusetts had been surveyed in 1876 by water quality expert and civil engineer James P. Kirkwood, who judged that the river water was "not merely repulsive or suspicious, but more or less dangerous for family use."[54] By the turn of the century, the Massachusetts Board of Health possessed considerable power.

---

*The common housefly is a perfect carrier of disease. Its intestines hold about 40 million bacteria, which it regurgitates frequently. In addition, flies give off sticky secretions that contain another 6 million bacteria. These secretions allow them to walk on the walls and ceilings of our living space. Recently, Dr. Peter Grubel of St. Elizabeth's Medical Center in Boston, Massachusetts, discovered that flies carry *Heliobacter pylori,* the bacterium causing most ulcers. They pick up *H. pylori* from human waste and deposit it on food. Countries with the poorest sanitation have the highest rates of *H. pylori.* ("What's That Fly Doing in My Soup?" *Newsweek,* July 28, 1997, 77.)

It established drinking water quality standards and reported annually to the legislature, recommending "measures for the prevention of pollution . . . and for the removal of polluting substances."[55] Most of the other states collected information, filed reports, and did little else.

At the federal level the passage of the Rivers and Harbors Act of 1899 prohibited lumber mills from dumping sawdust, which late nineteenth-century sportsmen claimed polluted the waterways and destroyed fish and their habitat. Sportsmen maintained that sawdust clogged the gills of fish, covered their spawning beds, "and that turpentine from pine shavings and tannin from oak killed eggs."[56] Four years after the Act's passage, however, Congress retreated and instructed federal agencies to limit their enforcement of the law to only polluted water "flowing from streets, sewers, and passing therefrom in a liquid state."[57] The Refuse Act of 1899 prohibited dumping into navigable waters. In 1912 Congress authorized the Public Health Service to conduct research on water pollution caused by sewage in navigable waters. The following year the Surgeon General of the United States appealed for federal controls over the growing contamination of interstate waterways. In 1924 the Oil Pollution Act prohibited oil discharge in coastal waters.[58]

Passing regulatory legislation at the federal level was mostly symbolic, however, despite growing awareness of water pollution. Uneven enforcement or no enforcement at all left most of the regulatory responsibility to local and state governments. Until the new environmental movement of the late 1960s and 1970s, federal agencies considered pollution only when it threatened navigation of the nation's waterways. Even then, the federal government ignored pollution problems in the navigable waterways that crossed state boundaries and it "ignored jurisdictional conflicts between states of the arid West over water rights."[59]

The West

As migration spread inland through the Midwest, to the semi-arid Great Plains and beyond to the western desert, settlers in the form of miners, ranchers, and farmers became preoccupied with the ownership of water. The Great Plains have been described as:

> [a] broad topographic plain with a semi-arid climate, grassland ecology, and an agricultural economy. Its most important climatic characteristics are its dryness and the unpredictability of the weather. For over a century, agricultural settlement has caused massive transformations in the region, with the eventual establishment of a vast dryland farming system for the production of grain.[60]

Climatic extremes, dry heat, and a parched landscape characterize the central high plains of the region. *In order to gain an understanding of the arid regions of the country, read document 3.3, a report by John Wesley Powell, explorer and government official of the late nineteenth century.*

Once bison were driven to the brink of extinction in the years after the Civil War, ranchers established their cattle empire on the Plains. After 1886, small family farmers came into the region to take advantage of the federal government's policy of giving away public land. The extensive use of barbed wire defined boundaries and restricted cattle grazing. The widespread use of economical windmills to draw groundwater to the surface converted much of the land to agriculture. As one historian has pointed out: "By the 1920s the region had been divided into thousands of relatively small family farms that grew one crop—wheat, as farmers converted the plains from an area of grasslands to one of cropland."[61] The region's population peaked in 1930.

Technological innovations including John Deere's steel shear plow and Cyrus McCormick's mechanical reaper were invented to overcome the adversities of farming the semi-arid Plains. The shear plow "busted the sod," breaking through the soil held in place by the thick-rooted multi-varied grasses of the Plains. The reaper cut across the wheat fields, mechanically cutting the harvest. No surface technology, however, would do for these Plains what tapping the vast groundwater Ogallala aquifer would do for agricultural productivity.*

Until 1910, farmers on the Plains drew small amounts of groundwater to the surface using windmills. However, western settlers were not the first to irrigate the Plains. As early as eight hundred years ago about 100,000 acres had been irrigated in the American Southwest by Hohokam Indians. They used "an elaborate 135 mile network of canals, many of them carved through tough volcanic outcroppings and lined with clay to prevent seepage. Other irrigators, including the Subaipuris and Pimas, succeeded the Hohokam civilization, which vanished around 1400."[62] After 1910, internal combustion engines and electric motors eliminated the need for windmills. Motors powered large capacity pumps that delivered a continuous volume of water to farms. The discovery of natural gas fields in the region provided a readily available source of energy for the pumps. A cheap energy source

---

*The Ogallala aquifer, a vast underground water resource created by retreating glaciers during the last stages of the Ice Age, extends from the Oklahoma–Texas panhandle north through eastern New Mexico to southwestern Kansas and eastern Colorado, covering almost the entire state of Nebraska plus eastern Wyoming and south-central South Dakota.

coupled with high capacity water pumps to raise water in the aquifers to the surface allowed farmers to extend their farmland further away from river valleys and water basins.[63]

Although farmers abandoned the Plains in the 1930s in the wake of the "Dust Bowl," one of history's catastrophic environmental disasters, advances in irrigation technology expanded rapidly across the Great Plains and into California and the Pacific Northwest. The advent of sprinkler technology in the 1950s extended the reach of farmers far beyond the water sources and allowed them to apply uniform amounts of water to the land. The invention of the center-pivot sprinkler expanded irrigation at an annual rate of 500,000 acres.[64] Today, pumping water out of the ground to irrigate crops accounts for nearly one-half of the nation's annual withdrawal of groundwater. As one historian of the West has noted: "Each year farmers pump from the Ogallala aquifer of the Great Plains more [water] than the entire flow of the Colorado River. That resource, left over from Pleistocene times, once the largest natural storage system of its kind anywhere, now has a life expectancy of about forty years."[65]

Water Rights

Beyond the land of the Ogallala aquifer lay more arid land and desert. There struggles for water became commonplace. The doctrine of prior appropriation gave preferential treatment to those miners, ranchers, and farmers who arrived first and established ownership. The doctrine included the concept of "beneficial use," which allowed owners to divert water from its natural course for irrigating the land for agricultural productivity, mining, and commercial activity, and later for western cities. The question of who owns western water and how much one pays for its use has come to dominate our thinking about the West today; yet, the region is as diverse and as fragmented as any other region of the country.

Although much of the West is arid, much is also covered by mountains and some of it receives abundant rainfall, including the Northwest's "great Pacific rain forest." Although water irrigates much farmland, dry-farming continues in large parts of the region. Although the size and scale of the West's public works projects—dams, canals, and aqueducts—during the twentieth century dwarf their nineteenth-century eastern and midwestern counterparts, those earlier projects, including the construction of the Erie Canal and the Croton Aqueduct system, were for their time engineering and construction feats.[66] Despite the West's diversity, disputes over water rights involving ownership and use became important features of the region's late nineteenth- and twentieth-century history.

The doctrine of prior appropriation gave owners the right to deny any users who lived downstream rights to water by diverting it for any purpose. If this policy were carried to its extreme, owners who claimed priority could deny water to downstream users. The concept of prior appropriation originated with mining rights. Western miners determined the source of the water they desired and then posted their claim to it and recorded that claim with the local land office. According to this practice the first person who came upon a stream had a prior right to exploit it. In practice this meant that: "A seniority system developed of which the basic principle was 'first in time, first in right.' "[67] Thus the origins of this doctrine did not emerge from disputes over irrigation but from the California Gold Rush:

> The discovery of gold in the Sierra foothills of California in January 1848 and the great mining industry that followed had a profound influence, not only upon the political and economic growth of California, but upon the development of water law in the state and throughout the West. The association of gold and water came about because much of the gold was extracted from the ground by means of hydraulic or placer mining processes in which the use of water was essential. Rights to the use of water therefore became fundamentally important.[68]

Appropriators could divert water to any place for reasonable beneficial use, an argument over the meaning of the term "reasonable beneficial use" often brought a waterway's many users into conflict. The principle of riparian or riverbank rights was the second part of the system of water rights. The riparian doctrine was brought by early English settlers to the east coast colonies, where water was plentiful and available to most settlers. Riparian owners could use water along their riverbanks for household and livestock use and to power waterwheels, but they could not reduce its flow or pollute it to the point where it was unusable to those downstream.[69]

The rules of right to ownership and use of water in the West developed as a complex system ranging from the doctrines of prior appropriation and riparian rights, which became the fault lines of water disputes in California, to state ownership and distribution of water in nineteenth-century Wyoming. Between these opposites, namely individual control of water as a right of property in California to state control in Wyoming, existed a range of water policies practiced by other western states.* Western states experi-

---

*Presently, nine western states adhere to the prior appropriation doctrine: Alaska, Arizona, Colorado, Idaho, Montana, Nevada, New Mexico, Utah, and Wyoming; while a dual system of prior appropriation and riparian rights exists in California, Oregon, Texas, Washington, Kansas, Nebraska, North Dakota, South Dakota, and Oklahoma.

enced continuing struggles among local water users who were determined to control this limited resource. In California an intense and constant struggle pitted users against each other. The state's water law of 1872 endorsed a dual system of prior appropriation and riparian rights, and the state legislature repeatedly passed laws promoting economic development through the irrigation of arid land. The legislators sided with upstream appropriators who wanted to divert rivers and streams, build water storage facilities, interrupt the natural flow of the waterways, and turn arid land into productive agriculture. Downstream riparian users, ranchers, miners, and farmers, claimed their entitlement to the uninterrupted flow of the waters. Disputes were argued before the California courts, where they were usually decided on behalf of the riparian users. The period from approximately 1872 to 1928 was one of continuous litigation over water. In 1928, an amendment to the state's constitution limited the rights of riparian owners to a "reasonable use" of water, changing California water law for the first time in almost forty years.[70]

Reclamation and Irrigation

In the years following the Civil War, much water policy was determined by individual action. Acting alone, miners, ranchers, and farmers were responsible for the diversion of streams. They settled into river valleys and along streams extracting a small amount of water. By acting alone, settlers exploited only a small fraction of an area's land. However, as cooperative ventures were formed to divert larger streams and rivers, capital and labor were employed to cultivate larger tracts of land. Canals were dug and water storage facilities were constructed to make reclamation of arid land possible. The passage of the federal Desert Land Act of 1877 encouraged land settlement and farming on a large scale. As the last of the important nineteenth-century land laws, the act provided settlers with 640 acres of land, four times the size provided under the provisions of the Homestead Act of 1862. Settlers paid twenty-five cents per acre upon filing a land purchase application and the balance of one dollar per acre after three years, when the land was reclaimed by irrigation. The size of the parcels was an inducement to settlers and a drain on the water supply.[71]

The Desert Land Act transformed the semi-arid and arid West. With the rush to settle came the need to build irrigation canals and water storage facilities. The formation of publicly held ditch companies soon followed. These were financed by selling stock to farmers, who received a guarantee for use of a specified volume of water from the canals in addition to shares in the newly established companies. In the Owens Valley, "Canal construction was done by the farmers themselves during the winter season using a team of horses and a primitive cast-iron scoop called a Fresno scraper, and they were paid for their labor in shares of stock."[72]

From this beginning, the scope and size of irrigation projects grew throughout the West, as mining enterprises resulted in the discovery of large, lucrative deposits of ore. Mining booms resulted in new capital investments in roads and railroads as miners moved in seeking their fortunes. To grow and prosper, the mining communities needed access to water delivered by canals and aqueducts. In addition, higher consumer demand for beef in the East and Midwest required larger irrigated and cultivated alfalfa fields for livestock feed. As the cattle industry expanded, small 160–acre parcels of land, the size specified by the Homestead Act of 1862, were purchased and combined into large cattle ranches. The trend was toward larger ranches, supported by even larger water irrigation projects. Once the mining and cattle booms stabilized in the last decades of the nineteenth century, the rate of population growth slowed in the West. To stimulate population growth and a robust economy, government invested heavily in irrigation projects. The goal was to expand agricultural development throughout the American West.

Federal government reclamation policy in the early years of the century helped to shape the West's economic development. The passage of the National Reclamation Law of 1902 was the result of years of lobbying Congress by a coalition of interested parties. *Senator Francis Newlands from Nevada became the author of the Reclamation Act of 1902 and the government agency that it established. His arguments for reclamation legislation appear in a 1901 speech and are presented in document 3.4.* The coalition included farmers, ranchers, and miners who attended annual irrigation conventions, the publishers of the trade journal *Irrigation Age,* and writers popularizing irrigation and reclamation themes in national periodicals such as *American Review of Reviews, Century Magazine, Forum, North American Review,* and *Atlantic Monthly.* In addition, the role of the Army Corp of Engineers in promoting massive public works to reclaim the western desert was instrumental in getting congressional approval. The law also had the support of Theodore Roosevelt, a powerful advocate of reclamation, irrigation, dams, and reservoirs. He believed that reclamation projects benefited the development of the West in much the same way as river and harbor public works had promoted the economic development of the East in the nineteenth century. A fundamental difference existed in the two kinds of public works projects, however. The nineteenth-century projects received local, state, and regional support. With the passage of the Reclamation Law of

1902, the role of the federal government in developing and funding water projects would become paramount throughout the twentieth century.

The Reclamation Law of 1902 created the Bureau of Reclamation in the Department of the Interior and authorized it to "locate, construct, operate, and maintain works for the storage, diversion, and development of waters for the reclamation of arid and semi-arid lands in the Western States."[73] The Bureau's work in irrigating the driest western states had the most dramatic environmental effect in the region. The law began a new era in the nation's history. For the first time the federal government became the West's dam builder. In addition, the Bureau diverted rivers and cut canals through the western deserts. Dozens of artificial lakes and reservoirs as well as aqueducts were built over the next seventy years to irrigate dry farmland and bring water to an increasingly concentrated population in western cities. The Bureau's activities spurred movement of settlers and capital into the region during the entire twentieth century. Its influence was so great that "by late 1979 the Bureau had responsibility for 138 water and power projects, along with 333 reservoirs, and the projects were said to supply the water used by 30 percent of the population of the West. More than 146,000 farms, covering about 9,000,000 acres, receive irrigation water courtesy of the Bureau."[74]

The impact of reclamation activity in California transformed its dry-land ecology into an agricultural oasis. One-fourth of the nation's irrigated land is located in California, and three-fourths of its agriculture now depends on irrigation. One could not have predicted this outcome, given the provisions of the 1902 law. The "family farm" concept in the provisions of the law allowed each family member to receive enough water to irrigate 160 acres of land. The family members were obligated to reimburse the water district in which they lived for the cost of the water. In fact, the interest rates on water use were so low that government costs were never fully recovered. Unfortunately, the "family farm" provision of the Act was not strictly enforced by the Bureau of Reclamation.

The Bureau began almost immediately after passage of the Reclamation Act to grant exemptions from the 160–acre provision. As a result, large-scale, corporate agricultural users benefited most from subsidized irrigation water. In effect, these corporate farmers never paid the full cost of reclamation, including dam construction, river diversion, and reservoir development and maintenance. These costs were paid out of the national treasury, continuously replenished by the taxpayers. Owners of tracts of land averaging 2,200 acres were the primary beneficiaries of irrigation water.[75] However, the Reclamation Act of 1902, which created the West's agricultural landscape, made no provision for supplying the region's urban water needs.

State laws, which encouraged the development of irrigation water districts for agriculture in the nineteenth century, did not provide for the domestic water needs of Los Angeles, San Francisco, and other western cities either.

Water, according to both riparian and appropriation doctrines, was a private resource, not a public good. As a result, a disproportionate amount of water served private interest groups rather than the general public. This imbalance in the allocation and distribution of water created substantial inequities among its many consumers. In California, for example, cities seeking access to water to meet the needs of its residents received no relief from the state. Consequently, the federal law of 1902, like the earlier state-wide agricultural irrigation policies, built an irrigation water colossus with taxpayer's money to enhance the region's agricultural productivity rather than its growing urban population. The irrationality of water policy can be understood by placing agricultural and urban water use in modern context. The same amount of water that it takes to serve the 20 million people in the greater Los Angeles area is used by farmers in the West to grow alfalfa on irrigated land for feeding cows. As one critic of western water policy has noted, the more one tries to understand this water policy:

> the less success one has. Feeding irrigated grass to cows is as wasteful a use of water as you can conceive. Pasture is hydrologically inefficient in the extreme, and, metabolically speaking, so are cows: You need seven or eight feet of water in the hot deserts to keep grass alive, which means that you need almost *fifty thousand* pounds of water to raise *one* pound of cow.... If the livestock industry earned California real money ... [it] might make a grain of sense.... In 1985, however, the pasture crop was worth about $100 million, while southern California's economy was worth $300 *billion,* but irrigated pasture used more water than Los Angeles and San Diego combined.... It isn't much different in any other western state.[76]

Los Angeles

Although California's irrigation of dry land to boost agricultural production proved successful in the decades before and immediately after the turn of the century, irrigation water policy ignored the rapid changes taking place in the state's urban areas. From 1860 to 1900, the populations of San Francisco and Los Angeles skyrocketed. During this forty-year period, the population of metropolitan San Francisco grew by over five times its size and Los Angeles grew by almost seventeen times its size. By 1900, 40 percent of the Golden State's population was concentrated in these two expanding metropolitan areas.[77] As these cities developed, they began to reach the limits of their domestic supply of water, made available by private water companies. Unlike all eastern and midwestern cities in 1900, neither of these burgeoning metropolitan areas controlled their water supplies at the beginning of the twentieth century. Since water for domestic use was not considered to be a commodity capable of creating enormous wealth, providing water for urban households was not a priority.

In contrast, water used in hydraulic mining was "capable of breaking down whole mountainsides or shifting stretches of entire rivers from their streambeds in order to reveal the rich deposits of ore."[78] Similarly, irrigated land made farms abundant in produce, greatly enriching their owners. However, private waterworks only remained profitable to stockholders if they made large capital investments in hydraulic systems, namely pumping stations, aqueducts, tunnels, and pipes. The rapid growth of both San Francisco and Los Angeles far outstripped the willingness of private water companies to keep up with the demand.

Ignoring the development of municipal waterworks led to a host of problems associated with short supply. The West's frequent droughts exhausted available water rapidly. Significant drops in water pressure were a constant irritant to urban residents and a serious problem for firefighters. A steady barrage of complaints about service was often coupled with increases in the rates charged for water by private companies. Droughts, poor service, and high water bills were the conditions that led western cities to replace private water companies with new public water utilities. As the coastal cities of California gained access to the rivers of the Sierra Nevada Mountain range, they were able to curtail the monopoly power of private water companies.

Los Angeles–Owens Valley Water Dispute

For Los Angeles, growth and development depended on building a major urban water system. Gaining control of the water in the Owens Valley and constructing Los Angeles' Owens Valley aqueduct proved to be the way to get the water. The Owens Valley and the origins of its water supply have been eloquently described in the following way:

> Here nature has created a tiny island of green in the middle of a wasteland. The valley is a graben, approximately 100 miles long and an average of 5 miles wide, confined on the east by the Inyo-White Mountains and on the west by the Sierra Nevada, which rises abruptly thousands of feet above the valley's floor. More than one and one half million years ago, when the vast granite blocks that form the modern Sierra Nevada first pressed upward, they carried the valley with them, lifting it to an elevation of nine thousand feet before it broke away and fell back to its present level. As they subsided, the

blocks forming the valley's floor twisted together, sealing the basin and closing its lower-lying southern end with pinched bedrock. When particles of block and soil were washed down the mountainsides in the thousands of centuries that followed, they were consequently captured in this watertight basin, forming alluvial fans of granitic soil which eventually covered over 275 square miles of the area between Owens Lake and the present site of Bishop. The mountains are thus the source of all the valley's richness, for they have provided both the soil that fills the valley today and the water to make it fertile.

In terms of climate, the valley is a desert. It lies in the rainless shadow of the Sierra Nevada and shares the characteristics of the barren lands to its south and east, which include the hottest, driest regions of North America. But it lies as well within sight of the living glaciers and perpetual snow fields along the crest of the Sierra. And every year the vast quantities of precipitation which the mountains capture from cloud masses pass down into the valley through rivulets and streams that run full in the summer months of June and July.[79]

It was the water diverted from these rivulets and streams that became the early twentieth-century source of Los Angeles water, taken at the expense of the farmers, ranchers, and residents of the lush and pristine Owens Valley. The gorgeous valley described here with its thriving economy became a depressed region without an adequate supply of water. After a decade of secret land purchases by agents for the city of Los Angeles, in which the city laid claim to a substantial flow of the Owens River, the construction of the 233–mile Los Angeles Aqueduct from the valley in the north and across the Mojave Desert and into the city was completed in 1913.

The aqueduct consisted of 142 tunnels, 500 miles of service highways, 169 miles of transmission lines, and 240 miles of telephone wires. In addition, the project required its own cement manufacturing plant for cement to line the tunnels, the exposed sections of the aqueduct, and its support structure.[80] An engineering marvel from the standpoint of the citizens of Los Angeles, it would seal the fate of the citizens of the Owens Valley by depriving them of the water they needed to irrigate their farms.

Water was the essential ingredient for turning Los Angeles into a twentieth-century metropolis. In 1920, the city's population had grown to 576,000. By the mid-1920s, as the region's oil fields were helping to fuel the nation's thirst for petroleum, the movie industry was thriving, and the port of Los Angeles surpassed San Francisco in tonnage. For example: "From 1921 to 1928, 3,233 subdivisions covering nearly fifty thousand acres were formed and 246,612 building lots were created."[81] The city's population doubled from 1920 to 1925, and the assessed value of real estate jumped 120 percent. The area was plagued by severe droughts throughout

Jawbone Siphon Construction Site. Courtesy Los Angeles Department of Water and Power.

much of the decade, however, and the Owens Valley aqueduct was unable to meet the city's growing demand for water within a few years after its completion. As a result, Los Angeles began purchasing land in the northern sections of the Owens Valley.

To compensate for the droughts, Los Angeles began pumping Owens Valley groundwater into its aqueduct diversion system. This angered some landowners, who retaliated by establishing the Owens Valley Irrigation District in 1922. The city retaliated by purchasing the largest irrigation canal on the Owens River before all the valley's farmers could join the new irrigation district. Infuriated by this water grab, some forty Owens Valley residents dynamited one of the aqueduct's spillway gates on May 21, 1924. Although the damage was minor, the emotional impact of this episode revealed the residents' willingness to protect the last vestiges of their water from an overpowering adversary. Similar bombings occurred many times throughout the decade.

In conjunction with its plans in the Owens Valley, Los Angeles planned to construct an elaborate system of aqueducts and reservoirs that would divert water from the humid northern region of the state to the arid agricultural south. These plans were thwarted by the state supreme court in 1926. The court upheld the rights of upstate riparian landowners to the water flowing through their property. As a result, Los Angeles had to look elsewhere for its water.

In the early years of the twentieth century, California had begun to irrigate its Imperial Valley with water diverted from the lower Colorado.* By 1904, 700 miles of canals in southern California irrigated 75,000 acres of the Imperial Valley in this way. The waters of this mighty river gained increased attention from Los Angeles after 1920, primarily because of the city's need for electric power. The proposed Boulder Canyon Dam on the Colorado would generate the hydroelectric power that a burgeoning Los Angeles would need to meet its future growth. Yet, as the city's insatiable demands for water became known, farmers in the Imperial Valley, ranchers, and residents of other Colorado basin states became worried about the city's intentions. With the Owens Valley–Los Angeles "water wars" as a point of reference, other water-laden areas became suspicious of the city's motives. Appearing before a congressional committee in February 1924, William Mulholland, the chief engineer behind the taking of the Owens Valley water, testified with regard to the Imperial Valley: "Our need is their need. . . . Our sympathies are with the people of the Imperial Valley. The people in the Imperial Valley are our customers and they are our citizens. They live in Los Angeles, they have to go out there to Imperial Valley and nearly roast themselves to death trying to raise crops for us; and they are as welcome as the flowers in May to come to Los Angeles to cool off."[82]

---

*The Colorado River is 1,400 miles long, draining land in seven states and Mexico. It passes through Colorado, Wyoming, Utah, Nevada, Arizona, California, and New Mexico before emptying into the Gulf of California. Six other rivers are its major tributaries.

From 1930 to 1931, three significant water projects commenced that would make more water accessible to Los Angeles. In May 1930, voters approved the sale of bonds to support the Mono Basin Extension Project, which lengthened the Owens Valley Aqueduct northward to Mono Lake.* Combined, the Mono Lake–Owens Valley conduit would be 338 miles long, from the Lake to Los Angeles.

In March 1931 construction began on the Boulder Canyon Dam on the lower Colorado River. In September of the same year, the voters of Los Angeles approved the sale of bonds to finance the construction of the Metropolitan Water District's Colorado River Aqueduct. The aqueduct would cover 240 miles from the river to the city and was approved by a margin of five votes to one. Voters no doubt believed what the aqueduct's boosters proclaimed, namely that the Colorado River's water would satisfy the city's needs to the year 1980.**

---

*Mono Lake in southern California is the remains of a 13,000–year-old inland sea that covered a vast area of approximately 300 square miles of the Mono Basin and the surrounding Aurora Valley. Left by retreating glaciers, the lake has shrunk in size to about 85 square miles, and its depth has changed by as much as 100 feet. The lake has no outlet to streams or rivers and as a result has been described as the Dead Sea of the West. However, Mono Lake supports an ample number of species, namely brine shrimp and flies. These very small inhabitants make the lake attractive to a variety of wildlife including gulls, grebes, snowy plovers, and migratory birds. Before the lake became a source of water for Los Angeles and its level began to drop about 1 1/2 feet each year, Negit Island on Mono Lake was the second largest rookery of California gulls in the world. However, decline in the water level exposed sections of the lake bottom. Land bridges allowed mainland predators to attack the rookery, endangering the gulls and any other species of waterfowl using the lake. (William L. Kahrl, *Water and Power: The Conflict Over Los Angeles Water Supply,* Berkeley: University of California Press, 1982, 429–430.)

**The Colorado River Compact of 1922 established rules for the allocation of river water among the seven states served by the river. The lower basin states, California, Arizona, and Nevada, receive 7.5 million acre-feet a year, and the upper basin states, Colorado, Wyoming, Utah, and New Mexico, are also allotted 7.5 million acre-feet. An acre-foot of water covers an acre of land one foot deep. It takes about 326,000 gallons of water to achieve this coverage. In October 1930 Arizona sued California in the United States Supreme Court over use of the Colorado River. Arizona asked the Court to nullify the Boulder Canyon Act, which had authorized the construction of the Boulder Dam on the Colorado River and also asked the Court to declare illegal the seven-state Colorado River Compact. By an eight-to-one majority, the Supreme Court rejected Arizona's claims that Congress had acted unconstitutionally in authorizing the construction of Boulder Dam and denied the state's claim that the compact represented an unlawful infringement on Arizona's water rights. As states in the upper basin of the Colorado River began to use their water allotments, it became clear to Arizona that little surplus water would be available unless the state asked the courts to review their circumstances. In 1952, Arizona once again asked the Supreme Court for relief. By then, California was

However, the citizens of Los Angeles discovered that the water from Mono Lake and the Owens Valley satisfied their needs amply and that Colorado River water was not crucial to the city's expansion. "In its first five years of operations, the Metropolitan Water District could find customers for only 2 percent of the Colorado River water it was capable of delivering. After the first ten years, this figure had risen to only 18 percent. And even as late as 1952, when the district had vastly expanded its service area in an effort to bring in new customers, its pumps drawing water from the Colorado were still operating only half the time."[83]

By the 1980s and through the 1990s, however, the availability of Colorado River water became essential for the continued expansion of the southern California area and its surrounding farmlands. Unlike the city of Los Angeles, many of the communities that now make up the Metropolitan Water District depend on Colorado River water to irrigate their farmland, water their lawns, fill their swimming pools, and quench their thirst. Citizens of Los Angeles prefer Mono Basin water in part because the quality of the water from the Mono Basin exceeds that of the Colorado River. In addition, Mono Basin water flows downhill on the Lake Mono–Owens Valley Aqueduct to the city, while water from the Colorado must be pumped over mountains to reach the counties of the south coast of California. In short, Mono Basin water is cheaper to transport than Colorado River water. Need has outstripped convenience and quality, however, and the city's response has been predictable. Los Angeles pumps millions of acre-feet of water from the river, and its citizens have paid more than $335

---

taking in an excess of 4,400,000 acre-feet annually from the Colorado River. At the time, the case proved to be one of the longest and most expensive cases in our nation's history. After a cost of $5 million and eleven years of testimony, on March 9, 1964, the Supreme Court decided that the Congress had the right to authorize the Secretary of the Interior to fairly divide mainstream Colorado River water among its lower basin users, namely California, Arizona, and Nevada. California would receive 4,400,000 acre-feet, Arizona, 2,200,000, and Nevada, 300,000. The Court also gave Congress authority over allocations of water shortages and surpluses and gave the states control over its tributaries. The victory was a large one for Arizona, since it curtailed the amount of water that California could take from the Colorado. In December 1997, Secretary of the Interior Bruce Babbitt decided to allow states in the Colorado Compact to sell water to each other. Rapidly growing populations in California, Arizona, and Nevada had placed excessive demands on the Colorado River. Under the new policy, water-rich states like Utah would be allowed to sell their surplus to states with increasing water demands. Since California and Nevada were exceeding their allotments of water from the Colorado, they would now be in a position to purchase water from other Compact states. Currently, California is exceeding its annual allotment of 4.4 million acre-feet by 800,000 acre-feet. Today, Southern California depends on the Colorado for 70 percent of its water.

Los Angeles Aqueduct and Mono Extension. From Norris Hundley, *The Great Thirst: California and Water, 1700s–1990s.* **Reproduced courtesy Madge Kelley.**

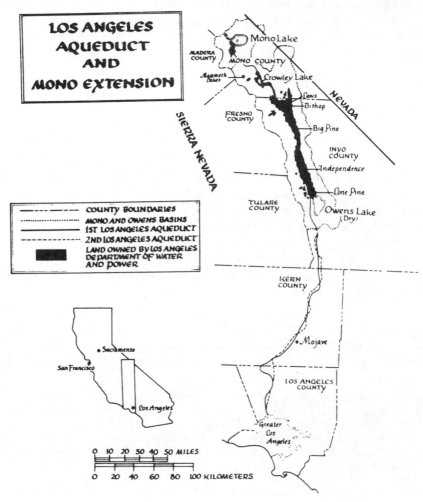

million to develop the Colorado River Aqueduct water system to provide what has become an important source of supply.[84]

East Bay

The major public urban water system in northern California was constructed in response to dissatisfaction with the water service of private water companies and conflicts over water rates charged by these companies.

Colorado River Aqueduct, All American Canal. From Norris Hundley, *The Great Thirst: California and Water, 1700s–1990s*. Reproduced courtesy Madge Kelley.

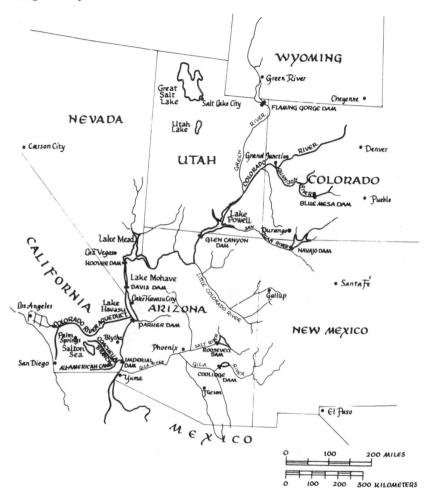

A long-lasting drought plagued the region from 1917 to 1924. Conditions were so bad that one private company, the California and Hawaii Sugar refinery, pumped water from the Sacramento River Delta and spent $30,000 a month to transport water by barge across the Bay to its factories.[85] As a result of these and similar hardships, the East Bay Municipal Utility District (EBMUD) was established by the city of Oakland and its neighbor cities, Alameda, Berkeley, and Richmond, to tap the rivers of the Sierra Nevada

Mountains. Between 1926 and 1929, water from the Mokelumne River, dammed at Lancha Plana, was carried by two 80–mile aqueducts to the East Bay cities.[86] However, the plan to build the Lancha Plana Dam and construct two major conduits did not go unopposed by two major water appropriators, the region's farmers and its rural population.

These groups failed in the courts to prove that all of the Mokelumne River water had already been appropriated, and they also failed to prevent the new water district from purchasing land along the proposed aqueduct routes. As with most water rights cases, those who lost in the lower courts appealed to higher courts to reverse lower court rulings. In this instance, the most important decision came in 1936, when the California Court of Appeals reversed a lower court decision that required the EBMUD to maintain the Mokelumne at a minimum level. Farmers and members of the region's rural population argued that the river provided much of the groundwater for the aquifer beneath the town of Lodi, California. The Appeals Court decided that much of the groundwater overdraft from the aquifer was caused by agricultural irrigation, not the cities or industries in the EBMUD.

The court's decision did not deny the water rights of residents in California's rural communities or their farmers. The court's decision included the proviso that "if EBMUD's project did endanger Lodi's water supply, the district would have to provide Lodi with water or increase the water level in Lodi's wells."[87] Industries and cities in the East Bay area had successfully challenged small agricultural enterprises in much the same way that Los Angeles overwhelmed Owens Valley farmers. As one historian has noted: "In 1920, the value of Alameda and Contra Costa counties industrial produce was estimated at just over $500 million, only $90 million less than the state's total agricultural output."[88] From 1910 to 1940, the growth of California's cities and manufacturing industries required the allocation of more water to them than had previously been necessary.

The Golden State's Central Valley Water Project* of the 1930s and the State Water Plan** of the 1960s as well as federally funded water projects

---

*The Central Valley Project (CVP) was turned over to the federal government in 1935 during the Great Depression because of the state's inability to raise money for the project through the sale of bonds. Dams were constructed by the U.S. Bureau of Reclamation on the upper Sacramento River and the Trinity River on the state's north coast. Water from the Trinity River is carried by tunnel eastward to the Sacramento River and the Shasta Dam, where it is stored and eventually exported to San Joaquin Valley for irrigation purposes.

**The State Water Project (SWP) consisted of a major storage facility in the Sacramento Valley and paralleled the Central Valley Project. However, the SWP was initiated after California's economy recovered from the Great Depression and was

State Water Project. From Norris Hundley, *The Great Thirst: California and Water, 1700s–1990s*. Courtesy Madge Kelley.

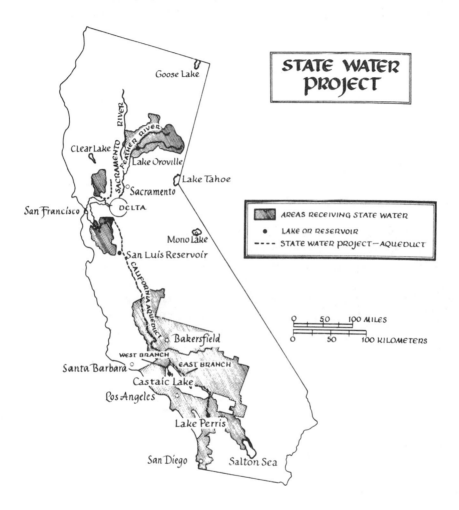

financed with state funds. As a result, it did not have federal restrictions placed on it. The SWP dam on the Feather River near Oroville used river channels to carry water to the Sacramento–San Joaquin Delta. There pumps lifted the water from the Delta into an aqueduct taking water south. A reservoir in the San Joaquin Valley was constructed and shared with the Central Valley Project. The proposed Peripheral Canal from the Sacramento River, traveling along the eastern edge of the Sacramento–San Joaquin Delta, was to be the conduit connecting the river to the Delta. (Harrison C. Dunning, "Dam Fights and Water Policy in California: 1969–1989" *Journal of the West* 29 (July 1990): 16, 19.)

were efforts to avoid agricultural versus industrial, urban versus rural conflict. However, these state and federal plans favored the large irrigation–agricultural producers, California industry, and its cities, not its small farmers.[89]

San Francisco

The third major public urban water system issue in California differed from the Los Angeles–Owens Valley aqueduct and East Bay water conflicts. In the more widely known San Francisco Hetch Hetchy project, the city successfully lobbied the federal government for a permit to submerge a portion of the Hetch Hetchy Valley in Yosemite National Park by building a dam. The proposed project originated in the 1880s, when San Francisco city engineers decided that access to Hetch Hetchy water would answer the city's insatiable water needs. It pitted Progressive conservationists, led by Gifford Pinchot, against the preservationists, led by John Muir. The Hetch Hetchy Reservoir controversy ensued over the proposed flooding of pristine park land and scenic landscape in order to bring water to California's fastest growing city. Hetch Hetchy brought federal, state, and private interests into conflict, thereby complicating San Francisco's proposed water project. As a result, it was the subject of many public hearings and repeated delays. *Excerpts from one of the most important congressional hearings on Hetch Hetchy appear as document 3.5.* Hetch Hetchy proved to be another example of the increasingly important role played by California's industries and cities in requiring access to the region's most scarce resource—its water.

Changes in California Water Policy

The government was responsible for funding numerous water projects, building dams, canals, and reservoirs. Diverting rivers and streams to irrigate arid and semi-arid land had significant impacts on the West's environment. Less water was available for fisheries and free-running rivers. The quality of the water deteriorated and, as a result, crop yields succumbed to the higher salt content of water in irrigated fields. The impact of these environmental changes has been noted in the following way: "The artificial plenty created in California's urban and rural areas crippled efforts to restock major game and commercial fish, and left the state's rivers and lakes saline, polluted, and ecologically impoverished."[90]

The completion of the State Water Project in the late 1960s signaled the end of unrestricted water development in California and in the West. By this time a greater environmental awareness competed with further water development proposals in deciding the future of California. The passage of the National Environmental Policy Act in 1969, requiring environmental impact statements before major changes in the land and water would be approved, occurred as Californians vetoed the further extension of the State Water Project to include the construction of the Dos Rios Dam and Reservoir. Blocking the Dos Rios plan further energized California environmentalists. In 1972, the California legislature passed the Wild and Scenic Rivers Act, which prohibited further water development on many north coast rivers and prevented developers from planning water projects on more than 20 percent of the state's land.

Until the passage of the Wild and Scenic Rivers Act, California water development had been guided by the view of water as a commodity. This view was prevalent in a 1928 amendment to the state's constitution, which required that "water resources of the state be put to the beneficial use to the fullest extent of which they are capable."[91] In other words, river and stream water was to be captured behind dams, stored, and conserved there for reasonable and wise use, and not allowed to be squandered or "wasted to the sea." The Wild and Scenic Rivers Act represented a fundamental change of thinking about the California environment and its system of rivers. The "wise use" policy of early twentieth-century conservationists was replaced by the new policy of the 1972 act, which declared that "certain rivers which possess extraordinary scenic, recreational, fishery or wildlife values . . . shall be preserved in their free-flowing state . . . such use of these rivers is the highest and most beneficial use and is a reasonable and beneficial use of water within the meaning of . . . the Constitution."[92] California's water policies of prior appropriation and riparian rights were changed by the Wild and Scenic Rivers Act.

The controversy about the destruction of the Mono Lake Basin in southern California during the 1980s represented another major change in California water policy. As it held a significant rookery for wild birds, the depletion of the lake and the disruption of the wildlife habitat in the Basin represented a potential environmental disaster. Also, depletion of the lake left behind an alkaline residue which became airborne in the dry desert climate, adding significantly to the region's air pollution. Led by the National Audubon Society, a number of environmental groups sued the Los Angeles Department of Water and Power on the grounds that its water rights based on prior appropriation violated the legal doctrine of public trust, which guaranteed the preservation of wildlife habitat. In addition, California Trout, an organization which promotes trout fishing in the state, argued that Department of Power and Water dams restricted stream flow in violation of the state's Fish and Game Code.

By 1989, the California Supreme Court had accepted the National Audubon Society's idea that the theory of prior appropriation was restricted by the protection of public trust values, which included the protection of wildlife habitat. As a result, stream flow from Mono Lake has been curtailed by 60,000 acre-feet each year, thereby protecting the level of the lake, which sustains the habitat of the wild birds. Also, the state legislature appropriated $65 million to protect the lake and limit water exports.[93] The passage of the Wild and Scenic Rivers Act and the court's acceptance of the public trust doctrine "permits challenges to all water projects which are operated in a way that seriously impacts fish, wildlife, recreation, and other public values related to navigable water."[94] The practice of constructing dams to conserve water and thereby avoiding the "waste to the sea" was no longer generally accepted by professionals and the public. Now California courts and those that followed California's lead were accepting arguments stating that the unimpeded flow of rivers was a public good, not secondary to arguments for "reasonable beneficial use," which in the past had meant water development projects. New dam projects in the West were no longer a foregone conclusion. Many proposals were defeated, and an effort to take some existing dams out of service has commenced.

As the era of federally sponsored dam building in the West slowed, the efficacy of existing dams was challenged by environmentalists. Although these existing dams provided electric power to hundreds of thousands of regional households and reservoirs provided recreation to thousands more, environmentalists pointed to the ecological and financial costs. Millions of tons of silt accumulate annually at the bottom of the reservoirs. Each year hundreds of thousands of acre-feet of water in the reservoirs evaporate into the dry desert air. The flooding of the areas behind the dams has resulted in extinction or near extinction of several fish species, destroyed habitat for songbirds, herons, owls, and beavers, and eliminated wild and scenic landscape and plant life. As drinking water and irrigation costs skyrocket, the surrounding natural environment deteriorates and the viability of the dam system becomes symbolic of a lost wilderness and a challenge to restore some of what has been lost.

However, dam construction nationwide has not abated. Although the largest number of dams in the United States were built between 1935 and 1986, the nation has experienced only a minor rate of decline since 1972. By 1980, reservoirs larger than 500 acres had flooded at least 15,000 miles of streams. Between 1935 and 1986, 68,000 dams were financed and built by municipalities, water districts, and states. The impact of this construction on the habitats of birds, waterfowl, fish, and other aquatic and plant life has been devastating. During the 1980s, surveys were conducted to identify candidates for the Wild and Scenic Rivers System. Less than 2 percent of rivers qualified ecologically because the flow of so many had been disrupted by dams built to generate hydroelectric power.

Changing the natural flow of rivers had become so prevalent that by 1990 only one river longer than 620 miles, the Yellowstone River in Montana, was free flowing. Most had been changed by a number of dams and artificial lakes. Only forty-two of the nation's rivers that were longer than 124 miles were free flowing. Nearly all of the altered rivers generated power for a nation whose hydroelectric power capacity doubled between 1970 and 1990. Smaller rivers were especially hard hit:

> Since most sites suitable for large dams have already been used, a large number of smaller projects are planned instead. According to the Federal Energy Regulatory Commission, which licenses hydro facilities, the eleven hundred-plus small projects planned as of 1988 would increase by more than half the total number of dam sites in the country, in return for a tiny (2 percent) increase in hydroelectric power and only 0.3 percent of the total electricity capacity in the country.[95]

Among the many negative effects of damming rivers and creating reservoirs are downstream river erosion and stopping the natural flow of river sediments, which results in silting and salination. Degraded water quality as magnified by a string of dams along major rivers and tributaries remains to this day a reminder of our power to change the course of our mightiest rivers without comprehending the negative consequences of our actions.

Clean Water Legislation

The building of a large system of dams increased river water temperatures and salt content while it diminished oxygen levels. As a result, the ecological integrity of our rivers was compromised. Although the federal government did not address the role of the nation's system of dams in reducing the quality of our country's fresh water and the role of free-flowing rivers in protecting fish life and wildlife, government policy in cleaning polluted rivers began to take shape in the years after World War II. Beginning in 1948 with the passage of the Water Pollution Control Act and continuing until the passage of the Clean Water Act of 1972, the government increased its financial commitment to building sewage treatment facilities throughout the country. By 1972, more than thirteen thousand grants totaling $1.25 billion were provided to ten thousand locations for sewage treatment. However, not until 1965, with the establishment of the Federal Water Pollution Control Administration, were states required to develop quality standards for their waterways.

Various private and public agencies reported in the late 1960s and early 1970s the amount of contamination in our rivers and streams and the dangerous levels of mercury and DDT in fish and water samples. In addition, these reports described elevated bacteria levels, which made drinking and swimming dangerous. They estimated the cost of water pollution at almost $13 billion a year. In response to these findings, the Congress passed the Clean Water Act of 1972. The Congress stated that, "The objective of this Act is to restore and maintain the chemical, physical and biological integrity* of the nation's waters."[96] To help achieve the integrity of the nation's waterways, the Congress established three national goals to guide water policy and practice: First, eliminate the discharge of pollutants into the navigable waterways by 1985; second, by July 1, 1983, wherever possible make water clean enough to protect fish, shellfish, and wildlife and make it usable for recreation; third, eliminate the discharge of toxins in life-threatening amounts from the nation's waters.[97] The Clean Water Act has been expanded since its passage in 1972. In 1977 and 1987, Congress sponsored new programs to eliminate pollution caused by chemical runoffs from farms, factories, and city streets, and to protect watersheds and estuaries from contamination.

The Clean Water Act of 1972, passed in an atmosphere filled with environmental reports, detailed: "the grim realities of lakes, rivers and bays where all forms of life have been smothered by untreated wastes, and oceans which no longer provide us with food."[98] Water, polluted by sewage, agricultural runoff, and industrial waste, contaminated fish and shellfish, our most common source of low-fat protein. This shift in policy represented a significant change in thinking about the chemical and physical health of our nation's waterways. At the beginning of the twentieth century, many public health officials supported the practice of discharging toxic effluent into the waterways in hope that the effluent would reduce the threat of waterborne disease.

Since the passage of the original act and its reauthorizations, has the public health been protected and improved? Most public drinking water is tested for bacteria and some for toxins. But most people cannot be assured that drinking tap water and eating fish caught locally will not result in immediate illness or in contributing to long-term health problems. Since

---

*Biological integrity has been defined as the "ability of an aquatic ecosystem to support and maintain a balanced, integrated, adaptive community of organisms having species composition, diversity, and functional organization comparable to that of the natural habitats within a region." (Robert Adler et al., *The Clean Water Act 20 Years Later,* Washington, DC: Island Press, 1993, 59.)

1971, there have been 740 reported outbreaks of waterborne disease caused by contaminated drinking water from public systems. Small water systems serving ten thousand people or fewer are more vulnerable to pollution than larger systems. Many of these smaller systems serve poorer populations, who are less able to afford the equipment and engineers needed to operate water filtration equipment. As a recent Environmental Protection Agency study pointed out: "Systems serving fewer than 500 people violate drinking water standards for microbes and chemicals more than twice as often as those that serve large communities."[99] However, larger communities are not immune. In 1993, as many as 183,000 people in Milwaukee, Wisconsin, became ill from drinking water which was not carbon-filtered. Livestock runoff was identified as the source of the contamination. Although this case proved to be the most high-profile example, it was certainly not an isolated one. For the years 1971–1985, more outbreaks of waterborne infectious disease were reported than in any previous fifteen-year period. Undoubtedly, more accurate reporting, use of more precise scientific equipment to detect pathogens, and a heightened national consciousness about the importance of clean water helped cause the jump in reported contamination. After 1985, a drop occurred in the number of infectious outbreaks caused by contaminated water, in part because carbon-based filtration systems were installed by increasing numbers of municipalities.

As we reduced pollutants in the waterways, the levels of contaminants in fresh water and sea water declined, resulting in lower level contamination of fish and shellfish. However, persons continue to face serious health risks in urban/industrial areas where past dumping of solid and liquid wastes occurred or where dumping has continued over time. Considering that the consumption of seafood has increased from 12.5 pounds per person annually in 1972 to 15.5 pounds in 1990, a large and increasing number of consumers face immediate illness and long-term health risks from waterborne pathogens.[100] Waterway erosion, the taking of wetlands for commercial and residential development, pesticide and fertilizer runoff, septic seepage, damming and siltation, and acid drainage from mining all contribute to the creation of weakened aquatic ecosystems. Concerns about contaminated seafood heighten our awareness about the precarious state of aquatic ecosystems repeatedly assaulted by human and animal waste and toxic chemicals.

The danger to aquatic species in North America from water pollution may be much worse than the danger faced by land-living species threatened by habitat damage and loss. More than 70 percent of the mussels and 60 percent of the crayfish in North America are threatened by water pollution. Threats to birds, mammals, and reptiles are serious, but the percentages seem small by comparison—11 percent of birds, 13 percent of mammals, and 14 percent of reptiles are classified as threatened species.[101] The Clean Water Act requires the federal government to protect aquatic life and to promote their propagation. Since the passage of the act, the destruction or loss of free-flowing streams and rivers and the loss of aquatic habitat continue to top the list of causes. Damming our free-flowing rivers, and draining and filling wetlands, floodplains, spawning grounds, and estuaries, initially for agriculture but in recent years for commercial and residential development, have wreaked havoc on the living and breeding places of aquatic life.

Threats to aquatic species from habitat loss and water pollution parallel the decline in drinking water quality for the public at large. One Environmental Protection Agency study points out that about 50 million United States residents live in areas where pesticides have polluted groundwater. Questions about the impact of the Clean Drinking Water Act passed in 1974 to regulate water quality as it flows from the tap are similar to those about the effect of the Clean Water legislation written to regulate river and lake water quality. Since clean water supplies result in clean drinking water, the links between the two pieces of federal legislation are obvious. The costs of cleaning drinking water because of surface and groundwater pollution are staggering. For New York City to filter its surface water for pathogens and solid waste, the cost was estimated to be between $1.5 billion and $5 billion for construction and an additional $300 million annually for operations.[102] Similar construction and operational estimates have been made for providing clean drinking water for residents of other urban areas. In the past, the contamination of drinking water by municipal sewage, and to a lesser degree by industrial pollution, were the concerns of engineers and public health officials. Now, our concerns focus on carcinogens found in drinking water arising from industrial wastes and agricultural runoff. We also need to consider the cost of new filtration technologies and investments in infrastructure to carry pure water from even more distant sources than we have used in the past.[103]

The contamination of our nation's waters "is part of a cascade of problems that causes pollution of air, land, and water."[104] In addition to fouling these three essential and renewable resources that make for a healthy environment, we threaten public health. When toxic chemicals enter the waterways, they not only enter the drinking water supply, they contaminate the air we breathe; as unstable organic chemicals, they evaporate when exposed to the sun's energy. Those organic contaminants that spill onto the land are dug up and burned in incinerators. They also add to the volume of air pollutants. To limit airborne exposure to toxins, some chemical compounds are buried in landfills, but those landfills that are unlined pollute surface and groundwater. The cycle thus will continue, until we reduce the environmental impacts of pollution and assign aesthetic and economic values to these precious natural resources.

❧

Document 3.1

Annual Report of the Water Commissioner in Somerville, Massachusetts (1911)

Frank E. Merrill

One of the most important branches of the department work continues to be the installation of water meters under the provisions of the Metropolitan Water Act. Some of our neighboring cities have finished the metering of all their services, and find, as a result of the consequent diminution in consumption of water, that the entire expense of their meter installation has been offset by the reduction in their state water assessment. It is pleasing to note a gradual dropping in the daily consumption of water in our own city, per capita figure for the year being 80, a decrease of four gallons from that of the previous year, and the lowest on record for this city. This is, no doubt, attributable to the increasing meter installation, which tends to reduce the water waste.

While we have not benefited to the extent that those municipalities have which have completed their meter installation, it is very gratifying to know that the work which has been accomplished by this department has had the effect of substantially reducing our state water assessment for the current year. The amount assessed by the state as this city's proportion of the Metropolitan water tax for 1909, was $112,573.20, and on account of an increase in the general levy on the water district and the increase in the valuation of our city, which serves as a basis for one-third the annual assessment, it may be fairly estimated that the city's assessment for water for 1910 would have been as high as $114,000, but on account of the reduction which we were able to make in our water consumption for the year, the amount actually assessed on us was but $110,056.25; making an estimated saving of $4,000 as a result of the present meter installation. As the cost of our meter installation for the year was but $4,632.73, it will be seen that the saving effected represents a large percentage of the cost of the work.

The natural increase in the water income which would take place under the old rating is being held well in check by the extension of the meter system, and it is reasonable to expect some reduction in the income ultimately, as many metered

Reprinted from "Water Meter Economies," *The American City* 5 (1911): 95.

consumers find their bills for water to be only one-third or one-half the amount they were under the old schedule. That the income is holding up well, however, is seen by comparison with the previous year, when the city was 43 per cent metered, the increase showing over $3,000 with 48 per cent of the services metered, and but $140 less than the high mark reached in 1906, with but 25 per cent of the services metered. While but 48 per cent of the city is metered, the accounts show that 55 per cent of the water income is derived from metered services.

∾

Document 3.2

Clean Water as a Municipal Asset (1911)

George C. Whipple

It needs no apology to say that one of the greatest needs of any community is a supply of good water. . . .

Last have come the standards of the bacteriologist and the sanitarian. Our water supplies are being judged not only by the chemical analysis but by the bacteria that are present or absent. Great stress is laid upon such organisms as the colon bacillus, which is taken as a index of fecal pollution, and of streptococci and other bacteria and tests for specific germs of typhoid fever and other water-borne diseases are likely to become more common as the technique of the bacteriologist improves. The absence of these objectionable bacteria is sometimes considered as giving a water supply clean bill of health. Such tests are indeed of value, and not to be omitted. Decency demands that such indications of pollution be absent from water used for drinking, but it should not be forgotten that there are other tests than these and that the homely virtue of cleanness is sine qua non for every public water supply.

It is common, also, to say that the best test of the purity of a water supply of any city is the typhoid fever deathrate among the consumers. As a general statement this is true, though here, as elsewhere, there are exceptions to the rule. Decreases in the typhoid fever deathrate following the filtration of a public supply are also used, and often justly so, though not always, for measuring the practicable efficiency of a filter plant. So much stress has been laid upon this by engineers and sanitarians that there is danger lest the public get the idea that filters are built for the express purpose of protecting the consumers against typhoid fever. This is a false notion—false because it is only a partial truth. The object of filtration is not to reduce the typhoid fever deathrate, but to get pure water—water that is safe, and water that is clean. Filters, properly built and well operated, do protect and efficiently protect the consumers against water-borne typhoid fever; but they do far more; they protect

Reprinted from George C. Whipple, "Clean Water as a Municipal Asset," *The American City* 4 (1911): 161–65.

consumers against other diseases as well, and they are able to furnish a supply of water that is clean, and acceptable, as well as safe.

Statistics abundantly prove that when a pure water is substituted for an impure water the health of the city improves by a far greater amount than can be attributed to the elimination of typhoid fever alone. Diarrheal diseases other than typhoid fever, children's diseases and also, in some cases, such supposed unrelated diseases as pneumonia, are reduced. Where filtration saves one life from typhoid fever it saves three or four or five lives from other causes, although just how it is not always possible to trace out. Furthermore, clean water tends to increase the general use of water for drinking, a thing good in itself. It also tends to reduce the use of other water supplies that may be of questionable quality, such as local wells and impure vended waters or vended waters distributed in unsterilized containers that go from house to house. It doubtless tends also to decrease the patronage of the soda fountain and the saloon. Again, clean water makes for greater personal cleanliness, and personal cleanliness makes for health.

The changing standards of purity have been, for the most part, rising standards, and it is a most gratifying fact that the quality of the water supplies in our cities, taken as a whole, is better now than ever before. But in our zeal for purity there is danger lest a backward step be taken. During the last few years chloride of lime has been much used for disinfecting water supplies, that is, for killing the bacteria that may be in the water. In spite of opposition and prejudice this germicide has won for itself a place in water purification from which it will not be soon dislodged. That calcium hypochlorite will kill such bacteria as B. coli and B. typhi must be admitted, yet it does not completely disinfect. For example, it is doubtful if it will destroy spore-forming bacteria to any great extent. . . .

[Potassium hypochlorite] does not improve the appearance of water, nor its taste, nor odor—on the contrary, its tendency is to add to the odor of some waters, especially if used in too large doses. It does not make a water visibly cleaner, it kills bacteria. Such being the case, its scope of usefulness is obviously limited. Those in charge of water supplies where the water is always clean or of supplies that need an emergency treatment to destroy a sudden infection may find in this agent a safe, effective and inexpensive germicide. As an adjunct to filtration the use of calcium hypochlorite in the future is likely to be large, as it offers an additional safeguard and supplements the work of the sedimentation basin and the sand bed. . . . There is danger, however, that this substance may be regarded as a means of purification complete in itself, that it may be employed with uncleaned waters without other means of purification, and that because of its cheapness it may find adoption in situations for which it is not appropriate. . . .

Large supplies of clean water are difficult to find in nature, that is, waters that are clear, colorless, and odorless throughout the entire year. Ground waters most often fill these conditions, but even ground waters are not infrequently discolored with iron or impregnated with sulphurous odors. Among surface waters the Great Lakes, at least, might be expected to furnish clean water. . . . The waterworks intakes of large cities do not extend much beyond four miles from the shore, while most of them are much shorter than this; nor are they often located at depths much greater than fifty feet . . . Even lake water, therefore, requires filtration in order to be perfectly clean at all times. . . .

River waters are always more or less turbid. In some the turbidity is occasional and not serious. Others are perpetually muddy. The attempts that have been made to obtain clean water from streams intermittently turbid are extremely interesting. . . .

In connection with all projects for the purification of water the prevention of pollution usually receives prominent consideration, and rightly so. It goes without saying that the greater the natural purity of the water the less work is demanded of a purification plant, and the greater is the margin of safety. It is possible, however, to overemphasize the relative results that can be accomplished by prevention of pollution, and many do not fully appreciate the functions of the common sewage disposal processes. It is of course desirable that our streams and lakes be kept pure, and this is especially true when such waters are used as sources of water supply. Nevertheless a small amount of pollution can be more readily and efficiently removed by modern devices for purifying water, and at much less cost, than by the methods of purifying sewage. That it is cheaper to purify water than it is to purify sewage should be apparent to anyone who thoughtfully considers the nature of these two liquids. Where a stream is contaminated it is desirable, from every standpoint, to have some purifying agent between the source of pollution and the water consumer. In serious cases it may be necessary to have more than one such mechanism. But where the pollution is relatively slight it will usually be found safer and cheaper first to filter the water, thus obtaining not only water that is safe but water that is clean.

It is a difficult matter to adjust the equity in sanitary matters between riparian owners. No very well crystallized opinions on this subject exist at the present time, either in the courts or among sanitarians, and this problem is one that is likely to give our American cities much concern in the near future. . . .

It is very gratifying to see how rapidly the water supplies of this country are improving. When one considers the number of filter plants in operation today, as compared with ten or fifteen years ago, the progress is truly remarkable. The cities of the middle west have done not a little to forward this movement. Louisville and Cincinnati will be long remembered as the places where mechanical filtration first received adequate scientific study, and Columbus will be noted for the first large installation of a municipal water softening plant. Associations like the Central States Water Works Association can do much to advance the cause of clean water, thereby making our cities better places in which to dwell.

Document 3.3

Report on the Lands of the Arid Region of the United States (1879)

J. W. Powell

To a great extent, the redemption of all these lands will require extensive and comprehensive plans, for the execution of which aggregated capital or cooperative labor will be necessary. Here, individual farmers, being poor men, cannot undertake the task. For its accomplishment a wise prevision, embodied in carefully considered legislation, is necessary. It was my purpose not only to consider the character of the lands themselves, but also the engineering problems involved in their redemption, and further to make suggestions for the legislative action necessary to inaugurate the enterprises by which these lands may eventually be rescued from their present worthless state. . . . but to the Arid Region of the west thousands of persons are annually repairing, and the questions relating to the utilization of these lands are of present importance. Under these considerations I have decided to publish that portion of the volume relating to the arid lands. . . .

The Arid Region

The Arid Region is the great Rocky Mountain Region of the United States, and it embraces something more than four-tenths of the whole country, excluding Alaska. In all this region the mean annual rainfall is insufficient for agriculture, but in certain seasons some localities, now here, now there, receive more than their average supply. Under such conditions crops will mature without irrigation. As such seasons are more or less infrequent even in the more favored localities, and as the agriculturist cannot determine in advance when such seasons may occur, the opportunities afforded by excessive rainfall cannot be improved.

In central and northern California an unequal distribution of rainfall through the seasons affects agricultural interests favorably. A "rainy season" is here found, and the chief precipitation occurs in the months of December–April. The climate, tempered by mild winds from the broad expanse of Pacific waters, is genial, and certain crops are raised by sowing the seeds immediately before or during the "rainy season," and the watering which they receive causes the grains to mature so that fairly remunerative crops are produced. But here again the lands are subject to the droughts of abnormal seasons. As many of these lands can be irrigated, the farmers of the country are resorting more and more to the streams, and soon all the living waters of this region will be brought into requisition.

Reprinted from J.W. Powell, *Report on the Lands of the Arid Region of the United States,* 2nd ed. (Washington, DC: Government Printing Office, 1879), 5–6, 10–11, 14–16, 19–22, 40–41.

Irrigable Lands

Within the Arid Region only a small portion of the country is irrigable. These irrigable tracts are lowlands lying along the streams. On the mountains and high plateaus forests are found at elevations so great that frequent summer frosts forbid the cultivation of the soil. Here are the natural timber lands of the Arid Region—an upper region set apart by nature for the growth of timber necessary to the mining, manufacturing, and agricultural industries of the country. Between the low irrigable lands and the elevated forest lands there are valleys, mesas, hills, and mountain slopes bearing grasses of greater or less value for pasturage purposes. . . .

Advantages of Irrigation

There are two considerations that make irrigation attractive to the agriculturist. Crops thus cultivated are not subject to the vicissitudes of rainfall; the farmer fears no droughts; his labors are seldom interrupted and his crops rarely injured by storms. This immunity from drought and storm renders agricultural operations much more certain than in regions of greater humidity. Again, the water comes down from the mountains and plateaus freighted with fertilizing materials derived from the decaying vegetation and soils of the upper regions, which are spread by the flowing water over the cultivated lands. It is probable that the benefits derived from this source alone will be full compensation for the cost of the process. Hitherto these benefits have not been fully realized, from the fact that the methods employed have been more or less crude. When the flow of water over the land is too great or too rapid the fertilizing elements borne in the waters are carried past the fields, and a washing is produced which deprives the lands irrigated of their most valuable elements, and little streams cut the fields with channels, injurious in diverse ways. Experience corrects these errors, and the irrigator soon learns to flood his lands gently, evenly, and economically. It may be anticipated that all the lands redeemed by irrigation in the Arid Region will be highly cultivated and abundantly productive, and agriculture will be but slightly subject to the vicissitudes of scant and excessive rainfall.

A stranger entering this Arid Region is apt to conclude that the soils are sterile, because of their chemical composition, but experience demonstrates the fact that all the soils are suitable for agricultural purposes when properly supplied with water. It is true that some of the soils are overcharged with alkaline materials, but these can in time be "washed out." Altogether the fact suggests that far too much attention has heretofore been paid to the chemical constitution of soils and too little to those physical conditions by which moisture and air are supplied to the roots of the growing plants.

Cooperative Labor or Capital Necessity for the Development of Irrigation

The diversion of a large stream from its channel into a stream of canals demands a large outlay of labor and material. To repay this all the waters so taken out must be used, and large tracts of land thus become dependent upon a single canal. It is manifest that a farmer depending upon his own labor cannot undertake this task. To a great extent the small streams are already employed, and but a comparatively small portion of the irrigable lands can be thus redeemed; hence the chief future development of irrigation must come from the use of the larger streams. Usually the confluence of the brooks and creeks which form a large river takes place within the mountain district which furnishes its source before the stream enters the lowlands where the waters are to be used. The volume of water carried by the small streams that reach the lowlands before uniting with the great rivers, or before they are lost in the sands, is very small when compared with the volume of the streams which emerge from the mountains as rivers. This fact is important. If the streams could be used along their upper ramifications while the several branches are yet small, poor men could occupy the lands, and by their individual enterprise the agriculture of the country would be gradually extended to the limit of the capacity of the region; but when farming is dependent upon larger streams such men are barred from these enterprises until cooperative labor can be organized or capital induced to assist. Before many years all the available smaller streams throughout the entire region will be occupied in serving the lands, and then all future development will depend on the conditions above described. . . .

Timber Lands

Throughout the Arid Region timber of value is found growing spontaneously on the higher plateaus and mountains. These timber regions are bounded above and below by lines which are very irregular, due to local conditions. Above the upper line no timber grows because of the rigor of the climate, and below no timber grows because of aridity. Both the upper and lower lines descend in passing from south to north; that is, the timber districts are found at a lower altitude in the northern portion of the Arid Region than in the southern. The forests are chiefly of pine, spruce, and fir, but the pines are of principal value. Below these timber regions, on the lower slopes of mountains, on the mesas and hills, low, scattered forests are often found, composed mainly of dwarfed piñon pines and cedars. These stunted forests have some slight value for fuel, and even for fencing, but the forests of principal value are found in the Timber Region as above described.

Primarily the growth of timber depends on climatic conditions—humidity and temperature. Where the temperature is higher, humidity must be greater, and where the temperature is lower, humidity may be less. These two conditions restrict the forests to the highlands, as above stated. Of the two factors involved in the growth of timber, that of the degree of humidity is of the first importance; the degree of temperature affects the problem comparatively little, and for most of the purposes of this discussion may be neglected. For convenience, all these upper regions where conditions of temperature and humidity are favorable to the growth of timber may be called the timber regions. . . .

The evidence that the growth of timber, if protected from fires, might be extended to the limits here given is abundant. It is a matter of experience that planted forests thus protected will thrive throughout the prairie region and far westward on the Great Plains. In the mountain region it may be frequently observed that forest trees grow low down on the mountain slopes and in the higher valleys wherever local circumstances protect them from fires, as in the case of rocky lands that give insufficient footing to the grass and shrubs in which fires generally spread. These cases must not be confounded with those patches of forest that grow on alluvial cones where rivers leave mountain canyons and enter valleys or plains. Here the streams, clogged by the material washed from the adjacent mountains by storms, are frequently turned from their courses and divided into many channels running near the surface. Thus a subterranean watering is effected favorable to the growth of trees, as their roots penetrate to sufficient depth. Usually this watering is too deep for agriculture, so that forests grow on lands that cannot be cultivated without irrigation. . . .

Water Rights

In each of the suggested bills there is a clause providing that, with certain restrictions, the right to the water necessary to irrigate any tract of land shall inhere in the land itself from the date of the organization of the district. The object of this is to give settlers on pasturage or irrigation farms the assurance that their lands shall not be made worthless by taking away the water to other lands by persons settling subsequently in adjacent portions of the country. The men of small means who under the theory of the bill are to receive its benefits will need a few years in which to construct the necessary waterways and bring their lands under cultivation. On the other hand, they should not be permitted to acquire rights to water without using the same. The construction of the waterways necessary to actual irrigation by the land owners may be considered as a sufficient guarantee that the waters will subsequently be used.

The general subject of water rights is one of great importance. In many places in the Arid Region irrigation companies are organized who obtain vested rights in the waters they control, and consequently the rights to such waters do not inhere in any particular tracts of land.

When the area to which it is possible to take the water of any given stream is much greater than the stream is competent to serve, if the land titles and water rights are severed, the owner of any tract of land is at the mercy of the owner of the water right. In general, the lands greatly exceed the capacities of the streams. Thus the lands have no value without water. If the water rights fall into the hands of irrigating companies and the lands into the hands of individual farmers, the farmers then will be dependent upon the stock companies, and eventually the monopoly of water rights will be an intolerable burden to the people.

The magnitude of the interests involved must not be overlooked. All the present and future agriculture of more than four-tenths of the area of the United States is dependent upon irrigation, and practically all values for agricultural industries inhere, not in the lands but in the water. Monopoly of land need not be feared. The question for legislators to solve is to devise some practical means by which water rights may be distributed among individual farmers and water monopolies prevented.

The pioneers in the "new countries" in the United States have invariably been characterized by enterprise and industry and an intense desire for the speedy development of their new homes. These characteristics are no less prominent in the Rocky Mountain Region than in the earlier "new countries" but they are even more apparent. The hardly pioneers engage in a multiplicity of industrial enterprises surprising to the people of long established habits and institutions. Under the impetus of this spirit irrigation companies are organized and capital invested in irrigating canals, and but little heed is given to philosophic considerations of political economy or to the ultimate condition of affairs in which their present enterprises will result. The pioneer is fully engaged in the present with its hopes of immediate remuneration for labor. The present development of the country fully occupies him. For this reason every effort put forth to increase the area of the agricultural land by irrigation is welcomed. Every man who turns his attention to this department of industry is considered a public benefactor. But if in the eagerness for present development a land and water system shall grow up in which the practical control of agriculture shall fall into the hands of water companies, evils will result that generations may not be able to correct, and the very men who are now lauded as benefactors to the country will, in the ungovernable reaction which is sure to come, be denounced as oppressors of the people.

ॐ

Document 3.4

Water Policy Speech (1901)

Francis G. Newlands

What improvements are required in our rivers? In the first place the navigable rivers are subject to floods, and we seek to prevent the overflow by constructing levees. . . . Another character of improvement is the dredging of the rivers for the purpose of meeting the period of drought in the summer when the rivers are low and when bars and shallows obstruct navigation. . . . [I]t is contended that by storing the flood waters in the mountains regions, caused by the rapid melting of the snows in the spring, a large proportion of the flood in the Missouri and the Mississippi rivers can be prevented and a more equal and sustained flow of the rivers thus promoted.

It should be remembered that the waters stored in these reservoirs are not the only waters which will be held back during the flood seasons. The character of all the mountain streams in the arid region is that they are torrential during April, May, and June, and that they are reduced to almost nothing in the following months.

Reprinted from *The Public Papers of Francis G. Newlands,* vol. 1, Arthur B. Darling, ed. (Boston: Houghton Mifflin, 1932), 58–65.

Large areas of arid land lie within reach of these streams, but the condition of the flow during the hot months of July, August, and September limits the area of reclamation; for whilst the waters of the early spring and summer months is sufficient for the requirements of vast areas of land, yet, if the waters were diverted over them and crops were planted, they would lack water at the period of greatest want when the crops were ripening for harvest.

The storage of water above enables a larger utilization of the flood waters which are unstored, and storage insures a supply during the period of greatest drought. The result would be that for every acre-foot of flood water stored there would be four or five acre-feet of flood water taken out over the arid lands, thus diminishing the flow of the streams tributary to the Missouri and Mississippi during the torrential period, and these great plains, now arid, would themselves be made the storage reservoirs of vast quantities of flood waters which would otherwise rush down to the Mississippi, so that the effectual storage will not be confined simply to the artificial reservoirs, but will be extended to these large areas of land which will be reclaimed and which will absorb annually a volume of water at least two feet deep over the entire surface. The diversion and overflow of flood waters over the arid lands above would diminish the overflow in the lower Mississippi and would diminish the cost of the levees intended for protection of the adjoining lands. The water carried over the arid lands above would penetrate the soil and would seep gradually back to the rivers and keep the streams below fuller during the hot months than they would be had not this water been diverted or stored. . . .

We contend that, by the construction of storage reservoirs at the head waters of these rivers in the Rocky Mountains, a large proportion of the expenditures for levees on the lower Mississippi will be saved and that a more equal flow of the main river will be maintained, and thus the expense of dredging during the hot season will be greatly diminished. Navigation, like irrigation, requires that the streams should maintain an equal flow; that they should not be torrents at one season and attenuated threads at another.

The evils which attach to both navigation and irrigation are the same. The streams are overflowing at a time when the water is not needed and they are attenuated threads at a time when the water is most in demand. We of the arid regions contend that both navigation and irrigation can be promoted by the storing of these waters at the sources of these mountain streams which are tributary to the great navigable rivers. . . .

But all the rivers in the arid regions are not tributaries to navigable rivers. Upon what theory, then, should the Government proceed to store water on such rivers? Our contention is that irrigation is a public use, just as navigation is; that it is subject to the control of the law, and that the Congress of the United States, under the "general welfare" clause of the Constitution, can do anything in the way of internal improvement that is calculated to promote the general welfare, and that the general welfare is promoted by maintaining an equal and sustained flow of a stream for irrigation as well as by maintaining it for navigation. . . .

Large areas of lands along these rivers have already been taken up by settlers, and they have been able to solve the easy problems of irrigation, consisting simply in the diversion of the waters over the adjoining lands, but they are not able to control the torrential flow which has its source perhaps hundreds of miles away from those settlements, nor have they been able to store the water so as to maintain the supply during the hot season of July and August, when water is essential to the ripening of the crops. The limit of reclamation and settlement has been reached unless the Federal Government, acting, as it can, without regard to state lines, makes a scientific study of each river and its tributaries and so stores the water as to prevent the torrential flow in the spring and to increase the scanty flow in the summer. By doing this its arid lands will be made available for settlers, and it can, if it chooses, secure compensation by a charge upon the lands.

It is estimated that there are about 600,000,000 acres of arid public lands in the West, and of this about 100,000,000 acres can be reclaimed if storage is afforded. It is also estimated that the storage of water will cost from two dollars to ten dollars per acre-foot; the average probably would be about five dollars per acre foot. The cheaper forms of storage would doubtless be attempted first, and the more expensive forms of storage would only be taken up years hence, when the pressure of population and the increased value of the lands would warrant the expenditure.

A convenient argument against the immediate prosecution of this work is that we have no estimate of its ultimate cost. Our answer is that if the Government had halted at the threshold of any great public work for inquiry as to what the prosecution of like work would cost within one hundred years, the estimate would probably have paralyzed the action of congressional bodies. For instance, when the first river and harbor bill was introduced, suppose some captious member of Congress had demanded a halt until it could be ascertained what the total cost over a period of one hundred years would be. I imagine that the statement, verified subsequently by events, that in one hundred years nearly $400,000,000 would be expended on the river and harbor bill would have staggered the imagination, and yet this amount has been expended and the country has not felt it.

It is impossible to forecast the future and state exactly what the storage in the arid regions will cost; but assuming that 100,000,000 acres of land are to be reclaimed; that this land on an average will require annually 200,000,000 acre-feet of water, and that at least four-fifths of this will be supplied by the flood stream, and that one-fifth will be supplied by the stored water, we will require within the next fifty or one hundred years a storage capacity equal to 40,000,000 acre-feet of water—that is to say, a storage equal to covering 40,000,000 acres one foot deep, or 1,000,000 acres forty feet deep. Assuming that the average cost of this would be five dollars per acre-foot, the total cost would be within a period of fifty or one hundred years about $200,000,000.

Expenditures of the settlers upon their lands would far exceed this; it would probably average from ten dollars to forty or fifty dollars per acre, dependent upon the cost of the main canals, the level or broken character of the ground, and the difficulty in leading out the water from the river. But one thing is assured, and that is that every acre of land reclaimed would be worth at least fifty dollars, and, as 100,000,000 acres are to be reclaimed, we would have a total increase in the wealth of the country in land alone, without improvements, of $5,000,000,000 by the expenditure upon the part of the Government of $200,000,000, and we would have a country opened up for the surplus population of the East and the Middle Western states.

There are two ways of legislating upon this work. One is to pass annually a bill similar to the river and harbor bill, providing, first, for the construction of projects which have been surveyed, estimated, and reported favorably, and, second, making appropriations for surveys, estimates, and reports as to projects that are contemplated. Such appropriations would come out of the National Treasury and would be raised from general taxation, just as the appropriations in the river and harbor bill are.

Another method would be to fasten the cost of the government work of storage upon the public lands susceptible of reclamation. Such a plan would involve the creation of an arid-land reclamation fund in the Treasury, into which all moneys received from the sales of public lands in the arid and semi-arid states would go. The receipts from the sales of public lands last year amounted to about $3,000,000, and including commissions and fees, to $4,000,000. So the sum available for the first year would be about $4,000,000. Provision should be made for investigation, surveys, estimates, and reports by the Geological Survey of various projects, and upon approval of a project by the Secretary of the Interior he should be authorized to withdraw from entry the lands in the reservoir sites and to withdraw from entry, except under the homestead act, all land susceptible of irrigation by reason of such project. He should then be given power to contract for the work; no contract to be made unless the money is in the fund. When the project is completed, the total cost should be ascertained, and the price of the lands susceptible of irrigation and of the water rights attached thereto should be so fixed as to compensate the fund in ten annual installments, thus maintaining the perpetuity of the fund for progressive work.

If the report should show that lands already settled required stored water, power should be given the Secretary of the Interior to sell water rights to such settlers upon the same terms as to new settlers. Right of entry under the law should be limited to eighty acres, and the sale of the water right to existing settlers should be limited to an amount sufficient for eight acres; the purpose of this being not only to prevent the creation of monopoly in the lands now belonging to the Government, but to break up existing land monopoly in the West by making it to the interest of the owner of a large tract of land made more valuable by the possibility of securing stored water to divide up his land and sell to actual settlers. The bill should be so framed as to make its operation automatic, progressive, and complete, to guard against improvident projects, to prevent land monopoly, to secure homes for actual settlers, and to promote the division of the large tracts of land which, under the unfortunate administration of state and national laws, have been created in the West.

Under this plan the West would reclaim itself without calling upon the general taxpayers for a dollar. It has been suggested that the cession of the arid lands to the states would produce the same results, and would relieve the Federal Government of a great work. My answer to this is that the Government has no right to abdicate the great trust imposed upon it by the ownership of 600,000,000 acres of land, upon which the homes of unborn millions are to be made. It cannot afford to intrust these lands either to the ignorance, the improvidence, or the dishonesty of local legislatures. The experience of all the Western states has been that the grants of land made by the Federal Government to the states for the purpose of education or local improvement have been maladministered and have resulted in the concentration of immense holdings of land in single ownership.

This country has today 70,000,000 of people; within one hundred years it will have 300,000,000 people. The pressure for land will be great. Imagine the discontent and disturbance which will result from an improvident administration of these great areas easily capable of supporting 100,000,000 people. . . .

Now, I ask, who should undertake this work? Who can undertake the work? The view of the people of the arid region is that this is a public work of internal improvement which ought to be undertaken by the Government of the United States. It resembles in character the old canals that were constructed years ago, or the interstate roads that were constructed by the general government, or those improvements that have been made for a number of years in dredging our rivers and improving our harbors—public improvements intended for the general welfare; improvements from which the Government does not expect a direct reimbursement, but simply the general advantage that comes to the entire country and the general welfare from the promotion of enterprises of this kind. And inasmuch as the rivers of the arid region as a rule are not navigable rivers, and the only public use to which we can put them is irrigation, not navigation, we claim that a fair and equitable distribution of the benefits of government requires that these streams should be maintained in equal flow by the system of reservoirs to which I have alluded.

❧

Document 3.5

Hearings: Hetch Hetchy Dam Site (1913)

The CHAIRMAN. The bill under consideration this morning is H.R. 6281, introduced on June 23, 1913, by Representative John E. Raker, of California. . . .

The bill involves the construction of a dam at the Hetch Hetchy dam site in California to catch the flood waters of the Tuolumne River. This is not a new matter. This bill in one form or another has been before Congress and the departments for the past 12 years. . . .

I have also requested Mr. Pinchot to be here. . . . I am informed you are anxious to get away?

Mr. PINCHOT. I am.

The CHAIRMAN. Then, Mr. Secretary Lane, you may proceed. . . .

Secretary LANE. San Francisco needs a new and adequate water supply. The water supply that she has now has been developed from time to time during the last 50 years, and the city has outgrown it.

After research by engineers under the direction of Mayor Phelan, the determina-

Reprinted from *Hetch Hetchy Dam Site,* Hearing before the Committee on Public Lands, House of Representatives, Hearings, 63rd Congress, 1st session (Washington, DC: Government Printing Office, 1913), 3–6, 25, 28–29, 166, 213, 235–38.

tion was that the best supply would come from the Tuolumne River. The water came down in the high Sierras, and there was an available dam site within the Yosemite Park. When I speak of the Yosemite Park, I do not speak of the Yosemite Valley; that is distant from the park, or the valley is distant from Hetch Hetchy Valley, and it in no way touches that beautiful scenic valley. . . . The question, and the only question which has ever been raised against the use of this valley for this purpose—I mean for the conservation of the flood waters of the Tuolumne—the question that has been raised has been the question of turning the bed of the valley into a lake. I think that I have as much appreciation of natural beauty as anyone and as much of a desire to conserve the natural beauties of my own home State as anyone, and my conclusion, after thinking of this thing a long while, has been that to turn that valley into a lake would add to the beauty of the whole thing rather than to detract from it in any way; but, of course, in matters of taste we all differ.

California needs water for other than municipal purposes, for irrigation purposes, and she needs this water that comes down from these high mountains for power, because she has no coal, so that it is probably a matter of but a very few years, even if this application were denied and if this bill should fail to pass, it would be only a very few years before you would find yourselves pressed by the State of California or by private parties with large public influence behind them to set aside this identical site as a dam site for the holding back of the flood waters which run to waste, so that those waters might be used for irrigation purposes and for power purposes, if not for municipal purposes, and it has seemed to me, in looking over the whole situation, that San Francisco's demand or request made to the Secretary of the Interior in times past was a perfectly reasonable one. My concern, as Secretary of the Interior, has been to see that the interests of the Government were protected. I have looked over this bill in the very brief time I have had and it seems to meet a great many of the objections that have been heretofore raised to such bills. . . .

Mr. PINCHOT. Mr. Chairman and gentlemen, we come now face to face with the perfectly clean question of what is the best use to which this water that flows out of the Sierras can be put. As we all know, there is no use of water that is higher than the domestic use. Then, if there is, as the engineers tell us, no other source of supply that is anything like so reasonably available as this one; if this is the best, and, within reasonable limits of cost, the only means of supplying San Francisco with water, we come straight to the question of whether the advantage of leaving this valley in a state of nature is greater than the advantage of using it for the benefit of the city of San Francisco.

Now, the fundamental principle of the whole conservation policy is that of use, to take every part of the land and its resources and put it to that use in which it will best serve the most people, and I think there can be no question at all but that in this case we have an instance in which all weighty considerations demand the passage of the bill. . . .

Mr. RAKER. Taking the scenic beauty of the park as it now stands, and the fact that the valley is sometimes swamped along in June and July, is it not a fact that if a beautiful dam is put there, as is contemplated, and as the picture is given by the engineers, with the roads contemplated around the reservoir and with other trails, it will be more beautiful than it is now, and give more opportunity for the use of the park?

Mr. PINCHOT. Whether it will be more beautiful, I doubt, but the use of the park will be enormously increased. I think there is no doubt about that.

Mr. RAKER. In other words, to put it a different way, there will be more beauty accessible than there is now?

Mr. PINCHOT. Much more beauty will be accessible than now.

Mr. RAKER. And by putting in roads and trails the Government, as well as the citizens of the Government, will get more pleasure out of it than at the present time?

Mr. PINCHOT. You might say from the standpoint of enjoyment of beauty and the greatest good to the greatest number, they will be conserved by the passage of this bill, and there will be a great deal more use of the beauty of the park than there is now.

Mr. RAKER. Have you seen Mr. John Muir's criticism of the bill? You know him?

Mr. PINCHOT. Yes, sir; I know him very well. He is an old and a very good friend of mine. I have never been able to agree with him in his attitude toward the Sierras for the reason that my point of view has never appealed to him at all. When I became Forester and denied the right to exclude sheep and cows from the Sierras, Mr. Muir thought I had made a great mistake, because I allowed the use by an acquired right of a large number of people to interfere with what would have been the utmost beauty of the forest. In this case I think he has unduly given away to beauty as against use.

Mr. RAKER. Would that be practically the same as to the position of the Sierra Club?

Mr. PINCHOT. I am told that there is a very considerable difference of opinion in the club on this subject.

Mr. RAKER. Among themselves?

Mr. PINCHOT. Yes, sir. . . .

Mr. RAKER. From your general knowledge of conditions in California, is it your opinion that this is the most practicable and accessible water supply for San Francisco, with all of the rules and regulations provided in this bill?

Mr. PINCHOT. From what little I know of California, I think the conclusions in this report are correct.

Mr. RAKER. Which report is that?

Mr. PINCHOT. The "Report of Advisory Board of Army Engineers to the Secretary of the Interior on Investigations Relative to Sources of Water Supply for San Francisco and Bay Communities," House Document No. 54, Sixty-third Congress, first session.

The essential statement in this report seems to me to be the following:

> The board believes that on account of the fertility of the lands under irrigation and their aridness without water the necessity of preserving all available water in the Valley of California will sooner or later make the demand for the use of Hetch Hetchy as a reservoir practically irresistible.

In other words, it is certain that this reservoir must be used some time.

The CHAIRMAN. And it is a question of whether now or to postpone it?

Mr. PINCHOT . The time to use it is when it is most needed. . . .

The CHAIRMAN. Are there any gentlemen here who wish to speak in opposition to the bill?

Mr. WHITMAN. I am one of them. . . . There is no doubt that the building of the roads which they propose will facilitate the ability to get in there, but my proposition is that they will find that there will not be any reason to go in there, except for people who want to go in and look at the lake and come out again.

Mr. KENT. Well, if it should be made a popular camping ground, what provision could be made for taking care of the people? The minute you popularize a camping ground and make it available for a vast number of people, you immediately destroy the very element which originally made it attractive as a camping ground, because you must provide camp regulations, install a water supply, provide sanitary arrangements, and then the character of the camping site is entirely changed.

Mr. WHITMAN. A few words in conclusion, gentlemen: You are asked to consider this park as it is at present, with almost nobody using it. Very little attention has been given to what may happen to this park by the year 2000. On the other hand, the city desires to focus your attention to the year 2000 for its water supply. They are getting along and can get along perfectly comfortably for a good many years for their local supply, but it is the year 2000 they want you to look to. If you look to the year 2000 in one way, I pray you to look to it in the other. What will that park be and what will the use of it be to the American public, winter and summer, in the year 2000?

Now, I have said nothing about nature. I have tried to put this thing on a practical ground, which will appeal to the American citizen, and I do not want to add anything as to nature. But I have a letter here addressed to the chairman of this committee from Robert Underwood Johnson, who was, with Mr. John Muir, the original cause of the establishment of this park, and he has put this matter so admirably in his letter that, as a few concluding words, I should like to read it. There is not very much of it. He says:

New York, June 25, 1913
Hon. Scott Ferris, M.C.,
CHAIRMAN House Committee on the Public Lands,
Washington, D.C.

Dear Sir:

I deeply regret that pressing private business here makes it apparently impossible for me to appear in person before the committee. I therefore respectfully submit for the consideration of its members some points which I think germane to the bill. . . .

There never was a time when there was a more urgent necessity for our country to uphold its best ideals and its truest welfare against shortsighted opportunism and purely commercial and local interests. The history of the country presents a thousand examples of the sacrifice of the good of all to the advantage of a part, and the waste of national resources at the dictation of selfish parties under specious pretexts. The enormous amounts of money lost to the Government for the enrichment of individuals in the careless disposition of the public lands and forests would have liquidated the public debt a hundred times over and have made life easier for every citizen of the United States in the past century and down to the present day. It is the subordination of the ideal to the material, the greater future to the lesser present, that has set us apart as the most wasteful and imprudent of nations. In 1889–90 came a awakening, largely through the efforts of John Muir, discoverer of the great Muir Glacier, a man combining in himself the ideal and the practical as have few men of our day. It was he who awakened the administration of President Harrison to the necessity of conserving the public forests instead of giving them over to the tender mercies of the chance comer.

The first step of importance in this awakening was the establishment of the Yosemite National Park, which led to the immense reservations made by the Harrison administration under the law of March 3, 1891, and to further reservations by each succeeding President, until at last the headwaters of all the great western streams are measurably secure against the perils of forest denudation. I think it is not too much to say that no Representative should consider himself competent to decide a question involving the dismemberment of a great national park until he has read the book of the late George P. Marsh, formerly American minister to Italy, entitled "Nature as Modified by Human Action," a work of singular imaginative force, in which the author, as early as 1850, pleaded with his countrymen to put an end to the passive policy of forest destruction, from which every Mediterranean country has suffered disastrously. Unless one can view the subject in the light of history and with the eye of imagination, he will remain indifferent to the large considerations involved in giving away to a corporation the use and control of fully half of the most beautiful of all our national parks. . . .

The opponents of the Hetch Hetchy scheme maintain that their position is not inimical to the true interests of San Francisco. They say if there were no other source of good and abundant water for the city they would willingly sacrifice the valley to the lives and the health of its citizens. The records of the hearing before the Senate Committee on Public Lands two or three years ago shows that two official representatives of the city (one, ex-Mayor Phelan) confessed that the city could get water anywhere along the Sierra, if she would pay for it. This is the crux of the whole matter. The assault upon the integrity of the park has this purpose— to get something for nothing. Mr. Freeman, the engineer employed by the city, has also stated that it is physically possible to get water anywhere along the Sierra. . . .

We believe, moreover, that a larger measure of attention should be given to the question of filtration. I have already called your attention to the system in operation at Toledo, under which typhoid fever has almost disappeared, and to the abandonment by the city of London of its project of a supply from the Welsh Mountains in favor of the same system of filtration. I earnestly suggest that the advantages of this method be made the subject of an official examination during the present summer by United States Government experts, for if such a system be feasible, it would be folly to destroy the valley and dismember the park to have it discovered later that they must, after all, be abandoned for a method both better and cheaper. . . .

I have not yet spoken of the great recreative, curative, and hygienic uses of the park. It contains three considerable camping spots—the Yosemite Valley, now greatly crowded every summer; the Tuolumne Meadows, and the Hetch Hetchy. The second is much more difficult of access than the third, and both would be withdrawn from public use by the operation of the proposed bill, for it would be idle to take the valley for a reservoir without giving to the city full control of the watershed, since a single case of typhoid infection would endanger the health of the city. The population of the San Joaquin Valley, in the hot and dusty summer, increasingly frequent the park as campers. These would be deprived of the use of these wonderful scenes. . . . Without this touch of idealism, this sense of beauty, life would only be a race for the trough.

i believe California would not consent to give up the great reservations. Moreover, I believe that the people of the State are opposed to the destruction of the Hetch Hetchy, and that this can be demonstrated if the bill can be delayed until the December session.

I have the honor to remain, respectfully, yours,
Robert Underwood Johnson.

Mr. WHITMAN (continuing). Mr. Johnson, as you all know, has been for many years the editor of the Century Magazine.

In conclusion, I wish there was some way in which this committee could see the Hetch Hetchy Valley itself. . . if you should see it for yourselves I know you would have an entirely different view of it.

4

Air Quality and Air Pollution

Introduction

The quality of the air that we breathe is affected by the particles and gases emitted from burning hydrocarbon fuels such as coal, oil, and gas. Like the water we drink in order to sustain our bodies and our lives, the air we breathe is a precious life-sustaining gift of nature. Pure and clean, the air is refreshing and healthy; contaminated and fouled by toxins and particles, the air is the cause of numerous respiratory ailments and life-threatening diseases. Until recently, we could say complacently that some substances "disappeared into thin air," or went "up in smoke." Now we know that what we put into the air comes back to us in the air we breathe.

Early History

No one knows exactly when early humans faced the challenge of controlling fire and putting it to human use, but the use of fire surely dates back at least 750,000 years to the inhabitants of the Escale cave near Marseilles, France, and their ancient hearths.[1] About 650,000 years later these early humans slowly began to leave the forests and tall grasslands and their life as hunters and gatherers. As they established settled communities, their agricultural productivity increased and their communities grew in population. The quality of their lives was improved by the life-giving products of the hunt and their newly created agricultural bounty. Burning wood in their growing communities increased the volume and concentration of indoor and outdoor (ambient) smoke and created the first smoky surroundings.

When agriculture finally replaced hunting and gathering as the primary source of food during the Neolithic Age, about 12,000 years ago, building a dwelling used approximately thirteen tons of firewood in the making of plaster for the walls and floor. Abundant woodlands were cut to meet the insatiable demands of early humans. The deforestation of many parts of premodern Europe occurred long before the Roman conquest. When the general Julius Caesar invaded Britain in 55 B.C., less forest existed than does today.

A thousand years later, before the invention of relatively efficient chimneys, people living in colder climates huddled around fireplaces built in the center of a room with a roof louvered high enough to partially carry away the smoke.[2] The smoke that was produced must have been an annoying but acceptable byproduct of a settled, agricultural life. Indoor smoke pollution is at least as old as the first fire. Humans could endure the smoke emitted from fires mainly because human populations remained relatively small by modern standards, and the smoke these populations created by burning mostly wood as fuel for warming and cooking was dispersed outdoors, over a wide geographical area. Millennia ago, ideas about energy efficiency and the conservation of resources were absent.

A good stove did not emerge until 1744 A.D. Benjamin Franklin's invention proved to be a momentous event for the forests and wood piles of America. The Franklin stove greatly reduced the amount of fuel required, but its widespread diffusion took a hundred years. Colonial Americans did not develop a manufacturing industry to produce Franklin stoves because wood was plentiful and cheap, economic growth was sluggish, and they were generally poor, with little money to invest in a newer technology. The price of Franklin stoves was simply too high for most colonial consumers.

Carbon Fuel Sources

Active cutting of the primordial forests resulted in a fuel crisis in the ancient eastern Mediterranean countries and, a thousand years later, in much of Europe. As scarce wood became more costly, coal was found to be an alternative and cheaper source of fuel. Although the burning of coal is now thought of as the "great polluter" of our clean air because of its carbon content, the combustion of wood, not coal, released higher carbon content into the atmosphere.

Wood, along with coal, oil, and natural gas, is a hydrocarbon fuel. Hydrocarbon fuels contain carbon (C) and hydrogen (H), but at different ratios. As energy is created by the burning of hydrogen and smoke and smog are the products of burning carbon, it is important for a energy source to have a low carbon to hydrogen ratio. As one economist has noted: "Wood weighs in heavily at ten effective (C) for each (H). Coal approaches parity with one or two (C) per (H), while oil improves to two (H) per (C), and a molecule of natural gas (methane) is a carbon-trim (CH_4)."[3] For more than two hundred years, humans have gradually improved energy efficiency by using fuels with progressively less carbon per hydrogen atom. Replacing wood with coal was the first step in this long historical process.

Since the burning of coal with a high carbon content coincided with rapid urbanization and industrialization, coal is identified with the air pollution and the smoky conditions of European and American cities in the last two centuries. Had plentiful supplies of wood been available, however, conditions would have been even less tolerable. Although we entered the long-term, slow evolution of the process of decarbonization centuries ago, the effects were hardly noticeable, given the growing concentrations of people and industries in cities.

The process of fuel decarbonization has taken place at approximately 0.3 percent per year, with about 40 percent reduction in carbon emissions since 1860.[4] Contributing to the rate of reduction is the concept of fuel efficiency. Over the long term, efficiencies have been achieved in generating, transmitting, and distributing energy. Replacing soft bituminous coal with hard anthracite coal, replacing the latter with petroleum, and, more recently, choosing natural gas have reduced carbon emissions significantly. Also, the devices that use energy have changed as the result of breakthrough inventions and evolutionary improvements.

Early History of Smoke Pollution

These slow historical "decarbonizing" changes tend to be ignored in studies of the early history of smoke. The replacement of scarce and costly wood with plentiful and cheaper sea coal from Newcastle, England, accelerated the decarbonizing process in thirteenth-century London. This coal was a boon for blacksmiths and lime burners, who used the new fuel for their furnaces and ovens. In the process they blackened the skies over the city. By 1257, Queen Eleanor of England issued from Nottingham the first recorded complaint about air pollution, and by 1306 a proclamation was issued by King Edward I prohibiting the use of coal in the furnaces of London while the Queen was in residence. Coal taxes were imposed by Richard III and Henry V.

With increasing prices for fuelwood and no other alternatives to coal, its use increased with each passing decade.[5] Coal as a fuel for residential use in lower-class sections of towns and cities first appeared in Scotland and northern England. With substantial increases in the price of fuelwood, the residential use of coal spread to the south of England, including London, in the sixteenth century.

Smoke's "Medical" Benefits

Despite the publication in 1661 of John Evelyn's *Fumifugium or the Inconvenience of the Aer and Smoke of London Dissipated* and in 1662 of John Graunt's *Natural and Political Observations . . . Upon the Bills of Mortality,* coal use escalated in London. In response to the darkening of the London sky by coal particles, ash, soot, and smoke, Evelyn recommended that all trades and industries, including brewers, dyers, and salt boilers, be moved five to six miles from the city limits. He also proposed a greenbelt of "fragrant Shrubs, Trees and Flowers" to serve as a buffer separating the city residents from these polluting industries. [6] In his popular treatise on the threat of smoke to human health, John Graunt observed that:

> whether a City, as it becomes more populous, doth not, for that very cause, become more *unhealthfull,* I [am] inclined to believe, that London now is more *unhealthfull,* than heretofore, partly for that it is more populous, but chiefly, because I have heard, that 60 years ago few *Sea-Coals* were burnt in *London,* which now are universally used. For I have heard, that *Newcastle* is more *unhealthfull* than other places, and that many People cannot at all endure the smoak of *London,* not only for its unpleasantness, but for the suffocation which it causes.[7]

Graunt's volume earned him a fellowship in the prestigious Royal Society and was reprinted four times in the three years after its initial publication. Based on information comparing the mortality of residents in a rural community and in London over a sixty-year period, he concluded that the average life span of Londoners was shorter than that of those living in the rural community.[8] Despite the conclusions drawn by Graunt, many physicians promoted the medicinal benefits of inhaling smoke, particularly during periods of widespread outbreaks of infectious disease. Many of these ideas about the therapeutic effects of smoke persisted in England and the United States into the later decades of the nineteenth century. One early twentieth-century survey noted that many people believed that smoke was beneficial for some diseases, including tuberculosis, and that it "has been for years a common custom for those affected with the disease to resort to coal mines, or to build fires and inhale the smoke."[9]

Many diseases, including tuberculosis (TB), influenza, pneumonia, measles, and other streptococcal infections are carried through the air. It is understandable that the frantic search for remedies led to some extreme measures. TB was responsible for as many as 15 percent of all the deaths in the 1860s and 1870s. The 20 million casualties worldwide from the influenza A pandemic of 1918–1919 caused as many as 25 percent of the deaths in some regions of the United States and probably larger percentages in Europe. With a half-million deaths in the United States alone, the pandemic depressed the average life expectancy in 1918 from fifty-two years to thirty-nine years. In addition, outbreaks of whooping cough, scarlet fever, and diphtheria were a constant reminder of the airborne transmission of germs in the nineteenth and early twentieth centuries. All of these diseases combined accounted for 30 percent of all deaths in the United States in 1900. It is no wonder that readily available smoke and coal dust were enlisted by some physicians and lay professionals as possible remedies in the war against aerial killers.[10]

The war against stench, symptomatic of these aerial killers, was initiated by leaders of the movement to clean up the nation's nineteenth-century cities. To them, eliminating odious smells meant ridding the cities of refuse and waste. They thought of the odor as either the cause or a contributing factor in the spread of disease. For much of the nineteenth century, fouled air commonly meant the stench emanating from decaying organic waste. Terms in common usage to describe such conditions included "foul miasmas," "sewer gas," and "offensive effluvia." By 1832, one of New York City's leading newspapers reported on the city's initiative to promote public hygiene:

> The measure taken to clean the streets, and to disinfect places which are ordinarily the receptacles of corrupt air, have been so effectual, . . . [one has] to ask himself if this is really New York, and if the pure breezes which he breathes, really belongs to that atmosphere which formerly in the summertime was so offensive.[11]

At the same time, the medical community held that synthetic chemicals created by the combustion of coal were relatively harmless when compared to the threats to human health caused by decaying "organic matter." This belief would change slowly, but by the end of the century most doctors acknowledged the harmful health effects of smoke.

The medical argument against smoke was a difficult one to prove since defining what precisely was hazardous about smoke was impossible. In the early years of the twentieth century the medical profession concluded in its official publication, the *Journal of the American Medical Association,* that "the direct harmfulness of smoke to the human organism is not wholly clear."[12] Studies that documented the higher rates of TB in cities when compared to rural regions and autopsies that showed higher instances of black lung among city dwellers had little effect on public perceptions about the dangers of inhaling smoke. Opposition to smoke needed to be made on other, nonmedical grounds, as a "public nuisance," a term with a long history in both England and the United States.

Briefly, the phrase meant that citizens were obliged to conduct themselves responsibly and use their property in ways that were noninjurious to others. Lawsuits against those who created a public nuisance by fouling the air and water and by disturbing the life and property of others were common in the last half of the nineteenth century. Black, sooty smoke descended on cities daily, choking and blinding their residents. A clean face and a clean shirt were anomalies on the streets of the business districts in urban America. The damage to personal and commercial property was staggering; retailers and shopkeepers struggled to protect their property and merchandise from the ravages of the omnipresent smoke. Closing windows during the stifling summer heat only added to the misery of the building's occupants, already plagued by poor indoor air quality and the enforced confinement caused by the poor quality of ambient air. In 1911, the U.S. Geological Survey estimated that the total cost of smoke pollution to all large and medium-sized cities was $500 million annually. Its chief engineer, Herbert M. Wilson, believed that it equaled "the total taxes [Americans] pay on their real and personal property, and . . . one third the total corporate debt of all American cities of this size."[13] *Document 4.1 is an article by the chief engineer describing the costs of this public nuisance in terms of human health and psychological well-being.*

History of Urban Air Quality in the Nineteenth Century in the United States

The abundance of smoke, soot, and dust in the nineteenth century in the United States was a byproduct of nineteenth-century industrialization and urbanization, which had occurred a century earlier in England. For much of the populace, including the nation's business and manufacturing elite, these byproducts possessed symbolic value. They represented a new-found prosperity for the nation as a whole—jobs and wages for the many, accumulated wealth and upward mobility for the few. At the very least, citizens were ambivalent about the smoke. On the one hand, some believed it was a nuisance, but for others it was an annoyance with some medicinal attributes and for many of the same citizens, the smoke meant progress.

When compared with familiar nineteenth-century conceptions of fouled air and the stench of decaying organic matter including human and animal waste, which littered the streets, lots, and alleys of most cities, noxious smoke was not nearly as offensive. Booth Tarkington captured the essence of the value of smoke in his 1915 novel, *The Turmoil :*

> There is a midland city in the heart of fair, open country, a dirty and wonderful city, nestled dingily in the fog of its own smoke. The stranger must feel

the dirt before he feels the wonder, for the dirt will be upon him instantly. It will be upon and within him since he must breathe it, and he may care for no further proof that wealth is here loved more than cleanliness.[14]

Although smoke and progress were synonymous for some, municipalities began passing antismoke ordinances to curb smoke nuisances. No such laws existed prior to 1880, but soon thereafter one city after another began to act on behalf of the public good. In 1881, Chicago passed the first antismoke law, and its initiative was soon followed by Cincinnati, Cleveland, Detroit, Kansas City, Pittsburgh, Salt Lake City, St. Louis, and St. Paul. By 1915, twenty-three of the nation's twenty-eight largest cities had passed laws or imposed regulations to control airborne pollutants.[15]

The passage of smoke-control legislation in cities combined with the absence of systematic enforcement characterized much late nineteenth- and early twentieth-century behavior toward airborne pollution controls. Although many legal suits against smoke-producing industries were found in favor of the defendants, some courts were sympathetic to the appeals by plaintiffs. In many cases in New York, Pennsylvania, and New Jersey between 1840 and 1906, the courts awarded financial compensation to plaintiffs.[16] Some courts understood the meaning of smoke nuisance for the residents of congested, poorly ventilated urban and industrial environments. Upton Sinclair's *The Jungle,* an early twentieth-century novel about worker exploitation and environmental decay, captured the effect of the smoke discharged from the chimneys of his imaginary Packingtown.

> [The smoke] came as if self-impelled, driving all before it, a perpetual explosion. It was inexhaustible; one stared, waiting to see it stop, but still the great streams rolled out. They spread in vast clouds overhead, writhing, curling; then uniting in one giant river, they streamed away down the sky, stretching a black pall as far as the eye could reach.[17]

When smoke began to be thought about as a nuisance rather than as a symbol of progress, it was described as a "problem," an "evil," or a "plague." Although many cities had passed antismoke laws, the phrase "air pollution" did not enter the vocabulary until much later.[18] In fact, in a modern sense the term "air pollution" was not used until the 1930s. According to one historian:

> The first entry under "air pollution" in the *Reader's Guide to Periodical Literature* was listed in 1915, and the entry said simply: "See Dust, Smoke, Soot, Ventilation." . . . In the annual *New York Times Index,* the first entry for "air pollution" appeared only in 1931. . . . [and] the Smoke Prevention Association, . . . became the Air Pollution Control Association only in 1950, after more than a decade's debate about the wisdom of adopting a new name.[19]

Packingtown. Union Stockyards from Ashland Avenue, cabbages in a vacant lot, Chicago, Illinois, ca 1910. Courtesy Chicago Historical Society (ICHi-01869). Photographer unknown

Smoke was mostly defined as particulate matter, such as ash, soot, and coal dust; the later definition of air pollution would include particulate matter as well as gases and toxins. *Document 4.2 is taken from an article published in 1913 about the chemical properties of soot and its damaging environmental effects.*

The birth of big industries in the United States in the mid-nineteenth century changed the landscape of the countryside and the towns and cities in much the same way that had occurred in England a century earlier. This was the age of coal and iron, then steel, petroleum, and coal-burning locomotives. By the 1880s, the burning of wood was eclipsed by fossil fuel consumption. By 1890, the combustion of bituminous coal supplied 41 percent of the nation's energy needs.* By the end of the century, bituminous

---

*In 1890, using British Thermal Units (BTUs) as the measure, bituminous coal produced 2,900 quadrillion BTUs (tBTU); wood 2520 tBTU; anthracite coal 1,160 tBTU; petroleum 156 tBTU; natural gas 257 tBTU; and hydropower 22 tBTU. (Indur M. Goklany, "The Federal Role in Improving Environmental Quality in the United States: Evidence From Long Term Trends in Air Pollution," paper presented at the American Society for Environmental History Conference, Baltimore, MD, March 1997, 5.)

coal had replaced wood and the cleaner burning anthracite as the leading source of fuel in the United States.

Coal combustion was the paramount symbol of an industrial society. The eastern seaboard cities of New York, Boston, and Philadelphia used coal from the hard, low-sulfuric, anthracite coal mines of eastern Pennsylvania. Burning soft coal, however, released enormous amounts of hydrocarbons in the form of smoke, soot and dust particles, sulfur dioxide, carbon monoxide, and carbon dioxide. Pittsburgh, Cincinnati, St. Louis, and Chicago suffered the most from burning soft, high-sulfuric, bituminous coal. As early as 1864 in St. Louis, a person named Whalen sued his neighbor Keith, arguing that smoke from the latter's shed made the former's house "almost untenantable." Missouri's Supreme Court awarded Whalen fifty dollars in damages.[20] In 1868, Pittsburgh attempted to control smoke emitted by coal burning locomotives without much success.

As Pittsburgh, Chicago, and St. Louis became heavily industrialized during the nineteenth century, they placed severe stress on ambient air quality. Heavy coal smoke was emitted in large volumes from office buildings, warehouses, and factories. It coated buildings and people's lungs with soot and grime.[21] The effects of these emissions were a blight on the environment. Yet in each of these industrialized cities with a pro-growth business philosophy, smoke symbolized prosperity and jobs. So, early on, supporters of economic progress and prosperity were pitted against groups committed to abating smoke for aesthetic, health, and environmental reasons. The interest of local chambers of commerce in abating smoke in some industrial cities peaked with their efforts to compete with other cities to secure world fairs and expositions.

Chicago

Similar to other midwestern cities, Chicago, according to one historian, faced:

> black smoke ... so heavy that it could barely float in the air. It often fell to the ground, creating almost solid banks of soot, steam and ash on city streets. An observer looking back on the smoke generated by the Chicago Edison plant on Adams Street noted that the smoke was "so dense that one could almost lie on it."[22]

The effects of such smoke on human health included a number of infections due to inflamed mucus membranes. Tuberculosis and chronic eye, nose and throat irritations, as well as a variety of respiratory ailments, plagued city residents.

Chicago became the nation's first city to respond to the blight caused by dense smoke. In passing the smoke control ordinance of 1881, the municipal government responded to the protests of the Citizens' Association, a business reform group. It ordered violators, those who emitted excessive smoke from tugboats, locomotives, and chimneys, to pay fines of between five and fifty dollars, depending on the density of the smoke. Enforcement proved as elusive in Chicago as in other late nineteenth-century cities. The absence of a sufficient number of inspectors and an unwillingness of violators to voluntarily obey the ordinance exacerbated the problem of enforcement. Only when the majority of Chicago's industries and businesses began to understand the value of a less smoky environment in the early 1890s did attitudes and behavior begin to change.

With the impending World's Colombian Exposition in 1893, the majority of the city's elite began to advocate the enforcement of the 1881 statute. Only after considerable agitation from reform-minded civic groups did city officials began to take action. In the vanguard of this agitation were women's groups who viewed smoke as a threat to civilized living, organized business groups who feared the loss of business, and the Union League Club, who represented groups of civic-minded residents. Their combined efforts led to the formation of the Society for the Prevention of Smoke in Chicago. Representing bankers, real estate developers, lawyers, manufacturers, cattle ranchers, and others, the Society's members hoped to educate their peers in the city's busy downtown about the value of smoke control. Remarkably, education had an important effect on the behavior of many smoke emitters.

Within six months after the process of education had begun, the Secretary of the Smoke Prevention Society reported "that the engineering staff [of the Society] had investigated 430 smoking steam plants and had sent out over 400 reports to owners about how to curtail smoke. He stated that about 40 percent of the owners of smoking buildings had voluntarily followed the engineers' recommendations and had practically cured their smoke nuisance." Also, several railroads had installed abatement equipment on their locomotives. Some 20 percent of the others had voluntarily installed abatement equipment, but were either not using the equipment correctly or not stoking their fires properly. Consequently, railroads continued to cause a smoke nuisance.[23]

Forty percent compliance would not prepare the city for the thousands upon thousands of visitors who would descend on the city for the World's Colombian Exposition, celebrating the four hundredth anniversary of Columbus's discovery of the New World. Since city promoters had lobbied Congress to make Chicago and not New York the official site of the celebration, dense smoke would most assuredly disrupt the city's planned festive atmosphere. Local business and industry wanted the celebration to become a showcase for Chicago's industrial, commercial, and technological prowess, not its debilitating and noxious smoke. These promoters "opted to house the fair in a group of huge, extravagantly designed, entirely *white* Beaux Arts buildings, called 'The White City,' [and] they feared humiliation if visitors encountered a pall of black smoke darkening and dirtying everything."[24]

Efforts to increase voluntary compliance failed. Many prosecutions resulted in fines that were never collected. In the case of some convictions, the courts refused to assess fines. Finally, the Society for the Prevention of Smoke hired its own engineers and inspectors as well as employing its own attorney, Rudolph Matz, to prosecute violators of the 1881 smoke abatement ordinance. With the agreement of the city government, Chicago had turned the power of enforcing the 1881 statute over to the Society, a private organization.

Initially, Matz's achievements were striking. Numerous prosecutions were followed by many convictions. The dogged opposition of tugboat owners, a class of small businessmen unaffiliated with the city's powerful commercial and industrial elite, hampered further progress. Unfortunately, the depression of 1893 doomed the efforts of Matz and the Society. However, the Society was soon replaced in 1907 by a government organization called the Smoke Abatement Commission; membership continued to be made up entirely of businessmen. One of the Commission's first actions was to require business and industry to apply for permits to construct new, and refurbish old, furnaces. The Commission used this new power to demand that efficient mechanical stokers be installed in new and reconditioned furnaces. *The workings of mechanical stokers in increasing the efficiency of furnaces and reducing smoke are described in document 4.3.* For years thereafter, the Commission strengthened ordinances to reduce smoke emissions and supported increased funding for the city's Smoke Inspection Department.

In a 1912 report about its progress, the Commission boasted that

> in one year it had brought 1,040 suits and collected over $25,000 in fines and costs; 3,000 out of 14,000 stationary combustion sources had been reconstructed; under threat of suit, tugboats and marine vessels plying the Chicago River switched to "semi-smokeless" West Virginia coal; and both locomotives and stationary sources changed operating practices to reduce smoke generation. All these measures helped reduce smoke by 75% in the central city.[25]

Dense smoke in Chicago dropped 50 percent from 1911 to 1933, while coal consumption nearly doubled. As in other cities, technological improvements in the form of efficient mechanical stokers, the use of smokeless coal, and new furnace designs for private residences, apartment buildings, and industrial and commercial establishments helped to reduce the number of dense smoky days in Chicago. Locomotives and tugboats replaced coal with diesel oil. The consumption of coal began to decline after the 1920s as oil, natural gas, and electricity replaced it in Chicago and elsewhere.[26]

St. Louis and Pittsburgh

Along with Chicago, St. Louis and Pittsburgh became bellwether cities in the nearly century-long efforts to rid cities in the United States of visible smoke. After decades of complaints about smoke pollution, the first attempts to control smoke emissions were made in St. Louis in 1867. "The atmosphere was so heavy that it retained the smoke poured into it," claimed the editor of the city's *Globe-Dispatch*.[27] As the city experienced population growth and industrial development during the later decades of the nineteenth century, a city ordinance was passed requiring that smokestacks be at least twenty feet higher than nearby buildings. Smoke pollution continued, however, to darken the cityscape. To complicate this process, the city's topography magnified its pollution problems. St. Louis has been described as a heat island, reflecting the sun's light while absorbing its heat in the day and releasing some of that heat after dark.* Also, hills on the

---

*Half of the nation's population lives in areas with "heat island" characteristics. These are areas where the average surface temperature is five to eight degrees higher than in nearby suburbs. Conventional wisdom tells us that "heat islands" occur because of crowded conditions and the emissions from factories and automobiles. The reality, however, is that "heat islands" occur because cities are filled with heat-absorbing surfaces such as asphalt streets, parking lots, and dark roofs. Replacement of these with lighter shades of roofing material, paving streets with Portland cement, and tree planting would reduce the effects of the heat-trapping materials and reduce energy costs by millions of dollars each year for each city.

A computer model of energy savings for Los Angeles has calculated that changing roofing and paving material and planting 10 million shade trees to cover 5 percent of the land area would reduce air conditioning costs by 18 percent, or $175 million each year. Trees are important, not only for the shade they provide but because of the biological process called "evapotranspiration." As a tree drinks up groundwater from its roots, it perspires from its leaves and cools down the surrounding air. A healthy tree transpires about 40 gallons of water each day, enough to offset the heat of thirty-eight 100–watt bulbs burning all day. (Peter J. Howe, "Lighten up, cool down, cities told," *Boston Globe*, August 4, 1997, C4–5). For more information about the issue of urban "heat islands," consult the Lawrence Berkeley National Laboratory web page at: http://www.eande.lbl.gov/eap/bea/hip/himain.html.

eastern side of the Mississippi River occasionally slowed the dispersal of moving pollutants causing the formation of stagnant, polluted air. For residents with pulmonary disease, pollution caused shortness of breath and other debilitating respiratory conditions. Stagnant air was most common in the fall and winter where smoke "hovered where it was made."[28]

The combination of urban and industrial density and a smoke-trapping topography had a devastating effect on St. Louis and its residents. According to calculations made by engineers, about 900 tons of solid waste per square mile fell on the city as a result of "black smoke" in the 1920s. The annual cleaning up cost of this "public nuisance" was estimated to be about $15 million.[29] The engineers were unable to calculate the cost of the permanent damage to gardens, shrubs, and trees caused by reduction in the daily number of hours of sunlight from coal combustion releasing sulfuric acid, coal dust, and soot. In 1905–1906 alone, it was estimated that smoke had killed about one-third of the trees in St. Louis. The devastating effects of smoke were evident in other industrial cities as well. In 1904, Cleveland's forester wrote that "the smoke from the factories and from the engines of the Lake Shore and Michigan Southern Railway is killing off the trees at the west side of Gordon Park. . . . Without constant care and attention, Cleveland will be treeless in a few years."[30]

Unlike St. Louis, Pittsburgh discovered a local supply of natural gas in 1886 and used it as a source of fuel until 1892. For this relatively short period of time, Pittsburghers experienced a much improved air quality. Once the city had depleted this natural gas supply, however, it had no real alternative except to return to burning soft coal. One observer noted: "We are going back to the smoke. We have had four or five years of wonderful cleanliness in Pittsburgh. We all felt better. We looked better. We all were better."[31]

"Going back to the smoke," was the Pittsburgh that travelers, detractors, and visitors had reviled since the early nineteenth century. The English writer Charles Dickens reportedly condemned the city as "Hell with the lid lifted." The social philosopher Herbert Spencer visited Pittsburgh at the invitation of Andrew Carnegie in 1887 and is reported to have quipped, "six months in Pittsburgh would lead a person to contemplate suicide."[32] City officials passed ordinances from the 1860s into the early years of the next century attempting to regulate dense smoke emissions from coal-burning railroad locomotives, industries, and other commercial enterprises. None of these ordinances proved to be enforceable, and no efforts were made to limit the combustion of soft coal by iron and steel manufacturers or for residential use.

In St. Louis, the pressure to recommend new emission controls forced the mayor, Edward A. Noonan, to appoint a commission of engineers in

1891. Working together to alleviate the city's smoke were the St. Louis chapters of the National Association of Sanitary Engineers and the Manufacturers' Association. These groups were instrumental in getting the city to enact the smoke abatement ordinances of 1892 and 1893. Opponents of smoke control, mostly businesses engaged in manufacturing goods and brewing beer and spirits, sought relief from the restrictions imposed by the legislation. They sued the city on the grounds that only Missouri's state legislature had the authority to declare smoke a nuisance. In 1897 the Missouri Supreme Court invalidated the city's smoke abatement ordinances. The opponents had won only a temporary victory, since the same legislature passed a law declaring smoke emissions in Missouri cities with 100,000 or more residents a public nuisance. Soon thereafter, St. Louis passed a series of ordinances against dense smoke, in 1901, 1902, and 1903.[33] As was the case in Pittsburgh, however, passing legislation to address the problem pointed out the futility of these early efforts at smoke control. Enforcement proved to be much more elusive.

To begin with, the Manufacturers' Association of St. Louis had convinced the Missouri legislature to limit the power of inspectors by including the following proviso in the state law: "Provided, however, . . . it shall be a good defense if the person charged with the violation shall show . . . that there is no known . . . [way] the emission or discharge of dense smoke complained of in that proceeding could have been prevented."[34] Even without this amendment to the state law, enforcement in St. Louis would have remained episodic. The city office of Inspector of Boilers, Elevators and Smoke Abatement employed only four smoke inspectors and one photographer to provide visual documentation of violations. Even a new Missouri smoke nuisance law in 1915 accomplished little.

To assist in the effort to improve the city's atmosphere and literally clean up the city, the elite women's Wednesday Club established the Women's Organization for Smoke Abatement. From 1890 to 1923, the Women's Organization was most influential in supporting smoke-control ordinances. As we have seen, women environmental reformers were also active in urban water reforms and protecting wildlife. Their view was that a city was a home shared by all of its residents. The Wednesday Club explained that: "The present condition of our city . . . endangers the health of our families . . . and adds infinitely to our labors and expenses as housekeepers."[35] In addition to lobbying for local smoke abatement laws, women became monitors of smoke emissions from city smoke stacks by reporting their findings to smoke inspectors. By 1910, the city's Women's Organization was providing the service of testing the technical effectiveness of new smoke-consuming devices.[36] However, conditions in the city remained bleak until the 1930s.

In 1911, Pittsburgh created a Bureau of Smoke Regulation both to instruct manufacturers in the use of efficient furnaces and to provide information about new technological equipment to control smoke emissions. Fuel efficiency, much like other kinds of efficiencies in the industrial workplace, was seen as a way to eliminate or curtail waste. Since smoke was an example of fuel waste, it needed to be brought under control.[37] In 1917, the bureau reported that for the last five years, during the peak smoky months from January to June, the number of days with dense smoke had dropped from twenty-nine to six. For the first time in either of these cities, regulating industrial and commercial emissions had had an effect on smoke abatement.[38]

Citizens of St. Louis elected a reform mayor in 1933 who was committed to bringing the oppressive smoke conditions under control, ending many years of Republican rule. Mayor Bernard L. Dickmann appointed Raymond R. Tucker to be Commissioner of Smoke Abatement. An engineer, Tucker believed that a smokeless fuel should replace cheap and plentiful bituminous coal for residential and industrial use. In addition, Tucker advocated the installation of mechanical stokers to feed coal efficiently into industrial furnaces, replacing the wasteful stoking practice of employing firemen to tend the boilers. Under the leadership of Dickmann and Tucker, the city passed the 1937 smoke abatement statute, which included an important provision called the "washing clause."

The washing clause greatly expanded the powers of the city government as they pertained to the combustion of fuel by "define[ing] acceptable smoke and ash emissions, limit[ing] the size of burnable coal to no more than six inches, and require[ing] all fuel exceeding those standards to be treated by a washing process (either with water or air) until it conformed to the ordinance's standards. It mandated the use of the Ringleman chart*—a simple visual, but 'practical' device that used different gradients of gray and black as standards—to measure smoke."[39] To strengthen the provisions of the 1937 statute, the city passed a second ordinance, regulating the sale, delivery, and distribution of fuel in St. Louis. Violators of these two new statutes would lose their permits as coal dealers. Although the new laws

---

*In 1898, Ringelmann developed a chart for measuring the density of smoke. For the most dense and blackest smoke, the replication of results from observer to observer could be very accurate. In subsequent decades, refined versions of the chart allowed observers to measure accurately less dense smoke. As a result, the chart became the single most effective method for enforcing smoke abatement regulations until the 1960s, when federal clean air legislation was passed. (Indur M. Goklany, "The Federal Role in Improving Environmental Quality in the United States," Baltimore, MD, 1997, 6.)

effectively regulated industrial and commercial smoke emissions by insisting on the combustion of higher quality coal, no limitations on fuel quality were placed on household stoves and furnaces. Since domestic use of unregulated coal accounted for approximately 50 percent of the city's smoke, St. Louis continued to experience smoke palls. Residents witnessed some of the worst smoke in the autumn of 1939. Visibility was so poor that one could not see across the main streets.[40]

Public outrage at the city's appalling air quality led to the passage of the 1940 Smoke Control Law, which required all of St. Louis either to use mechanical devices to eliminate smoke caused by burning bituminous coal or to burn smokeless fuel. Raymond R. Tucker, the mayor's advocate and initiator of the law, remembered years after its implementation how it changed "the buying habits of approximately 1,000,000 people . . . [and] the merchandising habits of practically all the fuel dealers in the city of St. Louis."[41] The power of city government was expanded, to require all businesses selling smoke-control devices to register those sales with the city office of smoke abatement. Smokeless fuel was defined as that which contained less than 25 percent volatile matter, meaning smoke-producing chemicals. Those citizens, businesses, and transport companies who did not comply with the provisions of the law had their furnaces and stoves sealed by the city after three violations in any twelve-month period. In a four-year period, from 1940 to 1944, almost 30,000 households replaced manual-fired stoves and furnaces with efficient mechanical starters and stokers.

During the same period, railroads replaced two hundred coal-burning steam locomotives, which had caused an estimated 20 percent of the smoke, with one hundred diesel electric ones.[42] Since emissions from household furnaces and fireplaces still continued, however, little progress was made in reducing dense smoke through the early decades of the twentieth century. The city's smoke abatement experts argued that: "the amount of black smoke produced by a pound of coal is greatest when fired in a domestic furnace and that domestic smoke is dirtier and far more harmful than industrial smoke."[43]

In Pittsburgh, with approximately 100,000 homes using coal-burning stoves and furnaces in the 1940s, enforcement of new regulations presented a small staff of inspectors with a nightmarish ordeal. The regulations required householders either to buy a new smokeless stove or furnace that could burn bituminous coal, convert existing equipment to burn natural gas, or use nearly smokeless anthracite coal in existing stoves and furnaces. Following a strategy already in use in St. Louis, Pittsburgh's inspectors focused on the thirty or more coal distribution centers and truck handlers, insuring that soft coal was neither sold nor delivered to households, rather than trying to monitor households themselves. *Document 4.4 describes the effects of poor indoor air quality on human health.*

In St. Louis, Pittsburgh, and other industrial cities, the effect of laws to prohibit household use of coal by the poor was mostly negative. They suffered the most economically from the transition to higher cost, cleaner fuel and the fixed costs of retrofitting older stoves and furnaces with more efficient technologies. Pittsburgh's new ordinance:

> fell hardest on poor families, because fuel costs composed a larger percentage of their budget than higher income groups and because of their fuel-buying habits. Working-class families often purchased their coal by the week in bushel lots from itinerant truckers, since they had neither the cash nor the storage space to buy larger amounts. In addition, the poor commonly used older, inefficient stoves for heating and cooking. Grave indoor air quality problems compounded the plight of the poor and working classes who used older stoves burning noxious soft coal and wood. While there had been considerable discussion in both the 1941 and 1946 hearings about special provisions for the poor, cash subsidies of a limited amount were provided only for public assistance recipients.[44]

Progress was slow, as the new ordinances required systematic enforcement. In Pittsburgh, for example, more than two decades of debate and delays were required before the Pittsburgh city council unanimously passed new smoke abatement regulations to eliminate the combustion of bituminous coal in 1941. The implementation of the ordinance was then delayed until 1946 since the effort to win World War II had a higher priority than smoke abatement. The passage of the regulation had been achieved by the combined support of the city's powerful business elite, its civic associations, the political leadership, the coal operators, and the miners' union.

The impact of the smoke-control laws on the St. Louis and Pittsburgh environment can be measured by the reports of the United States Weather Bureau that estimated that the winter weather in St. Louis had improved significantly in one year, from 1940 to 1941. Days with moderate smoke had declined by 70.3 percent and those with heavy smoke had decreased by 83.6 percent. In Pittsburgh, a similar striking rate of change took place. In 1940, 81 percent of its households burned coal and 17.4 percent natural gas (from Appalachian fields); by 1950, the figures were 31.6 percent coal and 66 percent natural gas. Almost half the city households had changed fuel type and combustion equipment by 1945. In Pittsburgh between 1946 and 1955 occurrence of dense smoke dropped from 298 hours to 10 hours per year, a 96.6 percent decline. For moderate smoke, the figures were equally impressive, with declines from 1,005 hours to 113 hours, or an 88.8 percent decline.[45]

Information about these success stories spread rapidly. City after city asked for information about the St. Louis and Pittsburgh smoke control ordinances; by 1944, some 230 cities had requested information. As other cities acknowledged that the smoke nuisance could be eliminated, they imposed strict regulations on polluters. In 81 percent of cities, however, weak law enforcement allowed households, factories, and businesses to emit smoke that obscured 40 percent of the visibility as measured on the Ringelmann chart in 1940.[46] The impact of smoke-control legislation, the use of alternative and cleaner fuels, the construction of gas pipelines in the late 1940s and 1950s that covered many hundreds of miles, and new combustion technologies eventually changed the outdoor atmosphere of most of the nation's cities, however. Los Angeles eliminated burning solid wastes in open dumps in 1947, thereby reducing particulate matter by 50 percent in two years.

The effect of the new ordinances improved the visibility and the air quality almost immediately in the country's industrial centers. Interestingly, the positive changes in air quality were not the result only of the new regulations but also of increased use of natural gas. Lower cost, cleaner natural gas became increasingly available after the end of World War II in 1945. Transported in pipelines from the southwestern states to the East and Midwest, natural gas competed with coal as an alternative source of fuel. Coal had become increasingly expensive; its supply diminished when mine workers went on strike over better working conditions and higher wages in the years immediately after the war.

Indoor air quality improved significantly as a result of cleaner fuels and modern combustion appliances. Pressure to rid cities of their dense smoke by passing regulatory ordinances contributed to achieving the goal of more smokeless and fewer gray days. However, an alternative fuel source in the form of plentiful and cheap natural gas contributed even more to ridding the cities of their smoky conditions. By 1960, burning residential coal nationally had declined significantly, as 68.4 percent of home heating was now done by natural gas.[47] By 1975, only 3 percent of cities accepted high levels of dense smoke.[48]

The Donora Catastrophe

Before air pollution problems received widespread national attention, an episodic air pollution catastrophe took place in Donora, Pennsylvania, an industrial town with 14,000 inhabitants, during a four-day period in October 1948. On the worst day of the episode, Saturday, October 30, seventeen people died in a twelve-hour period, while almost 600 became ill from near asphyxiation and thousands more were left gasping for air.[49]

The Donora disaster was the result of environmental and industrial factors. Located 30 miles southeast of Pittsburgh, in the basin of the Monongahela River Valley, the town is surrounded by 400–foot cliffs. Like Los Angeles, it is situated in the bottom of a bowl-shaped valley. Donora's mountains slowed the prevailing winds, preventing industrial pollutants from dispersing quickly into the atmosphere. Warm ground-level pollutants were trapped by this slow-moving air, which covered the area like a blanket. As the upper air temperatures rose faster than those of the ground air, temperature inversions produced haze and smog. Under normal circumstances, slow winds and stagnant air create inversions that trap industrial pollutants in the lower atmosphere.[50]

In the last days of October 1948, severe fog covered the Northeast and Midwest, playing havoc with airplane traffic control and covering the roadways with a slick residue. Residents with nose, throat, and lung ailments were rushed to local hospitals for oxygen.[51] These environmental conditions were exacerbated in Donora by the atmospheric effluent produced by the zinc works of American Steel and Wire Company, a subsidiary of the United States Steel Corporation. To produce the metal zinc, natural gas and soft coal were used as fuel in oxidizing zinc-bearing ores. The smelting process, namely the combined burning of fuel and ore to produce molten zinc, generated high temperatures and released sulfurous fumes, carbon monoxide, carbon dioxide and "a variety of heavy metal dusts . . . into the valley atmosphere."[52]

From Tuesday morning through Saturday evening, October 26 through October 30, 1948, the smog over Donora worsened. By Friday evening some residents crowded into local hospitals, while others sought relief from oxygen provided by local fire department volunteers. An ambulance passed slowly through the town's streets after dark "to ferry the dead and dying to hospitals or on to a temporary morgue."[53] The account of the Donora smog was broadcast to the nation on radio by the popular columnist Walter Winchell, whose flair for the sensational in news reporting alerted people and government to the "horrifying scene" in Donora. In the aftermath of the infamous Donora episode, the United States Public Health Service (USPHS) decided to study the health effects of air pollution, the first comprehensive investigation of its kind in the United States.

USPHS findings were inconclusive regarding the effects of the zinc smelting emissions on the health of Donora's citizens. The data collected by this investigation and subsequent studies confirmed, however, that the eighteen deaths during the five-day episode for a population of 14,000 represented:

15 percent of all deaths we would expect today from all causes in a full year in a population of equivalent size. Retrospective measurements indicated daily SO_2 (Sulfur Dioxide) concentrations in Donora may have been at least 1,800 micrograms per cubic meter or $\mu g/m$ (its mass in a fixed volume of outdoor air). PM (Particulate Matter) concentrations may have been at least 5,320 $\mu g/m$. By comparison, twenty-four hour U.S. public health-related ambient (outdoor) air quality standards adopted in 1971 for SO_2 and PM were 365 $\mu g/m$ and 260 $\mu g/m$, respectively.[54]

The Donora smog disaster proved to be a catalyst that brought the federal government, namely the Congress and the USPHS, into the policy debate about the health effects of air pollution. As one historian pointed out: "the air pollution episode at Donora, Pa. in 1948 stimulated the first flow of legislative proposals at the federal level in 1949."[55] The Clean Air Act of 1955, which provided funding for research and technical assistance, was a direct outcome of the Donora smog. With the end of worries about domestic smoke and the coming of the environmental movement in the decade of the 1960s, Americans were able to shift their attention to other air pollutants, especially those emitted by automobiles, and to factories and power-generating utilities using tall smoke stacks to disperse particulate and gaseous matter.

Cleaner fuels, namely natural gas and oil, replaced wood and coal as alternative energy sources in homes, factories, and businesses. The increasing population density of cities accelerated the process of substituting one fuel for another. The growth of cities and the expansion of surrounding agricultural land limited access of urbanites to woodlands. Increased density encouraged suppliers of natural gas to build pipelines to cities with their many potential customers. As a cost-effective alternative to coal, which faced strict regulation, natural gas and electricity became the energy sources of choice. In addition, new and cleaner furnaces and boilers replaced older inefficient models for homes, industry, and businesses. These newer technologies, along with the widespread use of alternative, cleaner fuels, reduced the amount of smoke inside buildings as well as outside in highly populated urban centers.

Los Angeles "Smog"

As the battle against domestic smoke was mostly won, concerns about air quality shifted to other pollutants, such as "smog" caused by leaded gasoline and other industrial emissions. Although Los Angeles prohibited the incineration of trash in open dumps in 1947, throughout the decade the city had experienced a new form of pollution, caused by the combination of the chemical elements found in smoke and the fog created by the city's peculiar geography and meteorology.

In the early 1940s, people living in the Los Angeles region experienced the negative effects of relying on the automobile for urban transport. Unlike the episodic smoke palls of the past, pollution now covered the region with a continuous hazy brown blanket. This photochemical air pollution was created by the interaction of chemicals and particulates emitted by automobiles with the region's topography, climate, and stagnant air. The Los Angeles area has been described as a:

> 1,600 square-mile bottom of a huge natural box. Three sides of the box are formed by mountains. . . . The fourth side of the box is provided by cool air currents moving gently but steadily in from the ocean. The air moving toward California descends, compresses, and heats. . . . As a consequence, when the warm air reaches the California coast, it is several degrees warmer than that at the land surface. Normally, air temperature decreases directly as altitude increases. Over . . . the Los Angeles region, the inverse is the case— the area is covered by a warm "inversion" layer.[56]

The inversion acts as an umbrella over the region, temporarily trapping slow-moving, polluted air. Eventually, the contaminated Los Angeles air reaches the mountains and has been heated sufficiently by the sunlight to dissipate the inversion. This allows the polluted air to move into the upper atmosphere, mix with cleaner air, and move through the mountain passes. As this air flow is completed, another cycle sharing the same characteristics has already begun. Without this movement, "polluted air would accumulate over the area in an ever-deepening layer."[57]

The role of sunlight in this complicated mix of air flow, topography, temperature, and ground-level pollutants is important to understanding the atmospheric conditions in the Los Angeles region. When sunlight interacts with motor vehicle emissions, it creates photochemical smog.* "Smog," the

---

*Los Angeles experiences temperature inversions between 250 and 340 days each year. About 120 of these days are ones in which inversions are severe, meaning that the atmospheric ceilings created by the inversions are about 1,500 feet from the surface of the land. This concentrates the pollutants closer to the ground. Inversions combine with weak wind currents do not possess the velocity to move air quickly through the region. As a result, stagnant air is a common phenomenon. For example, the average velocity of wind in the region is about six miles per hour, approaching three miles per hour during the summer months, the season when inversions are most severe. By comparison, New York City has an average wind current of eight miles per hour, the "windy city" of Chicago has an average wind speed of nine, and St. Louis's is ten. (James E. Krier and Edmund Ursin, *Pollution and Policy: A Case Essay on California and Federal Experience with Motor Vehicle Air Pollution, 1940–1975,* Berkeley, CA: University of California Press, 1977, 43.)

combination of smoke and fog, causes eye and membrane irritation and impaired visibility. It was a form of pollution that no one understood at the time. Observing the smog, as it was described then, did not begin to explain scientifically the causes of the region's air pollution.

In time, researchers discovered that automobile emissions, in the form of nitrogen oxides and hydrocarbons, synthesized when they came into contact with the bright California sunlight and created smog. Smog often combines with a number of other pollutants as well, including particulate matter such as dust, soot, and ash, to create a brownish haze familiar to inhabitants in many urban areas.

Not all of the evidence about the negative effects of auto transport were collected scientifically. Some of it was anecdotal and based on episodes with memorable characteristics. For example, as data was being gathered, an event took place which reinforced suspicions about the automobile's contribution to Los Angeles smog.

The event was an intercollegiate football game in 1949 on the campus of the University of California, Berkeley. While the game was being played, air pollution around the stadium was similar to the pollution first experienced by the residents of Los Angeles a decade before. The area around the stadium resembled Los Angeles in miniature, with a heavy concentration of automobiles and stalled traffic. Exhaust fumes, it was thought, must be a contributing factor to creating the pollution. In fact, pollution control studies in the 1940s pointed to the significance of internal combustion processes.[58]

In 1950 California biochemist A.J. Haagen-Smit noted the existence of photochemical reactions caused by the atmospheric combination of pollutants from automobiles and oil refineries. Initial resistance to his findings from the region's oil refineries and the nation's powerful automobile industry eventually evaporated, as the evidence accumulated about the contribution of the internal combustion engine to Los Angeles air problems. Haagen-Smit's research would be used in subsequent successful legislative efforts to curb oil refinery emissions and vehicular pollution in California, and the state would became a model for the eventual federal approach to automobile pollution.

The Clean Air Act and Amendments

The decades of the 1960s and 1970s were defined by the passage of air quality control legislation in California and in Congress. First, however, both passed laws in 1955 to investigate the causes and the environmental effects of air pollution. By 1956, eighty-two local governments had passed air pollution control programs. Oregon passed the first statewide program in 1951, and by 1954, fourteen other states had followed suit.[59]

Most of these local and state laws focused on controlling dense smoke coming from open fire pits, incinerators, and the smoke stacks of industrial and electric power-generating plants. Eliminating ground-level concentrations of dense smoke succeeded in improving air quality. For example, the total suspended particulate (TSP) in Los Angeles was as high as 1,000 µg/m in 1953. By 1970, TSP in the city had declined to 280 µg/m. The federal Air Pollution Control Act in 1955 provided research and technical assistance to the states. By 1960, the Congress had passed the Schenck Act, giving the Surgeon General authority to study the health effects of automobile emissions.

In the same year, California went much further than the Congress in passing air pollution control legislation. The state experienced increasing levels of photochemical pollution with one-hour ground-level ozone concentrations exceeding 1,200 ug/m. The California Motor Vehicle Pollution Control Act of 1960, the nation's first motor vehicle emissions law, identified vehicle emission standards for volatile organic compounds (VOCs) and carbon monoxide (CO). Also, it made California the first state to certify auto emission control technology for vehicles registered in the state. As California's legislators recognized air pollution as a statewide problem, the federal government became committed to air pollution controls and recognized the national importance of controlling auto emissions.

The Clean Air Act of 1963 provided research grants to states for the support of motor vehicle emission control programs and gave the Department of Health, Education, and Welfare authority to develop standards for measuring the effects of air pollution. With the passage of the 1965 Motor Vehicles Pollution Control Act, the federal government adopted the California vehicle emissions standards and extended them across the nation. These new standards became effective in 1968 for new automobiles. By 1967, however, Congress had recognized the weaknesses in the Clean Air Act of 1963 by passing an improved Air Quality Act.

This act greatly expanded the federal research budget, provided federal grants to states initiating inspection programs, and required petroleum companies to register the fuel additives they developed to improve engine efficiency. In addition, it established air quality standards and criteria for emission control technology. Under this legislation, the states were required to submit implementation plans meeting the criteria established by the act. Most importantly, the act denied to all states, except California, the right to impose emission control standards higher than those written by the federal government. California's emissions standards had become a national bellwether.

Unfortunately, none of these laws sufficiently challenged the states to reduce air pollution. However, the number of deaths caused by air pollution in a twenty-year period from the 1940s to the 1960s declined significantly. While domestic smoke emissions had been reduced, the public also demanded that the newer air pollution threats to human health be conquered.[60]

As the decade of the 1970s began, it was clear that air pollution caused by automobile emissions had not been curtailed nationally. For example, in Los Angeles county alone, the population had reached 7 million persons by 1970, an increase of over 1.5 million in fourteen years, while automobile registrations numbered 4 million, an increase of 1.2 million during the same period. In the same year, these same automobiles "were responsible for 90 percent of the total pollutant tonnage, and for 64 percent of all pollutants other than carbon monoxide. Vehicles contribute[d] virtually all of this latter pollutant."[61] The Clean Air Amendments of 1970 had begun the era of present air pollution policy.[62]

While the newly created Environmental Protection Agency was enforcing air quality standards, the 1970 amendment was written in response to the inactivity of the states in improving air quality. Specifically, Congress believed that the states had been negligent in carrying out the automobile inspection programs budgeted in the Air Quality Act of 1967. In addition, an "environmental crisis" had been proclaimed in 1969 and 1970 by the critics of our nation's economic policies and a government slow to respond to their environmental concerns. In interviews, documentaries, and news broadcasts, the news media brought the message of an impending crisis to the public. Earth Day was celebrated in April 1970 with public demonstrations, seminars, and conferences to publicize the condition of the nation's environment. Opinion polls taken in the same year showed that environmental problems were among the public's top concerns.

The Clean Air Amendments of 1970 required the Environmental Protection Agency (EPA) to develop two air quality standards for each pollutant. The primary standard was written to protect public health. Since the public health concerns of air pollution were first raised during the investigation of the Donora episode in 1949, state and federal clean air and air quality laws had been written to protect human health. A secondary standard written to promote public welfare included provisions to protect plant and animal life and maintain aesthetic and material well-being.

In many states, efforts were misplaced in trying to develop air quality standards. Energies could have been spent more appropriately in developing implementation plans. Also, some states were vulnerable to large industrial employers who threatened to move elsewhere unless less stringent standards were implemented statewide. By the beginning of the 1970s, however, it became clear that uniform national air quality standards were the only way in which to protect the nation's health. In addition, it became clear to both pollution control experts and critics of government policy that the goal of clean air could not be achieved across the nation without additional major reductions in automobile emissions.[63]

The Clean Air Amendments of 1970 gave the federal government expanded authority in dealing with air pollution. The law gave the EPA the authority to develop and enforce national ambient air quality standards (NAAQS). As one researcher noted: "among the most effective features of federalization are the NAAQS, which established an objective yard stick for people to gauge whether their air quality was 'healthful.' Their very presence creates pressures to improve air quality."[64] Also, the law set deadlines for meeting this "healthful" air standard. The deadline was set for 1975 but replaced with new deadlines after subsequent more stringent amendments to the act were passed. The amendments' most significant provision established automobile emission standards requiring 90 percent reductions in hydrocarbons (HC) and carbon monoxide (CO) by 1975 and in nitrogen oxides (NO_x) by 1976. Finally, it gave the EPA enforcement authority and oversight of state programs and policies, and provided citizens with the opportunity to sue violators of the amendments' provisions.[65]

In order to establish NAAQS, the Environmental Protection Agency began establishing standards for sulfur oxides (SO_x), carbon monoxide (CO), and nitrogen oxides (NO_x) in 1971. All of these chemicals contribute pollutants to the atmosphere. Sulfur oxides damage vegetation and cause respiratory and lung infections and disease. In the form of sulfuric acid mist, such oxides act as a corrosive agent. Carbon monoxide, a poisonous gas, is formed by the incomplete combustion of hydrocarbon-based fuels. Incomplete combustion occurs when the carbon is not oxidized fully to form carbon dioxide. As a result, carbon monoxide gas is released, as in automobile exhaust. Since breathing CO limits the oxygen-carrying capacity of the blood, it causes various human impairments. These include the loss of psychomotor functioning, and cardiovascular and pulmonary diseases; exposure to high concentrations of CO causes death.

Nitrogen oxides are also produced by the combustion of fossil fuels. The high temperature and pressure conditions of the automobile engine promote the formation of a variety of nitrogen oxide compounds, commonly referred to as NO_x. High concentrations of these substances have immediate and sometimes lethal health effects; short-term, low dosages of NO_x contribute to respiratory problems. Claims about the negative long-term health effects of exposure to these chemicals in low dosages, however, remain controversial.[66]

Compliance with the new federal standards regarding toxic motor vehicle and smoke stack emissions remained difficult for the states because replacing existing vehicles and manufacturing and power plants with new ones would occur gradually. If the cost of new vehicles rose sharply from installing new automobile emissions technology, consumers would be deterred from making new purchases. Retarding consumer purchases would further slow the transition from older, fuel-inefficient vehicles. In order to meet the EPA's compliance deadlines on emissions, the automobile industry turned to the use of catalytic converters to reduce unburned volatile organic compounds (VOCs) and carbon monoxide (CO).

Now common in the exhaust systems of motor vehicles, catalytic converters decompose toxic gases into mostly benign byproducts, namely water and carbon dioxide. Hot engine exhaust gases pass through the converter, whose surface is constructed in a honeycomb design to maximize catalytic surface area. The inside of the converter is coated with metals such as platinum or palladium, which oxidize the toxic exhaust gases as they pass through the converter at the very high temperature of 600°F.*

Long before there was a need for catalytic converters to meet the new federal emissions standards, the petroleum industry, in cooperation with the automobile manufacturers, added lead to high octane gasoline as a lubricant for engine valves to prevent knocking. Lead-based additives, however, destroyed the ability of catalytic converters to render harmless the toxic gases produced by the internal combustion engine.

To meet federal guidelines while assuring consumers that engine knock would not return, an organic-compound-based additive was found to replace lead, making way for the various types of unleaded fuel available to consumers today. At the same time that unleaded gasoline was introduced, converter-equipped vehicles became available to the consumer. When new

---

*Originally, standard catalytic converters were ineffective in controlling automobile emissions, because gases released during cold starts constituted up to 80 percent of total emissions during an average trip. To overcome the limitations of standard converters, a smaller electrically heated catalytic converter (EHC) was designed to perform until the larger converter could reach the proper lightoff temperature of 500°F. Later, the location of the EHC was changed to improve efficiency and electrical demand. It was placed directly before the main converter. By 1981, automobiles were able to meet the standards set by the Clean Air Amendments of 1977 through design improvements, including the three-way converter, which was able to oxidize three types of gaseous compounds—hydrocarbons, carbon monoxide, and nitrogen oxides. This technology incorporates the use of two converters, one located next to the engine, which heats up faster than the main converter placed near the tailpipe. Together, they reduce lead and nitrogen emissions by 90 to 95 percent. Combined with an onboard computer and oxygen sensor to self-regulate emissions, these newer devices replaced earlier standard converters. In order to safeguard against faulty equipment, cities and states established inspection and maintenance programs. Such programs required periodic testing of all passenger vehicles to monitor their emission control systems.

NAAQS for lead were established in 1978, compliance was achievable in most urban areas.

Reducing lead emissions from gasoline, paints, and smelter and battery plants has resulted in improvements in human health. As one researcher has pointed out, "lead in blood samples, a far better indicator of the public health impact of lead than outdoor air quality, has declined substantially. Between the late 1970s and 1991, the proportion of people having more than 10 micrograms [of lead] per deciliter of blood declined from 78% to 4.3%."[67]

The Environmental Protection Agency continued to fine-tune emissions control regulations. In 1985, the EPA adopted stringent emission standards for diesel-powered trucks and buses. These standards became effective in the early 1990s, after stricter limits were placed on the sulfur content of diesel fuel. Later in the decade, the EPA set fuel volatility limits for the first time, aimed at reducing evaporative emissions that account for a significant percentage of emissions from newer model automobiles. The federal government's contributions to reducing motor vehicle emissions through the past decades have proved to be very effective.

Although California demonstrated that a state could be quite effective in reducing emissions, federal intervention established national emissions standards. Progressively more demanding federal standards insured that the improvements achieved from existing regulations would not be lost. Yet, one researcher noted that "given . . . the diminishing returns from further tightening new source emission standards, the later should be frozen at current levels with the states being responsible for making them more stringent in their own jurisdictions."[68]

The Clean Air Amendments of 1990 recognized the contribution of nitrogen oxides (NO_x) and sulfur dioxide (SO_2) to the nation's acid rain and ground-level ozone (O_3)* problems. These amendments required further reductions in SO_2 from the tall stacks of industrial sources. Emissions from

---

*Ozone is a molecular form of oxygen consisting of three connected oxygen atoms (O_3). This ground-level ozone should not be confused with upper atmosphere ozone, which is developed naturally and serves as a shield to protect human and animal life from the cancer-causing ultraviolet radiation of the sun. Ground-level ozone, however, is an extremely hazardous pollutant formed when nitrogen oxides (NO_x), volatile organic compounds (VOCs), and hydrocarbons combine in the presence of sunlight and warm, stagnant air. On hot summer days, urban areas with high concentration of motor vehicles, the single greatest source of ozone-producing pollutants, are primary locations for the production of ground-level ozone. However, atmospheric conditions are capable of carrying the ozone hundreds of miles from its primary source, affecting many more people and a larger part of the environment than the primary site. Changes in weather patterns contribute to differences in ozone concentrations in different cities at different times of the year.

these point sources contribute to the production of sulfuric acid in the atmosphere, a major ingredient in the acid rain.

The Acid Rain Controversy

Acid rain is caused primarily by power plants in the midwestern states burning coal and emitting sulfur dioxide (mostly as soot) and nitrogen oxide (mostly as soot and smoke) from their exceptionally high smoke stacks, many exceeding 1,000 feet in height. A third gas, carbon dioxide, contributes little to the formation of acid rain but does contribute to global warming. Airborne sulfur dioxide in the upper atmosphere combines with other chemicals to become sulfuric acid mist. Wind currents carry the mist in an easterly direction toward the Middle Atlantic and New England states, where acid rain is primarily responsible for destroying plant life and the forests in the regions. To reduce acid rain emissions, the 1990 Clean Air Amendments established an innovative but controversial program of emissions trading among polluting industries. This program allows power companies to continue to pollute at current levels by purchasing credits from another power company that has reduced pollution more than is required by the 1990 Clean Air Amendments.

The 1990 amendments require utility companies to reduce sulfur dioxide emissions to 1980 levels. To achieve these emission levels, they have three basic options. Many of them have chosen to install giant scrubbers to wash away the sulfur before it becomes airborne, contaminating the New England countryside. As a second option, companies can gain credits by burning higher priced low-sulfur coal. By making the capital improvements either by installing scrubbers or by burning more expensive and cleaner fuel, companies can not only reduce emissions to 1980 levels, they can receive pollution credits from the federal government. These credits are then made available at a price to companies who fail to meet the 1990 amendments. This is the third option.

Originally power plant owners opposed the measure, predicting that a shortage of pollution credits would result in a cost of $1,000 to buy a single credit. The price has been closer to $100 because many companies chose to become competitive by building expensive scrubbers and purchasing low-sulfur coal, largely from Wyoming. As a result, a surplus of pollution credits became available to companies choosing to do nothing to comply with the new regulations. At the same time, utilities constantly scrapped old coal-fired plants and replaced them with newer, more efficient facilities, eliminating their need to buy pollution credits.

An important weakness in the 1990 amendments, however, was the failure to control nitrogen oxide emissions, another major contributor to the acidification of the soil. Acids leach important plant nutrients such as calcium from the soil. A decline in nutrients reduces the total amount of living matter or biomass in an ecosystem and stunts the growth of plants and trees. As Dr. Gene Likens, Director of the Institute for Ecosystem Studies, points out: "sensitive forest regions need the buffering quality of calcium compounds to neutralize acid rain."[69] With the amount of acid in the soil already, and the continuing release of nitrogen oxide emissions from power utilities, it will take decades for the woodlands to recover from the damage of past and present acidification.

The 1990 Clean Air Amendments did introduce a comprehensive set of programs aimed at further reducing pollution from motor vehicles. For example, the amendments encouraged an expanded inspection and management program (I/M), a higher standard for reducing gaseous emissions from vehicle tailpipes, and a new program that required cities with excessive ozone levels to initiate commuter programs to encourage increases in the average number of passengers in each vehicle.

The 1990 standards were followed two years later by the first federal standards setting automotive emission limits for carbon monoxide at cold temperatures (20°F). Accompanying these "cold start" standards was the arrival of oxygenated gasoline, introduced in cities such as Denver, Colorado, where carbon monoxide (CO) exceeded the levels permitted under federal pollution standards. In 1993, a new regulation outlawed production of vehicles that burned leaded fuel.

Finally, in 1994, on-board diagnostic systems and emission control systems were required for new automobiles to meet federal warranty provisions. Clearly, progress in improving the nation's air quality has been noteworthy since the passage of the Clean Air Amendments of 1970. Progress, however, does not translate into unqualified success because many areas of the country are in noncompliance. As of January 1997, despite a substantial weakening of the original 1979 emissions control standard and renaming it the ozone standard, sixty-eight areas were in noncompliance for the ozone NAAQS; thirty for CO; forty-three for SO_2; and one for NO_x.[70]

How Clean is Clean Enough?

The Clean Air regulations of 1997 responded to the widely recognized conclusion that the 1990 regulations limiting ozone concentrations equal to 120 parts per billion were not sufficiently strict to protect public health. As a result, the new standard of 80 parts per billion replaced the old standard. The new standard on ozone requires auto makers, truckers, petrochemical producers, and power-generating utilities to develop newer technologies to cut emissions further.* Also, the new standards defined airborne, microscopic particles of soot of 2.5 parts per million as dangerous to public health. Ultrafine particles escape the numerous natural human barriers located in the mucus membranes, nose, and throat and become lodged more deeply in the lungs. Since the largest quantity of ultrafine particles are produced by coal-fired electric utility plants, the utility industry will be forced to invest in more efficient chimney scrubbers and new pollution control equipment.

Presently, the electric utility industry is the nation's largest stationary source of air pollution. It accounts for almost one-third of all the ground-level ozone-producing nitrogen oxide and carbon dioxide emissions and two-thirds of the sulfur dioxide emissions, the primary cause of acid rain.

Currently, the EPA is implementing an agreement reached by thirteen East Coast states to reduce nitrogen oxide emissions by 75 percent by the year 2003.[71] Utility plants also account for the high mercury levels in the waterways of the Northeast. In 1997, the EPA reported that coal-fired power plants and municipal incinerators are major sources of mercury emissions that harm aquatic and bird life and at very high levels cause neurological damage in humans. The report went on to point out that municipalities need to prohibit the burning of batteries, fluorescent light bulbs, thermometers, and other sources of mercury in incinerators.[72] One researcher has pointed out that "you want to do some technology-forcing early on, before industry commits to plants that may eventually require costly modification."[73]

The Contribution of Our Energy-Hungry Society to the Phenomenon of Global Warming

A growing consensus exists among scientists that warming of the atmosphere is caused by the carbon dioxide and other gases emitted by burning fossil fuels. The combustion of coal, petroleum, and natural gas by motor vehicles, factories, and power plants along with the burning of the world's woodlands are the major sources of airborne pollutants. Although scientists

---

*In early 1998, auto makers announced plans to begin building gasoline-powered cars that eliminate 99 percent of smog-producing emissions. These conventional internal combustion engine automobiles would be equipped with advanced catalytic converters and electronic engine control systems that further reduce the emissions of hydrocarbons and nitrous oxide. Before auto makers begin production, however, they want California and many northeastern states to drop the requirement for the auto makers to begin selling zero-emission electric cars in these states by the year 2000. Many states require that 10 percent of total automobile sales be zero-emission vehicles by the year 2000.

do not know this with absolute certainty, the consensus is that global warming is caused by heat-trapping "greenhouse" gases. Without high concentrations of the gases, the sun's heat in the atmosphere would be reflected back into space. Mainstream scientists believe that the high emission of heat-trapping greenhouse gases during the past century of rapid industrialization have caused the average surface temperature of the planet to rise about one degree Fahrenheit. They point out that about half a degree rise has occurred in the last forty years, with temperatures rising faster the farther away one moves from the Equator.

They base their findings on the long-accepted theory that the earth's atmosphere is much like the glass ceiling in a greenhouse. The atmosphere, similar to a glass ceiling, lets in the sunlight and traps some of the sunlight's warmth. If the atmosphere did not act like a greenhouse and possessed no heat-retaining ability, the planet would have an average surface temperature of 0° Fahrenheit.* Which of the atmosphere's elements have heat-retaining properties, however? As it turns out, the two most abundant elements, namely nitrogen and oxygen, discovered by the British physicist John Tyndall in the 1850s and representing 99 percent of the atmosphere, possess no heat-trapping properties.

In effect, this means that two heat-trapping gases, carbon dioxide (CO_2) and water vapor, are responsible for warming the earth's atmosphere. Without CO_2 the air around us would be twenty degrees colder, and without water vapor in the air the earth would become a frozen planet. Scientists know that these gases exist in only small trace amounts in the atmosphere—they are measured in parts per million and even in parts per billion. It has been noted that atmospheric carbon dioxide concentrations have risen from 280 parts per million before the launching of the Industrial Revolution in the 1750s to 360 parts per million today. At this level, these measurements still represent small trace amounts. Mainstream scientists have observed, however, that these small but growing amounts of trace gases may exert a powerful effect on global climates.

---

*The average global surface temperature reached its highest point in a century in 1997 at 62.45°F. Surface thermometers and satellite instruments measure the earth's temperature in different parts of the climate system, and they show a warming trend of 0.13 degree for each decade. From the perspective of most scientists, this change is not significant on a decade basis, but the trend could be alarming. Many believe that a new record will be achieved by the year 2000. While the earth has warmed generally, some sections of the United States, namely the East and South, have actually cooled, while the West has grown warmer. The twentieth century began with an average global surface temperature of 61.5°. Since that time, a general upward trend has occurred.

The effects they foresee include the following:

> The seas would rise . . . inundating many coastal areas and swamping small island nations. The world as a whole would become rainier, with most of the increase coming in the big downpours that cause floods. At the same time, drought-prone areas would get more droughts.
>
> Climatic zones would shift away from the poles. Since the warming would be unusually rapid, many natural ecosystems might be unable to adjust, and whole forest types could disappear. Growing seasons are already lengthening in northern latitudes, and temperate-zone agriculture might benefit in the long run. But in dry areas, like much of Africa, warming could bring agricultural ruin. Tropical diseases like malaria and dengue fever could spread. And while temperate-zone winters would be milder, summer heat waves would be more intense and deadly.[74]

Although such predictions are filled with uncertainty, the potential threat of these climatic changes cries out for human action. According to some experts, additional global warming is inevitable because only about one-half of the full impact of already emitted greenhouse gases has been felt by the climate systems of the planet. The oceans, which absorb millions of tons of these gases, act as a drag on the heating of the atmosphere; thus, the planet's climate systems respond slowly to the changing carbon load in the atmosphere.

Greenhouse gas emissions since the beginning of the Industrial Revolution have resulted in a one degree Fahrenheit rise in average surface global temperatures. The world scientific community predicts that emissions at the same level throughout the twenty-first century will result in a rise of two to six degrees. If this nightmarish scenario occurred in 2100, then the earth's average temperature would be higher than it had been for the last 120,000 years. One scientist, who carries the calculations out another one hundred years to 2200, contends that within five hundred years, the average surface temperature could be twelve degrees higher than at present. The point being made by this scientist is that "if too little is done too late, the world may in time regret the consequence. If you get to where you don't like, there's not a lot you can do about it—you're wired in for a long time."[75]

Other scientists contend, however, that much of the warming occurred before 1940, while much of the greenhouse gas emissions were released after that date; so, according to them, only some of the warming can be attributed to human activity. Others believe that regardless of the causes of global warming, some warming of the planet will have beneficial effects, as it did during Europe's medieval period from about 800 A.D. to about 1400 A.D. During this period, climate conditions favored the expansion of agriculture, which resulted in economic progress and improvement of the general

Grinnell Glacier, 1910. Courtesy Glacier National Park Archives.

welfare. Today, warmer climate conditions with higher CO_2 levels could stimulate plant growth and reduce plants' need for water. The result would be longer growing seasons in the northern hemisphere and higher agricultural productivity. Despite the complexity of the debate and the present limitations of science to explain the trend, there is growing agreement among scientists that warming is a potential threat to life as we know it.

For those who do not accept the explanation offered by most scientists, what alternative explanations are there to explain the warming? Explanations include the natural variability in the earth's climate and the solar activity of the sun; that is, natural activity such as sun–earth interactions offer a probable competing explanation for the planet's warming. For centuries, scientists have known about the cyclical variations in the sun's activity, ranging from its solar storms to its sunspots and flares lasting about eleven years. In the last decade, some scientists have begun associating these activities of the sun with the shifts in the earth's climate. They have focused on three characteristics of the sun which may affect our weather patterns. They include:

> the sun's overall brightness, which is seen as affecting temperatures; the sun's ultraviolet rays, which are seen as affecting winds and ozone produc-

Grinnell Glacier, 1931. Courtesy Glacier National Park Archives.

tion high in the atmosphere, and the sun's storms of magnetic fields and subatomic particles, which are seen as affecting rainfall and the amount of cloud cover.[76]

Knowledge of the relationship of the sun's brightness and the earth's climate can be traced back in time to when information about changing temperature conditions began to be gathered. Between 1640 and 1720, the earth's average temperature fell two degrees Fahrenheit. As a result, snowfall on glaciers exceeded normal accumulations. The path of winter storms, especially in Northern Europe, grew wider and they lasted longer. Generally, the winter season lengthened. Scientists also observed a significant drop in the number of sunspots during this same eighty-year period. Sunspots have been described as dark blemishes on the sun with relatively low temperatures. Until recently, it was assumed that their disappearance would cause the sun to glow brightly, causing a rise in the earth's temperature.

Now we know the reverse to be true. The sun glows brightly when there is maximum sunspot activity and dimmer when it disappears. The bright patches on the sun called *faculae* accompany sunspots in an eleven-year

Grinnell Glacier, 1997. Courtesy Glacier National Park Archives.

solar cycle and overpower the dimming effect of the sun's dark blemishes. All of the scientific evidence suggests that the sun's brightening has an ancient and variable rhythm.[77] If the sun's brightness may account for some of the earth's heating, what else, if anything, can explain climate change?

Sunlight in the ultraviolet range is known to change oxygen (O_2) in the upper atmosphere into ozone (O_3). Ozone in combination with heat is alleged to cause changes in temperature and the path of winter storms. Since many scientists dispute the impact of these solar events on climate change, a third kind of solar activity is enlisted to explain sun–earth interactions. This activity is not brightness but the velocity of the solar "winds" of particles and magnetic fields: "on Earth, the solar wind is well known to produce the aurora borealis, or northern lights. When it is blowing strong, it can also cause transformers at power plants to burst into flames, radio communications to fail and satellites to stop working or even fall from the sky."[78] The effect on earth's climate has also been observed during periods of low solar winds and high cosmic rays, which produce high electric charges on clouds, contributing to rainfall. However informative these findings are about the relationship of solar activity and the earth's climate, though, skeptics remain unconvinced that solar activity explains more about climate change than the effects of human pollution.

The Atlantic "Conveyer" and Its Effect on Climate Change

One of the more disturbing ideas about global warming concerns its effects on the current of the Atlantic Ocean, called the Atlantic thermhaline circulation. The circulation or "conveyer" begins near Greenland, where cold salt water sinks to more than a mile deep and moves southward, passing South America. Warmer water on the surface of the ocean moves northward, becoming the "Gulf Stream" as it passes North America. The breadth of this warm water flow is so extensive that it warms the air above it, providing warmth as far east as Europe. The importance of the salt content of the water in the North Atlantic cannot be minimized, for the salt content causes the water to sink to the depth of one mile and gets the conveyer moving. Increased salinity would cause the conveyer to speed up, amplifying temperature changes. Decreased salinity would prevent water from sinking off the coast of Greenland and might dramatically slow down or turn off the conveyer entirely.

What would reduce the salinity of the ocean water? A rise in the average temperature of the earth could cause increased rainfall and a more rapid melting of the Arctic glaciers. Fresh water melt and precipitation into the ocean off the coast of Greenland would slow or stop the Atlantic conveyer, and the warm water flow from the south Atlantic would be altered significantly. If this occurred, Europe might enter an era of extreme cold and, even worse, the entire earth might get considerably colder. As one earth and environmental scientist has concluded: "a slight weakening of the ocean circulation could be likened to a sledgehammer blow—one that could conceivably bring the present interglacial to its knees."[79]

In light of the new knowledge about the effects of the Atlantic conveyer, the predictions of gradual climatic changes caused by the buildup of greenhouse gases may have to be changed by mainstream scientists. Since they believe that greenhouse gas emissions are probably responsible for at least part of the rise of one degree in average global temperature in the last century, it is fair to estimate that unless emissions are reduced, there will be a further rise of perhaps 3.5 degrees in the next century. By comparison, the temperature of the earth has warmed between five and nine degrees since the last Ice Age, 13,000 years ago. A disruption of the Atlantic conveyer could trigger immediate catastrophic changes in the world's climate. The same scientist quoted above concluded by saying: "there's no way to predict whether this is going to happen. We can get some indication that we're approaching the edge of the cliff, but there's no way to say if it's 1 chance in 2 . . . or 1 chance in 200. It's Russian roulette where you don't know how many chambers are in the gun."[80]

United States Contribution to Atmospheric Warming

A little more than 4.7 percent of the world's population lives in the United States, yet the United States possesses 22 percent of the world's wealth, and each year it consumes 25 percent of the world's energy production. Automobiles and trucks driven by Americans account for 5 percent of all human-related carbon dioxide emissions.* Burning one gallon of gasoline releases 19 pounds of carbon dioxide. The lifetime emissions of a car getting twenty miles per gallon total 50 tons. For 20,000 cars the lifetime emissions total is one million metric tons. When 166 countries met in 1992 for the Earth Summit in Rio de Janeiro, Brazil, they reached an agreement to voluntarily reduce emissions of greenhouse gases by 2000. The United States has not come close to achieving the goals established at the Rio Summit. Since 1992, United States emissions of carbon dioxide from motor vehicles and power plants have grown nearly 10 percent. In 1995, 19.9 metric tons of carbon dioxide were produced for each American.[81] By way of comparison, on a per capita basis Europeans contribute 7.9 metric tons of carbon dioxide.

Entering the era of mass consumption, China has increased its energy usage by more than 200 percent since 1970 and will double its energy consumption in the next decade. Similar changes are occurring in India, Indonesia, Mexico, Brazil, and the other emerging market economies of Asia and Latin America. With 40 percent of the world's population, China, India and Indonesia account for about 15 percent of the world's carbon dioxide emissions. This percentage will increase as the per capita incomes of these countries rise, and consumers have more disposable income. Thus, efforts to stabilize atmospheric carbon dioxide at current levels of 360 parts per million will also become a challenge to new industrial countries.

---

*Automobiles and industrial smoke stacks are viewed as the primary reasons for carbon dioxide concentrations in the atmosphere. However, as scientists calculate the world's total CO_2 concentration, they need to include emissions from volcanoes, hot springs, and other thermal features of the earth. For example, the thermal features of Yellowstone National Park in Wyoming vent millions of tons of CO_2 annually. The Yellowstone Mud Volcano area emits about 176,300 tons of CO_2 each year, and the total for the entire park is approximately 44 million tons annually. In contrast, a middle-size power plant releases about 4.4 million tons of CO_2 per year. ("Yellowstone Park Emits Tons of Carbon Dioxide, Study Finds," *New York Times,* December 26, 1997.)

With carbon dioxide levels at 450 parts per million at the end of the twenty-first century, a realistic figure to many scientists, the total temperature increase from the end of the twentieth century to the end of the twenty-first century will be about two and one half to three degrees Fahrenheit. Carbon dioxide concentrations could grow unchecked if industrial countries continue their present practice of adding CO_2 tonnage to the atmosphere and if developing countries conduct "business as usual" in their quest for economic growth and personal comfort.

The older industrial countries need to stimulate action to replace existing capital stock, such as power plants and industrial facilities, while the newer industrial and developing countries need to begin the industrializing process using more energy-efficient capital stock, including nonfossil fuel installations. Currently, neither is taking place rapidly enough. Transitions are slow, and investments in new capital stocks often occur over a long time period. Economies are not changed overnight. However, if lower concentrations of greenhouse gases are desired, reductions must be made sooner rather than later.

∾

Document 4.1

Smoke Worse than Fire (1911)

Herbert M. Wilson

The smoke nuisance is one of the greatest dangers of modern times, insidiously attacking the health of the individual and lowering his vitality, increasing the death rate, and causing untold loss and injury to property. The damage this evil inflicts can hardly be estimated in money; it is equally impossible to estimate the amount of suffering, disease and death, and the general effect of lowered vitality caused by this nuisance.

A careful inquiry was recently made by the government concerning the toll paid by the people of the United States on account of smoke. Unfortunately few cities have investigated the costs involved, but for those that have furnished data, the results are almost startling. Summing up the results of inquiries in a number of cities the estimate is made that smoke causes more than $500,000,000 damage each year in the destruction of merchandise, the defacement of buildings, tarnishing of metals, injury to human life and plant life, the greatly increased labor and cost of housekeeping, and the losses to manufacturers due to imperfect combustion of coal.

Reprinted from Herbert M. Wilson, "Smoke Worse than Fire," *The American City* 4 (1911): 210–212.

In our great and middle-sized cities live more than 30,000,000 people, and these suffer all the loss shown in the total of $500,000,000. This means a per capita loss of $17 each year to every man, woman and child in these cities. This sum is so vast that it fails of comprehension. It would build nearly a Panama Canal and a half every year. But more startling still, considered as an annual per capita tax, the losses incurred by the inhabitants of American cities equal the total taxes they pay on their real and personal property, and equal one-third the total corporate debt of all American cities of this size.

The Loss Estimated

Those figures are so astounding as to be almost unbelievable, and it is but fair to tell on what this estimate was based. A short time ago smoke officials of Chicago, after careful inquiry, reported that the city lost $50,000,000 each year through smoke. Cleveland conducted a similar inquiry among its merchants and placed the smoke damage at $4,000,000. St. Louis, in estimating the damage on merchandise alone, gave it at $1,000,000. The city of Harrisburg showed a $120,000 loss for the year.

The Smoke Committee of Cleveland, discussing the losses occasioned by smoke reported:

> There are approximately 400 retail dry goods stores in Cleveland doing business of from $10,000 to $3,000,000 or $4,000,000 a year. The owners of some of these stores estimate, and the same estimate is given in other cities, that on all white goods a clear loss of 10 per cent must be figured. Taking the single items of underwear, shirt waists, linens and white dress goods for the eleven department stores, the proprietors conservatively estimate their combined loss at $25,000. Consider then the loss in all lines of light goods for all 400 stores. The wholesale dry goods houses show a similar loss. In Cleveland there are 55 men's furnishing stores, and the conservative estimate of loss in these stores is placed at $15,000 annually. The stores mentioned represent only a small portion of the trade affected.
>
> Aside from the damage to stock an annual cost for cleaning, particularly among retail houses, must be included. One retail establishment in Cleveland paid, just a year after painting and decorating its walls and ceilings, $1,800 for repainting and redecorating, made necessary entirely by smoke. During the same year the bill of this house for window cleaning was $2,000, for laundry purposes $1500. This in a measure was due to the smoke nuisance. Multiply these figures by the thousands of business houses needing the same attention, and some estimate of the total cost in this direction may be obtained. To this should be added the cost of lighting, particularly in retail stores, factories and offices, made necessary by the smoky atmosphere.

Damage to Homes

But a greater cost than all of these must be considered in the loss to the 100,000 homes in Cleveland. The constant need of cleaning walls, ceilings, windows, carpets, rugs and draperies, for redecorating and renewing, can be realized only by the house owner or housekeeper. To this should be added the increased laundry bills for household linen, the cost of dry cleaning clothing, and the great additional wear resulting from this constant renovation, necessitating frequent renewal. Consider also the permanent injury to books, pictures and similar articles. Though impossible of computation, it will be seen that the total of these items aggregates millions of dollars.

In Chicago one prominent merchant of State Street asserted that in his establishment alone the price of goods was reduced to $200,000 in one year because of being soiled, most of the damage having been done by smoke in the atmosphere.

A St. Louis dry goods merchant estimated that from 7 1/2 to 12 per cent on the cost is not an excessive estimate of the loss which St. Louis dry goods merchants are called upon to sustain in depreciation of the value of merchandise on account of the smoke nuisance, exclusive of the expense incident to the care of merchandise, to which merchants are subjected to prevent a greater loss. Another merchant of St. Louis said:

> Our porter and cleaning bill runs about $17,000 a year and much of it would be unnecessary were it not for the extra dirt due to smoke.

A St. Louis book and stationary dealer testified that:

> A very conservative estimate of our damage due to smoke would be $10,000 annually. We employ three boys whose sole duty it is to clean the soot from the stock.

Trees Killed

The City Forester of St. Louis declared that more than 4 per cent of the city trees are killed every year by smoke. In that city it has been found impossible to grow evergreen conifers, except the dwarf juniper and the Austrian pine. Only the hardiest of roses grow in that city. The trees which suffer the greatest injury are the oaks, hickories and conifers, and these are especially ideal park trees and far more valuable for beauty and permanence than the softer wooded varieties.

Turning now to the losses in fuel combustion: our present method of burning coal with smoke is costing the people of this country, unnecessarily, $99,000,000. It is estimated that 8 per cent of the coal used in the production of power, light and heat, or in all about 20,000,000 tons of coal, are going up the chimneys each year in smoke. This coal costs the people at least $40,000,000. It is further estimated that in the production of coke 25,000,000 tons of coal are wasted in the air. This coal is worth $50,000,000.

Loss of Life

While this total loss of $90,000,000 due to imperfect combustion, added to the losses due to damaged property, aggregates a vast sum, it is as nothing compared with the injury to life which the smoke inflicts in the great cities. The smoke nuisance means uncleanliness, wretchedness, disease and death. Comparing physical and vital assets as measured by earning power, vital assets are three to five times the physical assets. Dr. Irving Fisher, in his report to the National Conservation Commission on the subject of human vitality, writes:

It is found that fifteen years, at least, could be at once added to the average human lifetime by applying the science of preventing disease; more than half of this gain would come from the prevention of tuberculosis, typhoid, and five other diseases, the prevention of which would be accomplished by purer air, water and milk. The prime source of the pollution of the atmosphere is smoke. The death rate is higher in the city than in the country, and the larger the city the higher the death rate.

In a report to the London City Council a scientific expert said:

Pure air is essential to a thoroughly healthy life, and the effects of smoke in vitiating the atmosphere are shown by the fact that children born and bred in big towns are usually of inferior physique, and this degeneration is growing in succeeding generations of town dwellers. Indeed, the standard of health in towns is only kept up by the constant influx of people born and bred in the country, and there is little doubt that a smoke-laden atmosphere diminishes the vitality of those who continually breathe it, increases their liability to disease, and finally shortens their lives. Also it is more than probable that living in a foul atmosphere which diminishes the vitality, increases the desire for stimulants, induces drunkenness and concomitants—brutality, immorality, and crime.

It Shuts People In

Dr. John W. Wainwright, of New York, states:

One effect of the smoky atmosphere, even worse than breathing it, is found in its indirect effect in causing people to keep their windows closed, and so breathe a more vitiated atmosphere within. It has been recognized for some time that one of the conditions most favorable to consumption is to be found in defective ventilation, the breathing over and over of the same foul air. Another effect not to be lost sight of is that the presence of soot in the atmosphere shuts off and obscures sunlight, which is so important to a healthy life. The eyes are subjected to a continuous overstrain, bringing on headaches and a whole train of nervous diseases. A smoky atmosphere by its exclusion of light, its content of sooty, acrid and irritating particles suspended in it is harmful to the tissues of the nose, throat, eyes, and especially to the lungs and air passages, whether in a healthy or other condition; aggravates the discomfort of all those suffering from all forms of ordinary diseases, increases the distress of those with nervous complaints, lowers the tone of general health, is a peril to the aged, diminishes the buoyancy of spirits, and reduces still further the already lowered resistance of disease.

What smoke costs in reduced vital energy is forcefully shown in the figures given by Rollo Russell, who estimates that the shifting pall of smoke which hangs over London costs Londoners as much as $25,000,000 a year. It is estimated that owing to the perpetual haze lying between sun and city that London gets only 50 per cent of the sun's light between November and February and only 84 per cent from May to August. Sir Frederick Treves, a famous physician, said that in three days fog in Manchester it was calculated that for every square mile 150 pounds of sulphuric acid and 1,300 pounds of soot were deposited. A similar examination in Chelsea showed that for every square mile there were 6 tons of soot. Sir Frederick said that from what he had seen of the lungs of dead persons in London they were absolutely black both on the surface and down to their depths. He declared that smoke kills people not by scores but by thousands.

Smoke a Poisonous Gas

It must be understood that smoke, aside from the looks and tangible shapes in which it presents itself, is one of the most poisonous gases polluting the very air we breathe. So apparent is this fact that physicians in our larger cities state their ability to tell at a moment's glance at the lungs in a postmortem examination whether the man has lived more than thirty days in such a city or not. In the former case their examination proves that the blood, instead of showing red, is black as soot can make it.

Medical men the world over are unanimous in the declaration that the breathing of coal smoke predisposes the lungs to tuberculosis and even more violent lung trouble, such as pneumonia, as well as to many other acute diseases. We know that lung diseases are more prevalent in smoky cities; that the death rate of children due to diseases of the respiratory organs is especially great in coal and iron districts; that tuberculosis is more rapidly fatal in smoky regions.

According to the report of the National Conservation Commission, 150,000 persons die each year in the United States from tuberculosis, and 500,000 are suffering from that disease at the present time. The statement is made that, with the proper hygienic conditions and the absence of smoke, three-fourths of the deaths from tuberculosis are preventable. In other words, we are wasting of that most precious of all resources—human life—112,500 men, women and children each year. If we appraise each life lost at $1,700, as some European insurance companies do, and each year's average earnings as $700, the economic gain to be obtained from preventing tuberculosis through impure atmosphere and bad hygienic conditions would be $270,000,000 in one year. It is this sum which, added to the losses in property damage and fuel value previously considered, make the total of $500,000,000 first stated as the estimated losses due to the smoke nuisance.

In addition to all the above; there is the psychological effect of smoke. The city enveloped in a sooty fog is a gloomy city and the children reared therein are in danger of growing up with too much toleration for dirt and too little of that full enthusiasm for the beautiful and clean things of life which sunlight and God's blue sky encourage about as well as anything else in this world.

As more than one-third of the people of the United States live in cities, the smoke nuisance has become a national pest. The fuel division of the Geological Survey is charged with conducting investigations into the fuel resources of the country looking to the best utilization of the supply, and thus prolonging the life of the coal fields. That this is absolutely necessary is seen from the fact that during the past ten years nearly as much coal has been used in this country as had been produced during the preceding century. The increase in the use of coal has been so great that if the present ration of increase were to continue the coal fields of this country will be exhausted before the end of the next century.

Document 4.2

Fortunes That Have Literally Gone Up in Smoke (1913)

Edward J. Wheeler

About one-half of the soot is carbon, which is commonly known in the form of charcoal or graphite, or in a still purer state as the diamond. A form of carbon, which is much more like soot, is called lampblack, and this is used for making black paint. Those familiar with lampblack paints know that it takes very little of the paint to blacken a large surface, and this is also one of the properties of soot, the one which makes it so injurious to delicate fabrics and even to more ordinary clothing.

In addition to the carbon, soot contains about one-fifth of its weight of tar and oil, and these very sticky substances cause soot to have somewhat the properties of paint, and make it much more difficult to remove the black substance from any kind of cloth. This tar and oil seem to be somewhat caustic in their action, and cause the soot to have an injurious effect on the leaves of plants; but much more injurious than this is the sulphuric acid, amounting to about one-twentieth of the weight of the soot. This acid eats up the cloth, the leaves of trees, and even into stones or the steel rails of the railways. It may not eat holes in the cloth, but it weakens the fabric, and on leaves it often causes the formation of spots.

Besides these substances soot contains a large number of ingredients of interest to a chemist, which are here put down in order to show its complexity. It contains ammonia, best known as a cleaning fluid; phosphate of lime, a constituent of bones; from one-tenth to one-fourth of its weight of sand; and small quantities of potash, soda, lime, magnesia, iron, phosphate of aluminum, chlorine, sulpho-cyanogen, carbonic acid, water, and traces of other substances.

Reprinted from Edward J. Wheeler, editor, "Fortunes that Have Literally Gone up in Smoke," *Current Opinion* 54 (January 1913): 72–73.

Document 4.3

The Smoke Problem (1907)

David Townsend

It is practically impossible to secure perfectly smokeless combustion in any ordinary furnace fired by hand, under the usual conditions of natural draft as existing today in the majority of plants. Some device is therefore necessary to accomplish this result. There have been innumerable appliances devised to consume or prevent smoke, but nearly all of these aim to do so by purely mechanical means, with usually indifferent results, because the fundamental laws governing combustion are chemical laws rather than mechanical principles.

The usual solution of the smoke problem, so far, has come from the introduction of mechanical means of handling the coal, which gives a uniform feed to the fuel and a corresponding delivery of air for combustion. The use of mechanical stokers has been brought about by the mutual demand for machine handling in large power plants as more economical than human labour, rather than by a philanthropic desire to benefit the community. It has been estimated that one able-bodied man with a shovel and slice-bar can take care of 200 horse-power of boilers. With good mechanical stokers he can handle double, and with complete coal and ash-handling equipment, three times this amount.

Stokers may be divided into three general classes: inclined shaking grates, travelling or chain grates, and under-feed stokers. The inclined grate has a hopper in front and slopes down and back, having a clinker grate just in front of the bridge wall; while the double incline has a magazine on either side and slopes in two planes parallel to the axis of the boiler, meeting in a clinker grate at the bottom. The principle of action is practically the same and involves the slow coking of the coal on a dead plate, the pushing forward on the top of the incline and the gradual descent, impelled by oscillation of the grate bars, until the combustion has left nothing but ash and clinker at the bottom. Air is usually admitted both below and above the grate and the hydrocarbons which are distilled at the top of the grates pass through the intense heat of the burning coke on their way to bridge wall. The double incline usually has a revolving clinker bar which disposes of some of the ash automatically, but as a rule both forms need considerable cleaning. When used with a fuel which does not cake or clinker too much, and when not crowded too hard, these stokers reduce the amount of smoke considerably. If, however, it becomes necessary to slice and poke the fire, on account of coking coal or overcrowded boilers, unburned masses of coal are rolled to the bottom and holes are made in the fire through which cold air rushes. Both of these circumstances make for poor combustion and a smoky fire. As a rule, firemen poke the fire on stokers too much, doing more harm than good.

The under-feed stokers operate on an entirely different principle, the coal being

---

Reprinted from David Townsend, "The Smoke Problem," *Cassier's Magazine* 32 (October 1907): 541–542.

fed in underneath the grate and forced up through the rectangular opening in the center. A forced blast is used and the air for combustion is blown up through the coal, the tuyeres being on either side of the rectangular opening just mentioned. By this arrangement the fresh coal is always underneath and the distilled gases are obliged to pass through an incandescent mass of fuel in company with the air. The ash and clinker are now at the top of the fuel, which forms a gradual rising mound in the center and pushes the clinker over to either side, whence it is removed by hooks through doors at the front. The heat generated is such that the ash generally melts and forms a sheet of clinker which can be removed without disturbing the fire.

In the American stoker the coal is forced under the grate and up by a revolving screw, somewhat similar in shape to the ordinary gimlet-pointed lag screw. In the Jones underfeed stoker, a plunger driven by steam operates to feed the coal. This plunger can be arranged to start and stop by hand or to run automatically.

Another method, and one which is apparently based upon correct chemical principles, is that known as the Cornell economizer, this system utilizing the waste heat passing over the bridge wall to dissociate a small amount of steam to oxygen and hydrogen in cast-iron retorts, the resulting gases being passed through the fire and furnishing oxygen to combine with the otherwise unburned carbon and hydrogen to burn itself in the furnace. The presence of oxygen renders it unnecessary to have an excess of air, and thus prevents the chilling of the furnace, while the proportions may be made such as to effect practically a complete and smokeless combustion, independently of the method of firing the solid fuel.

The economy resulting from the abatement of smoke is naturally a potent argument in its favor. This phase of the subject has, however, little to do with the ethics of the question, as every community has a right to insist on its abatement regardless of economical considerations.

As a general proposition smoke consumption means economy of fuel, as it is the result of perfect combustion and the combination of carbon and oxygen to form a colorless, unburnable gas. Of course, it must always be remembered that a smokeless chimney does not always mean economy, as an excess of air may dilute the chimney gases sufficiently to cause a serious waste of heat.

Document 4.4

Annual Report of the Metropolitan Board of Health of New York (1868)

Edward Dalton

Narrow and filthy streets, crowded, ill-ventilated, and dark dwellings, lack of provision for drainage, and of facilities for personal and general cleanliness—these were the causes of pestilence no less in medieval Europe than at the present day. It needs but a glance to see how the frequency and virulence of epidemics have decreased with the application of improved sewerage, the introduction of plentiful supplies of water, the destruction or remodeling of crowded and filthy quarters, and the removal from populous districts of such processes and manufactures as contaminate the atmosphere, and so reduce the vigor and degrade the *morale* of the inhabitants.

It was a consideration of these facts, together with the daily increasing evidence that the city of New York, or at least a large portion of it, was already in a condition, not only to foster such ordinary forms of disease as depend upon foul air and general uncleanliness, but to invite and rapidly develop contagion and pestilence, that some six years since stimulated the legislative action which resulted in the establishment of the Metropolitan Board of Health.

Many portions of New York and Brooklyn, but especially of New York, had become densely populated, not only, in fact not chiefly, with native citizens, but with immigrants from abroad. Every week added largely to this population. The older portions of the city, where the laboring classes congregated, were becoming overcrowded to a degree that rendered cleanliness and decency almost impossible.

Diseases of every kind, but especially such as have their origin directly or indirectly in the lack of pure air, personal cleanliness, and nutritious food, prevailed constantly and to an alarming extent among the inhabitants of these districts. The mortality was very great, particularly among children; and it was from time to time startlingly evident that the almost utter neglect of sanitary regulation was leaving the city a victim to the poisonous influence of these sources of sickness, which were daily extending their limits, and every year more imminently threatening to destroy the salubrity of a city to which Nature had afforded special facilities for the preservation of life and health. . . .

On the 26th of February, 1866, a Health Law was passed by the Legislature. . . .

This law created a Metropolitan Sanitary District, comprising the cities of New York and Brooklyn and several adjoining counties, which was to be under the control, in all matters bearing upon the public health, of a Board of Health, to be composed of four health commissioners, three of whom should be medical men, the fourth a layman, the commissioners of police, four in number, *ex officio*—and the health officer of the port, *ex officio*—also the officer, a medical man, who had

Reprinted from Edward Dalton "Annual Report of the Metropolitan Board of Health of New York," *North American Review* 106 (April 1868): 351–53, 355–57.

charge of the quarantine. It provided likewise for the appointment of a sanitary superintendent, an assistant superintendent, sanitary inspectors, clerks, employees, etc.

The Board organized its corps of officers and employees without delay, and commenced at once upon its labors. A plan was perfected by which the district should be under constant and rigid inspection, and the Board notified of the result. . . .

In New York alone there are eighteen thousand five hundred and eighty-two tenement-houses, that is, houses occupied by several families, living independently of each other, but having a common right in the halls, stairways, yards, cellars, and sinks. Of this number, when first examined by the inspectors, fifty-two per cent were found in bad sanitary condition, that is, in a condition detrimental to the health and dangerous to the lives of the occupants, sources of infection to the neighborhood, and of insalubrity to the city at large. Thirty-two per cent were in this condition purely from overcrowding, accumulations of filth, want of water supply, and other results of neglect. The danger to the public health from this state of things, especially in the event of an epidemic, is not, however, adequately expressed by these figures; for while in the upper and newer parts of the city the tenement-houses are comparatively well built and properly looked after, there are many localities where almost entire blocks are composed of such houses, all of which were found to be in bad condition, and where the danger was greatly increased by this grouping.

The causes of the improper sanitary condition of tenement-houses may be classed under two heads, namely: first, those due to faults in the original construction of the buildings; and second, those due to overcrowding and neglect.

Prominent under the first head is—First, *the custom of erecting a front and rear tenement house on a single lot.* By this plan the rear end of each rear house is within a short distance, varying in different instances from six inches to two feet, of the rear end of the rear house situated upon the reverse lot fronting on the next street, above or below as the case may be. The result of this is, that the back rooms of the rear houses are entirely cut off from direct sunlight, and the ventilation is necessarily very imperfect. The spaces, too, between houses thus contiguous are always damp, and very frequently, from being made receptacles for garbage and other offensive matters, give off the foulest exhalations, which are either diffused through the houses, or compel the tenants to keep the rear windows constantly closed, and thus preclude the slender means of ventilation which they might otherwise afford. Even the front rooms of such houses suffer in a similar manner, though not to so great a degree—the presence of the high front house, separated only by a narrow court, allowing but a meagre share of direct light and fresh air.

Second, *deficient ventilation* is a very common evil in tenement-houses. The halls are close, rarely, except on the lower floor, extending to either front or rear wall, so as to admit of a window. Therefore, as the tenants keep their room-doors closed, the hall is entirely cut off from the external air, save by the chance opening of the street entrance. The dwelling-rooms have no provision for ventilation, except such as may be afforded by the windows, which are usually on but one side of the room. The sleeping-apartments open from these dwelling-rooms, and are simple closets, with absolutely no ventilation.

Third, *absence of light.* For the same reasons that the halls are unventilated, they are also dark and damp. No sunlight can enter them. The space allowed for the hall is so narrow that a proper well is impossible, and no adequate skylight is provided. A large proportion of these halls are so dark that at midday it is difficult to discern objects in them without opening some adjacent room-door. In many instances the floors are damp and rotten, and the walls and banisters sticky with a constant moisture.

Fourth, *basements, or cellars.* The basements, or cellars, are often entirely under ground, the ceiling being a foot or two below the level of the street, and are necessarily far more damp, dark, and ill-ventilated than the rest of the house. Many of these are constantly occupied, and not infrequently used as lodging-rooms, having no communication with the external air save by the entrance, and the occupants being entirely dependent upon artificial light by day as well as by night. In the lower streets of the city they are often subject to regular periodical flooding by tide-water, to the depth of from six to twelve inches, frequently so as to keep the children in bed until ebb-tide.

Fifth, *deficient drainage.* A large number of tenements have no connection with the common sewer, and no provision for drainage but surface gutters, by which all the house slops are conducted across or immediately beneath the sidewalk into the street gutter, where, from lack of the proper grade, they remain stagnant and putrefying during the summer, and during the winter freeze and turn the flow into the cellars. Indeed, at all seasons, much of the fluid matter deposited by the tenants in the yards makes its way into the cellars, and it is by no means exceptional to find entire blocks of houses where the cellars are constantly flooded to a greater or lesser extent from this cause. In other instances, the flow from the different sinks and wash-basins on the successive floors is conducted by pipes, devoid of traps, to a common wooden drain of inadequate dimensions, running immediately beneath the basement floors of contiguous houses, and thence passing into the street sewer. The current through these drains is generally sluggish, frequently obstructed by accumulations of solid matter or by the decay and consequent breaking down of the drain itself. In the event of such accidents, collections of stagnant and offensive fluids take place beneath the basement floor, or in the cellar, if there be one; the whole house becomes permeated with a disagreeable stench, the cause of which is not discovered until sickness or intolerance of the odor leads to complaint and investigation. These drains are not infrequently furnished with ventilators, consisting of flues immediately connected with the interior of the drain, and thence passing up through the house, with openings in the various apartments, through which the gases resulting from the decomposition below are diffused. The lack of proper traps gives rise to the same difficulty—the exhalations from the stagnant contents of the drain finding their way up through the waste-pipes into the halls and rooms.

Notes

Introduction

1. Paul Harrison, *The Third Revolution: Population, Environment and a Sustainable World* (New York: Penguin Books, 1993), 89.

2. Donald Worster, "Transformations of the Earth: Toward an Agroecological Perspective in History," *Journal of American History* 76 (March 1990): 1088.

3. David M. Potter, *People of Plenty: Economic Abundance and the American Character* (Chicago: University of Chicago Press, 1954), 1.

4. Donald Worster, *The Wealth of Nature: Environmental History and the Ecological Imagination* (New York: Oxford University Press, 1993), 9.

5. Ibid., 17.

6. Alfred W. Crosby, *Germs, Seeds & Animals: Studies in Ecological History* (Armonk, NY: M.E. Sharpe, 1993), 167.

7. David Donald, *Lincoln Remembered: Essays on the Civil War Era* (New York: Vintage Press, 1989), 217.

8. William Cronon, *Changes in the Land: Indians, Colonists, and the Ecology of New England* (New York: Hill and Wang, 1983), 21.

9. Maurice Dobb, *Studies in the Development of Capitalism,* rev. ed. (New York: International Publishers, 1963), 7.

10. Karl Polanyi, *The Great Transformation* (Boston: Beacon Press, 1957), 44.

11. Carl F. Kaestle, *The Evolution of an Urban School System: New York City, 1750–1850* (New York: Hill and Wang, 1983), 102.

12. David B. Tyack, *The One Best System: A History of American Urban Education* (Cambridge: Harvard University Press, 1974), 37.

13. Donald, *Lincoln Remembered,* 216–17.

14. Samuel P. Hays, "Three Decades of Environmental Politics: The Historical Context," in *Government and Environmental Politics: Essays on Historical Developments Since World War II,* ed. Michael J. Lacey (Baltimore: Johns Hopkins University Press, 1991), 24.

15. Samuel P. Hays, "The Central Role of Habitat," *Environmental Forest Brief,* [sphl@pitt.edu], 13 January 1997.

16. Hays, "Three Decades of Environmental Politics," 29.

17. Joel A. Tarr [jt03@Andrew.cmu.edu], "The City and the Natural Environment," [h-aseh@h-net.msu.edu], January 1998, 1.

18. Hays, "Three Decades of Environmental Politics," 22.

19. Ibid., 23.

20. Chris Hendrickson et al., "Introduction to Green Design," *Green Design Initiative,* [http://www.ce.emu.edu/GreenDesign/introed.htm].

21. Ibid.

22. Jesse H. Ausubel, "The Liberation of the Environment," *Daedalus* 125 (Spring 1996): 8.

23. Ibid.

24. Mary Graham, "Why States Can Do More: The Next Phase in Environmental Protection," *American Prospect* 36 (January/February 1998): 66.

25. Ibid., 65–66.

Chapter 1

1. Robert Mason and Mark T. Mattson, eds., *Atlas of Environmental Issues* (New York: Macmillan, 1990), chapter 6.

2. Gary G. Gray, *Wildlife and People: The Human Dimensions of Wildlife Ecology* (Urbana: University of Illinois Press, 1993), 173.

3. Ibid., 173.

4. G. Tyler Miller Jr., *Living in the Environment* (Belmont, CA: Wadsworth, 1990), 287.

5. Ibid., 285.

6. Ibid., 287.

7. Charles McCoy, "Cut Down: Even a Logger Praised as Sensitive to Ecology Faces Bitter Opposition," *Wall Street Journal,* April 1, 1993, 1, A16.

8. Philip G. Terrie, "Forever Wild Forever: The Forest Preserve Debate at the New York State Constitutional Convention of 1915," *New York History* 70 (July 1989): 251–75.

9. "Unit to Let Owners Clear Park Lands," *New York Times,* November 11, 1995, 25–28.

10. Catherine Caufield, *Beloved of the Sky,* ed. John Ellison (Seattle: Broken Moon Press, 1993), 163.

11. Ibid.

12. Richard G. Wood, "A History of Lumbering in Maine 1860–1861," *The Maine Bulletin* 37, no. 7 (1935): 21.

13. William Bradford, *Of Plymouth Plantation: 1620–1647* (New York: Knopf, 1952), 62.

14. Michael Williams, *Americans and Their Forests: A Historical Geography* (New York: Cambridge University Press, 1989), 11.

15. Roderick Nash, "The Roots of American Environmentalism," in *Perceptions of the Landscape and its Preservation* (Indianapolis: Indiana Historical Society, 1984), 34.

16. William Cronon, *Changes in the Land: Indians, Colonists and the Ecology of New England* (New York: Hill and Wang, 1983), 111.

17. Wood, "A History of Lumbering in Maine," 8, 19.

18. Williams, *Americans and Their Forests,* 61.

19. Michael Williams, "Clearing the United States Forests: Pivotal Years 1810–1860," *Journal of Historical Geography* 8, no. 1 (1982): 14.

20. Ibid., 14–15.

21. Carl Bridenbaugh, "Yankee Use and Abuse of the Forest in the Building of New England, 1620–1660," *Proceedings of the Massachusetts Historical Society* 89 (1977): 32.

22. Cronon, *Changes in the Land,* 120–21.

23. Williams, *Americans and Their Forests,* 79.

24. Michael Williams, "Products of the Forest: Mapping the Census of 1840," *Forest History* 24 (1980): 6, 10, 14–15.

25. Williams, *Americans and Their Forests,* 81.

26. Williams, "Clearing," 16.

27. Cronon, *Changes in the Land,* 111.

28. Thomas R. Cox et al., *This Well Wooded Land: Americans and Their Forests From Colonial Times to the Present* (Lincoln: University of Nebraska Press, 1985), 76.

29. Ibid., 77.

30. Ibid., 75.

31. Caufield, *Beloved of the Sky,* 163.

32. Cox et al., *This Well Wooded Land,* 89.

33. William G. Keller, "Henry Marie Brackenridge: First United States Forester," *Forest History* 15 (January 1972): 12–23.

34. Williams, *Americans and Their Forests,* 144.

35. Ibid., 144–45.

36. Ibid., 145.

37. George Perkins Marsh, *Man and Nature* (Cambridge: Harvard University Press, 1965), 7–14. J. Donald Hughes, *Ecology in Ancient Civilizations* (Albuquerque: University of New Mexico Press, 1975), 128. J.V. Thirgood, *Man and the Mediterranean Forest: A History of Resource Depletion* (London: Academic Press, 1941), 158–62.

38. Philip Shabecoff, *A Fierce Green Fire: The American Environmental Movement* (New York: Hill and Wang, 1993), 58.

39. Caufield, *Beloved of the Sky,* 163.

40. William G. Robbins, *Lumberjacks and Legislators: Political Economy of the United States Lumber Industry, 1890–1941* (College Station: Texas A&M University Press, 1982), 3.

41. Wallace P. Gates, *The Wisconsin Pine Lands: A Study in Land Policy and Absentee Ownership* (Ithaca: Cornell University Press, 1943), 70.

42. Cronon, *Changes in the Land,* 159.

43. Williams, *Americans and Their Forests,* 201.

44. Ibid., 218.

45. Wood, "A History of Lumbering in Maine," 31–32.

46. R. Newell Searle, "Minnesota Forests," in *Encyclopedia of American Forest and Conservation History,* ed. Richard C. Davis (New York: Macmillan, 1983), 433.

47. Cronon, *Changes in the Land,* 153.

48. James Willard Hurst, *Law and Economic Growth: The Legal History of the Lumber Industry in Wisconsin, 1836–1915* (Cambridge: Harvard University Press, 1964), 432–37.

49. Williams, *Americans and Their Forests,* 201–02.

50. John N. Yogel, *Great Lakes Lumber on the Great Plains* (Iowa City: University of Iowa Press, 1992), 41–42.

51. Ray Raphael, *Tree Talk: The People and Politics of Timber* (Washington, DC: Island Press, 1981), 12.

52. Ibid., 14.

53. Cronon, *Changes in the Land,* 154.

54. Theodore C. Blegen, "With Ax and Saw: A History of Lumbering in Minnesota," *Forest History* 7 (Fall 1963): 4.

55. Hurst, *Law and Economic Growth,* 435.

56. Ibid., 435.

57. Nash, "The Roots of American Environmentalism," 37.

58. N.H. Egleston, "Methods and Profit of Tree-Planting," *Popular Science Monthly* 21 (May 1882): 1–2.

59. Blegen, "With Ax and Saw," 2–13.

60. Hurst, *Law and Economic Growth*, 433.

61. Williams, *Americans and Their Forests*, 232.

62. Vernon Carstensen, "Cutover Lands," in *Encyclopedia of American Forest and Conservation History*, ed. Richard C. Davis (New York: Macmillan, 1983), 123–25.

63. Robert S. Maxwell, "The Impact of Forestry on the Gulf South," *Forest History* 20 (April 1973): 31.

64. Donald J. Pisani, "Forests and Conservation, 1865–1890," *Journal of American History* 72 (September 1985): 340–59.

65. Frank H. Taylor, "Through Texas," *Harper's Monthly* 59 (October 1879): 703–18.

66. William Bartram, *Travels Through North and South Carolina, Georgia, East and West Florida* (Dublin: Moore, Jones, McAllister, and Rice, 1793), 129–30.

67. John Muir, *A Thousand Mile Walk to the Gulf* (San Francisco: Sierra Club, 1919), 39–41.

68. James I. Pikl Jr., "Pulp and Paper in Georgia: The Newsprint Paradox," *Forest History* 12, no. 3 (1968): 6–19.

69. Williams, *Americans and Their Forests*, 238.

70. R.D. Forbes, "The Passing of the Piney Woods," *American Forestry* 29 (March 1923): 134.

71. Ibid., 131.

72. Maxwell, "The Impact of Forestry," 34.

73. James M. Curry-Roper, "19th-Century Land Law and Current Land Ownership Patterns," *Geographical Review* 77 (July 1987): 261–78.

74. Williams, *Americans and Their Forests*, 252.

75. John G. Mitchell, *Dispatches in the Deep Woods* (Lincoln: University of Nebraska Press, 1991), 29.

76. Ibid., 26.

77. Caufield, *Beloved of the Sky*, 167.

78. D.E. Booth, *Valuing Nature: The Decline and Preservation of Old-Growth Forests* (Lanham, MD: Rowman and Littlefield, 1994), 30.

79. Thomas R. Cox, *Mills and Markets: A History of the Pacific Coast Lumber Industry to 1900* (Seattle: University of Washington Press, 1983), 55.

80. Helen Betsy Abbott, ed., "Life on the Lower Columbia, 1853–1866," *Oregon Historical Quarterly* 83 (1982): 254.

81. John Muir, *Steep Trails*, ed. William Frederick Bade (Boston: Houghton Mifflin, 1918), 206.

82. Williams, *Americans and Their Forests*, 293.

83. Raphael, *Tree Talk*, 22.

84. Williams, *Americans and Their Forests*, 315.

85. Raphael, *Tree Talk*, 22.

86. Williams, *Americans and Their Forests*, 317–18.

87. Ibid., 319.

88. Shabecoff, *A Fierce Green Fire*, 62.

89. Booth, *Valuing Nature*, 9.

90. Shabecoff, *A Fierce Green Fire*, 64.

91. Robert Gottlieb, *Forcing the Spring: The Transformation of the American Environmental Movement* (Washington, DC: Island Press, 1994), 28.

92. Mitchell, *Dispatches in the Deep Woods*, 60.

93. John Muir, "The Hetch Hetchy Valley: A National Question," *American Forestry* 16 (May 1910): 263.

94. Booth, *Valuing Nature,* 12.

95. Alfred Runte, "Preservation Heritage: The Origins of the Park Idea in the United States," in *Perceptions of the Landscape and its Preservation* (Indianapolis: Indiana Historical Society, 1984), 66–67.

96. Shabecoff, *A Fierce Green Fire,* 82.

97. Donald Worster, *The Dust Bowl: The Southern Plains in the 1930s* (New York: Oxford University Press, 1979), 220–23.

98. Thomas R. Cox, "Closing the Lumberman's Frontier: The Far Western Pine Country," *Journal of the West* 33 (July 1994): 59–66.

99. Booth, *Valuing Nature,* 13.

100. James N. Tattersall, "The Economic Development of the Pacific Northwest to 1920," (Ph.D. dissertation, University of Washington, 1960), 185–207.

101. Samuel P. Hayes, "The Environmental Movement," in *Encyclopedia of American Forest and Conservation History,* ed. Richard C. Davis (New York: Macmillan, 1983), 144–48.

102. John H. Cushman Jr. and Timothy Egan, "Battles on Conservation Rack Up Ratings Points," *New York Times,* July 31, 1996, 1, A 12.

Chapter 2

1. Robert J. Mason and Mark T. Mattson, eds., *Atlas of United States Environmental Issues* (New York: Macmillan, 1990), 189.

2. Gary G. Gray, *Wildlife and People: The Human Dimensions of Wildlife Ecology* (Urbana: University of Illinois Press, 1993), 176.

3. Ibid., 176–77.

4. D.E. Booth, *Valuing Nature: The Decline and Preservation of Old Growth Forests* (Lanham, MD: Rowman and Littlefield, 1994), 104–106.

5. Roderick Nash, "The Roots of American Environmentalism," in *Perceptions of the Landscape and its Preservation* (Indianapolis: Indiana Historical Society, 1984), 34.

6. Thomas A. Lund, *American Wildlife Law* (Berkeley: University of California Press, 1980), 58–60.

7. David Quammen, "National Parks: Nature's Dead End," *New York Times,* July 28, 1996, E13.

8. Ibid.

9. Gerald Goddard, ed., *Saving Wildlife: A Century of Conservation* (New York: Harry N. Abrahms, 1992), 234.

10. Hal Glen Borland, *The History of Wildlife in America* (Washington, DC: National Wildlife Federation, 1975), 12.

11. Nash, "The Roots of American Environmentalism," 32.

12. Paul S. Martin, "The Discovery of America," *Science* 179 (1973): 972.

13. Gray, *Wildlife and People,* 15.

14. Borland, *The History of Wildlife in America,* 55.

15. Ibid., 45.

16. Ibid., 48.

17. Ibid., 55.

18. Peter Matthiessen, *Wildlife in America* (New York: Viking Penguin, 1987), 81.

19. John Godman, *American Natural History* (Philadelphia: R.W. Pomeroy, 1831), as quoted in Matthiessen, *Wildlife in America,* 81.

20. Nash, "The Roots of American Environmentalism," 32.

21. E.P. Hill, "Beaver Restoration," in *Restoring America's Wildlife 1937–1987,* ed. H. Kallman et al. (Washington, DC: U.S. Fish and Wildlife Service, 1987), 281–84, as quoted in Gray, *Wildlife and People,* 81.

22. Borland, *The History of Wildlife in America,* 55.

23. Ibid., 57.

24. Gray, *Wildlife and People,* 74.

25. James A. Tober, *Who Owns the Wildlife* (Westport, CT: Greenwood Press, 1981), v.

26. Lund, *American Wildlife Law,* 29.

27. William Cronon, *Changes in the Land: Indians, Colonists and the Ecology of New England* (New York: Hill and Wang, 1983), 100.

28. Matthiessen, *Wildlife in America,* 57.

29. Tober, *Who Owns the Wildlife,* 24.

30. Matthiessen, *Wildlife in America,* 59–63.

31. William T. Hornaday, *Thirty Years War for Wildlife* (New York: Arno Press, 1970), 99–100. Reprint of 1931 edition.

32. Cronon, *Changes in the Land,* 23.

33. Matthiessen, *Wildlife in America,* 56–57.

34. Borland, *The History of Wildlife in America,* 87.

35. James B. Trefethen, *An American Crusade for Wildlife* (New York: Winchester Press, 1975), 63.

36. Lisa Mighetto, *Wild Animals and American Environmental Ethics* (Tucson: University of Arizona Press, 1991), 28.

37. Charles Elton, *Animal Ecology* (New York: October House, 1966), 105.

38. Trefethen, *An American Crusade for Wildlife,* 64–65.

39. George Plimpton, "Death in the Family," *New York Review of Books* 15 (March 4, 1993): 30.

40. Matthiessen, *Wildlife in America,* 168.

41. Robin W. Doughty, *Feather Fashions and Bird Preservation* (Berkeley: University of California Press, 1975), 20.

42. Ibid., 21.

43. Ibid., 22.

44. John F. Reiger, *American Sportsmen and the Origins of Conservation* (New York: Winchester Press, 1975), 64.

45. Carolyn Merchant, "Women of the Progressive Conservation Movement: 1900–1916," *Environmental Review* 8 (Spring 1984): 73.

46. Ralph H. Lutts, *The Nature Fakers: Wildlife, Science and Sentiment* (Golden, CO: Fulcrum, 1990), 28–29.

47. Peter J. Schmitt, *Back to Nature: The Arcadian Myth in Urban America* (New York: Oxford University Press, 1969), 10.

48. J.H. Shaw, *Introduction to Wildlife Management* (New York: McGraw Hill, 1985), 8.

49. Reiger, *American Sportsmen and the Origins of Conservation,* 27.

50. Ibid., 120–25.

51. *The American Sportsman* 6 (June 13, 1874): 344, as quoted in Reiger, *American Sportsmen and the Origins of Conservation,* 41–42.

52. Rachel Carson, *Silent Spring* (Boston: Houghton Mifflin, 1962), 1.

53. James Turner, *Reckoning with the Beast: Animals, Pain, and Humanity in the Victorian Mind* (Baltimore: Johns Hopkins University Press, 1980), 125.

54. William T. Hornaday, *Our Vanishing Wildlife* (New York: New York Zoological Society, 1913), 220–21.

55. Nash, "The Roots of American Environmentalism," 45.

56. William Cronon, *Nature's Metropolis: Chicago and the Great West* (New York: W.W. Norton, 1991), 215.

57. Borland, *The History of Wildlife in America,* 109.

58. Richard Irving Dodge, *The Plains of the Great West and Their Inhabitants* (New York: Archer House, 1959), 132–33. Reprint of 1877 edition, as quoted in Cronon, *Nature's Metropolis,* 217.

59. Borland, *The History of Wildlife in America,* 110.

60. Nash, "The Roots of American Environmentalism," 45.

61. Reiger, *American Sportsmen and the Origins of Conservation,* 119.

62. "Save the Park Buffalo," *Forest and Stream* XLIL (April 14, 1894): 1.

63. David E. Brown and Neil B. Carmony, eds., *Aldo Leopold's Wilderness* (Harrisburg, PA: Stackpole Books, 1990), 68.

64. Goddard, *Saving Wildlife,* 43.

65. Ibid., 42.

66. Stewart L. Udall, *The Quiet Crisis* (New York: Holt, Rinehart and Winston, 1963), 156.

67. Ibid, 155.

68. Hornaday, *Our Vanishing Wildlife,* 225–26.

69. Thomas R. Dunlap, "Values for Varmints: Predator Control and Environmenal Ideas, 1920–1939," *Pacific Historical Review* 53 (May 1984): 141.

70. Ibid., 144.

71. Hornaday, *Our Vanishing Wildlife,* 140.

72. Dunlap, "Values for Varmints," 144.

73. Stanley Young and E.A. Goldman, *The Wolves of North America* (Washington, DC: American Wildlife Institute, 1944), as quoted in Mattheissen, *Wildlife in America,* 193–94.

74. Donald Worster, *Nature's Economy: A History of Ecological Ideas* (New York: Cambridge University Press, 1985), 259.

75. Borland, *The History of Wildlife in America,* 138.

76. Worster, *Nature's Economy,* 259.

77. Ibid., 271.

78. Dunlap, "Values for Varmints," 151.

79. Ibid., 157.

80. Worster, *Nature's Economy,* 259.

81. Thomas R. Dunlap, "Wildlife, Science, and the National Parks, 1920–1940," *Pacific Historical Review* 59 (May 1990): 192.

82. Ibid., 192–93.

83. Ibid., 193.

84. Thomas R. Dunlap, "American Wildlife Policy and Environmental Ideology: Poisoning Coyotes, 1939–1972," *Pacific Historical Review* 55 (August 1986): 351.

85. Worster, *Nature's Economy,* 259.

86. Dunlap, "American Wildlife Policy," 353.

87. Worster, *Nature's Economy,* 265.

88. Curt Meine, *Aldo Leopold: His Life and Work* (Madison: University of Wisconsin Press, 1988), 242.

89. Ibid., 259–60.

90. Jared Orsi, "From Horicon to Hamburgers and Back Again: Ecology, Ideology

and Wildfowl Management, 1917–1935," *Environmental History Review* 18 (Winter 1994): 20.

91. Ibid., 26.

92. Meine, *Aldo Leopold,* 263.

93. Gray, *Wildlife and People,* 159–60.

94. Meine, *Aldo Leopold,* 277.

95. Gray, *Wildlife and People,* 165.

96. Ibid., 164.

97. Worster, *Nature's Economy,* 272.

98. Aldo Leopold, *A Sand County Almanac* (New York: Oxford University Press, 1949), 214.

99. Ibid., 129–32.

100. Worster, *Nature's Economy,* 261.

101. Gray, *Wildlife and People,* 221.

102. Douglas H. Chadwick, "Dead or Alive: The Endangered Species Act," *National Geographic* 187 (March 1995): 22.

103. Plimpton, "Death in the Family," 30.

104. Steven Lewis Yaffee, *The Wisdom of the Spotted Owl: Policy Lessons for a New Century* (Washington, DC: Island Press, 1994), ix.

105. Mary Elizabeth Johnson, "Wildlife Conservation," *Atlas of United States Environmental Issues,* eds. Robert T. Mason and Mark T. Mattson (New York: Macmillan, 1990), 709.

106. Linda Greenhouse, "Court Opens Species Act to Wider List of Challenges," *New York Times,* March 20, 1997, 20.

107. A.P. Dobson et al., "Geographic Distribution of Endangered Species in the United States," *Science* 275 (January 24, 1997): 551.

Chapter 3

1. William Graves, "Introduction," *National Geographic Special Edition: Water* 184, no. 5A (November 1993): inside cover.

2. Allen Hammond, ed., *The 1993 Environmental Almanac* (Boston: Houghton Mifflin, 1993), 36.

3. David A. Franko and Robert G. Wetzel, *To Quench Our Thirst: The Present and Future Status of Freshwater Resources of the United States* (Ann Arbor: University of Michigan Press, 1983), 117.

4. Ibid., 117.

5. Graves, "Introduction," inside cover.

6. Ibid., 20.

7. Ibid., 24.

8. Richard White, *The Organic Machine: The Remaking of the Columbia River* (New York: Hill and Wang, 1995), 6.

9. Franko and Wetzel, *To Quench Our Thirst,* 5–6.

10. Ibid., 16.

11. Ibid., 17.

12. Michael Parfit, "Water," *National Geographic Special Edition: Water* 184 no. 5A (November 1993): 26.

13. Hector St. John Crevecoeur, *Sketches of Eighteenth Century America,* ed. Henri L. Bourdin et al. (New Haven: Yale University Press, 1925), 39.

14. Letty Anderson, "Hard Choices: Supplying Water to New England Towns," *Journal of Interdisciplinary History* 15 (Autumn 1984): 213, 216–18.

15. Nelson Manfred Blake, *Water for the Cities: A History of the Urban Water Supply Problem in the United States* (Syracuse: Syracuse University Press, 1956), 178.

16. Fern L. Nesson, *Great Waters: A History of Boston's Water Supply* (Hanover, NH: University Press of New England, 1983), 1.

17. Ibid., 2.

18. Joel A. Tarr, "The Horse—Polluter of the City," in *The Search for the Ultimate Sink: Urban Pollution in Historical Perspective* (Akron, OH: University of Akron Press, 1996), 323–33. In this essay, Tarr describes the effects of the horse on the nineteenth-century urban environment in the following way: "Piles of manure collected by street cleaners bred huge numbers of flies and created 'pestilential vapours.' Litter from wealthy residential neighborhoods was often dumped in poor neighborhoods and left to rot. Streets turned into virtual cesspools when it rained, causing women to accumulate filth on their dresses.... Other complaints derived from the pulverized horse dung that blew into peoples faces and houses and that covered the wares of merchants with outside displays. The paving of streets accelerated this problem, as wheels and hooves ground manure against the hard surfaces and amplified the amount of dust." (p. 326.)

19. Nesson, *Great Waters,* 6.

20. Ibid., 7.

21. Peter S. Canellos, "Crowding, Conflict, and Conflagration," *Boston Globe Magazine,* March 2, 1997, 22. In this article, a quote from *Harper's Weekly,* 1872, dramatizes the nation's awareness of the seriousness of the 1812 blaze. "The Old South [Meeting House] and Faneuil Hall are in Boston, but they are the treasures of the country. The painful, almost gradual approach of the flames to the old church as watched by the spectators was shared by those in distant parts of the country who could see only by the telegraph."

22. Nessen, *Great Waters,* 72.

23. "Boston Seeks to Add a Second Water Supply Pipeline," *U.S. Water News Online,* January 1996. [uswatrnews@aol.com]

24. Edward Wegmann, *The Water Supply of the City of New York, 1685–1895* (New York: John Wiley and Sons, 1986), 3.

25. Charles H. Weidner, *Water for a City: A History of New York City's Problem from the Beginning to the Delaware River System* (New Brunswick, NJ: Rutgers University Press, 1974), 17.

26. Ibid., 18.

27. Wegmann, *The Water Supply of the City of New York,* 6–7.

28. Nelson P. Blake, "Water and the City: Lessons from History," in *Water in the City: The Next Century,* eds. Howard Rosen and Ann Durkin Keating (Chicago: Public Works Historical Society, 1991), 61.

29. Weidener, *Water for a City,* 22–23.

30. Ibid., 29.

31. Blake, "Water and the City," 143.

32. Weidener, *Water for a City,* 57.

33. Blake, "Water and the City," 277–78.

34. Weidener, *Water for a City,* 65.

35. Ibid., 130.

36. Ibid., 191.

37. Blake, "Water and the City," 35.

38. Ibid., 86.

39. Ibid., 89.

40. Ibid., 275.

41. Elaine M. Koerner, "Guardian Angels or Agitators?: A Century of Women at the Helm of Grassroots Environmental Activism," paper presented at the American Society for Environmental History Convention, Baltimore, MD, March 1997, 1–2.

42. Sam Alewitz, *Filthy Dirty—A Social History of Unsanitary Philadelphia in the Late 19th Century* (New York: Garland, 1989), 73.

43. Blake, "Water and the City," 263.

44. Craig E. Colten, "Industrial Wastes in Southeast Chicago: Production and Disposal, 1870–1970," *Environmental Review* 10 (Summer 1986): 96.

45. Harold L. Platt, "Everlasting Purity: Science, Engineering and the Chlorination of Chicago's Water Supply, 1880–1920," paper presented at the American Society for Environmental History Convention, Baltimore, MD, March 1997, 5.

46. Stuart Galishoff, "Triumph and Failure: The American Response to the Urban Water Supply Problem, 1860–1923," in *Pollution and Reform in American Cities, 1870–1930,* ed. Martin V. Melosi (Austin, University of Texas Press, 1980), 48.

47. Platt, "Everlasting Purity," 27, 29.

48. Galishoff, 40, 49–51.

49. Joel A. Tarr, "Water and Wastes: A Retrospective Assessment of Wastewater Technology in the United States, 1800–1932," in *The Search for the Ultimate Sink: Urban Pollution in Historical Perspective* (Akron, OH: University of Akron Press, 1996), 182.

50. Ibid., 183.

51. Ibid., 187.

52. Nancy Tomes, "The Private Side of Public Health: Sanitary Science, Domestic Hygiene, and the Germ Theory, 1870–1900," *Bulletin of the History of Medicine* 64 (Winter 1990): 509–39.

53. Blake, "Water and the City," 264.

54. Joel A. Tarr "Industrial Wastes and Public Health: Some Historical Notes, 1876–1932," *American Journal of Public Health* 75 (September 1985): 1059.

55. Donald J. Pisani, "Fish Culture and the Dawn of Concern Over Water Pollution in the United States," *Environmental Review* 8 (Summer 1984): 123.

56. Ibid., 121.

57. Ibid., 127.

58. Robert A. Shanley, "Franklin D. Roosevelt and Water Pollution Control Policy," *Presidential Studies Quarterly* 18 (Spring 1988): 320.

59. Pisani, "Fish Culture and the Dawn of Concern Over Water Pollution in the United States," 127.

60. Joel A. Tarr, "Environmental Risk in Historical Perspective," in *The Social and Cultural Construction of Risk,* ed. Brandon Johnson and Victor Covello (Norwell, MA: Reidel, 1987), 317.

61. Ibid., 17–18.

62. Donald J. Pisani, "Irrigation, Water Rights, and the Betrayal of Indian Allotment," *Environmental Review* 10 (Fall 1986): 158.

63. R. Douglas Hurt, "Agricultural Technology in the Twentieth Century," *Journal of the West* 30 (April 1991): 71.

64. Ibid., 68.

65. Donald Worster, *The Wealth of Nature: Environmental History and the Ecological Imagination* (New York: Oxford University Press, 1993), 127.

66. Donald J. Pisani, *To Reclaim a Divided West: Water, Law, and Public Policy, 1848–1902* (Albuquerque: University of New Mexico Press, 1992), xiii–xiv.

67. Robert A. Sauder, "The Agricultural Colonization of a Great Basin Frontier:

Economic Organization and Environmental Alteration in Owens Valley, California, 1860–1925," *Agricultural History* 64 (Fall 1990): 83.

68. Marc Reisner, *Overtapped Oasis: Reform or Revolution for Western Water* (Washington, DC: Island Press, 1990), 62.

69. Pisani, *To Reclaim a Divided West,* 11–12.

70. M. Catherine Miller, "Riparian Rights and the Control of Water in California, 1879–1928: The Relationship Between an Agricultural Enterprise and Legal Change," *Agricultural History* 59 (January 1985): 22–23; M. Catherine Miller, "Water Rights and the Bankruptcy of Judicial Action: The Case of Herminahaus *v.* Southern California Edison," *Pacific Historical Review* 58 (February 1989): 84–85.

71. Sauder, "The Agricultural Colonization of a Great Basin Frontier," 93.

72. Ibid., 94.

73. Fred Powledge, *Water: The Nature, Uses, and Future of Our Most Precious and Abused Resource* (New York: Farrar Straus Giroux, 1982), 111.

74. Ibid., 113.

75. Ibid.

76. Marc Reiser, *Cadillac Desert: The American West and its Disappearing Water* (New York: Penguin Books, 1993), 514–15.

77. William L. Kahrl, *Water and Power: The Conflict over Los Angeles' Water Supply in the Owens Valley* (Berkeley: University of California Press, 1982), 2.

78. Ibid., 5.

79. Ibid., 32–33.

80. Ibid., 227.

81. Ibid., 260.

82. Ibid., 265.

83. Ibid., 349.

84. Ibid., 349.

85. Sarah S. Elkind, "Industry and Water Distribution in California: The East Bay Municipal Utility District, 1920–1930," *Environmental History Review* 18 (Winter 1994): 67.

86. Ibid., 66.

87. Ibid., 81.

88. Ibid., 82.

89. Ibid., 84–85.

90. Ibid., 85.

91. Harrison C. Dunning, "Dam Fights and Water Policy in California: 1969–1989," *Journal of the West* 29 (July 1990): 19.

92. Ibid., 19.

93. Ibid., 20.

94. Ibid., 21.

95. Robert W. Adler et al., *The Clean Water Act 20 Years Later* (Washington, DC: Island Press, 1993), 83.

96. Ibid., 7.

97. Ibid., 8.

98. Ibid., 7.

99. "Safe Water," *News Report* 41 (Fall 1996): 6.

100. Ibid., 42.

101. "News 3," *Biodiversity Network* 46, no. 3 (1990): 7.

102. Adler et al., *The Clean Water Act 20 Years Later,* 100.

103. Joel A. Tarr, review of *Great Waters: A History of Boston's Water Supply,* by Fern L. Nesson, *The New England Quarterly* 57 (June 1984): 301.

104. Adler et al., *The Clean Water Act 20 Years Later,* 101.

Chapter 4

1. Jesse H. Ausubel, "The Liberation of the Environment," *Daedalus* 125 (Spring 1996): 4.

2. Ibid., 3.

3. Ibid.

4. Ibid.

5. Peter Brimblecombe, *The Big Smoke* (New York: Methuen, 1987), 16–18. Peter Brimblecombe, "Attitudes and Responses Toward Air Pollution in Medieval England," *Journal of the Air Pollution Control Association* 26 (Winter 1976): 941–45.

6. John Evelyn, "Fumifugium or the Inconvenience of the Aer and Smoke of London Dissipated," in *The Smoke of London: Two Prophecies,* ed. J.P. Lodge (Elmsford, NY: Maxwell Reprints, 1969), 40. Reprint of 1661 edition.

7. John Graunt, *Natural and Political Observations . . . Upon the Bills of Mortality* (1662), available at http://rowlf.cc.wwu.edu:8080/stephan/Graunt/graunt.html (January 8, 1997) 70, as cited in Indur M. Goklany, "The Federal Role in Improving Environmental Quality in the United States: Evidence From Long Term Trends in Air Pollution," paper presented at the American Society for Environmental History Conference on Government, Science, and the Environment, Baltimore, MD, March 1997, 60.

8. Indur M. Goklany, "The Federal Role in Improving Environmental Quality in the United States," 4.

9. Ibid., 5.

10. Ausubel, "The Liberation of the Environment," 11.

11. Nelson M. Blake, *Water For the Cities: A History of The Urban Water Supply Problem in the United States* (Syracuse, NY: Syracuse University Press, 1956), 131.

12. Adam W. Rome, "Coming to Terms with Pollution: The Language of Environmental Reform, 1865–1915," *Environmental History* 1 (July 1996): 16.

13. Christine M. Rosen, "Businessmen Against Pollution in Late Nineteenth Century Chicago," *Business History Review* 69 (Autumn 1995): 354.

14. Booth Tarkington, *The Turmoil* (New York: Harper, 1943), 1–2; reprint of 1915 edition.

15. Rome, "Coming to Terms with Pollution," 18.

16. Christine Rosen, "Differing Perceptions of the Value of Pollution Abatement Across Time and Space: Balancing Doctrine in Pollution Nuisance Law, 1840–1906," *Law and History Review* 11 (Winter 1993): 341.

17. Upton Sinclair, *The Jungle* (London: Penguin Books, 1986), as quoted in Adam Markham, *A Brief History of Pollution* (New York: St. Martin's Press, 1994), 11.

18. Rome, "Coming to Terms with Pollution," 6–8.

19. Ibid., 14–15.

20. Goklany, "The Federal Role in Improving Environmental Quality in the United States," 5.

21. Rosen, "Businessmen Against Pollution in Late Nineteenth Century Chicago," 352.

22. Ibid., 353.

23. Ibid., 360.

24. Ibid., 363.

25. Goklany, "The Federal Role in Improving Environmental Quality in the United States," 8.

26. Ibid., 9.

27. R. Dale Grinder, "The Battle for Clean Air: The Smoke Problem in Post-Civil War America," in *Pollution and Reform in American Cities, 1870–1930,* ed. Martin V. Melosi (Austin: University of Texas Press, 1980), 84.

28. Joel A. Tarr and Carl Zimring, "The Struggle for Smoke Control: Achievement and Emulation" in *Common Fields: An Environmental History of St. Louis,* ed. Andrew Hurley (St. Louis: Missouri Historical Society Press, 1997), 200–201.

29. Ibid., 201.

30. Grinder, "The Battle for Clean Air," 87.

31. Ibid., 84.

32. Harold C. Livesay, *Andrew Carnegie and the Rise of Big Business* (Glenville, IL: Scott, Foresman, 1975), 126.

33. Tarr and Zimring, "The Struggle for Smoke Control," 204.

34. Grinder, "The Battle for Clean Air," 91.

35. Ibid., 86.

36. Ibid., 88.

37. Joel A. Tarr, "Changing Fuel Use Behavior and Energy Transitions: Pittsburgh Smoke Control Movement, 1940–1950," in *The Search for the Ultimate Sink: Urban Pollution in Historical Perspective* (Akron, OH: University of Akron Press, 1996), 231.

38. Goklany, "The Federal Role in Improving Environmental Quality in the United States," 8.

39. Tarr and Zimring, "The Struggle for Smoke Control," 211.

40. Ibid., 212.

41. Ibid., 215.

42. Ibid., 215–17.

43. Tarr, "Changing Fuel Use Behavior and Energy Transitions," 231.

44. Ibid., 249–50.

45. Tarr and Zimring, "The Struggle for Smoke Control," 217.

46. Tarr, "Changing Fuel Use Behavior and Energy Transitions," 252.

47. Joel A. Tarr, "The Search for the Ultimate Sink: Urban Air, Land, and Water Pollution in Historical Perspective," *Records of the Columbia Historical Society of Washington, D.C.* 51 (1984), 13.

48. Goklany, "The Federal Role in Improving Environmental Quality in the United States," 11.

49. Lynne Page Snyder, "The Death-Dealing Smog over Donora, Pennsylvania: Industrial Air Pollution, Public Health Policy, and the Politics of Expertise, 1948–1949," *Environmental History Review* 18 (Spring 1994): 117, 121.

50. Ibid., 123.

51. Ibid., 117.

52. Ibid., 119.

53. Ibid., 121.

54. Goklany, "The Federal Role in Improving Environmental Quality in the United States," 11–12.

55. Snyder, "The Death-Dealing Smog over Donora, Pennsylvania," 132.

56. James E. Krier and Edmund Ursin, *Pollution and Policy: A Case Essay on California and Federal Experience with Motor Vehicle Air Pollution, 1940–1975* (Berkeley: University of California Press, 1977), 42.

57. Ibid., 42–43.

58. Ibid., 6.

59. Goklany, "The Federal Role in Improving Environmental Quality in the United States," 12.

60. Ibid., 15.

61. Krier and Ursin, *Pollution and Policy,* 209.

62. Ibid., 10.

63. Ibid., 201.

64. Goklany, "The Federal Role in Improving Environmental Quality in the United States," 38.

65. Ibid., 16.

66. Krier and Ursin, *Pollution and Policy,* 20–21.

67. Goklany, "The Federal Role in Improving Environmental Quality in the United States," 27.

68. Ibid., 39.

69. Michael Kranish, "The Politics of Pollution," *Boston Globe Magazine,* February 8, 1998, 25.

70. Goklany, "The Federal Role in Improving Environmental Quality in the United States," 18.

71. John P. DeVillars, "Cheap Energy, and Clean Air," *Boston Globe,* May 13, 1997, C4.

72. A complete copy of this Environmental Protection Agency report can be obtained at http://www.epa.gov/airlinks.

73. Peter Passell, "The Air Standards Are Set, But How Clean Is Clean Enough?" *New York Times,* July 3, 1997, D2.

74. William K. Stevens, "In Kyoto, The Subject Is Climate; The Forecast Is for Storms," *New York Times,* December 1, 1997, E11.

75. William K. Stevens, "Warming Could Bring Some Cold Surprises," *New York Times,* September 9, 1997, C2.

76. William J. Broad, "Another Possible Climate Culprit: The Sun," *New York Times,* September 23, 1997, C1.

77. Ibid., C8.

78. Ibid.

79. David L. Chandler, "Earth's Past Offers Chilling Global Warming Scenarios," *Boston Globe,* December 2, 1997, A10.

80. Ibid.

81. Scott Allen, "U.S. Lifestyle Choices Take Toll," *Boston Globe,* May 26, 1997, A8.

Index

About the Author

Anthony N. Penna is a professor of history at Northeastern University. Among his many publications are *The Americans: A History of the United States* and *Living in Urban America.* He has received fellowships and grants from a number of agencies and foundations, including the Carnegie Corporation of New York, the General Electric Foundation, the Fulbright Fellowship Foundation, the Buhl Foundation of Pittsburgh, the National Endowment for the Humanities, the National Science Foundation, and the Andrew W. Mellon Foundation.